Legacy and Redemption

To the twins & lucky Mother
with my best wishes
of a Twin Blessing
Alison & Jillian Cogan
from
Joseph Kennedy
June 11/06
Wash. D.C.

Legacy and Redemption

| A LIFE RENEWED |

by JOSEPH E. TENENBAUM

with an introduction by ELIE WIESEL

**THE UNITED STATES HOLOCAUST MEMORIAL MUSEUM AND
THE HOLOCAUST SURVIVORS' MEMOIRS PROJECT**

This book is published by the United States Holocaust Memorial Museum, 100 Raoul Wallenberg Place, SW, Washington, DC 20024-2126.

Copyright © 2005 by Joseph E. Tenenbaum

All rights reserved, including the right to reproduce this book or portions thereof in any form.

The Holocaust Survivors' Memoirs Project, an initiative of Nobel Peace Prize laureate Elie Wiesel, is under the auspices of the United States Holocaust Memorial Museum and the World Jewish Congress. The Project was launched through a generous grant from Random House Inc., New York.

Editor-in-Chief:	Menachem Z. Rosensaft

Editorial Advisory Board:	Sam E. Bloch, Dr. Eva Fogelman, Dr. Alfred Gottschalk, Rabbi David M. Posner, Dr. Romana Strochlitz Primus, Thane Rosenbaum, Elan Steinberg

The assertions, arguments, and conclusions contained herein are those of the author. They do not necessarily reflect the opinions of the United States Holocaust Memorial Museum, the World Jewish Congress, or the Holocaust Survivors' Memoirs Project.

ISBN: 0-89604-163-8

Printed in the United States of America.

CONTENTS

Introduction by Elie Wiesel	vii
Acknowledgments	xi
A Letter to My Children	xiii

Part I

Dzialoszyce	3
Our Household	13
Heder	19
Talmudic Piecework	27
Secular Education or without *Peyes*	31
The Gerer *Shtibl*	37
Shabes in Dzialoszyce	41
Joseph—The Youngest	47
Mischief and Other Pastimes	51
Our Store and Other Commerce	55
Family	61
Giving from the Heart and Not Giving	69
Beyond the Theoretical	73
Girls	77
German Occupation	83
Shame	93
Thwarted Romance	97

Part II

The Expulsion	105
Ten Thousand Worlds	109
Chosen for What?	113
The Zatorska Street Camp	119
Krakow/Plaszow	125
Separated Again … and Again	135
To Appease a Lonely God	143
Die Stollen—The Tunnels	151
Ebensee	157

Part III

Liberation	165
To Palestine	173
Derailed	181
Kaddish	185
Going Underground	189
Headaches	195
Life in Munich	205
The Princess in the Woods	211
Honeymoon	221
Still the Youngest	227
Monkey Business	231

Part IV

One Foot in the New World	241
Odd Jobs and Odd Behavior	245
Davy Crockett and the Bandits	253
The Dynamics of Dynamic Electronics	257
Truth in Advertising and Everyday Life	271
Selling Houses	279
Every Bit of It	281
The Manhattan Store	287
Closing a Chapter	295
Construction	299
Yahrzeit	305
Digging for Truth	309
Back to the USA	315
Visiting the Lubavitcher Rebbe	319
Friends and Heroes	323
Closing a Chapter—Again	327

Part V

8 Stayner Avenue	345
Not the Mouse but the Hole	349
A Squirrel at the Floodgates	355
From Where the Legs Grow	357
Rabbis	365
Elie Wiesel	369
Roosters, Hens, and Torn Scrolls	375
Partner	381
On My Own	385
Developing Land	397
Hangouts	401
Drinking Wine by the Glass	405

Part VI

More Rabbis and Warriors	417
Holocaust Denial	421
"Crush the Arrogant"	429
Zion, Friends, and Poets	431
Revisiting Sodom	439
Wolgelernter—An Alternate Return	451
"Tell Thy Children"	455

Epilogue   459

INTRODUCTION

by Elie Wiesel

The collection of survivors' testimonies—and Joseph Tenenbaum's is one of them—represents for some among us both an obligation and a challenge: a challenge to all-too-comfortable forgetfulness and an obligation toward those who want to combat it by sharing the memory of their suffering. Will that obligation be felt by the public at large? It surely will be felt in the heart of the informed reader.

In spite of its urgency, this project did not begin yesterday.

In the beginning the survivors tried to express their travail in words. People refused to hear them. As in the case of the tragic messenger in Kafka's work, they tried to deliver the message, but the message was not received. Then they chose to close down, and after, silence. Now and then when they were asked, apropos of nothing in particular, they would respond, "What's the point in talking about it? You would not understand; you cannot understand."

Then with years, under the pressure of the occasional old friend, they agreed to make the effort. They understood the uniqueness of their roles. Are they not more or less the last of the survivors? Are they not the bearers of incomparable memories which are unique in and of themselves? Do they not have the sad duty to reveal them rather than carry them to the grave? The historian Shimon Dubnow, did he not, before collapsing in the Riga ghetto, call out to all his brothers and sisters of misfortune, to write, to write with their last breath?

It was an irrefutable argument, and it had an effect on a number of us. This collection, published with a profound feeling of gratitude, is one of its fruits.

The author of this work, Joseph Tenenbaum, may serve as an example. For a long time, he also doubted the power of words. However, he had things to say about the incredible pathways he trod as he went from the small Polish-Jewish town of Dziaoszyce, where peace and love of life prevailed, to the camps of Plaszow, Mielec, Mauthausen, Melk, Ebensee, and others where cruelty and death reigned.

As in almost all autobiographies of the same genre, as he plunges into his most distant past, he first evokes the engulfed and shattered world of his childhood. They were sunny years, punctuated by holidays and discoveries: *heder*, first teachers, first punishments for having preferred football over Talmud, adolescence and first emotions, the first death, the first suicide, quarrels and reconciliations. The beauty of Hebrew, the Zionist dream. The typical *shtetl* society with its rabbis and students, businessmen and beggars, its sages and criminals: he gives names to them all, individually, as if he were anxious simply to protect them from being erased from memory.

Picturesque and funny people, the town crier who mixes up words, the *melamed* who stays glued to his chair; some too naive, others too cynical. Curious and by nature mischievous, little Yossele wants to observe everything, learn everything, try everything, even risk everything, often to laugh and to make others laugh and always to enrich his memory. An entrancing period, and one hit by small anxieties and large joys: it could have continued thus in calm and expectation until the end of time, until redemption.

Yossele had not yet reached his bar mitzvah age when war breaks out. With the arrival of the Germans, change becomes absolute. For Jews nothing will ever be the same as before. Plundering, expulsions, humiliations, separations, breakups, punishments: Hitler's will quickly replaced destiny's will.

The stages that Yossele went through resemble a dizzy descent into hell. He is not alone. Resourceful and fearless, he finds a way to help his parents and brothers. Around him, his family circle is brutally and implacably shrunk. First, his mother's death: she is carried off by angels of destruction wearing the SS uniform and gassed at Belzec. The description of his father's death, standing in the snow, freezing, brings tears to the eyes.

Without the slightest indulgence Yossele recounts the agony of Jewish prisoners. He evokes the disastrous activities of certain informers—Jewish policemen and guards—whom he denounces with anger. He finds their behavior immoral, criminal, ugly. But he is far tougher on the Polish and

Russian antisemites who tormented their fellow Jewish prisoners; had they not learned anything?

And what about God here? This boy who was raised as a son of a Gerer Hasid takes Him on as well. Without denying or renouncing Him, he often questions Him: why did He permit the enemy to massacre His people? But God remains silent.

The adolescent grew up quickly. Constantly watched, always in danger, never losing courage, he surmounts traps and obstacles placed by an enemy that seems omnipotent and omniscient. Is it the will to survive beyond the assassins of our people that saved him? His desire to show the enemies of Israel that each Jew is the measure of their defeat? Is it something else? The fact is that at the time of the liberation, the orphan that he is, is not confused or resigned to his fate. He regains his self-control and decides to give meaning to his survival.

He is not yet 18 years old and already he is assuming political responsibilities. A militant Zionist, an active member of the secret *Irgun* group in Germany and Italy, he organizes illegal immigration to Palestine, recites by heart the burning poems of Uri Zvi Greenberg, marries Gena, and goes off to establish himself first in America and then in Canada.

Much of this book deals with the postwar period: on the rubble of their lives, the victims of yesterday have remained human and are capable of grandeur and generosity.

Full of imagination and energy, and humor as well, Yossele confronts his new existence and its innumerable difficulties. He knows how to parry them in the same way he learned how to banish the reasons that might have made him bitter.

His story is that of an epoch that left its mark on the consciousness of the Jewish people and also, on another level, that of humanity in general.

You have to read it to understand the importance not only of the memoir but of the use to which it will be put.

Translated from the French

DEDICATION

To the memory of my dear parents, Tuviah Zisman and Chaja Grina Tenenbaum, victims of the Shoah.

To the everlasting memory of six million innocent Jews murdered by the Nazis and their brutal helpers.

To the victims who did survive and, despite pain, went on to build new lives and fought for the State of Israel.

Let this book be a reminder and a consolation to them that "… *netsah Yisrael lo yeshaker*" (The eternity of Israel will never falter) 1 Samuel 15:29.

ACKNOWLEDGMENTS

I would like to thank Elie Wiesel for planting the seed that grew into this book. By listening to my account of experiences during and after the war, Elie was a constant source of encouragement and advice. This memoir took years to germinate, but it has finally come to fruition. My testimony bears witness to the horrors of our century.

When I begin to thank Elie Wiesel, I can hear his gentle words: "Yossele, stop. It is not necessary." Nonetheless, my gratitude to him is boundless and must be expressed.

Dr. Linda Bayer did a superb job in the first go-round of editing my manuscript—even though she removed sufficient material to fill another book. After all, what are good editors for? I also appreciate Jeanette Friedman's work in this regard. I would like to thank Menachem Z. Rosensaft of the Holocaust Survivors' Memoirs Project for his hard work in making this book a reality.

My son Sid Tenenbaum took over where Dr. Bayer left off. He could not let well enough alone, and knowing my stories as well as anyone can, he coaxed out of me colorful details that were more in keeping with what I had shared over the years around the Friday night table. Sid is also a stickler for logic and consistency. My memories did not always organize themselves in the sequence in which they occurred, and it was very important to me that this testimony stand the test of historical scrutiny. As an architect, he has a good sense of how a story is structured, and he helped see to it that this narrative construction had good foundations and elegant lines!

My son Gary Tenenbaum gave constant profound advice and strengthened my work in many different areas. He also taught me to do the impossible—use a computer! Hours of unwavering, patient explanation were a task for a psychologist as well as a computer whiz. He did such a good job that I now can't imagine my life without the computer. Gary also handled all the technical issues relating to the manuscript over the course of the many years that it took me to write.

To know to what extent my children—all of them—have internalized my experiences has moved me greatly. My daughter, Tamara, and her husband, Uli, busy with their young family, and my daughters-in-law, Judy Cardozo Tenenbaum and Louise Tenenbaum, never ceased to encourage me and to follow my progress in this project.

And *akharon, akharon khaviv* last but dearest, Gena, my love—your patience, your influence, your subtle and not-so-subtle remarks, your constant balancing, your transcribing, your accompanying my *meshugas* and getting up at 5 a.m. to type—all your hard work helped me reach my goal. Without your love, support, and encouragement, this work would never have reached publication.

A LETTER TO MY CHILDREN

Only beware and guard well your soul that you do not forget the things which your own eyes have seen ... but make them known unto your children and your children's children.

Deuteronomy 4:9

Dear Sidney, Gary, and Tamara:

I am in Miami, in the condo. It is noontime and I am alone, looking out the window. All I can see is sky and ocean, waves undulating endlessly, with myriad colors ranging from pale to deep green and shades of blue darkening to indigo. A thought enters my mind and repeats itself with the rhythmic rise of waves, "You are getting older; time is short; time does not stand still."

Children, I decided to write you a letter. I never took a course in creative writing, but I feel compelled to put my thoughts into words so that you can read what is on my mind. I am speaking into a tape recorder. Later, my thoughts will be transcribed. It is hard for me to express my need to write.

Where do I start? How do I proceed? I have so much to tell you—this letter will go on and on like the waves in the ocean. I will try to string together words and events like beads in a necklace. However, the strand is long. The letter might become a book. Perhaps I will never finish it. Yet I want to leave you something of myself. You knew me all these years, but you were not always with me. Before you were born, I lived through a nightmare that still haunts my sunny days. I want to leave you a side of myself that I haven't fully expressed. This memoir is a legacy that may bring me closer to you and reveal a person who is sometimes misunderstood. I am anxious to speak now because my memory of the past is beginning to fade. I become angry when I forget faces, events, names, and dates.

Maybe I am also afraid of the memories. Are the fading memories running away from me, or is it really I who am running away from them?

Yet retreat is impossible. Reality must be faced. So I write to capture my past and myself. I approach this undertaking without preparation or notes. The thoughts I address to you, my dear children, flow freely from the inner man who is your father. My life has risen and fallen like the waves I am watching; cresting with the happiness of my childhood, sinking in a trough of despair when the town of my youth was obliterated, and rising again with the joyous occasions of my postwar life. Other Holocaust survivors have had experiences similar to mine and have written of their ordeals. So many papers, books, and films have detailed the horror and the lives that were lost. Professional writers, journalists, and historians have chronicled the tragedy. Why raise another voice?

I will take the time to contribute one more account for the same reason each new soul is added to the universe. Our tradition teaches that the world was created for each individual person and that each person is himself a world. Every person resembles others but is unique, and each unique story must be told. By relating the specific, we testify to the universal tragedy that befell us and to the universal condition that is the existential condition of each person. The telling of this story might just be one more protest against mortality.

A few years ago, I started to do some estate planning and spent much time on that project. No matter how much I planned and how many accountants and lawyers drew up agreements, all the work would have been worthless without considering the beneficiaries of the estate. That is why I wanted to involve you in plans for my retirement from day one. And if I invested effort in planning the material estate, I would certainly invest no less effort in planning the "spiritual estate," and that is what this letter/book is meant to be. I leave this legacy to you and to my grandchildren, the ones who are here and the ones who have yet to be born.

The beauty of talking to a tape recorder is that nobody interrupts me. Without interference, without external pressure, I can speak at my own speed. My internal pressure is sufficient to fuel the flow of words, except that I do my own interrupting with thoughts coming at me from everywhere. My recollections may not be in chronological order, as I am compelled to record these distant memories as they surface in my mind. I am dictating very rapidly, yet I am scarcely able to keep up with my memories of events.

Faced with this daunting task, I keep asking myself, "What will my story add?" and I answer myself that my story will bring my world, my being, to the people most dear to me. I am a witness who was saved from a fire. In Anne Michaels's book *Fugitive Pieces*, the protagonist says, "Write to save yourself, and someday you will write because you have been saved."

With my parents and grandparents, I lost some of the facts that fit together to form my history. The lost pieces, and the ones I retain, are my testimony for the living and the dead. I bear witness for my children, grandchildren, and offspring to come so that they can know and understand, remember and not forget what my family and my generation endured. The past is within me, not behind me; it accompanies me wherever I go. More than 80 generations are looking down upon me. Therefore, I must do the proper thing. I cannot presume to write for my fellow survivors, but if I do not expose my own experiences I might as well be among the dead. Perhaps the Almighty has spared me in order to bear witness.

I continue to feel that the task I have undertaken is a very difficult one for me. Throughout my life, steps appeared before me. Often, I only had to rise one step. Sometimes the steps were difficult or hazardous, but I considered them unavoidable. I refused to back down. The challenge of the steps has become one of the principles in my life. Occasionally the steps stopped, and I could not continue. Then I prayed to the Almighty to take me the rest of the way. I did not want to fall. I pray that He will not let me fall here so that I can tell you my story.

PART I

*Since wars begin in the minds of men,
it is in the minds of men that the defenses of
peace must be constructed.*

Preamble to the Constitution of the
United Nations Educational, Scientific and
Cultural Organization, November 16, 1945

DZIALOSZYCE

In the beginning, there were my parents. They gave me a wonderful home, three older brothers, grandparents, uncles, aunts, cousins, a business—*'olam u-melo'o*—a world with everything in it. I received the blessing of *ahavat olam* (eternal love) from my parents. Although the spiritual world given to me was broad, it was the little town of Dzialoszyce, Poland, that circumscribed the boundaries of my physical world. Before World War II, Dzialoszyce was a town of 8,000 to 9,000 people, about 80 percent of them Jewish. The Gentiles lived mostly on the outskirts of town. Some were local or government officials, very few were prominent or wealthy, most were craftsmen and of the working class. The latter were often employed by the Jewish population to help on *Shabes*, the Sabbath—making fires in the ovens and carrying water from the well. Poles administered the town, although the vice-mayor was a Jew, and there were some Jewish Council members. Mr. Zwolinski, the mayor, owned a tobacco and cigarette store.

As a child, I was fascinated by the many boxes of tobacco, cigars, and cigarettes that were lined up in an orderly fashion. His store, which he kept in meticulous order, was a marked contrast to our store.

The Jews of Dzialoszyce were wholesalers, retailers, stallkeepers, traveling merchants, manufacturers, and craftsmen—tailors, tinsmiths, shoemakers, tanners, oilmakers, soapmakers, stockingmakers, metalworkers, hatmakers, bookbinders, bakers, goldsmiths, and barbers. Their livelihood depended on the peasants living in the surrounding villages who came to town on Tuesdays and Fridays, the weekly market days.

Located in the center of town, the market was the size of about a quarter of a soccer field and comprised roughly 100 stalls. The villagers sold goods and bought the town's wares with the proceeds. Most of the stores, workshops, and factories belonged to the Jews, as did most of the homes. The majority of Dzialoszyce's Jews were Orthodox; a smaller percentage were "observant"; very few were what we would have called back then "*frayers*"—free of religious observance.

I was born in Dzialoszyce on February 9, 1927. Hinda Rock, the midwife who delivered me, was a giant woman who brought many babies into the world. Hinda was strong and walked at a quick pace, despite her great weight and height. I was the youngest of four boys born to Zisman and Grina Tenenbaum. Avrum (also called Art, Avremel, or Abraham) was ten years older than I. Next in line, born three years after Art, was Chaim-Leizer (Chaim, or Hymie). Velvel (Willie, or Volvele) was closest in age to me, and he was three years older.

One of my earliest recollections is of having a terrible earache when I was just three years old. The pain was excruciating. Mother held me, putting my ear to her breast. Soon, my pain went away. When I slept in her bed, she noticed that my heart did not have a normal rhythm, causing her great alarm. She took me from one doctor to another to check out the problem. Finally, they decided that although my heartbeat was abnormal, it was normal for me. One doctor said, "With this kind of beat, one can live a long time!"

We lived in a three-story townhouse that was flanked by several other homes. As far as I know, my mother's grandparents built the building. Mother inherited the home and shared it with her sister, Henna. Her other siblings were paid in cash for their share of the inheritance. There were two storefronts on the ground floor—Uncle Yoyev's and ours, which was a small department store. The sign above the entrance read: "Warsaw Textiles and Clothing." Our store was one of the four largest textile establishments in the city, so we were considered financially well off.

At the back was a storeroom for extra merchandise. The shelves were full, and boxes were stacked right up to the ceiling. The storeroom had a trapdoor about three feet square that led to a basement where more merchandise was kept. When winter approached, summer items were put away and winter fare was displayed. When summer approached, the process was reversed. From the storeroom, a door led to a small backyard and an alley about 15 feet wide. We could enter our house from there.

Two brothers married to two sisters occupied the whole building. The two heads of the families were my father, Zisman, married to my mother, Grina, and his brother Yoyev, who married her sister Henna. Yoyev and Henna had three children. The eldest, a son, was named Alter and was my brother Willie's age. Their daughter Royzele was my age, and another daughter Cesia was younger than me.

My family occupied 60 percent of the building and lived primarily on the second floor. My uncle's family occupied the balance of the house. The kitchen was in the front of the house and had a window overlooking Koscielna Street. It was furnished with a table, chairs, and a wooden piece of furniture that resembled a long box. During the day, this box was a surface that held two enamel water pails and some other kitchen items. When we opened it at night, it became a double bed for Willie and me.

Because the house had no indoor plumbing, the kitchen also contained a barrel that we filled with pails of water we brought in from the well. Human waste was disposed of manually, and the laundry was done in a large cauldron in the kitchen. The combined cooking range and oven were used to heat the house, and in this way, our kitchen was quite special by prewar Polish standards. Our oven had a two-foot by two-foot wood storage bin and was covered with shiny white tiles that made our kitchen look pretty and modern.

As the youngest, I was delegated the "honorary task" of emptying the chamber pot. It really was not a very difficult thing to do. I took the pot filled with liquid waste to the rear balcony and emptied it into a steel sink that drained into the open sewer in the middle of the courtyard behind our house. This, in turn, led to another open sewer that ran in swales alongside the marketplace and emptied into the river. Yes, the same river that provided water for laundry was polluted with our wastes. Solid excrement was taken to the outhouse. It was a valuable commodity that farmers eagerly purchased to mix with straw to make fertilizer for their fields, resulting in better corn and bread for us. We recycled it all.

I studied in my parents' bedroom. They had separate beds that stood high, headboard to headboard, probably because my mother was very pious. She always covered her hair with a kerchief or wig made by Shaindele Sarna, who was the best wigmaker in town and a very nice lady. Exposing one's hair to anyone other than one's husband was considered immodest. The separate beds were also because of religious dictates separating the sexes during menses. The room was large enough to be used as a dining room, living room, and study.

The room, in which the dining table doubled as my study table, also held two huge, made-to-order armoires. One of them had three sections—two bookcases flanking a clothes closet. The other large closet was filled with all the books of the Babylonian and Yerushalmi Talmud, the Five Books of Moses, the Prophets, and many other religious books by famous rabbis and scholars. The books were packed tightly from top to bottom and stacked in double rows that made the closet so heavy the floor beneath it sagged. My two oldest brothers, Art and Hymie, slept on the third floor of the house in a large room next to the *sukkah*.

The *sukkah*, used for celebrating the Feast of Tabernacles, had a two-part roof that we opened with two long poles. The *sukkah* was large enough to accommodate our family and a few neighbors. Two attics flanked the *sukkah*—the attic on the right had a skylight, and it belonged to Uncle Yoyev, who lived with his family in one room on the second floor behind our living room. Their window faced the alley, but our apartment had a balcony facing Koscielna Street, the main thoroughfare to the marketplace in Dzialoszyce.

It was nice having a balcony overlooking Koscielna Street. On Sundays, we watched the crowds going to church, and on Saturday afternoon we would see beautiful young people promenading on the *corso*—the boulevard. After the Sabbath meal on pleasant Saturdays, at about 3 p.m., the boys would meet the boys, and the girls would meet the girls. These groups would stroll past each other, stealing glances from the corners of their eyes. My mother and her sisters Frimche and Esther often sat on the balcony to observe and comment: "This one looks nice, that one not so nice. This one is the daughter of so and so. This one would make a pretty bride for Avrumele; that one would suit Chaim-Leizer." Analyzing everyone took some time. Occasionally, my two older brothers joined my mother and aunts because they wanted to check out the young ladies, but they were too religious to make comments.

There was an exuberance to life in town on Saturday nights, as evidenced by the rowdiness emanating from young men and women in their late teens and early 20s who parked themselves on a stone ledge on the *corso*. Late one Saturday night, a group including Benjamin Mandlebaum and Chanine Yasny was particularly noisy, shouting out loud and singing. They began to chant the names of the merchants on the block: "Yoyness, Yoyne, Yoyev, Zisme." It was late, and the streets were deserted, but they persisted in their chanting.

My mother, who was still at work late that night, walked out of the store and chided them, "I don't mind if you shout out loud, but at least call my husband by his proper name." "What should we call him?" they asked. "Zismele," she replied, using the diminutive of his name, her form of endearment for him. And so they continued chanting, now using the corrected version.

The balcony also offered a perfect bird's-eye view of the parades that took place on civic holidays, such as Constitution Day on the 3rd of May or Polish Independence Day on the 11th of November. Parades began at the new schoolyard behind the church and passed right in front of our house. We watched as young and old from various organizations marched by. To mark these national occasions, we decorated the balcony with beautiful velvet covers and displayed portraits of the president and marshal of Poland.

I remember when the Polish government launched a campaign to support Lot, the Polish airline. I do not know how many airplanes Poland had, but Mr. Lokai, the master tinsmith in town, made a huge model airplane—about six feet wide by eight feet long—out of shiny sheet metal. The airplane was a good imitation, with a propeller in the front and small mirrored windows that reflected the sun. It hung by two wires attached to our balcony and two tied to a balcony across the street that belonged to the Alexanderer *shtibl* (the study house of the Alexanderer Hasidim). The plane floated over the street, the thin wires unnoticed, and for the month that the fundraising campaign lasted, the children thought the airplane was heart-stoppingly exciting.

This balcony was also good for airing out our books before Passover and for storing food we wanted to keep fresh during the winter. We kept geese in the basement and fattened them up in summertime, then slaughtered them in December around Hanukkah time. My mother cut the geese into quarters, boiled them in huge pots, and then prepared about a dozen pots of fat she rendered from them. This provided delicious food during the winter and produced enough for us to give one or two pots to our aunts in Chozow, in Silesia. During the winter, I would come home from *heder* (religious school) and be entranced by the tantalizing aroma of goose and gravy cooking on the stove. My brothers and I helped ourselves to dried-up tidbits of skin that were left after the fat melted away. That treat, which was delicious with bread, tasted like heaven.

Until midwinter, we kept the pots covered with plywood, sealing them well against snow, ice, and birds. Out on the balcony, food stayed fresh and cold.

We took the pots inside as we used them, but one day when I went out to bring in a pot, I discovered that they had all been stolen. I did not know exactly when the theft occurred, but I had a good idea who the culprits were—some recent boarders in the apartment across the way. Nothing was left for us to eat that winter.

Fastened to the balcony railing was a birdhouse that I had built from plywood salvaged from the store. Bolts of fabric had been wound around the planks. My parents allowed me to build it as a reward for studying Talmud and gave me a few hours off from studying to devote to the project. I had compassion for the poor birds in winter and put out bread and seeds for them. I was also happy about the way my tiny house turned out. Once, I caught a bird, brought it into the house, and let it fly all around. My parents could not figure out how it got inside. When they saw the bird, I cried out, "A bird just flew into the house!"

"It's wintertime," my parents said. "The windows are closed, the doors are locked, and Yossele's birds are flying into the house!" Later my folks discovered that I had turned the birdhouse into a trap by hinging a small plywood flap to the birdhouse controlled by a string that went through the balcony door opening. From inside our warm house, I watched through the window, and when a bird stopped to eat crumbs, I waited for the little creature to get inside the closed area and pulled the string to release the trapdoor. Then I took my cute prisoners indoors and played with them as pets. It was fun and made me feel masterful, but in the end, I always gave the birds back their freedom.

I remember the place outside our house where I played with my friends, on the pavement in front of our store, so Mother could keep an eye on me. We collected old buttons and played a tossing game, the point of which was to have your button land on the others so you could take all the played buttons. We played a similar game with hazelnuts, aiming them into a small hole.

Since I was not given toys, I had to create my own. I remember finding an old pail, removing the metal hoop ringing the bottom, and rolling the hoop in the street by guiding it with a stick. One time, my friend Yossel Wolfe tried to make off with the hoop, and it took a little bit of "physical convincing" to get it back.

My mother sometimes sat in front of the store. Once, catching my reflection in one of the doors, she turned around to look at me. I came running and embraced her. She said to me: "Yossele, will I ever live to see you settled?" I recall those words distinctly. "Will I ever live to see you settled? You shouldn't run so fast."

Our house was on the road to Kazimierz, a town about 15 kilometers away, site of a sugar factory. Farmers from the outlying villages drove huge, horse-drawn wagons loaded with white sugar beets through Dzialoszyce. As they came by, people with long, nail-tipped sticks picked beets off the wagons. At times, my friends were also tempted to take a few beets, and I went along with some of these pranks.

The market square was on Koscielna Street, about 50 meters from our house. One of the square's main features was a monument to the Polish hero Tadeusz Kosciuszko. This military engineer volunteered to fight on the side of the American rebels shortly after the American colonies declared their independence from Great Britain. Kosciuszko, through his ingenuity, helped the colonists win the Battle of Saratoga and became a famous general. Upon returning to Poland, Kosciuszko fought against the Russians and was wounded at Maciejowice.

The Kosciuszko monument served as a gathering place for young people and was where all important announcements on behalf of the *magistrat* (city hall) were made. The town crier, Fygiel, had a few front teeth missing. When he blew loud blasts of his oversized trumpet, people of all ages, especially children, congregated around him. Fygiel often became confused and mixed up his words so that the announcement did not make sense. Once, he proclaimed, "Gentlemen cattle, the mayor got lost and he asked me to announce ...." Everyone burst out laughing. He was one type of intelligentsia that existed among the public servants of our town, though there were others who were somewhat more sophisticated.

Dzialoszyce was a *shtetl* and, as such, its inhabitants often had a folk view of the universe. Many people wore red *bintl* (ribbons or strings) to ward off the evil eye. My own mother was superstitious. I remember an occasion when Chawzie Lazniaz visited in our store. My mother took a lunch break, and the two women chatted about their respective businesses (Chawzie's husband, Itchele, was a master goldsmith) while my mother ate something. When Chawzie left, my mother started feeling nauseous and opined, "It could only be the evil eye."

The folk culture of the *shtetl* sometimes extended to medicine as well. Leibish Seniawski, nicknamed the *felsher* (folk healer), worked as a family practitioner. Leibish had a remedy called Ichtiol, a dark brown ointment with the consistency of plum jam that he packaged in small wooden containers. Whenever anybody had a complaint, be it a headache or backache, whether serious or trivial, Leibish treated it with this ointment. Amazingly, Ichtiol worked most of the time, and it helped me. Another folk remedy was a little harder for us children to take. If any of us had croup or got a really bad cough, we were taken to Uncle Aaron Yasny's stable. Urine was collected from his mare and my parents made us drink it. This was supposed to cure us. I do not know if it helped our coughs, but we all survived the treatment in good health.

The logic of the *shtetl* sometimes approached the logic of Chelm, a topsy-turvy *shtetl* where twisted reasoning was a purported commonplace and, as such, the subject of humorous folktales. I recall one incident involving the same Lazniaz family. Chawzie, a very tall woman, was walking along the main street looking for a pair of galoshes with her husband, a very short man. The contrast in their heights alone was enough to elicit a smile. (Add to that Chawzie's domineering character versus Itchele's demurring nature to complete the sketch.) As luck would have it, Itchele was pleased to find a pair of rubber galoshes that fit his diminutive foot. On the way out of the store after having made the purchase, Chawzie noticed in the window display a large pair of size 11 galoshes marked for sale at two zloty. Chawzie commented, "Look, Itchele, the price for the larger galoshes is the same as for the ones you bought. For the same money, take the larger ones!" Itchele hesitantly replied, "But the bigger ones won't fit me. They will get stuck in the mud and come off. They are much too big. How can I wear them?" Chawzie shot back, "For the same price, even if you break your legs, you will wear the larger ones!" Itchele, as usual, was defenseless in the face of his wife's overbearing "logic."

If the street was where I learned about relationships and life as a child, it was also where I learned about death. When I was about six years old, Chane Delesete died. She had a little grocery store a step up from Chmielowa Street, at the other end of town near the first school I attended. I followed the funeral procession on its way to the cemetery. On the corner of Dziekanowice Street, between the marketplace and the cemetery, a woman came out of her house, wailing, whenever a funeral passed by. People carrying and following Chane's coffin cried too, but as they neared the cemetery, this woman—who was a professional crier—started an earnest rendition of her act. She was given a few groszy as she kept on crying, bringing the others to tears. She repeatedly proclaimed, "Such a nice person, and to die so young." Afterward, I overheard her asking, "Who died? What did he die of?"

I followed Chane's coffin all the way to the grave, and when they opened it one last time to put twigs in her hands and clay shards over her eyes, I saw her lifeless face. That was the first time I saw a dead person. I thought about that face for weeks and months, and I remember every detail of it, even now. At the entrance to the cemetery, there was the tomb of a saintly rabbi whose name I do not recall. I do remember my grandparents' grave markers and a little monument for a year-old infant who may have been my aunt.

I was also exposed to a suicide. Suicide in a small town had a tremendous impact on the whole community—especially the younger generation. The first suicide I knew about before the war was that of Leibel Silber, an officer in the Polish army. I remember his splendid uniform and his cross-shaped hat sporting a feather on its left side. He was religious, very Orthodox, yet he served in the Ulany, the Polish cavalry. Leibel's father, Avrom Silber, had standing in the community and was known as a very tough, tenacious person.

Leibel used to come to the Gerer *shtibl* (Gerer Hasidim—followers of the Rabbi of Gory Kalwaryjskie in Polish, "Ger" in Yiddish) because his father prayed there. When Leibel walked into the synagogue dressed in his military uniform, he looked so grand and proud, as if he had been born in the uniform and belonged on a horse. He was often given an *aliyah* (the honor of being called to the Torah for a blessing).

Nobody ever found out the real reason for Leibel's suicide. Perhaps the tension between his upbringing as a Gerer Hasid and his position as a Polish cavalry officer contributed. Some speculated that he was in love with a girl his father did not allow him to marry. When the *hevre kadishah* (burial society) did the *taharah* (Jewish ritual washing) on Leibel's corpse, it turned black because of the arsenic he had taken. According to *halacha* (Jewish religious law), suicide is a sin, and one who takes his own life cannot be buried inside the regular cemetery boundaries. Instead, he was interred just outside of the cemetery's stone fence.

OUR HOUSEHOLD

My parents divided their responsibilities between them. Father concentrated on educating his four sons and did the buying for the store. He took three or four trips per year, usually to Warsaw and Lodz. The rest of his time he spent studying religious texts, forever searching for new insights. Mother looked after the day-to-day operation of the store and the household and had servants who helped her with the household chores. One of the girls, who worked for us for years, was responsible for cooking and preparing all meals. While some aspects of running the household have not changed, even in the 21st century, others differed radically.

Laundry is a case in point. Today, we have washing machines and dry cleaners. We do not give much thought to tossing a hardly worn garment into the hamper. In Dzialoszyce, laundry was a major undertaking. First, one had to get water from the river because well water was too hard for washing and was useful only for drinking or cooking. Rainwater, collected in large vessels stored on the balconies, was also used, all handled by the laundress, who came to our home for this specific purpose.

Clothes were put in a big cauldron on the stove and boiled for a long time to kill bacteria and loosen dirt. We used large quantities of dried-up soap that was manufactured in town. The laundress lathered the dirty linen and scrubbed it on washboards. Then she dipped the clothes in a vessel of clean water and rinsed the garments again and again. Finally, the clean clothes were wrung out by hand. In later years, the clothes were put through a wringer, which left them almost dry. Helpers took the clothes up to the attic where the clean laundry was hung on ropes attached to the rafters. The dry laundry was taken down, and larger pieces, such as sheets, were stretched and folded by the seamstresses we contracted to sew merchandise for our store. Later, using irons heated by coal, the laundry was ironed and folded. Although she was fully occupied with running the shop, Mother always directed the help when they did the laundry.

My parents treated the servants who cared for us like their own children. These people were usually between 20 and 30 years old. My mother prepared dowries for them so that they could marry in proper weddings and enter their new lives with trousseaus that contained all the essentials.

I especially remember a particular case that exemplified the relationship my parents had with their employees. One year, Minda, one of the house servants, decided to go home to her parents on the day before Pesach (Passover). The next evening, my father returned from *shul* (synagogue), and we prepared to begin the seder. Our family and the invited guests were all assembled when Father noticed that Minda was missing. When he asked where she was, Mother explained her absence, and Father got upset. He declared that he would not sit down for the seder without Minda because a person who worked in our household should feel enough a part of our family to participate in holiday celebrations with us. Father left and went to Minda's house to make sure that she felt at home in our place and was being treated properly. After he insisted that she return for the seder, Minda complied, and we proceeded with the service.

Father's responsibilities in the household were generally limited to special projects that were usually connected to Jewish ritual or festivals. Making wine for *kiddush* was a useful hobby of his. He kept many bottles of homemade wine locked in a cabinet in the attic. He tied paper over the tops of the grape juice–filled bottles and made little air holes with a pin so that the wine could ferment. From time to time, he checked the wine, sometimes taking me with him when he tasted samples to see which bottles were good and which needed sugar. Sometimes he blended bottles to produce a very good wine. As time went on, I learned more about winemaking from him and decided to surprise him with my talent.

I went out to the meadow, picked certain blue-petaled flowers, and put them into bottles filled with water and sugar. I kept the bottles hidden so that he would not see them. When they were ready, I offered him a sample of this wine without revealing its source. After tasting it, Father agreed that it was very good. When I told him what it was, he was proud of me and pleased with the wine I made for him out of meadow flowers.

Sometimes Father's projects did not turn out so well. Our family had a tradition of making borscht before Passover—three or four pails, at least, so there would be enough for the holiday and for my aunt and her family. It was special borscht, and large pails of it were lined up on the sleeping bench. The pails, which were enameled white inside and blue outside and trimmed beautifully at the rim and base, were filled with red beets and water. We had to be very careful making the borscht and covered the pails with cardboard to make sure that no bread or other type of *homets* fell in. (On Passover, we are commanded to remove all leavened products like bread and fermented products, such as beer, from our houses. The purpose of this removal is to recall the flight from slavery in ancient Egypt, a time when Jews had to leave so quickly that they did not have time to let their bread rise.) The borscht had to be 100 percent kosher for Passover and could not be contaminated.

One year, Father checked the pails on the day before Passover and instead of borscht found a congealed mass. He was so embarrassed that early the next morning I dumped them in the outhouse, making sure nobody saw me do it. When I put the last pail on top of the garbage pile, it flipped over and the mass held together like a Jell-O mold.

Amid the general Passover cleaning—changing the straw in the mattresses, airing out all the books on the balcony, brushing out the crumbs that would fall between the pages, and reshelving the books—we had to carefully watch over a sack of wheat. Any dampness could cause the wheat to ferment (or rise), which would have rendered it *homets*, forbidden on Passover. Because the prohibition is so strict, Father took a personal hand in supervising the process. To make sure the wheat contained no *homets*, it was inspected by spreading small amounts on a white sheet of paper and removing suspected impurities, such as black grains, one by one. We then ground the wheat into flour from which we baked *matzah shmura* (matzo given extra attention in preparation).

Sukkoth (the Feast of the Tabernacles) was the one holiday where my brothers and I took primary responsibility for the centerpiece of the holiday, the *sukkah*—the tabernacle. Sukkoth commemorates the wanderings of the Israelites in the desert, living in temporary shelters, or *sukkoth*. What made our *sukkah* "temporary," though its walls were permanent, was its roof that opened. One could then gaze straight into heaven. What made our *sukkah* unique was its size and its upper-story location—with its windows above the roof of Yankel Bergman's house next door and facing south toward the market square—that provided a view over most of the town.

On cold autumn days, one side of the *sukkah* was warmed by the white brick chimney wall that passed through it. That is where the children sat. We enjoyed our *sukkah*, even when it was not Sukkoth. Being in this special place made the spirit of the holiday last the whole year.

We started the preparations for the holiday by making ornaments out of whatever we could find. Willie and I went to the church garden where there were lots of chestnut trees and collected in a large pot the green, thick-skinned nuts lying on the ground. If there were not enough of them for our use, we climbed the trees and shook the branches or took a stick and hit the chestnuts until they fell. Afterward, we brought the chestnuts to the attic, which we entered through a door in the *sukkah*. Then we split the shells open and took out the beautiful, shiny nuts and strung them together with colorful string. It took a long time to wash our hands because they were black from peeling chestnuts.

My dear older brother, Chaim-Leizer, sat on the steps leading to the *sukkah* and, in addition to doing the physical work of decorating the *sukkah*, considered how we would finance its decoration. He devoted most of his time to the store, where his help was much needed. He advised us to take colored paper, crayons, and other materials we needed from the bookstore and deduct the cost from the money the establishment owed Father. In addition to good ideas, Chaim-Leizer gave us 50 groszy for what we needed to buy, like a large pumpkin to hang in the middle of the *sukkah*. Our parents also gave us gifts we could use to decorate the *sukkah*. Willie, the maid, and I made all kinds of colorful chains with each link a different color. We cut out Hebrew lettering for quotations related to the holiday and worked for at least a week before the holiday to clean up, paint, install lights, and finish decorations. Everything was tightly secured, especially the pumpkins, so they would not fall down into the plates or on the heads of people sitting around the table.

The pièce de résistance was the pumpkin that I carved and hollowed out to use as a lantern. But we needed to solve the problem of getting power to it since we still did not have electricity. There were, however, a chosen few along the length of Koscielna Street who could afford electricity and for whom wiring had recently been installed. For me, the distance between the wiring and three small windows in our attic was tantalizingly close. On the eve of Sukkoth, I hooked into the electrical wires and got power to the *sukkah*. When Father came back from his *shtibl* with our guests and saw the light, he had mixed feelings. On the one hand, he liked how the electric light added to the festive atmosphere. On the other hand, he could not condone taking electricity without paying for it. Furthermore, my jerry-rigged hookup was dangerous, and Father feared the possibility of a fire. A week after Sukkoth, Father ordered electricity to be legally connected to the whole house. This pleased the owner of the hydroelectric company and the electrician, who was happy to have another job.

HEDER

My parents started sending me to *heder* when I was about four years old. On the first day, my parents gave me several groszy—back then, two could buy an ice cream, three, a bagel. The newly minted coins were shiny and I happily kept the treasure in my pocket. I was happy to go to *heder* and play with more children my own age. At home, my siblings had their own friends and did not include me in their games. Though the *heder* was not far from home, the walk was interesting because I had to pass the bakery and shoe store, and I could look at the goods displayed. A man who held janitorial jobs at several buildings in town also lived along my route, and I liked to see all his dogs.

At *heder*, the teacher was Heshele, a short man with a long beard, who looked tall from our diminutive perspectives. We called him Heshele *Kaker* (a Yiddish word referring to excrement) because his *heder* included many very small children, and many of them were not yet toilet trained. Heshele told us stories from the Bible and taught us some basic prayers, but in reality, the *heder* was just a nursery.

Across from the *heder* was a laundry with a mangle, a linen wringer. This contraption consisted of a very large box filled with stones that sat on top of a set of rollers. When the housewives or their maids put the linen through the rollers, the rolling weight smoothed and pressed the linens. It was often more interesting to look out the window to watch the goings on at the laundry than it was to listen to Heshele, who would often chase us around the *heder* when our minds wandered.

When I was five years old, my parents sent me to another *heder* run by Rabbi Yosef-Leib. This school was on the second floor of a house located in an alley off the town's market square and had two entrances in its facade. The second floor was shared with the Szliwinskis and two other families. The *heder* was near the Sancygniowka River, named for its source in the village of Sancygniow. The rebbe's face, framed by a long beard, was punctuated by dark, deep-set eyes. Although his posture was slightly bent, he stood tall.

At this *heder* we started learning *Humash* (the Five Books of Moses) and *siddur* (the prayer book) orally and began identifying the printed letters of the Hebrew alphabet. We got to *heder* at 8:30 a.m. and recited three or four basic prayers in unison. Then we were given letter charts with vowels, one to a pair, and the rebbe started us off in the singsong *"kometz aleph-o,"* similar to A-B-C rhymes kindergarten children sing today. Some students brought food with them, but most of us went home for lunch then returned to *heder* for the afternoon. In the winter it got dark early, but most of my 12 classmates and I had to stay in school until 7:30 or 8 in the evening. I was always jealous of Norman Kamelgard, whose sister Hannaleh picked him up by 7 p.m., well before the end of the school day.

Chiel Garfinkel was another lucky boy whose older sister came for him after classes. Because I was the youngest in my family and had three brothers who could have picked me up, staying in school well after nightfall made me feel abandoned. When it was time to go home, because it was dark and I was little, I would run all the way. Fortunately, my home was closer to the *heder* than those of most of my friends. Since Dzialoszyce did not have streetlights, we carried homemade lanterns made of cardboard and translucent paper with candles inside. Some of the children from more comfortable families had store-bought tin lanterns.

Once, when I misbehaved, Rabbi Yosef-Leib sent a fellow student to fetch Father so that he could have a hand in my punishment. Because Father had not yet arrived when the rest of the class was dismissed, I decided to make a break for it because I knew Father would scold me. There were two entrances to the building, each having its own address, and though I had not yet started to learn *Gemara*, I was already starting to reason in Talmudic patterns. Number 8 was closer to where Father was coming from, so I thought of escaping through Number 10 to avoid him. Then I reasoned that Father would probably anticipate the exit I chose, so I selected the other one. This reversal brought me back to Number 8, where I bumped right into him. He grabbed my arm and took me back to the rebbe. My usual punishment was a good scolding and the withholding of my allowance.

We students were a rebellious group and often had fun because of it. One time we put glue on the rebbe's chair and after he sat down, much to our amusement, he could not get up. Whatever we did manage to learn was due to the rabbi's *kanchik*, a whip with a handle that had several strips of leather at its end. Rabbi Yosef-Leib always had his *kanchik* with him and seldom put it down. Once the students hid it, and the rabbi spent hours trying to find it while we fooled around and learned nothing. Yet, when he had the *kanchik* in hand, he used it quite often, and its force kept us on our benches.

Leibel, the son of Beryl the shoemaker, also attended the *heder* of Yosef-Leib, the *melamed*. Leibel was a tall, handsome, strong fellow, whom the rabbi once punished by putting a heavy pot of water on his shoulders and telling him to stand at the wall with his hands up. The rabbi sat down and proceeded with the lesson. Leibel stood there for a minute or two, but was unable to withstand the punishment. He threw the pot to the floor with a crashing sound, and with lightning speed, he jumped the three high steps leading out of the classroom door and was gone. He never came back. I offered to take Leibel's books home to him, but the rabbi refused my request. The books were expensive, and not everybody could afford them. In *heder* we used old, torn books, and even those were not plentiful.

A typical *heder* term lasted six months, from Passover to the end of Sukkoth and from Sukkoth to Passover. *Hadorim* and their *melamdim* catered to specific age groups and academic levels, causing students to change schools as they matured and advanced to different levels of study.

After attending Yosef-Leib's *heder*, I transferred to the *heder* of Rabbi Yaakov Lehrer on Chmielowa Street, farther from home. To get to school, I had to cross the Sancygniowka River over a little bridge, which was at a very narrow point near the mill, right behind the *heder*. It was 1933, and when I was six years old, I studied there in the afternoons, because newly enacted Polish regulations required us to go to public school every morning.

This particular *heder* differed from the others because, in addition to the standard curriculum of the Five Books of Moses with its various commentaries, the Yiddish language was taught as a subject. For the first time, we had a blackboard and chalk in the classroom and learned to write the Hebrew alphabet, which is also used for writing Yiddish. We were also given notebooks in which to practice our handwriting.

Rabbi Yaakov Lehrer's second-floor *heder* had two rooms, one of which held a large chest. It was always filled with dried-out bagels and bread—goodies that the rebbe scavenged from the uneaten food the children left behind. I don't know what he did with his hoard; perhaps he gave it to the poor or fed it to pets or birds. This rebbe also had a passion for sour pickles, and every day he sent one of the students to buy some for him. The pickles were brought to him in the pitcher that we used for ritually washing our hands before the blessing on bread. They were large pickles, and when he squeezed them, the juice squirted out. Yaakov Lehrer's wife did not come up to the second-floor schoolroom, but stayed downstairs. On our way out, she asked for money from students whose parents had not yet paid tuition. She never asked me, which I took as a sign that my parents always paid on time.

My good friends Norman Kamelgard, Hershel Mandelbaum, and Chiel Garfinkel were also my *heder*-mates. We often played a game called "two fires" in the summer. The objective was to throw a ball as hard as we could at the other team members (11 per team) so they would not be able to catch it. If it hit the ground after touching one of them, that person would be out of the game. In the winter, we slid down the hill near Norman's house. My second cousin, Meilach Yasny, an excellent soccer player, also attended our *heder*.

When I was ready to leave Rabbi Lehrer's *heder*, my father sent me to Rebbe Meyerl's *heder*, also located on Chmielowa Street, but farther away from the center of town. It was near the Stawisko, a sports field at the north end of town, on the road to the village of Chmielow. Stawisko came from the Polish word for pond, reflecting the area's much earlier incarnation as a small lake. On occasion it was so muddy we wondered if its earlier incarnation had come back to haunt us. We had to cross another bridge over the Sancygniowka River to get to the Stawisko to play football and other field games.

More students attended Rebbe Meyerl's *heder* than had attended my previous *hadorim*. We were 20 students, ranging in age from seven to nine. The group included Schmelke Balderman, the twins David and Yankel Balderman, the Stoleks, and the Huberwasser children. Schmelke was the oldest and the strongest of the boys. He once hit me so hard I cried, so the rebbe offered me his *kanchik* and I let Schmelke have it. He remembered that beating for a long time.

Rebbe Meyerl was a short, heavy, older man with a white beard. He had some sort of skin disease and was always scratching himself. He was a good teacher, but we were still troublemakers and gave him a hard time. Our antics included peeing into the washbasin or the garbage pail when we went to the washroom. The *heder* consisted of two rooms that were really the rebbe's living quarters. We never went into the second room, which was the rebbe's bedroom. With so many students and such close quarters, the rebbe's wife had to help her husband with disciplining the class. When she got angry, she would yell at the top of her lungs and hit us with both hands.

The *heder*'s clock stood on a shelf in a cabinet with glass doors. Often, we moved the hands of that clock so that we could take midday breaks sooner. We were young boys with lots of pent-up energy; we just wanted to get out of *heder* to play. In the winter, we slid down a nearby hill on homemade skates that we made of wire rods attached to the bottoms of wooden blocks. When we returned to *heder* red-faced and perspiring, the rebbe would ask sarcastically, "How come you are so blue?" Then he would hit one of us because he knew we had been skating instead of studying *Humash*.

Rebbe Meyerl had a daughter named Sheindel, who was a quite beautiful 17-year-old. We all liked her because she was compassionate and tried to restrain her father when he wanted to hit us. She later married Shloymeleh, a learned person and one of the teachers who was forever studying.

Not far from Rebbe Meyerl's *heder*, at the foot of the hill, near Beryl the shoemaker's place, there lived a rebbe named Kopel Unger. In time, I studied Talmud with him. Rebbe Kopel Unger was frail, and his *heder* differed from the others. We learned to concentrate and take the texts seriously—otherwise, slaps could land on any part of our body. This rebbe had a unique approach to discipline. If a pupil did not behave, the rebbe would pinch his thighs with a large spoon, grabbing flesh between the spoon and his thumb. The pain was excruciating.

My older brothers had also studied at Kopel Unger's *heder*. Father was very Orthodox and knew his *Humash*, the commentaries, and the Talmud very well. He wanted me to learn more than I was learning and to advance at a quicker pace. He sent me to study at other *hadorim*, including one run by Chaim Chiel on Dziekanowice Street at the southern end of town. He taught advanced classes to boys nine and ten years old.

The second-floor *heder* was located near the Dina-Danas Bakery, not far from a number of kosher slaughterers. Hershel Lubelski, the very smart son of Reb Leibish, the *shoykhet* (ritual slaughterer), was one of my *heder*-mates. Moshe Drobiarz, who lived across the hall, had a beautiful daughter to whom we all liked to talk. I was not studious, although most of the day was spent on religious texts. As an active, energetic boy, I liked to do things quickly and was rarely able to sit still.

Hebrew was the language of the Bible, but when I wanted to study modern Hebrew, Father was not too happy about it. He wanted me to concentrate on the Bible's content, on Talmud, and on *halacha* (Judaic law). Even the Prophets were not 100 percent to his liking, but he compromised. Modern Hebrew and Zionism were not part of his world. In fact, he did not support the idea of Jews returning voluntarily to the land of Israel. He believed in the coming of the Messiah, who would bring redemption to the Jewish people and lead them all back to Jerusalem on the wings of eagles.

Balcia Bergman, my next-door neighbor, accidentally introduced me to Zionism. I was visiting one time and noticed a large photograph of a bearded man. It was sitting on a shelf, locked up in a large breakfront that held precious objects. Balcia asked me what I was looking at because I could not take my eyes off the photo. Except for his side-curls and a shorter haircut, Father closely resembled the image in the photo. I was having a hard time believing it was not Father in a different incarnation, but Balcia said it was Dr. Theodor Herzl, of whom I had never heard. Balcia explained who he was and also told me that the Zionist organization to which she belonged was called the Zionist Youth Group and proudly showed me her uniform. I begged Balcia to give me the photograph, but she would not part with it.

My wish to learn Hebrew intensified when I met Professor Joseph Landau, a new face in town. He was a very short man with a bit of a paunch and no facial hair, which in Dzialoszyce made him stand out as a secular person. He was a genius who spoke eight or ten languages fluently. (After the Germans invaded, the Professor became the town's chief interpreter.) I insisted on studying Hebrew with him. Father refused to pay for the lessons, but Mother was more understanding. She went to Professor Landau's house and made a deal: in exchange for Hebrew lessons for me, she would give him clothing every month. I loved Hebrew. Whenever my brother Art was out of the house, I unlocked the drawer where he kept his Hebrew dictionaries and used them to learn new words.

I was inspired by my exposure to the Po'alei Agudat Israel, an observant religious-Zionist umbrella organization to which Art belonged. Benjamin Mintz, who had immigrated to Palestine to work on Kibbutz Chofetz Chaim, sent us magazines and *Baderech*, another publication from the Yishuv, and I used them to practice. The young members sang a hymn in Hebrew that began with the words, "Gather brethren, youth of Agudath Yisrael." Despite Father's views, the rest of my family was active in the organization.

I also wanted to learn Hebrew so that I could read my brother's personal letters. He corresponded with friends such as Meyer Wolgelernter, brother of Chaim Yitzchak, who was a scholar and the son-in-law of Yachet Platkiewicz. Although I played with friends my own age, I was always curious about what the older fellows were doing.

Professor Landau conducted several Hebrew classes, and I took more than the regular number of class hours because I came early to listen to the lessons of the other students. When they did not understand a Hebrew word and Professor Landau noticed me waiting to speak (because I was in a lower grade), he would call on me. Usually, I gave him the correct answer. He was proud of me, and I took a great liking to him.

Professor Landau also taught French and English. His class was the first time I ever heard the English language. I learned a few words just by listening to him and felt he was a wonderful teacher.

TALMUDIC PIECEWORK

Father was dissatisfied with my progress in the *hadorim*, so he engaged Rebbe Meyerl's son-in-law, Shloymeleh, as a private tutor. He came to our house to study with me daily, while Father kept an eye on my three brothers, my teachers, and me.

While I studied with Shloymeleh, Father would get me up early to review the text I had learned the previous day and test me from five to seven o'clock every morning. He sat at the table and, in the lamplight, reviewed sections of Talmud. I studied with Shloymeleh from noon until four o'clock. Father paid Shloymeleh ten groszy for every page of Talmud he taught me. This arrangement was designed to accelerate my pace of study. Then Shloymeleh paid me two groszy per page if I knew the material.

For me, two groszy constituted a small fortune. For this sum, I could buy an ice cream; four groszy bought a bar of chocolate. Each bar was wrapped with one letter of the word "chocolate," and anyone who saved all the letters to make the word could redeem them for a free candy bar. If I had two or three of the same letters, I traded them with friends I met on *Shabes* in the *shtibl*. As soon as *Shabes* was over and the candy store opened, I hurried there with all my letters.

The storeowner, however, was superstitious. She was convinced that the success of her business rested on making a real sale as her first order of business each week. For her, redeeming goods for no profit before making her first real sale was a bad omen, so she refused to give me the chocolate.

On one such occasion, instead of wasting time and waiting for the woman

...went home to study. The following morning Father tested... ...derstood the contents of three pages, he would have to pay ...oszy, and I stood to earn six groszy for my cut. Learning three pages... ...enge. I wanted to cover even more, but the sages' questions, answers, and interpretations in the *Mishnah* and *Gemara* were so intricate and complicated, I could barely manage three. If I learned the material superficially or inaccurately, I would have to return the money to Shloymeleh. But when I studied with Shloymeleh, I did not want to waste time asking questions about material I did not fully understand because I wanted to get more pages under my belt. After all, I was being paid for "piecework."

When Father tested me before he went to *shul*, I sometimes did not know the intricacies as well as he expected me to, and his tests flustered me. He would often prove I really hadn't studied properly. After a while, to compensate for the quickened pace of my studies with Shloymeleh, I decided to do nightly reviews of what I had studied during the day. I would begin reviewing after 6 p.m., and some nights I would ruminate on what it all meant until 11 p.m.

In winter, it was so cold our windows were often covered in ice. Father would feed and warm me each morning. One day I woke early, covered myself with the blanket, kept my eyes closed, and pretended to be asleep. I must have been seven or eight years old at the time and still sleeping in Mother's bed. I sneezed, and Father said, "Yossele, one doesn't sneeze when one is sleeping. If you sneeze, that means you're awake, so open your eyes." Another time, he did not deliberately wake me, but he was breathing on me in such a way that I could not help but wake up. When I woke, he wrapped me in heavy blankets and proceeded to check if I really understood my previous lesson.

On one hand, I felt under the gun. On the other hand, I was competitive, and wanting to know more than the others was more important than the pressure I felt. Besides, if I knew the material, Father would give me almost anything I wanted. If I did not know it, all I got was aggravation.

As time passed, I explained to Father that I wanted to study things in addition to the Holy Scriptures and the Talmud, but he objected. We continued to have heated discussions about the matter, day after day, week after week. Father kept the books he did not want me to read behind the first row of books in the book cupboard. These books contained Hasidic stories by the Kotztker Rebbe (Rabbi Menachem Mendel of Kotzk), Reb Simcha Bunem of Pshysche, Rabbi Yitzchak Meyer of Gur, the Alexanderer Rebbe, and others. These Hasidic books contained legendary tales about different rebbes and their dynasties. Father also did not allow me to study the Zohar or other kabalistic works. These were mystical works that speculated on the nature of God, the angels, the afterlife, and other esoteric aspects of theology. In fact, the rabbis suggested that one should not study kabala until one married or reached the age of 40. They reasoned that a certain level of maturity was required before one delved into such heady subjects. When my father caught me reading such works, he said, "Yossele, it's good to eat potatoes with a little bit of gravy. But if you just eat gravy, you'll get sick to your stomach. It's not healthy." He was comparing potatoes to the study of Talmud, which he considered scintillating. To him, these stories were the gravy. Nevertheless, I was drawn to these books.

Father kept important documents and money locked in a drawer inside the book cupboard. One day in 1937, when I was ten, I helped Father count money from the store before it went into the drawer. Father tallied the paper money while I counted five-*zloty* coins, which I loved doing. Father kept the coins in metal boxes because collecting them was something of a hobby for him. While he watched to see how well I handled the money, I said to him, "Father, after 120 years, when you leave an inheritance and divide all your material possessions among us, please don't forget one thing. You can give my three older brothers anything you like, including all the money, but you should leave all the books that are in this cupboard to me."

"Avrumele (a diminutive, endearing form of Art) can keep the dictionaries you gave him for a present, but all the rest, all the books on the shelves, I want." Father liked what I said and often repeated it to others, which was embarrassing for me. Once, after I heard him tell the story, I said, "Father, this was supposed to be between you and me. Why do you tell others what is between us?"

SECULAR EDUCATION OR WITHOUT *PEYES*

Father, an ultraorthodox Gerer Hasid, did not want his sons going to public school. Public schools were coeducational, and Christian prayers were recited in the classrooms. One could not enter a room without having to confront an image of Jesus nailed to a cross. All these things were taboo for a religious boy. In the mid-1930s new governmental regulations required all Polish children to receive a government-sanctioned secular education. Nobody taught us math, science, or Polish in *heder*. In fact, the rebbe often did not even know Polish. Father had to bite the bullet and send me to public school.

For me, public school was a very strange place. As luck would have it, my friends Norman Kamelgard, Hershel Mandelbaum, Chiel Garfinkel, and Mottel Leschman were enrolled in a different school. There were about 35 boys and girls in my class. In the strange environment with the girls, the crucifixes, my ignorance of the Polish language, and the children from radically different backgrounds, I stuck out like a sore thumb. Hasidic boys wore unique caps and long topcoats that reached below our knees, and my *peyes* (earlocks) looked like coiled springs. If I stretched one out, it would extend a foot. Our hair was cropped close enough to see our scalps. (The one time my brother Art let his hair grow just a bit, Father reprimanded him and told him to get a haircut because the top of the head was for *tefillin* [phylacteries], not long hair. When Art failed to obey immediately, Father cut his hair while he was asleep.)

The first few days of school were hell for me. The other children made fun of my *peyes* and strange garb, and it was especially embarrassing to be teased by girls. Hanusia Glatkiewicz, the daughter of the local constable, was one little girl who I thought was very nice. I must have had a crush on her because the day she laughed at me, she broke my heart. That afternoon when I came home from school, I took a pair of scissors from the shop and chopped off my *peyes*.

When Father saw me without *peyes* he shouted angrily, "Who cut off your *peyes*? What happened?" Antisemitism had been growing in Poland, and Father assumed I was a victim. Because he frightened me, I lied and told Father that my teacher, Mrs. Zlodzinska, had cut them off. Father grabbed my hand and began to drag me back to the school. Realizing that my doom was before me, I changed my story and blamed the incident on the principal instead. I hoped that Father would be as afraid of the principal as I was and would back off from the confrontation. That did not happen.

The principal, Maciek Kozminski, lived in a house behind the church. (I remember his signature from the report cards, and I can still sign his name exactly as he did, with a prominent "K" repeated under his name.) When we got to the principal's house, my father asked him about the *peyes*. Mr. Kozminski, of course, denied having any knowledge of the incident. At that point Father turned and glared at me. When we got home, I was spanked first for lying and second for cutting off my *peyes*.

The curriculum in public school included Polish grammar, mathematics, geography, and even religion. David Wdowinski, a Jew, taught Judaism to Jewish students. I was always ahead of the class in this subject. In fact, I probably knew as much about religion as the teacher, because he was not Orthodox and lacked a real understanding of religious texts in Hebrew. Only Jewish students with the most minimal religious upbringing could benefit from his lessons.

I found the geography class taught by Mr. Kovalsky to be most interesting. Once during exams, the principal visited the classroom, and our teacher wanted to show off how well we knew our lessons. Mr. Kovalsky talked about Poland's borders with other countries. I knew Germany was west, Czechoslovakia lay south, Hungary was southeast, Russia was to the east, and Latvia was northeast. The Baltic Sea was due north. When the teacher asked about the significance of the Baltic Sea for Poland and no one else responded, he called on me. I came forward and used the pointer to locate the Baltic Sea and Polish border. Then Mr. Kovalsky asked again, "How is the Baltic Sea significant to

Poland?" I knew the answer he expected but said I did not know, not wanting to embarrass the rest of the class and make enemies.

"You ass!" snapped the teacher. "Don't you know that the Baltic Sea is a window to the world?" I replied, "If the Baltic Sea is a window to the world for Poland, then the Mediterranean Sea is an open gate to Palestine." The patriotic teacher, an officer in the Polish army, became very angry. He reached for a wooden pencil case and hit me with it twice on my hand. Then he sent me home to get my parents and bring them to school. My father listened to the teacher's complaint and then scolded me for not answering the question.

The teacher's overreaction reflected growing antipathy to the Jews. In the government, a movement began to prohibit *shkhite* (ritual slaughter). Fortunately, the movement, proposed by Madame Pristofer, an antisemitic Polish minister, assisted by a priest named Czeciak, did not work. "Jews to Palestine" was a cry often heard, and Jewish children quickly learned the difference between visions of a homeland flowing with "milk and honey" and the bitter reality of Polish hatred. Jewish students were often taunted and attacked with stones. The schools were also full of students from outlying areas who came to Dzialoszyce for schooling. To accommodate so many out-of-town pupils, a new school was built behind the church. When I passed the church on the way home from school, I had to watch out for those who, at any time, might decide I was a suitable target.

We Jews were the town's majority, but not the majority in the area. In the mid-1930s, Polish antisemites formed hate organizations. They would stand on the main street and chant anti-Jewish slogans such as "Don't buy from the Jews!" and "To each his own!" to promote Gentile businesses. These groups circulated leaflets and pasted antisemitic posters on the retaining wall of the church, along the main street. One such poster was a caricature of a huge, fat, hook-nosed Jew pumping blood into himself from a small, thin, emaciated non-Jew. The caption beneath the caricature read, "Buy from your own."

Tradesmen who came into our home to do work for us never bothered to restrain themselves. When my parents hired the Adamczyk Tile Company to tile over the oven and stove, I took a keen interest, looking up from my Talmud to watch the workmen. When the tilers realized what I was studying, they started making antisemitic jokes. Another time my father ordered new furniture from a fine cabinetmaker named Schab, who was a very religious Catholic. He discussed the Bible with Father, for whom sacred scripture was the Old Testament alone. The cabinetmaker expounded his beliefs; Father could not accept, and the two men disagreed.

In an attempt to lighten the conversation, Mr. Schab told a joke. My father had no time or patience for jokes but had to listen to this one. Mr. Schab described a Jewish woman who was complaining about smoke coming through her wall. The male neighbor on the other side of the wall had installed a stovepipe, but, instead of connecting it into the chimney, had simply put it through the wall, with the smoke exhausting right into the Jewish woman's apartment. When pleading did not help and the woman could not stand the smoke anymore, she took the man to court and pleaded her case before the judge.

At this point, Mr. Schab affected an exaggerated Jewish accent, mimicking the woman: "Listen, Judge. He took his pipe, he put it into my hole, and I can't take it anymore." The story was lewd, and it was told with the kind of Polish bigotry that we encountered all too often in our lives. It bothered me that Father had to listen to it.

The liberals in Poland who were "good for the Jews" were not entirely innocent of using the Jews for their own ends. On May 12, 1935, Jozef Pilsudski, the Polish marshal, died. All public institutions, including the school I attended, displayed portraits of Pilsudski draped in black ribbons. The entire country went into mourning. Speakers delivered eulogies, poets wrote sentimental, patriotic poems, and musicians composed mournful songs with wistful melodies. One song went like this:

> It's not true that you are not alive,
> It's not true that you are lying in your grave,
> When the whole Polish country is mourning,
> And all the people cry.

My classmates exclaimed, "Our grandpa died." Everybody wore black armbands. Though I was still quite young, I was personally affected, caught up in the patriotic fervor being expressed all around me.

Pilsudski had fought for an independent Poland, organizing the working classes in their struggle against the Russian czarist regime. The Russians exiled him to Siberia after falsely accusing him of plotting the czar's assassination. Although he later fought with the Germans against the Russians in World

War I, the Germans incarcerated him for insisting on an independent Poland. With the collapse of Germany in 1918, Pilsudski got his wish. He created the first Polish government and was elected head of state. The general opinion was that Pilsudski was Poland's savior.

Pilsudski was a Socialist who believed in equal rights and therefore had a reputation as someone whose politics benefited Polish Jewry. However, in 1997, I was told an interesting story that someone heard from his grandfather, Shmuel Goldstein, of Nowy Korczyn, Poland. In 1920, when Pilsudski campaigned in Ukraine against the Russian advance on Warsaw, he desperately needed money. Pilsudski entered Nowy Korczyn, took ten Jews hostage, and demanded 10,000 rubles for their release. Pilsudski threatened to hang the Jews if his demand was not met. With great effort, the money was raised, and the hostages were released. Afterward, Pilsudski sent a handwritten letter to Goldstein to apologize for his behavior and explained that it was dictated by the exigencies of the times. Children of the former hostages who survived the Holocaust corroborate the story.

Despite this generally hostile atmosphere, not every Gentile I encountered during my public school days was antisemitic. One of my teachers, Mr. Pawlowski, was a very fine man and a high-ranking officer in the Polish army. On Independence Day and other national holidays, Mr. Pawlowski would wear his very impressive medal-bedecked uniform.

Father took primary responsibility for our education and attended the parents' meetings held at school. Two hours were reserved for parents to have interviews with the teachers, and then the students returned to their classes. On one such occasion, Father arrived after the conclusion of the parents' session and walked in right in the middle of our lesson.

Mr. Pawlowski said to Father, "*Panie* Zysmanie [Mr. Zysman—Father was known by his first name], you did not have to come. However, since you are here, I might as well tell you that your son, Jozek [the Polish version of my first name], is doing very well in all subjects. He knows how to study, he knows the answers, he does his homework, and he is good."

Father turned around and looked at me while I was sitting in the class among all the other students. He replied, "Mr. Pawlowski, what are you saying? Do you know what he does, my son? He fools the rabbi, he fools me, and now I can see he is fooling you too. He doesn't know enough; he should know much more!"

I started crying because Father had insulted me in front of all my classmates.

Now, as I look back and think about it, I understand that Father, in his own way, used the situation to prod me to do better.

I liked my teacher very much and when we would meet him in the streets of our town, the girls would curtsy and the boys would doff their hats. We followed him around like ducklings. Mr. Pawlowski moved gracefully, his body gliding like a dancer's. Once he noticed that I had forgotten to button the fly of my pants and, pointing to my crotch, noted, "You know, Jozek, on the Sabbath the stores are supposed to be closed, but your store is open."

In wintertime, on my way home from school, I would usually go skating on the fish breeder's pond in the meadow, and once, I fell through the ice. By the time I got home, my clothing was frozen and had icicles hanging from it. Father and Mother undressed me immediately, put me to bed, and, fearing I would come down with pneumonia, cuddled me.

THE GERER *SHTIBL*

Father was a follower of the Rabbi of Gur, Reb Abraham Mordechai Alter, also known as the *Imre Emet*. Reb Alter had inherited the title from his father, Reb Yehudah Aryeh Leib, who was known as the *Sfat Emet* (from the title of a commentary he had written), under whose leadership Ger became the largest Hasidic group in Poland. Three times a year Father would travel to the city of Gur, not far from Warsaw, to be with his rebbe.

There were about 150 Gerer Hasidim in our town. There were Hasidim who were followers of other rabbis as well—Alexanderer, Chenciner, and Dzialoszycer to name a few—who prayed at their own *shtibls*. The chief Rav, Staszewski, and the *dayan* (community judge) had their own congregations. The town also had one large central synagogue and a large *Beit Midrash* (study hall). There was no local Gerer rabbi, although sometimes there was a visiting rabbi. We *davened* (prayed) at the Gerer *shtibl*.

Before the beautiful new Gerer *shtibl* was built, we attended services closer to home. Our Gerer *minyan* prayed near Yatkes' butcher shop in the small, lower level of a row house close to the river. It was wedged between other houses and had no room to expand. The new Gerer *shtibl* was a large, freestanding building on Krakauer Street erected on a large lot donated by Hershel Drobiarz, a prominent, well-to-do Hasid. Hershel was also one of our *ba'alei tefilah*, a prayer leader who chanted the liturgy with a devotion that was immensely inspiring. Even though Hershel was such an outstanding member of the Gerer community, his sons Shmuel and Moshe chose not to be Hasidim.

It became a tradition for Father to give a *kiddush* (collation after services) in our house on Simchat Torah (the holiday on which we complete and begin anew the reading of the Torah with rejoicing and dancing) for all the Hasidim from the Gerer *shtibl*. I remember one Chune Edelist who was very short but had an extremely long beard and mustache. After a few drinks, he acted like a clown, splitting the hair of his beard into two parts and tying the ends to his mustache while he danced on top of a table.

Kalmen Blade was another "colorful" Hasid. He lived near the old Gerer *shtibl*, his ground-floor apartment windows facing the river, as did those of the *shtibl*. When we looked through Kalmen's windows, we saw some very odd behavior. He would walk around his home banging pots and pans. Another time we saw him put *tefillin* on one of his legs. Although we laughed at the strange things this Hasid did, as children we were also somewhat frightened.

On Yom Kippur, before we all went to the *shtibl* for Kol Nidre, Father would bless us. It was a memorable event because it was one of the few times a year that he expressed his love and devotion to us. I savored the serenity of the moment. We would cry, pray, and then walk to services.

Before we started Kol Nidre, Father would put on his *kitl* (a white robe signifying purity), closing it at the waist with a white *gartl* (a silky sash separating the upper/spiritual parts of the body from the lower/earthier parts). The *kitl* is worn only on a few important occasions: on seder nights, on Yom Kippur, for one's wedding, and as a shroud. While the garment reminds us of our mortality, by its whiteness, it allows us to emulate angels and kings.

One memorable year, we were in the middle of Kol Nidre when someone came into the *shtibl* and told Father that our house was on fire. He ran back to the house, half wrapped in his *talis* (prayer shawl) and holding on to one end with one hand as it floated after him. Father's glasses, kept on a lace around his neck, fell off. He looked like an apparition. I ran after him, and when we got to the apartment, we found the holiday candles my mother had lit and a handkerchief she left on a silver tray glowing in the reflected light of the candles. To people looking in from the Alexanderer *shtibl* across the street, the crumpled handkerchief resembled flames. Thank God, there was no fire, and we returned to the Gerer *shtibl*, where Reb Abraham Shenker, the *ba'al tefilah*, had delayed the service until we returned.

Reb Abraham usually led the *Musaf* service, the midmorning service, on holiday mornings. It seemed as if his powerful voice made the walls tremble.

Chiel Englender, another fine *ba'al tefilah*, led *Shacharit*—the morning prayers. Avrom Frouman was one of the better *ba'alei tefilah*, but he mostly traveled out of town to conduct services for hire, so we rarely got to hear him. He and his family lived behind Rabbi Meyerl's *heder*. Chaim Kleiner, another Gerer Hasid, also led prayers from time to time. He had a beautiful voice, and he also taught music and religious studies at the Agudath Israel yeshiva high school. It was a pleasure to listen to him. Chaim, the son-in-law of the miller, was not a native Dzialoszycer. He had come to town, as had many young men from the larger cities, to marry the daughter of one of our wealthy citizens.

I remember an extraordinary occasion, one that doesn't take place many times in a Jew's life: the Gerer Hasidim welcoming a new Torah scroll that had been donated to the *shtibl*. People dressed in costumes and celebrated in the streets with a parade. My mother's cousin, Chanine, a fine horseback rider, led the parade. As he stood in the stirrups, he held the Torah in one hand and the reins in the other, a striking sight.

SHABES IN DZIALOSZYCE

On *Shabes* in Dzialoszyce, just about every store in town was closed. The barbershops, owned by nonobservant Jews who worked on *Shabes*, usually kept their front doors closed. If someone needed a shave or haircut, he would use the rear entrances, because even nonobservant Jews were reluctant to openly violate the Jewish law.

Our family never worked on *Shabes* or opened the store, except under extraordinary circumstances. Rabbi Staszewski, our town rabbi, had notes for various emergencies prepared in advance and delegated tasks depending on circumstances. For example, there was one *Shabes* when a Christian family came to the rabbi and said they needed clothing for a family member who had just died. Rabbi Staszewski gave the bereaved the appropriate note, who brought it to us. My brothers and I opened the back door to the store and then locked them from the inside so no one else could enter. The store was dark because we could not open the shutters, so the Gentile lit a candle and took the clothing he needed. Then he deposited the payment in a drawer because we were forbidden to handle the money ourselves.

Preparation for *Shabes* began on Thursday. The maid cooked the meals and usually prepared a pot of *tsholnt*, a slow-cooked meat stew, for *Shabes* lunch. Since Orthodox Jews do not cook on *Shabes*, *tsholnt* was the perfect hot meal. A mixture of meat, potatoes, beans, and barley was prepared in a heavy pot and brought to the baker's oven late on Friday morning. By the time *Shabes* arrived and the fire could no longer be attended, the *tsholnt* would be three-quarters cooked. The bakery oven was a massive brick oven and retained heat well into the next day, allowing the *tsholnt* to finish cooking and stay hot until people came to retrieve their pots for *Shabes* lunch.

Another of the maid's jobs was to take chickens to the *shoykhet*. There were several of them in town: *Shoykhet* Yoinesin, Leibish Lubelski, and Avrumele Cohen. But our maid usually used Itche Meyer because he was a Gerer Hasid who davened with us and was the Torah reader at our Gerer *shtibl*.

Special foods, which were served on *Shabes* to make it more festive, became part of the *mitzvah* of sanctifying the day. The maid baked lots of goodies, and that interested me the most. Mother, however, wanted to make sure that the cakes and cookies would last until *Shabes*, so she would hide the goodies on top of the book cabinets or lock them inside, where she also hid the chunky, dark chocolate our visiting relatives would bring us. My sense of smell was extremely sharp—like a bloodhound's on a trail. As soon as I walked in from school, I would follow my nose to the hiding spot. If it was unlocked, my early discoveries spelled the end of the baked goodies. Once I started eating, my brothers would join me in the feast, and by *Shabes* very little would be left.

Late Friday afternoon, the *klaper* (knocker) would go from store to store and house to house, knocking on the doors with a wooden hammer. With that announcement, the Jewish community of Dzialoszyce was reminded that *Shabes* was approaching and that it was almost time to close up shop and light the *Shabes* candles. Mother would rush upstairs to deal with last-minute household preparations. I would accompany Father to the *mikveh* (ritual bath) where we took a steam bath, washed, and dressed in *Shabes* clothes. It was as a child at the *mikveh* that I first realized that the Almighty did not make us all equal. After finishing at the *mikveh* we would stop at home before going to the Gerer *shtibl* for *Kaboles Shabes*, the prayer service ushering in *Shabes*.

On our return home, the room glowed with the light emanating from the *Shabes* candles in their silver candlesticks. The atmosphere was festive, and the table was beautifully set. Although Mother served delicacies that were fit for a king—fish, soup, meat, and desserts—I personally preferred the plainer weekday fare. I simply was not a fan of cooked food. I preferred bagels and bread with butter and lots of sugar on top. During the week, we would buy two kilos of bagels and soft pretzels as well as two kilos of bread each morning. With four boys in the family, we could finish them all at one meal. I also loved naturally grown tomatoes dipped in sugar. Farmers from the surrounding villages brought these and local fruits, such as apples, pears, and plums, to exchange for clothing at our store. We always had plenty of fruit before the war.

One Friday night someone in the Gerer *shtibl* announced that any animal slaughtered by Avrumele Cohen was *treyf* (not kosher). Our food was all prepared, the table was set, and Father was getting ready to make *kiddush* so that we could sit down to our festive meal when he asked the maid where she had taken the chickens to be slaughtered. Normally, Father would not have asked, expecting that they had been taken to Itche Meyer, as usual. Because of the announcement at the *shtibl*, however, he wanted to make sure. When the maid answered that this week she had gone to Avrumele Cohen instead of Itche Meyer because the former was charging only 20 groszy as opposed to the latter's 50, Father, without causing a commotion, immediately gathered the chicken pot, the serving tray, and any other utensil that had been touched by the chicken and took it all to the outhouse. We had much less to eat that Friday night.

The next morning at the *shtibl*, word spread that Father had thrown away our food and dishes. We came home and just as Father was pouring wine in his goblet for *kiddush*, people streamed in with all kinds of food to replace what had been thrown out. We had never feasted on such a wide variety of delicacies as we did on that *Shabes*, and what added to the flavor was the extra ingredient of caring and goodwill that accompanied each dish. Ironically, a few days later the prohibition on Avrumele Cohen's *shkhite* was lifted.

On Saturdays, an elderly non-Jewish woman, Mrs. Mikolaikowa, came to our house to do work that was forbidden for Jews on *Shabes*. She kindled the fire in the oven so that we could warm the food that had been prepared before *Shabes* and knew exactly where to find the fee that was left for her. We always gave her some challah (braided egg-bread). She knew many of the laws connected with our tradition—perhaps even better than some of our own people do today. She spoke Yiddish, as did the letter carrier, Mr. Rogulski, who could also read and write it. Because he could read our postcards, keeping one's correspondence from Rogulski's prying eyes incurred the additional expense of sending a sealed letter.

Father expected me to review my lessons while he took his weekly *Shabes* afternoon nap and while my brothers read the newspapers to which we subscribed (both the Polish *Nowy Dziennik* and the Yiddish *Togblat* daily).

I was a rebel because Father forced me to study so much, even on my day off, that I had little time to play soccer with my friends. Therefore, I would sneak out to play. The positions I played were first back, second back, left wing, right wing, and sometimes even center because I could advance the ball quite well. One *Shabes*, the team to which I secretly belonged arranged an afternoon match. That day our *Shabes* routine went along as usual, except that after we finished saying grace after the meal, Father took my shoes and locked them away. He must have gotten wind of the game to take such a precaution. Father asked me to review my lessons of the week and went off to sleep. I reluctantly sat down to study, but my mind was elsewhere. I wanted to go play with my friends, but my shoes were in detention. I needed a solution.

What did I do? After making sure he was asleep, I took Father's shoes. They were actually beautiful short boots made of delicate leather with elastic inserts on either side. I put the boots on, but, because they were much too big for me, I had to stuff them with rags to make them stay on my feet. I sneaked out and went to meet my teammates at the field. Just a few kicks of the ball separated the sole from the upper, so I tied up the boot with a piece of cord and continued playing.

After a while, I could see Father heading toward me in his long black *kapote* (silk overcoat) tied with a *gartl*. As he came closer, I had visions of this being my last day on earth, yet I could not let my team down by leaving in the middle of the game. The solution was to change positions from back, where my father could catch me, to left wing. Then I ran up and down the field through the mud puddles, slipping and covering myself with dirt. The game ended with our team winning three to two. The whole incident lasted only ten minutes, but to me it felt more like ten hours. I was sorry that Father could not catch me, but I was angry at him because he embarrassed me in front of my teammates and distracted me from my game. What's more, I imagined that when I got home he would at least kill me, if not worse—the rebellious son who disobeyed, did not study, and publicly desecrated *Shabes*.

Back at home, I changed as much of my clothing as I quickly could. Tense with fear, I opened a large book of the Talmud and started to repeat my lesson in a loud voice. I did not leave the book for a minute. I had learned from the story of King David that the Angel of Death has no power over those engaged in religious study and remembered how David, knowing that he was going to die on *Shabes*, would study continuously on that day of the week to avoid his fate. Half an hour passed, then two hours, then three. *Shabes* was over, the family had eaten the third meal of the Sabbath, had made *havdalah* (the prayer separating the holiness of the Sabbath from the ordinariness of the week), and I studied through it all. At 10 p.m., I was still sitting and studying. At 10:30, my father went to bed. I continued studying because I knew that as long as I continued, my father would not hit me.

I slept for two or three hours and the next morning began studying again. I wouldn't move away from the table, turning page after page, reading loudly so that Father could hear me. At the same time, I kept thinking, "Please, God Almighty, let him come and hit me already. Let it be over." Finally, I broke down and said, "Father, I can't take it anymore. I can't go on like this. Please come hit me and let's get it over with." Father answered, "I will hit you when I am ready; not when you are ready."

As strict as my father was, there was a side to him that was very charitable and forgiving. There wasn't a *Shabes* on which my father failed to bring home poor people who had nowhere else to go.

I particularly remember a visitor by the name of Jigan. He would sit at our table, sharing our *Shabes* rituals. My father began with the *kiddush rabbah* (the daytime blessing over wine), passing around the wine followed by cake and cookies. He washed his hands before the blessing over the challah, Jigan and the children following. Mother, as usual, took off her rings and put them on the silver tray that held the candlesticks before she went out to wash her hands. Father was already making the blessing over bread when Mother discovered that the rings were gone. This normally would have provoked rage; instead, Father merely looked around as he chewed on a bite of challah. Mother said not a word.

Then Father looked at Jigan and holding out a handkerchief, said gently, "You have something in your mouth." The man spat the rings into the cloth, which Father then folded over the jewelry and slipped into his pocket. Father signaled that we should continue eating the first course—the fish. We resumed the meal; not a single remark was made to embarrass the desperate man. Father encouraged him to eat more and made him feel comfortable; Jigan behaved as though nothing had happened. My father acted in a charitable way; everyone present learned a great lesson.

JOSEPH — THE YOUNGEST

Though we sold suits in our store, when we needed festive clothing for ourselves, my parents went to Avrumele Schneider, Abraham the tailor, who was so short that he stood on a chair to take measurements for our *khalatls* (long overcoats). He usually arrived before Passover and the High Holy Day festivals so that my parents could get us to look presentable in suitable overcoats and *yibitses* (knee-length jackets made of heavy silk). We had to select both the quality of fabric and style of garment and often spent days making decisions. The color range was limited to modest grays or black, and, as for weight, the heavier the better. We were experts in the field because fabric was our business.

To test our knowledge, Father would let us choose the material we wanted. "Very well, children," he would say. "You decide what you would like to have for your long-coat." My own choices for new garments were seldom accepted, however. Father would explain with authority the reasoning behind the changes he made. In my case, it was an academic exercise. I almost never got a new garment.

When the reality of the situation hit me, my dear mother tried to console me with tender love, hugs, and kisses. Since we were four boys, the oldest got the new *khalatl*. In turn, Art's old coat would be given to Chaim, and his *khalatl* went to Willie. Before Chaim's coat was made over for Willie, it was taken apart and reversed so that the less worn face of cloth was exposed to make the coat look better. When Willie outgrew the coat, the garment was cut to size again and measured to fit me.

When the tailor arrived, I started praying, hoping, asking, and negotiating for a new *khalatl*. Sometimes I succeeded in getting what I wanted. When I walked down the street in new clothes with my friends, I felt good—especially if they admired my outfit. If I did not succeed in getting a new coat or jacket, and that was most of the time, I acted out. I did not talk much and stopped studying. I refused to run errands for Mother—like taking packages to the seamstress or bringing in water from the well. I would not take out the night pot filled with human waste. I broke many rules for not getting a new *khalatl*, especially when one of my older brothers did.

Shoes, on the other hand, were treated differently from other clothing. Each of us received handmade shoes measured to fit our feet. We all had different-sized and shaped feet. Even if our feet were similarly shaped, by the time one of my brothers outgrew his shoes, the footwear was completely demolished. Occasionally, my father saved the goatskin leather uppers and consulted with the shoemaker about adding a pair of soles, but that was for reuse by the same brother who wore out the shoes before outgrowing them.

I liked Beryl, the shoemaker, because when I came to pick up shoes for the holidays, he would allow me to watch him work. It was interesting to see the way he sat on the low stool near the table, bent over the soft leather uppers, pinning them with wooden pegs to the hard soles. But when I looked around that small, dark room screaming with poverty, I felt sorry for him.

Beryl's son Leibel was a very good soccer player who had a leather soccer ball his father helped him make from leather pieces of different colors wrapped around a rubber balloon. We blew air into the balloon with our mouths and then tied the ball up with a lace so that it was smooth and hard. We played soccer, just the two of us, in front of the shoe shop every time I went to pick up shoes. While I was waiting, Leibel and I would try to outmaneuver each other to get control of the ball. Any activity was better than studying—or so I thought at the time.

Being the youngest was a disadvantage when it came to clothing, and it also permeated other aspects of my existence. Art, the oldest, sometimes accompanied Father on buying trips to Warsaw, and they would often detour to visit the Gerer Rebbe in Gur. Even when Art did not travel with Father, I felt left out. Once Father returned from Warsaw with books and dictionaries for my older brother—and he made me very jealous. Art had dictionaries in Hebrew, Yiddish, and Polish and locked them up in the lower drawer of the closet so that he would not have to share them with me. At the time, I felt that he had all these volumes simply because he was the oldest. The reality was that he needed these dictionaries because he was getting a higher education.

Art belonged to the Agudath Israel and studied in a yeshiva college with male students between 17 and 20 years old in a group that was quite advanced. The students were often from well-to-do homes and considered to be very eligible bachelors. He used the dictionaries to look up unfamiliar words. I wanted to look up words, too, but I had no access to his sources and thus had no way to expand my knowledge. And to complicate things, Art did not want his little brother to touch his things.

There was a time our Aunt Esther visited and brought Art a flashlight. Typically, my brother locked his new treasure in the off-limits drawer where he kept his dictionaries—out of my reach. Once, I managed to get into the drawer and took the flashlight. As I played with it, I accidentally broke the bulb. When my brother returned and saw the broken flashlight, he got angry. I had saved some money and kept it in our heavy, wooden wall clock because I thought nobody would ever think of the clock as a hiding place. Art went straight to the clock and took all the money. Then *I* got upset. We straightened things out between us and restored the peace only after a couple of good fights.

Art was slim and had a delicate constitution. Consequently, he was given all the bananas, oranges, and grapes my aunt would send us from Chozow. These were expensive imports in prewar Poland, but it was thought that the vitamins in them would fortify him. There always seemed to be a rational reason for the preferential treatment Art received from our parents, but that did little to assuage the visceral feelings of jealousy that lingered inside me.

There was, however, one time when I was not envious of him at all. That was when Art was called up for his army physical. He stopped eating regular food and consumed almost nothing but pumpkin seeds. To lose weight, he jogged for miles every day and stopped sleeping at night, so that in addition to looking emaciated, he would also look anemic. Art did whatever he could to get a rejection. Before Art went to Pinczow, my father went to the Gerer Rebbe to pray that Art would not be accepted. When Art returned, he told us he met Jozek, our Polish neighbor from across the street, at the induction center. Jozek asked Art if he had lost so much weight in order to avoid military service. Statements of that sort could have been damaging, leading to criminal charges and conviction. Luckily for Art, he was rejected.

MISCHIEF AND OTHER PASTIMES

When I was nine, I often got into trouble. The store was usually full of customers on Fridays because it was a market day. Some arrived on horseback, and when a farmer tied up his mount, Father would ask me to guard it at the entrance to our store. Sometimes I untied the horse and went riding, showing off throughout the town. Once, Father came looking for me and caught me riding the horse I was supposed to be watching. I returned the animal immediately, expecting the worst, but Father did not say anything. I figured he was going to spank me, but he did not. Perhaps he was inwardly pleased I had the courage and skill to ride the horse. For me, galloping on a horse was an exhilarating change from sitting and studying all the time.

On another Friday, instead of studying, I went swimming with some friends. I did not know how to swim, and I must confess that I still don't swim well. Still, I wanted to learn, so I went upriver about two or three kilometers north of town to a spot near the brick factory's kiln. I don't know how Father discovered where I was, but he came to fetch me. Surprisingly, when he saw me in the water, he seemed happy. Again, he said nothing. I came out of the water and dressed myself. Father took me by the hand, and we went back home. He wanted me to sit down and start studying again, which I did eagerly just to escape the beating I expected.

I never stopped trying to find ways to evade studying. On yet another occasion, when I looked into the store and saw it was filled with customers, I figured that my parents were so busy they wouldn't notice my absence. I again decided to go swimming—this time at Lisowice, a village four or five kilometers south of town at the large dam next to the flour mill. Older boys and adults from Dzialoszyce went there because the water was deep enough for stronger swimmers to enjoy themselves. I was standing close to the riverbank, watching people swim and dive. The wide river was very cold on this particular day, but I was hamming it up, showing off my nonexistent aquatic skills. I was pretending to strike a diver's pose when one of my friends pushed me into the water. Since I did not really know how to dive or swim, I went under and started to drown. Luckily, somebody jumped in and pulled me out. By the time my rescuer brought me ashore, I felt close to death. People in the area tried to revive me by holding me upside down and then pounding my chest to get the water out of my lungs.

My friends saw me lying there unconscious and thought I was dead, so they ran back to Dzialoszyce to tell my parents. When my friends reached the store, they were afraid to go in to tell my father, so they paced back and forth out front. Father noticed them and went outside. When he heard the news, he left the store full of customers and ran all the way to Lisowice. By that time, I had recovered sufficiently, and Father took me home. I expected to be punished, but the blows never came. For my part, I never went to Lisowice again.

In the summertime, when parts of the river dried up, my friends and I would take off our shoes and walk in the riverbed, looking for whatever we could find. We often found rings or bracelets, which was pretty exciting for boys who had no toys. We did not even know what toys were. Our toys were books. Meyerl, a mentally unbalanced adult who got a little crazier in the summer, liked to wade in the river when the water was shallow. A pious Jew with a beard, he never paid attention to the children running after him, making fun of him.

I once found a little white dog and brought it home. This was a novelty because we never had pets other than the geese we kept in cages in the basement for later consumption, the birds I occasionally caught, and the porcupine that ate bugs in the store. As I sat on the steps holding the dog, my mother noticed it was full of fleas, and she fainted. Willie and Chaim-Leizer saw her, ran for water, and brought her back to consciousness. They then gave me a beating. I had not realized the dog was infested and did not know my dear mother was so sensitive. I quickly gave the dog away.

In addition to the *groshn* I got for studying, I also received two *groshn* a week from Uncle Yoyev and Aunt Henna. When they withheld my allowance, I got angry. One Friday, Uncle Yoyev's store, which was similar to ours, was filled with people. The store had a rather small window, and the only other source of natural light was a pane of glass in the inside door. I went over to Uncle Yoyev and asked for my money. He said in Yiddish, "Leave me alone. I have no time to talk to you." My response to his dismissal was to go out and close the two outside doors, jamming the chain with a piece of wood so that they could not open the door from the inside. One can imagine how much aggravation I caused that day. Naturally, I later got what was coming to me: a beating from my parents.

I used to play with a neighbor my age, Alchu, the son of Srul-Yosel and Esther Federman, who lived in a house two doors away. As an only child, Alchu was pampered, and his parents focused all their attention and worry on him. In the mornings, when I came to pick him up for school and his mother saw my bagels slathered with butter and sugar on top, she turned to her husband and said, "Take a look at the way Yossele eats, and Alchu doesn't want to eat. He has no appetite."

Alchu and I used to play "buttons," and when Alchu lost, he would grab buttons that were not his to take. Since he had been spoiled, he did not play fairly, and because he cheated, I gave him beatings. As a result, Alchu's mother came to our store and complained, "Reb Zisme, Yossele was hitting my Alchu." Father called for me and asked what happened. I explained that Alchu tried to grab buttons that were not his to take, and it was not right. The game was supposed to be played according to rules. Father then said to Esther, "The best way is to let them fight and settle the dispute on their own."

Alchu's mother, who also happened to be Mother's second cousin, said, "They shouldn't fight because I have only one boy. You have four sons so you don't mind if they beat each other up." My father replied, "Esther, I, too, have only one son. I have only one Yossele. To me, Yossele is an only son, and so are the others. Every one of them is an only son. Therefore, the best way to handle the matter would be as I suggested before. Let them straighten out their own accounts."

Father did not always follow his own advice when it came to not getting involved. I was friends with Yitzchak Wakschlag, younger brother of David and Meyer, son of Yankel and Carka. Yitzchak reacted very violently when we got into disagreements. Once he stabbed me with a sharp pencil; I still have the scar on my hand. Another time he stabbed me in the buttocks with a sharp tool—his father was a fine goldsmith, so he had access to tools—and I bled profusely. My parents could no longer abide by their hands-off policy and brought me with them to the Wakschlags to complain about Yitzchak's aggression. Nevertheless, I admired Yitzchak because of his unique intelligence, and in spite of our disagreements, we maintained an interesting relationship. After the war, his brother Meyer told me that the Nazis shot him in a concentration camp.

OUR STORE AND OTHER COMMERCE

Our store was open for business from Saturday night after the conclusion of *Shabes* until Friday afternoon when we closed early to prepare for *Shabes*. Although Polish law did not allow us to be open on Sunday, we unofficially sold merchandise from the back of the store, with the customers coming in through the rear entrance.

When I was about eight years old, I liked to stay in the store after it closed and watch my mother cut fabric for undergarments and shirts. This was then sent to contractors who sewed the pieces together. There was a lot to do, and she often worked late into the night. Often when I tired, I lay down on a pile of blankets and fell asleep. Father would carry me upstairs and put me to bed. My brothers and I delivered bundles of cut fabric to the many seamstresses who worked for us—Yitta Shventa, Lea, and Branche were among the crew. A few days later, we would pick up the finished garments and bring them back to the store. Farmers from surrounding villages purchased these ready-made goods after they bargained over the price.

Picking up merchandise had side benefits. When I accompanied Father or my older brother to the redhead Yankel Spokojny's store, one of two stores in town besides ours that sold cloth, I would get the plywood from his bolts of fabric from Hollanderski or Podolanski for my projects. I used the plywood, which was not readily available in Dzialoszyce then, to build my birdhouse, my pencil cases, and noisemakers for Purim.

Straightening out inventory and carefully watching the merchandise were also part of my job. There were two villages not far from Dzialoszyce, Kosciejow and Glupczow, that were known as dens of thieves—a song was even written about them! When people from these villages came to our store, it was to steal, not to buy. Women pretended to try on garments but hid sweaters or shirts beneath voluminous skirts or tucked our clothing around their bosoms. I kept count of the sweaters on the counter and then put them back on the shelves to prevent shoplifting.

When Father suspected that someone was a thief, he would say loudly, "Hello, welcome. Take a look who is here." This signal alerted our family to shady customers. Father mostly came to the store in the afternoon because he was busy studying and praying in the morning. It took considerable time to go to the *mikveh*, pray, and study every day. Sometimes, he recited half his prayers in the synagogue and completed the rest in the back of our store. He would come out and see customers while still wearing his *talis* and one of the two sets of *tefillin* that he put on every weekday. (The ultraorthodox put on two different types of *tefillin* every day, one following the tradition of Rashi and one following the tradition of Rabbeinu Tam, so that they would fulfill the *mitzvah* if only one of the two traditions were correct.)

When Father made his buying trips to Krakow, Lodz, and Warsaw for two weeks at a time, he would buy items that we did not make, such as fancy ready-made shirts, heavy knits, hats, ties, and suits. When Father returned we would greet him at the train station. I would kiss his hand, and he would hug and kiss me and give me extra pocket money.

There were two disasters before the war that affected our store. One took place in the bakery, two doors down, where we used to bake matzoth for Passover. Volf, the baker, and his wife, Fradel, owned the busy bakery. He was a short, elderly man who walked with a cane. A joker, he liked to play with the children by stretching out his arm and asking someone to pull his small finger. When the kids did, he would pass wind. He and his wife were helped in the bakery by their daughters, Leah and Chavche.

One advantage of being close to the bakery was that we were never cold. But there were disadvantages. Our first disaster took place when some sparks from their oven reached our warehouse and caused a fire that did considerable damage. I can still remember the smell of charred merchandise, but luckily we managed to save most of the store.

The other disadvantage, besides the risk of fire, was that we had little visitors from the bakery—bugs. To get rid of them, my parents bought a porcupine I considered a pet, but a pet that I was not allowed to feed. Whenever I came near it, it rolled up into a ball—its defensive posture—and extended its long needles that I was afraid to touch. Secretly, however, I gave the porcupine black beer to drink, which he seemed to enjoy following a buggy meal.

Not long after the fire, we had another disaster, one with far-reaching consequences. On May 22, 1936, we were resting and reading after our traditional *Shabes* afternoon meal. At about two o'clock the skies suddenly darkened. Fifteen minutes later, they were pitch black and rain came down in torrents. It was as if a water bomb had exploded. Whereas on a normal *Shabes* we would look out the window to watch people strolling, this *Shabes* the street was deserted and flooded with rising water that coursed down at full speed.

Two rivers, the Sancygniowka to the west and the Yakobowka to the east, ran parallel to Dzialoszyce, embracing our town. As the rain poured down, the water from the two swollen rivers rose on both sides of town, zigzagging in and out of Dzialoszyce, flooding the streets. The church and a building belonging to Moshe Grosswald were high on a hill, our house was on middle ground, and from there, the land sloped down to the marketplace. When the floodwaters rose, some of the houses were completely covered. At eight feet, the water almost reached the balcony at the front of our house. We watched small wooden houses floating by with lit candles still glowing in their windows and children in their cribs still inside. These smaller homes were mostly from villages farther north that had been carried several kilometers by the strong current. The scene was unforgettable.

As the waters rose with tremendous speed, powerless people screamed in fear at this confrontation with furious Nature. Since that *Shabes* in 1936, whenever I study the chapter in the Bible about Noah and the ark or try to imagine the ancient chaos before Creation, I visualize this catastrophe that killed 40 people and wrought such havoc in Dzialoszyce and its environs.

After a day, the flood subsided and left behind a huge mess. Bridges were destroyed and the damage to the city was extensive. Our basement was completely flooded. People helped us pump out the water, but the more we pumped, the more water came in from neighboring basements. The mayor sent out calls for help, and the fire brigade came with more people and more pumps. Afterward, a minister from the government of Rydz-Smigly in Warsaw came to Dzialoszyce with an entourage to investigate the damage and fatalities. I remember the colors of the kayak on top of his bus—red and white, the

Polish national colors. By the time he arrived the water had subsided, but bringing help was a nice gesture that comforted the community.

All the merchandise in the basement was soaked and soiled with mud. Cleaning specialists brought large vats of cleaning chemicals in an attempt to reclaim as much merchandise as possible. The white fabrics were so badly stained that they could not be properly cleaned. Eventually, we sold them to shoemakers in our town and surrounding areas, where lots of people supported themselves by making shoes for shoe stores in the larger cities. These shoes were handmade, and the upper part was lined with fabric often purchased from us. We sold the goods very cheaply. When word got around about the fabric sale, we took in quite a bit of extra money because shoemakers from far and near came to buy the damaged fabric at bargain prices. It proved so profitable we soon took good merchandise, dipped it in water to appear damaged, and sold it at a profit. This strategy helped us make up the tremendous losses we incurred in the flood.

We needed to be resourceful to keep ahead of the competition, especially when our strongest competitor was my Uncle Yoyev Tenenbaum, right next door. Although his store was smaller than ours, it stocked similar merchandise. We had to find ways of producing goods at rock-bottom prices to attract customers. For instance, we cut a roll of damask fabric into pieces four feet by eight feet, took out four inches of thread all around to make fringes, and sold the finished product as tablecloths. Everybody wondered how we could sell tablecloths at such low prices, especially when some expensive rugs had similar fringes. We sold many of these items, especially to young couples. We also specialized in fringed, flowered Turkish kerchiefs. When the farmers' daughters dressed for church or to meet young men, they wore these red kerchiefs on their heads.

We also made pleated fabric using a rather primitive method. My father bought corrugated cardboard, and we laid out two sheets on a long table. We put fabric between the two sheets and rolled the sandwich together, taking care to match up the corrugations so that one fit into the other. Afterward, we took a kettle of boiling water and let the steam penetrate the sandwich to create pleats in the cloth. In the end, the pleated fabric was sewn into skirts that girls wore for their school uniforms. We all contributed to this effort, and our store was a prosperous family business in every way.

There was, however, at least once every year when we made a concerted effort to appear less prosperous. That was when Butzke, the tax inspector, came to Dzialoszyce to assess every business in town. Butzke was from Pinczow, the regional tax department. When we heard rumors that he was coming, we tried to empty our usually packed store of much of its merchandise. We wanted Butzke to see as little as possible so that he would levy a lower tax. Antisemitism was everywhere, and Jews were taxed above the normal rate. We were just trying to protect ourselves from this unfair taxation.

Our store, so close to the market square, was part of Dzialoszyce's commercial hub. Up the block, Nattanson ran a store similar to ours, but it was much smaller and less prosperous. Next came the barbershop owned by two of Nattanson's sons, both of them literally deaf and dumb. We went there for haircuts and trims. The bakery was next. Near it was a store owned by Chaim Mandelbaum. He began his business as a sign painter and later opened a fabric shop, but neither venture was successful, though he was a fine man. Next door was the grocery that belonged to Israel and Esther Federman, the parents of my friend Alchu. Israel was the son of Shye Federman, a Jewish farmer from the village of Lipowka. They weren't too well off, but they made a living. Next to Uncle Yoyev's shop was Yoyne Friedman's store for farmers. There was also the fabric store of Yoyne Nattanson, who was a cousin of the other Nattanson.

Aside from regular retail establishments, there were many small workshops scattered throughout Dzialoszyce. People worked from their homes as tailors, dressmakers, knitters, shoemakers, and jewelry makers. The Lazniaz family, who lived just across the alley behind our house, were gold- and silversmiths. Itchele taught the trade to his oldest son, Michael, and the two worked together making jewelry, engraving monograms, and setting precious stones in brooches. I was fascinated by their skill and often had the opportunity to watch them work because I was friends with the Lazniaz's younger son, Chaimel. Mrs. Lazniaz would go to the marketplace to find customers, a function that suited her domineering personality. Unfortunately, not a soul from the family survived the war, nor did any members of their extended family. Raizel and Yossel Kamelgard on Pinczower Street manufactured ladies' coats. Srulke, their son, went to the Agudah yeshiva with my brother Art, and Norman, their youngest son, is, to this day, a very dear friend.

FAMILY

Mother was the second of seven Platkiewicz children. Her older brother Chaim was married to Bracha. They had two children, Lolek and David. Her brother David was married to Hinda, and they had one son, Lolek (or Leizer, in Hebrew), named for his grandfather. Their grandmother was Rose. The next sister in line after my mother was Henna. She and her husband, Yoyev, my father's brother, had three children: a son, Alter, and two daughters, Royzele and Cesia. Then there was Frimche, who was married to Mottel and had four children. Aunt Esther's husband was Uncle Shloyme. They had two children, Lolek and Hanusia. The youngest sister was named Itkele, and her husband was Harry. They had one son named Lolek. These dear ones were part of my extended family, and except for Uncles David, Chaim, and Harry, they were all murdered by Hitler and his henchmen.

Some of the sisters lived with my parents when they were young because they were, by that time, orphans. Even after the sisters were married, our house was the family gathering place, even more so after they moved back to town at the war's start. (My mother's brothers tried their luck in Warsaw but ended up settling in Chozow, a town near the German border. Esther and Itkele also moved to Chozow after they married.)

Our home was open, warm, and hospitable, but jealousy, authority, independence, finances, and inheritance—all the spices that complicate family life—also came into play. My Aunts Esther and Frimche were having a conversation one *Shabes* afternoon, when suddenly Aunt Henna barged in.

She lived right next door on the same floor and probably overheard something not to her liking. A heated quarrel broke out between her and my Aunt Esther, who was my mother's favorite. Aunt Henna was jealous of my mother, her older sister, Grina, who had four boys. At the time, Aunt Henna had two girls and one boy.

The taunting went something like this: "What do you have, and what do I have?" (referring to their children). Henna said, "You, they will ask how much do you want? Me, they will ask how much do you give?" This complaint referred to the fact that she would have to provide dowries and financial assistance. With her four boys, Mother was off the hook. In fact, dowries were always a matter of negotiation. The terms depended on the family's financial status and social standing in the community.

The argument became so intense that Uncle Yoyev (Henna's husband) got involved and ended up hitting Mother above her eye with a soup ladle. I immediately started crying. I will never forget that Saturday afternoon when I looked at Mother's bruised forehead. I had very bitter feelings toward my uncle. I shook until the next day, when in revenge, I took a pot, went out to the rear balcony, and broke all the glass in Uncle Yoyev's windows. My uncle did not catch me in the act, and I avoided him for a few days. Eventually, he suspected that one of my brothers or I had been the perpetrator, but there was nothing he could do about it.

The bitterness I felt toward my uncle affected how I related to him. At the beginning of the war, I tricked him into purchasing fake cigarettes from me. Uncle Yoyev wanted cigarettes, so I told him to pay me in advance. He refused to do so. I got back at him by picking clover, crumbling it up into very fine pieces, and filling empty filter-tipped cigarette tubes with my concoction. I filled a box with 100 of these "cigarettes," sealed it, and sold my uncle the product. Soon he wanted more, suspecting that the war was going to last a long time. I sold him many boxes, thinking that this was the best way to repay him for injuring my mother. When Uncle Yoyev started smoking these cigarettes, he began coughing and couldn't stop. He came to me and asked, "What did you sell me?"

"I sold you what I got. That's all I have, and that's it." That was the way I dealt with him. It was unfortunate that I disliked Uncle Yoyev. Even though he was a strong, husky man and I was a young, fragile boy, I felt that I had to do something to avenge Mother's honor.

I have mixed feelings about relating that story because neither Uncle Yoyev nor anyone from his immediate family is alive today to tell his side of the story. I wish I had the opportunity to quarrel with them today, but there is no one left with whom to argue.

Mother's brother David was an innovative man with good ideas who was loved by all. Although Uncle David was not terribly religious, he was asked to sit on the court of the advisory council to the rabbi in Chozow because he was considered a man of broad experience. Jews did not usually sue one another civilly in the prewar *shtetl*. If a person had a grievance, he brought the offending party before a rabbi for a *din Torah*—a ruling based on Jewish law. Usually, one, two, or even three rabbis listened to the adversaries and then issued a ruling. Very often, Uncle David was invited to sit in on these discussions, listen to the complaints, and give counsel to the rabbis. My uncle asked questions and his Solomon-like wisdom made him very good at ascertaining the truth.

Uncle David also met with people who sought his advice or help in negotiating deals. He moved back to Dzialoszyce after the war started and held court of a different kind, in a restaurant where he could enjoy some roasted duck or goose washed down with a stiff drink. When he came home to his wife, who waited to serve him the dinner she had prepared, he no longer felt like eating. Not wanting to hurt her feelings, he would pretend to have one of his frequent headaches. "Hindele, please give me two *Kogutki* (a Polish headache remedy in powder form as popular as aspirin is today). I need to lie down and don't feel like eating," he would say to his wife. Poor Hindele believed him and felt sorry for him, thinking the headaches ran in the family because Mother suffered from migraine headaches that were exacerbated by tension and long hours cutting fabric.

Aunt Frimche, who suffered several miscarriages and had a child who did not survive past its first year of life, had three children with Uncle Mottel. There was Royzele, a girl; a little boy whose name I can't remember; and Hershel, who was my age. Hershel was a genius and very observant, but he was extremely naive about matters other than Talmud. One fall day, while decorating the *sukkah*, we hung paper chains from the roof. Hershel wanted to see if the chains could catch fire, so he lit one. The *sukkah* went up in flames, and the entire town came running to watch.

My father did not like the way Hershel's parents treated him. He wasn't nourished properly, did not sleep enough, and was deprived of a good, secular education. Consequently, Father proposed that Hershel live with us for a while. Father's motivation may not have been entirely altruistic. He probably wanted Hershel around so that his good influence would rub off on me and get me more involved in my Talmudic studies. For Hershel, Father wanted less study, more rest, and better food. For me, Father wanted more study, more learning, and more prayer. When Hershel and I went to have our studies evaluated by Reb Itche Meyer, the *shoykhet*, Father asked him what he thought of us. Itche Meyer was very smart. He answered, "If we could take both of them, grind them up, mix them thoroughly, and divide the resultant product, we would have two perfect boys."

There was one distant relative of Mother's that my parents would have been very happy for me not to know at all. Mottel Platkiewicz, whose father, Leizer, was a very fine man, was a total rogue. One Yom Kippur I came out of my house to meet Alchu and saw Mottel in the vestibule of his house brazenly eating kielbasa (Polish smoked sausage) in public. This was the holiest day of the year, a day on which even the less-observant Jews of our town dared not eat, and the children fasted until noon. Apparently Mottel wasn't afraid of being struck by lightning.

I remember Mottel's mother telling mine about her disappointment in her son. In 1937, Mottel moved from Dzialoszyce to assert his independence. Once, he came from Chozow in Silesia to visit his parents, but he was very elusive. When he hung up his jacket, his mother noticed a paper sticking out of his pocket. It turned out to be a marriage certificate. She told Mother how hurt she was that her son had told her nothing about his marriage.

Mother's uncle, Aaron Yasny, lived to the north of the mill, near the Stawisko sports field. Aaron had a beautiful family, a horse and wagon, an abundance of chickens and geese, a stable, and a barn. On the barn's second floor, he kept hay for the horse. Sarah was the Yasnys' oldest daughter, followed by Hindele. Balcia, the next, was a slim girl; then Itka, who was gorgeous; and then Bronia and Rushke. There were three sons: Chaim, the oldest; the middle one named Chanine; and the youngest, Meilach, who was my friend. He and I belonged to the only Jewish sports club in Dzialoszyce. We played soccer together, and Meilach was particularly good at the game.

Cousin Chanine was a very strong man. Mother was once taken 60 kilometers to a hospital in Krakow for an operation. When she returned, she could not walk. Chanine picked her up in one swift movement, as if she were no heavier than a child, and put her in the wagon. But he did not know his own strength. My mother winced and said, "No, no, you have to be more gentle." I was there to welcome Mother because I loved her so much.

Mother's uncle Aaron had a butcher shop in the area where all the butchers in Dzialoszyce were located. There were about ten of them, and most of them sold kosher meat to Jewish customers. We bought our meat supply from Uncle Aaron every week. One *Shabes* afternoon, I remember visiting him with Mother, where for the first time I ate *galarete* (garlicky beef aspic) and large egg cookies. Now, every time I eat egg cookies or *galarete*, I am reminded of the first time I ate those foods at Uncle Aaron's house.

Apart from Aunt Frimche, Mother's sister, there was also Aunt Frimche, Mother's aunt. I remember visiting Mother's aunt when she was on her deathbed, but still conscious and able to talk to us. At one point she asked me to bring her a bedpan. I went out and brought her a glass of milk to drink instead. She asked me why I brought the milk, and I answered, "Milk will make you healthy, not the pot to pee. Milk is good for you." My mother, who was standing at the foot of the bed, burst out laughing along with the other visitors. For a minute, the pall was lifted from the room; then I fetched the bedpan.

Most of Father's family lived in the town of Chenciny and in Kielce, about eight kilometers away. Father's sister, Rachel, her husband, and their two children (a son and a daughter) lived in Kielce. They were in the furniture manufacturing business. Father's parents lived in Chenciny at 39 Malagoska Street, near the entrance to town. My paternal grandfather's name was Eliyahu, and my paternal grandmother was Esther-Reisel. They had a store that stocked grain, seeds, flour, and related products. My grandfather's brother, Nathan Tenenbaum, and his family lived next door to my grandparents and were in the same business. (I find it amusing that both Father and his brother Yoyev also ended up in competing businesses in Dzialoszyce.) Father's Uncle Nathan had two sons, Jehoshua and Leibel.

In the summer of 1936, when I was nine, I spent three weeks in Chenciny with my grandparents. I have wonderful memories of that visit, especially of jumping up and down on sacks full of grain. In the back of my grandparents' house, there was a large garden overgrown with wildflowers and weeds. Nearby was a store selling all kinds of drinks, such as *kvas*, a local beverage that tasted like cola, and other tempting treats. After playing in the garden or running around with friends, I liked to go into the store, order a cool drink, and charge it to my grandparents' account. The storeowner was a tall, handsome man, 35 to 40 years old, who was related to my grandparents.

Grandfather was the head of the *hevrah kadishah* (the burial society), which ritually prepared the dead for burial. According to *halacha*, a corpse must be handled with dignity. It is washed, dried, and dressed in a *kitl*. Broken clay shards are placed on the eyes of the deceased, and twigs are put in the deceased's hands. Grandfather was also elected chairman of the Radeszycer Synagogue and acted in that capacity for more than 15 years.

I was lucky to have many friends in Chenciny, including Sendor Charnocha, the son of one of Father's good friends. Sendor's family owned a down-and-feather business. On my vacation in Chenciny, Sendor and I went to visit the rabbi and the *heder* our parents had attended as children. My friend introduced me to Reb Meyer, who was, by then, an elderly man. I asked the rabbi questions about Father during the days when Reb Meyer was his teacher, but the rabbi said, "If you will study like Zisme, you will be all right, and you will know." Father had been a diligent, intense student, and I was eager to learn more about Father's relationship with his younger brother, Yoyev, since both boys had attended this *heder*. His rebbe, however, wouldn't tell me anything. Later that week, on *Shabes* afternoon, and for the following two *Shabesim*, I attended classes on *Ethics of the Fathers* (*Pirkei Avoth*) taught by Rabbi Meyer.

Chenciny had two marketplaces: the old one was in the historic narrow-laned center of town, and the new one was larger and more easily accessible, facing what we called "the mountain," really just a tall hill. Looking down at the city from the top of "the mountain," the view was spectacular. The *schloss*, a castle-fortress on top, was a most impressive edifice. On *Shabes* afternoons, my friend and I would climb up to it. We always wondered what had gone on inside the abandoned castle. One *Shabes*, ignoring the *tehum* (limiting distance to how far one can halachically walk beyond the city limits on *Shabes*), some friends and I decided to walk to Kielce, several kilometers away, where we visited my aunt and uncle, Rachel and Yankel Birnbaum.

I had a good time that summer despite the fact that I feared my grandfather, who was very strict and demanding. No matter what I did or how much I tried, the results were never good enough for him. Grandfather was a rigid man who showed little affection for me. However, my grandmother, who was kind and protective, always defended me. She cooked special dishes that she knew I liked, such as sugar beans (similar to fava beans).

It would have been easier to remember all these family members if I had a family album to consult, but ultraorthodox Jews usually did not have their pictures taken. Even before the war, we only had two photographs in our possession. One of them was taken because Uncle Shloyme and Aunt Esther, who lived in the city of Chozow, wanted to have a picture of us. Mother arranged for Mr. Goldkorn, the photographer and Selig's father, to meet us in the little park next to the fire station. There, under a tree, they took a picture of my brother Willie and me wearing our long *khalatls*. The other picture was of Mother and her relatives, taken while on a visit to Chozow. I would give anything to have those photographs of the child I used to be and of my wonderful family.

GIVING FROM THE HEART AND NOT GIVING

My parents were very charitable and always provided the poor with what they needed. Whether in smaller or larger amounts, donations in money or in kind were always given to those who asked. Canvassers who collected for specific institutions, such as private schools or burial societies, were never turned away.

One time, Itche Meyer demanded that my father donate 20 zloty to some worthwhile cause. After a prolonged discussion, Father offered him 5 zloty. He would not accept that amount and walked out of the store. About ten minutes later, he returned and wanted to settle for 18 zloty. My father softened a bit and offered 10. Itche Meyer left again.

We had two sets of doors to the front of the store. The outer set was made of heavy metal. The inner set was glass and in the reflection of an open door we could see who was approaching. We could even see down the block. Father watched Itche Meyer's reflection approaching other stores at the end of the block, and when he saw that he was about to leave the area, Father sent me out to call him back. They started haggling with each other anew, perhaps because he wanted to be the judge of what sum matched the need, but in the end, Father would never let anyone go away without giving a donation.

Father loaned money without interest to people in town. The amounts were 10 zloty, 20 zloty, 30 zloty, and more. Father had a long list of perhaps 50 people who owed him money at any given time. About three or four o'clock on Friday afternoons, he would hand over a copy of the list and send me out to collect the debts. Friday was market day, so Father expected that, after a week of business, borrowers would be able to pay back loans. Father said to me, "When you go into Moshe David Pomeranc (a store that sold soap, salt, and kerosene), say nothing but make sure he sees you. If he doesn't give you any money, walk away." (Reb Moshe David was about 70 years old.)

I would proceed to another store. When the stationer had no cash, he repaid his loan with something in trade. We took whatever school supplies we needed. On Fridays, it took hours to make the rounds—until about five or six o'clock in the summertime. I ran from store to store and, every so often, stopped at our house to empty my pockets, not wanting to carry around lots of money.

Often, very little of the money loaned was repaid. Once, Father sent me to collect on a loan that had grown too large. When I returned and told Father the borrower had torn up the note, he wondered why. Upset because the man had been unkind and confrontational, I suggested that Father not loan him any more money. Even though Father was disturbed and angry, he told me not to judge the man too harshly.

Visiting the sick was a *mitzvah* in which both my parents participated. If Mother learned that somebody was ill, she would leave work to bring them food and to see to their needs. *Erev Shabes* was a time that she was especially mindful of delivering meals to those less fortunate.

When Luser Ehrenreich, a well-educated, venerated older man greatly admired by the Gerer Rebbe, moved to town, Father became his friend. When Mr. Ehrenreich came down with typhus and the doctor put him in quarantine, Father still brought him food every day. My older brother complained to Father, "By visiting a man with an infectious disease, you are risking your own life and that of your entire family." Father taught him at that moment that to save a human life, we must do whatever we can—even at risk to ourselves, especially while someone is in isolation.

Father washed his friend and did what was necessary. He focused on realities and considered the consequences, but that did not stop him from doing what he thought was right. Later, when Luser was cured, he examined me on my knowledge of Talmud and promised me his granddaughter as a wife if I learned enough Talmud. (He was a widower, and she lived with him.) She was a young girl, slightly older than I was, and very beautiful. By using her as my inspiration, Luser encouraged me to keep studying and explained difficult passages of Talmud to me.

I had been studying the tractate connected with Hanukkah because the holiday was approaching, and I carved a menorah out of wood, accidentally cutting myself. Making the best of it, I stained the menorah with my blood because I did not have any paint. I gave the menorah to Mr. Ehrenreich as a gift of gratitude for his kindness. He looked at the detailed carving and asked, "Why is the menorah a reddish color?" I explained how my own blood had colored the menorah, and he responded with a pun: "This menorah is *norah* [can be translated as either "awesome" or "awful" in Hebrew]. I will cherish it because you made it with your own hands."

Charity was also a matter of deportment. The highest form of charity is *gemiles hasdim*, helping someone make a living. For example, Mother had me buy goods from Alchu's parents, Srul-Yosel and Esther Federman. Though the sugar and other staples we bought there were more expensive than elsewhere, Mother wanted us to patronize them because they were struggling to make ends meet. It was a way of giving, and they maintained their dignity.

Mother's greatest act of kindness was one she took on as a young adult—the responsibility for her four sisters and two brothers after her parents died. Her main concern was to ensure that the girls had decent dowries and found husbands that their parents would have approved of. Both my parents and my grandparents worked hard to save for them. Mother told us about the dowries in order to explain to my brothers and me the respectful distance that our family kept between them and her Uncle Mendel.

Mother's Uncle Mendel Silber was a quite-wealthy landowner in and about town. A heavyset man, he walked with a silver-handled cane and tried to conceal his goiter with his long, white beard. Sometimes he wore white gloves. My grandparents reckoned that the best way to increase the money they had saved for the girls' dowries was to rely on Uncle Mendel's business acumen—after all, he was rich—and have him invest the family savings. They gave him quite a lot of money to buy land or property or invest in some other venture.

After World War I, when Mother demanded funds for the dowries, Uncle Mendel said, "Come and get the box full of money." He gave Mother old rubles, a currency that was no longer in circulation and completely worthless. Mother asked whether the cash had been invested in land or property and learned that neither had been done. Uncle Mendel said, "Your parents gave me rubles, and here they are." Mother was about to call Uncle Mendel to a *din Torah*, but could not because my Uncle David announced he would act as a witness for Uncle Mendel, testifying that the money was offered to him before it became worthless. David decided to take Uncle Mendel's side because he was in love with Escia, one of Uncle Mendel's daughters. The feud lasted quite some time. Uncle Mendel could well have afforded to act charitably, but he never did. Mother's sisters were married off despite his miserliness. Our family ostracized Uncle Mendel, but we still treated him with respect when we chanced upon him.

BEYOND THE THEORETICAL

The most important aspect of my existence, from my parents' perspective, was my studying. Father wanted me to learn day and night. For me, all this learning was theoretical. When I studied the section in *Bave Batra* (a tractate of the Talmud) about two property owners who wanted to build a dividing wall between their properties and how they allocated responsibility, it was all well and good, but it really had no bearing on my existence. I learned about title to land and property, the mercantile responsibilities of fruit growers, laws governing shipping of commodities, and a code of business ethics. I was a little boy in a little town, and all this theoretical studying did not interest me nearly as much as the day-to-day goings-on of the tradesmen. I wanted to get my hands dirty and produce something like they did.

I have my Uncle Mottel to thank for getting me beyond the theoretical. He let me literally get my hands dirty. An Orthodox Jew, he was a *ba'al tefilah* and, in my opinion, a saint. At the same time, he was an excellent roofer with several employees. There were other roofers in town, but not everyone was as experienced as he was. Still, there was much rivalry between Yakker, one of the other roofers, and my uncle.

I apprenticed during the summertime by helping with the tar, which came in large, hard, glazed blocks that looked like coal. My job was to split the blocks with a hatchet and put the tar into vessels that were heated by coal or wood. The tar had to be liquefied to be spread easily with large mops, and I had to ensure that containers of the very flammable material did not catch fire. After the tar boiled, I transferred it to pails, brought them up to the roofs, and handed them to Stash, one of the helpers. While I made the transfer, someone else had to watch the drums of boiling tar. Once I knew how to patch, my uncle taught me how to install a new roof. Stash made good money, but I received only pennies for my work. Uncle Mottel said I had to learn the trade first, and then he would pay me more. There were so few opportunities to learn a trade in Dzialoszyce that I went along with it. Besides, anything was preferable to sitting and studying.

In those days, most roofers were also tinsmiths. When it rained or was too cold to work outdoors, my uncle and I did metalwork. We produced ovens, stovepipes, washboards, carbide lanterns, and the sieves farmers used to purify milk. I also fixed pots. I still know how to construct a bathtub with a metal rim. First, you join one-inch-thick boards for the tub base and cut them into the appropriate shape. Place a sheet of 16-gauge zinc on the surface and mold the tub by using studs nailed as supports for the rim to hold the shape. Fit the zinc sheet metal to the inside of this mold, nailing it to the form. For the rim, take a strip of sheet metal and make a long tube by bending it around an iron bar suspended between two chairs, soldering the seam, and rolling it until a tube is formed. Then fill the tube with hot sand so that it can be bent to the shape of the wooden mold and solder it to the tub. Remove the wooden mold, turn the tub upside down, and add a metal cover to the wooden bottom. Solder all joints, seams, and nail holes; make sure everything is solid and waterproof. Sand any roughness, clean and smooth the tub carefully (zinc is a delicate metal), then paint it with a good enamel. The finished product is a masterpiece. I would use all these tinsmithing, roofing, and painting skills in the darkest hours of my life in the concentration camps.

I learned a little bit about carpentry when the second-story balcony of our house disintegrated. Hershel Spokojny, who was pushing 40, was hired to construct a new balcony. I became his self-appointed helper, handing him nails and wooden planks as needed. I watched him work and learned a lot. For instance, I learned that the joists that supported the balcony were cantilevered, with the midpoint of the joists at the exterior wall, so that they were extended as far into the house as out and attached to floor joists running perpendicular to them.

There was a difference between the rough carpentry used for balcony repair and the fine cabinet-making techniques employed by Mr. Schab in his cabinetry shop. Whenever my father ordered armoires and furniture from his shop on the outskirts of town, I would watch him work, paying particular attention to the detailed joinery and the fine finishing process.

I learned about construction techniques when the Wakschlags, who lived across the street, enlarged their home. The Szmolarczyk family's hardware and iron store was on the ground floor, the Alexanderer *shtibl* was on the second floor, and the Wakschlag residence and jewelry workshop were on the third floor. They added a fourth floor by raising the roof inch by inch, inserting rows of bricks and blocks, one at a time. The work was painstakingly slow and took several weeks. In the meantime, everything below went on as usual.

Because we stocked our store with sweaters produced by Mr. Zilberberg on Krakower Street, I also had a chance to see how knitting machinery worked. Whenever I had to pick up merchandise, I would watch Mr. Zilberberg work his machine by hand, using long back and forth strokes. There were many types of yarn and different designs, and so the process was intriguing. I saw a different knitting process used by Leibel and Shmuel, the sons of Avrom Frouman, the cantor. They manufactured socks and stockings with a five-inch circular machine that produced knit tubes that were cut and finished as necessary. The brothers worked out of their home, behind Reb Meyerel's *heder*, and I visited often when I did not feel like attending to my studies.

GIRLS

As a young Hasid, I was taught to stay away from girls and to relate to female family members with reserve. But that did not stop me. I was already interested in girls when I was five years old. I was playing with my cousin Cesia and our wrestling became slightly titillating and intimate. I was curious. My brother Willie and her brother Alter caught us playing doctor and broke up our play. I did not quite understand what all the commotion was about.

I also did not quite understand a Polish song taught to me by Bronia Yasny, Meilach's sister. I understood it was naughty, but I did not fully get its meaning. The song was about King Cwieck's beautiful daughter, Princess Lizelotta, a virgin. To keep her chaste, the king ordered his army, air force, and navy to surround Lizelotta's castle. Lo and behold, the king discovered Lizelotta was pregnant. In a fit of rage, the king commanded the guilty party to step forward and confess, and everyone in the army, navy, and air force stepped forward to claim paternity. I—a boy from a pious home who learned Talmud every day—enjoyed learning this song because it sounded ribald. Though the Talmud I studied every day contained stories on sensitive topics, I had not yet found anything like this one in my studies.

As I grew older, I became more and more aware of the opposite sex. My older brother Willie and his friends used to hang out at the Kosciusko monument in the town square. I would sneak up and hide behind the adjacent fence to eavesdrop, and their conversations inevitably turned to girls. There was one in particular, Helen Drobiarz, a beautiful blonde, who fascinated me.

Helen and her friend Pola Vaga were older than I was and ahead of me in school. I met them at Professor Landau's because we were all in the same class. Pola's father, Isaac-Meyer, owned a profitable fabric store and was considered the richest man in town, but that did not faze me. Helen awakened certain feelings in me. Pola and Helen had a sled and would go sledding down the hill across from the fire station and Norman Kamelgard's house. I would sneak up behind them just as they were ready to take off, jump on their sled, and ride down the hill with them. My long jacket was too thin for playing outdoors in the winter, but sitting close to the girls on a sled kept me warm enough.

When the weather was warmer, I needed a different pretext to get close. I decided riding a bicycle would work, only I did not have enough money to rent one, let alone buy one—and I did not know how to ride. To raise the money, I negotiated a deal with my father that involved studying extra hard. The bicycle rental shop was just outside the town near the Jewish cemetery. After I rented the bike, I found a remote location where nobody could see me practice. Once I mastered the art of cycling, I rode to a place where boys and girls often met and enjoyed taking one of the girls for a ride on the frame of the bike.

Sometimes I managed to borrow a friend's bike. Willie's friend, Selig Goldkorn, had one and so did his older brother, Beryl. In Dzialoszyce, having two bikes in a single family was a luxury. To top it off, Selig's father had a motorcycle that Selig could use, and he would occasionally take me for a ride on the back. Although my parents were better off financially than the Goldkorns, my parents would never buy a bicycle for any of us, so Willie and I envied the Goldkorn brothers their good fortune. Apart from the cost, anything that might distract us from studying was discouraged. Furthermore, cycling was thought to be an improper pastime for boys from Orthodox families. Nevertheless, Willie and I longed for a bicycle, so we often went down to the end of the marketplace where the Goldkorns lived, hoping for a chance to ride.

On one occasion we were given the use of Selig's bicycle for a short time in exchange for helping him with Talmud homework. The arrangement was a good one all around. For my turn, I rode in large circles on the *Yanklowka* (green fields) a few times. Willie, in his turn, wanted to show off for his friend and me, so he started to speed, lost control, and smashed into a tree. We were shocked and remorseful when we saw the condition of the wrecked bicycle, but Selig was extraordinarily kind. Nice boy that he was, he told his mother he had smashed up the bike. He did all this maneuvering for the sake of his friend. Willie and I offered to pay Selig for the damage out of our meager allowances, but he refused to take it. He assured us that his father and Beryl could fix it.

One of the enduring smells of my childhood emanated from the apothecary, a shop that afforded me the opportunity to earn a little and learn a little. The pharmacist, an elderly man in a white coat and rimless glasses, paid me for the empty bottles I collected and washed out, one or two groszy each, depending on the size. Young men in their 20s would pay me, too, but for a different service. They were too embarrassed to buy their own condoms, so for two groszy per visit, I would do the purchasing for them. I learned all about the different types and brands. Olla Gum was the favorite. The kindly old pharmacist was amused to find a prepubescent Hasidic boy buying condoms from him and once asked ironically if I used them. My answer—"I don't need such expensive balloons"—was met with a hearty laugh.

Another source of my sexual education was *The Study of Sex*, a Hebrew book that was hidden away behind a double row of books in Father's book armoire. I notched the book's spine so that I could reach into the dark depths of the armoire and identify the book just by touch. My parents spent most of their time out of the house, so some days I would feign illness, stay home, lock the door, and head for the book closet. I enjoyed this book along with several others on Jewish mystical and Hasidic texts that Father did not want me to see.

The sublimation of sexuality is a given for a young Hasidic boy, but an incident involving two boys in the community caused me to question the wisdom of such severe repression. While working for Uncle Mottel, I met the three Luria sisters, who lived right across the street. (Their parents dealt in calcium used for whitewashing houses.) The Luria girls, all of marriageable age, were much older than I. Rabbi Staszewski, the chief rabbi of Dzialoszyce, lived next door to Uncle Mottel and had two grandsons, Simche and Moishe. Simche was a genius who learned a great deal of Talmud and also played the violin, which impressed many people. Moishe was not considered to be as bright as Simche. They all lived in the same building.

In the second-floor *shtibl* where their grandfather prayed, an ark housed the holy Torah scrolls behind a handmade ark curtain. The *shtibl* also served as a *beit midrash* (study hall) for young men between 18 and 22 years old. I was curious about the activities of the Staszewski brothers and sometimes followed them to the *shtibl* to see how they studied and what they discussed and discovered that they were interested in the Luria girls. The boys teased them and tossed their hats to them as their adrenaline levels rose. For Hasidic boys, removing one's hat in front of girls was a prohibited, almost lewd, act. The girls laughed, threw the hats back, and the game continued.

Another time, when the boys were supposed to be studying, they locked the door to the *shtibl* and would not let anyone in. Looking through a keyhole, I saw one of them standing in front of the ark, swaying fervently back and forth in the manner that was customary during prayer, holding the ark curtain and singing a song that translated, "Oh girl, girl, lift up your skirt. Show what you have, and tell me how much it costs." These young men, among the most devout in the city, were behaving in a most improper way. I was shocked, but part of me wanted to join them in this rebellion against religion, this expression of repressed sexuality.

Rabbi Staszewski's *shtibl* was also where one went for a *din Torah*. One such *din Torah* contributed to my "education." In 1938, Leibish Sieniawski's niece came from the nearby town of Proszowice to work for him in his folk-healing practice. Ever since Leibish's wife had died, he was uncomfortable about being home alone at night, to the point that often my mother would send me or one of my brothers to stay with him. When his niece came to work for him, she took over the "babysitting" and moved into his house. Zysman Sieniawski, Leibish's quite handsome nephew, lived close by in the mayor's building. Soon, a romance developed between the two young people, who went out together and loved each other. In time, they had sexual relations, and the girl got pregnant. Zysman liked the girl, but he did not want to marry her.

The girl's parents came from Proszowice and called Zysman to the rabbinical court for a *din Torah*. As an inquisitive boy, I was interested in everything that was going on and in anything other than my studies, so I tried to get into the *din Torah*. Naturally, they did not let me in, so I stayed just outside and spied through a keyhole, listening to the heated discussion between the girl's parents on one side and Zysman and his backers on the other side.

Zysman acknowledged that he had had relations with the girl, but added that other people had slept with her as well—he was not the only one. The girl started screaming hysterically. Then the rabbi asked, "Who else was there?"

Zysman named the others but said that they all preceded him. When the rabbi's wife came out to go to another room, I had to run away so as not to be caught eavesdropping. The rabbi asked Zysman, "Were you the last one?" Zysman answered in the affirmative. Then the rabbi gave his verdict: "She was probably made pregnant by you because you were the last one." Zysman had to marry the girl.

I once counted several unmarried pregnant girls in our modest and very religious small town. How did this happen? It began with walking on the *corso*. That, in turn, led to the "Jewish *Doly*" (Jewish Valley), a romantic, picturesque spot north of the Jewish cemetery not far from the dogcatcher's house. While young couples rolled around in the grass, various things fell out of their pockets. That was how I benefited from all the romance. I went to the "Jewish *Doly*" to hunt for "treasures" and combed the grounds to find coins—two-*groshn*, five-*groshn*, and even ten-*groshn* coins. I once found a beautiful little pocketknife with four separate blades, which I treasured.

GERMAN OCCUPATION

At the beginning of 1939, rumors of an impending war began to circulate. News of what had already transpired in Europe created a strained atmosphere, and tension hung in the air. In August, the Soviet Union and Germany signed a nonaggression pact, and on September 1, 1939, Germany attacked Poland. There had already been a general call-up of soldiers and reserve officers, but with the outbreak of war, there was a call for full mobilization.

Two of our town's public school teachers, Mr. Samczyk and Mr. Yanas, both high-ranking officers in the Polish army, were among those mobilized. Each of them gave a patriotic speech to the large group of people gathered at the Kosciuszko monument. In strong voices, our teachers proclaimed their devotion to their country and promised to conquer the enemy. When the speeches were over, they shook hands in the crowd and vowed to meet soon again in Berlin. They were assigned to battalions headed in different directions, but their hopes were thwarted by reality.

The Polish army was not heavily mechanized or set up defensively. Nor was German aggression ended by the declaration of war on September 3 by Britain and France. In a few short days, Germany occupied all of Poland with the exception of the southeast, which was left in Russia's purview, consistent with the terms of the nonaggression pact between Hitler and Stalin. Mr. Samczyk and Mr. Yanas were taken prisoner, and I never heard from either of them again.

In Dzialoszyce, the locals who were not mobilized immediately worked on civil defense. Many of them, like Simcha Jurysta, a fine man and a Gerer Hasid, volunteered to dig trenches. On the fourth or fifth day of the war, the first German plane flew over our town and dropped a single grenade, but people thought it was a bomb. It killed Simcha while he was digging trenches; he became the first war victim in our town. His youngest son, Abie, was ten years old at the time, about two years younger than I was.

On Friday morning, September 8, we woke to the roar of heavy, motorized cars, the deep rumbling of massive tanks, and the shouts of foreign voices. There was suddenly a new presence in our town; the conquering Germans had arrived with terrifying speed and determination. The mood in Dziaoszyce was gloomy and grim.

The Germans set up headquarters in one of the most prestigious buildings on the marketplace. The building belonged to the Szentails, but it was rented to the Jutczenkas, an ultra-Orthodox family with a son and two daughters. They owned a store called Jutczenka Haberdashery, one of the places I visited every Friday to collect repayment on a loan. After the war, Leibel Jutczenka, the son, moved to Israel. I don't think any other members of his family survived.

The Germans implemented their policies gradually, increasing the harshness of their decrees in increments, so that psychologically we would get used to intolerable conditions and not offer much resistance. It started by implementing the Nuremberg Laws passed in 1935 and forcing Jews to wear yellow armbands and chest patches imprinted with the word *Jude* in the center of a Star of David. Jews were not allowed to leave town without special permits. Jewish children were no longer allowed to attend public school.

The Poles, watching our degradation at the hands of the Germans, heartily joined in. Our neighbors and compatriots would taunt us with, "Now Hitler is going to teach you a lesson! Hitler is going to take care of you Jews!" Their church did not rein in these evil rabble-rousers. In fact, the Catholic Church contributed heavily to the atmosphere of hatred. Cardinal August Hlond, Primate of Poland, issued a pastoral letter, which, among the many lies it contained, accused Jews of spreading atheism. Our Catholic neighbors rejoiced in our misfortune. With no one to turn to for help, we felt increasingly alone. Our only solace was in our prayers for the Messiah's speedy arrival and the safety of our families.

Some people succumbed to despair immediately. Reb Simche Zalsberg had relatives who lived in Germany, and right after the occupation, terrible news about his relatives reached him. A deeply pious man, the fine gentleman could not cope with what he heard, went up to his attic, and hanged himself from one of the rafters. His son Alter was a close friend of Art's. We tried to conduct business as usual, but after the Germans began motorcycle and foot patrols through town, it became increasingly difficult. At first, the soldiers would come into the store to demand 20-inch squares of cloth to wrap around their feet as padding for their new boots. Then they graduated to taking more substantial items.

Father understood what was happening and immediately began removing most of the goods stored in our basement and hiding them among a group of non-Jewish families we hoped we could trust—the Novaks, Piotrkowskis, and Rogulskis among them. We had lots of merchandise, and some of it was fairly expensive—suits, shawls, and kerchiefs. At some homes we left several suits, at others a few rolls of fabric. Whatever we could reasonably remove was hidden behind armoires, under beds, in basements, or in attics. We were careful to choose people who could not be easily connected to our business, and we also entrusted goods to peasant customers from other villages who brought in the goods by horse and wagon.

The goal was to spread the merchandise out in as many places as possible to minimize the risk of detection. In our naïveté, we did not expect the war to last very long, and we hoped that these people would return our goods in the near future. Father calculated that the risk of not getting the goods back was worth taking when he was faced with certain confiscation by the Germans.

We hid other items in our house in a gable above the attic, where the *sukkah* was located. Between the rafters and joists, there was a long, empty space about two feet high. The place was full of straw, which served as insulation. I crawled into this opening, removed the hay, and slowly packed in quantities of merchandise, covering it with straw when I was finished. Every time I went there, I came out black from all the dust that had accumulated. I was the only one who could fit because I was the youngest and still relatively small. Sometimes, I had to come out just to catch my breath.

We hid some smaller items with other Jews who had room to take a few things. One of them was Moishe Chiel, a rabbi, *dayan* (religious judge), and civil judge, son-in-law of Chief Rabbi Staszewski. I hid several pieces of fabric behind a closet at his home, making sure the merchandise was well hidden. I was fond of his beautiful, redheaded daughter, but in her presence, I was a little shy. For a religious boy and girl, just a forbidden look at one another was exciting, and she was the reason I spent extra time there.

While we were beginning to cope with the new situation, Jews from Silesia, the western part of Poland along Germany's border, streamed into Dzialoszyce, especially those who had relatives living in town. Because of the preponderance of *Volksdeutsche* (ethnic Germans) in Silesia, conditions for Jews worsened there faster than they did farther east. By the end of 1939, all of Mother's family from Chozow was back in Dzialoszyce. There were David and Hinda, Chaim and Bracha, Esther, and Itke and Harry. Aunt Esther came with her children, leaving Uncle Shloyme behind.

Uncle Shloyme was a reserve officer in the Polish army, a demolition expert and a sapper who was mobilized as soon as war was declared. After the Germans overran Poland in the first week of the war, many soldiers returned, but Uncle Shloyme was not heard from. A week passed, then a month, then two months, and Aunt Esther still waited. The survivors had come back by then, with no word of Shloyme. I remember Aunt Esther leaning on the corner wall of Galonski's shoe store, long-suffering in her waiting, crying for her husband. We all felt sorry for this beautiful, redheaded woman and for Hanusia and Lolek, her two small children. Hanusia spent quite a lot of time with us as a young girl, and I remember how we tried to feed her when she did not want to eat. My mother and father kept saying "swallow."

Finally, one day, Uncle Shloyme came walking up from the marketplace. When Aunt Esther noticed him coming, she ran into our house and starting screaming and crying with joy. Dressed in tattered civilian clothes, we washed and cleaned Shloyme—his feet were completely swollen because, afraid to use the train, he had walked for hundreds of kilometers. He told us about daily risks to his life and the nightmares he had experienced as he tried to get back to his family. The only things he kept were his military boots, their tops hidden under his baggy, ill-fitting pants. When the Germans came, they looked for Polish officers, whose uniforms were expensive and of good quality. I still have a photograph of Hanusia in her *Krakowiak* ethnic outfit that Uncle Shloyme sent me after the war.

I once witnessed an incident involving two officers who tried to evade detection. They ran into public outhouses behind our house, took off their uniforms, threw them away, and changed into civilian clothes. After Uncle Shloyme returned, he, Aunt Esther, Hanusia, and Lolek set up housekeeping in the room upstairs next to the *sukkah*. My brothers Art and Chaim-Leizer, who used to sleep there, moved down to the kitchen and dining room. It was starting to get a little crowded, but we were far better off than the hundreds of refugees crammed into the *beit midrash*.

As soon as the refugee Jews arrived in Dzialoszyce, the Germans put them to work. They organized work details to clean the streets, shovel snow, and do community work—like guarding quarantined homes. A family living near the tannery contracted typhus and was consequently quarantined, and every day someone stood watch to make sure nobody left or entered the house. Uncle Shloyme was assigned the task, but the job bored him, so he asked me to do it.

While I stood guard, I noticed a white horse tied to a post not far from the house, and unable to resist the urge, untied the animal, mounted it, and rode away, down the road and across the fields. When I returned, I saw that Dr. Grenbowsky, the regional supervisor of the health department, had come to inspect the quarantined house, and when he saw that no one was watching the house, he was furious. I dismounted the horse, and after he ascertained that I was derelict in my duties, he sent me to the town jail, two barred rooms near the city hall. I was in a cell by myself, and my friends came by to tease me about being a jailbird. As they drew closer to the window secured by iron bars, I took a bucket of water and poured it on them through the grates. I was soon released because my imprisonment was a lesson to teach people that guarding a quarantined house was a serious matter.

Around the time my uncles moved to town, the Germans put a *Treuhänder* (trustee/manager) into our store. These managers were usually *Volksdeutsche* who were collaborators. There was still lots of merchandise in the store we had not managed to hide, and the presence of the German manager made it all the more difficult. Somehow, before he took a complete inventory, we did manage to hide some additional goods.

Uncle Shloyme's cousin, Black Laya, whose son was a tailor in the marketplace, lived on the outskirts of town on the second floor of a two-story house. The family had a large attic where we hid the bulk of our stock. We removed the attic doors and walled up the entrance, thus sealing and camouflaging it. We paid a weekly fee as rent, and though we wanted to operate as clandestinely as possible, her son insisted that his employer hide some merchandise there as well.

Then the confiscation of all Jewish property began. The Germans collected everything, including personal items of value, silver, cash, jewelry, diamonds, and furs. Mother gave her Persian lamb and raccoon coats to Mrs. Novak, whose family had been our customers for years. She also entrusted them with our monogrammed linens. Mr. Novak had as close a relationship with Father as a land-owning Gentile and a Gerer Hasid could have back then. Father even gave the Novaks matzos at Passover because, notwithstanding the Church's vile slanders, many of the country folk considered eating matzo a blessing. Father hid our valuables in various spots, helped by Uncle David, who was very handy. He was good at camouflaging openings in walls by putting bricks back in a way that could not be easily detected.

Soon after the confiscations began, and around the time of my 13th birthday, Father took me down to the basement and started to dig a hole in the dirt floor, crying all the while. He had in his hand the bar mitzvah watch his father had given him. He handed me the watch and said in a tone full of feeling, "Yossele, now is the war, we cannot make you a bar mitzvah. I don't know if I will live to make you a bar mitzvah at a later time, but this is my present to you."

Father explained the gift's significance and described watches as life's time-tellers. They show how precious time flies. One should use time wisely. Father's parents had given him this watch to symbolize the value of time. Father reiterated that he gave me that same watch to make me understand that he did not know what the future would bring, and he asked me to remember this event in the passing of time. Together, we buried the precious watch under the house in which we had both lived so much of our lives.

The Germans soon impounded the store and sealed the front and back doors. They warned us that removing the seals and entering would result in death by firing squad. Before the doors were sealed, the *Volksdeutsche* manager had taken inventory and missed the items hidden in the basement. He was long gone, so before the Germans came to cart away the contents, we made a last-ditch effort to liberate some merchandise. We knew how to get into the basement without breaking any of the seals. Stealthily, Uncle David, Hymie, and I went to work switching cheaper merchandise for more expensive goods. For example, the manager's inventory listed 40 suits, but did not specify what kinds of suits, so we exchanged good men's suits worth 15 zloty for ready-made children's suits from the basement worth a fraction of that.

Things, of course, got worse. The store was gone, and our merchandise was scattered throughout town and in nearby villages, making it difficult to access. From time to time, we sold some off and, little by little, retrieved our possessions and sold them as well, piece by piece. I was the courier. My father was well organized and kept records of where the stock was hidden. We managed by secretly inviting farmers to our home for private sales and using the money we earned to sustain ourselves. We also resorted to barter and exchanged goods for grain we could grind into flour to bake our own bread.

As the Germans decreed harsher and harsher regulations, the Poles continued to rejoice in our misery and informed on us. Many of the regulations were simply mean-spirited and designed to degrade us, with no practical benefit to the Nazis. Jews were forbidden to have facial hair, a direct affront to the Orthodox community, which read the biblical commandment of not "cutting the hair of the five corners of the head" as a prohibition against shaving. In order to comply with *halacha* and evade the Nazis, Father wrapped a kerchief around his head and face to hide his beard, pretending he had a toothache. A curfew was instituted. Anyone caught in the street after 9 p.m. was sent to jail or to a labor camp—or he could be shot on the spot.

As time passed, demand for Jewish forced labor increased. The Germans transported Jews by train to work in villages surrounding Dzialoszyce, with 50 or 60 people squeezed together in a single boxcar. Even I, a young boy, was sent to work in the fields of Nieszkiev, where I loaded and unloaded hay. The Germans went to the *Gmina*, the town's Jewish community council, to demand bodies to provide slave labor. The *Gmina* members, threatened with their own survival, acquiesced to Nazi demands, as did we all. We did not understand the insidiousness of the process and where it would lead.

Then, around Passover of 1940, the Germans issued a decree ordering each family to send one male member to a labor camp outside the city. We did not know what to do. They said that if a family male went to the camp, the rest of the family would be spared. We panicked.

Hymie was most involved in what was left of the business. He had a good head for business and, before the war, had helped in the store during the day and studied Torah at night. Now he managed the clandestine distribution of our goods. I was too young, having just turned 13. Therefore, the fate of going to a labor camp fell to Volvele. Father and Mother, all of us, were overwhelmed with sadness and tears. The first *Shabes* Volvele was gone was particularly heart wrenching. Father sobbed his way through *kiddush*, and we all sobbed with him.

Volvele was in a group of 150 men from Dzialoszyce in their midteens to early twenties who were taken by train to Krakow and then by truck to Kostrze, where they worked for Richard Strauch Hoch und Tiefbau, a company that built waterworks, sewage systems, and other infrastructure. We sent Volvele food and clothing packages, and though we knew he was alive, we understood how hard it was for him and how he suffered. We worried.

Volvele's first job was to dig a drainage system for a flooded valley. Later, during the expulsions from Dzialoszyce, those selected for labor (as opposed to death) joined him in the wet fields near Kraków. (I was sent there, too.) We spent endless hours every day standing in two to three feet of water and in soft mud, digging and digging, turning swamps into productive fields.

Before that happened, I continued to work in Nieszkiev, Siedlce, Sancygniow, and other villages around the town. As time went on, the physical labor grew more difficult. Jews were pressed into working in quarries. In 1941, I was sent to Drozdowice, halfway between Dzialoszyce and Skalbmierz, to work with a gang blasting stone. We removed boulders, hammered them into gravel for paving roads and then sorted the gravel by size using large metal screens. The work was backbreaking, the dust affected our lungs and health. My assignments were daily tasks, so I was able to go home to my parents and my brother Hymie until the expulsion in 1942.

When informers told the Germans where our merchandise was hidden, it was carted away. Everyone was generally depressed about life being difficult, and living conditions continued to deteriorate. I no longer received an allowance, so I did business on my own. First, I bought and sold hard-to-get cigarette rolling papers. Then I sold cigarettes. Later, I dealt in candies I bought from Drziewienski's son, my friend Hershel (whose father became mentally unbalanced every June or July and would wade in the river). Drziewienski manufactured the candy himself and sold it at wholesale prices to shops, stalls in the marketplace, and to me. He took plain sugar, boiled it in pots, rolled it, put sesame or poppy seeds on top, and cut the rolls into pieces. I sold these candies retail by walking around the marketplace with a box-tray hanging from my neck that displayed my wares. I tried to compete by selling for a *groshn* less than the stalls.

As people struggled with the oppressive conditions, life inexorably marched on. My parents wanted to marry off Art because he was already 20. In our circles that was the right age, so my parents put the word out. Father wanted Art to marry Reb Simche Zalsberg's fine daughter. (Her father was the one who hanged himself in despair.) The family manufactured and sold soap and was among the finest families in Dzialoszyce. The daughter was a beautiful, fair-skinned girl who wore rimless glasses. Perhaps Art was not yet ready for marriage or perhaps he did not like girls who wore glasses, so he declined the match. Other possible matches considered appropriate by Father were Rabbi Epstein's daughter and the daughter of Yachet Platkiewicz. Both girls were nice, had good reputations, and came from good families with backgrounds similar to ours. But those girls were Father's choices, not Art's, who had his own ideas. He was smart and had good taste, so in addition to the attributes my father searched for, Art wanted a beauty. In 1940, at age 23, he married Manya.

Art met Manya through Abraham Dayan (the judge), a learned gentleman with a relative in Skalbmierz, where Manya lived, a town eight kilometers from Dzialoszyce. We were all very happy with the match because Manya was nice *and* beautiful, and we all loved her. The wedding took place early in 1940, but I could not attend. Movement between towns was severely restricted, and even a moderate gathering of people attracted too much attention. Jews were not allowed on the trains after the Nazi order of January 26, 1940, so Uncle David rented a horse and wagon to take my parents to the small ceremony. I managed to visit the young couple on my own several times, using the occasion to do business in Skalbmierz. Traveling alone attracted less attention, though I did risk a fine, jail time, or both.

I rode the trains surreptitiously, grabbing a handhold and hanging onto the exterior of the last car just as it started moving, thus avoiding conductors. The little coal-fed train ran on narrow-gauge tracks and never really reached great speeds on the short run between towns. As the train slowed before reaching the station, I would jump off. Within ten months, Manya had her first baby, but mother and child never made it past the baby's second birthday. They were among the innocent children of Israel whose lives were barbarously cut short by the Germans.

Life's forward movement continued to assert itself with the death of my grandmother, Esther Reisel. She was a gentle woman, delicate of voice, fine-featured, and quite ladylike. She was very different from my grandfather, who was powerful in stature. When Father and Uncle Yoyev heard the bad news, Jews had already been forbidden even to leave town. They risked their lives to travel to Chenciny to sit *shivah* (mourn) with their lonely father, who was heartbroken at the death of his wife.

SHAME

And for the informers, let there be no hope…
(added to the *Shemoneh Esreh* prayer during the
Hellenic occupation of Israel)

As conditions worsened, people took bigger risks to survive, and ethical standards deteriorated. Art was doing business and taking chances. Once he went to Krakow by horse and wagon with others to buy merchandise, bring it back, and sell in Dzialoszyce. He bought a sack of sugar, which was scarce and expensive. He negotiated a very good bargain at the market and had opened the sack to make sure that it actually contained sugar. To cover himself in case the Germans checked and caught him smuggling, he hired a non-Jewish driver. Even so, Art was afraid and hid the sack of sugar by covering it with straw. When he came home and wanted to start selling the sugar, he found salt underneath the upper layer. This kind of fraud went on with increasing frequency during the war.

Most of the people I knew in my youth were pious, honest, honorable, and hardworking. They cared about one another and were decent folks. Our youths, though less observant, were more sophisticated, intelligent, and cultured. Perhaps those who were middle-aged and older did not have great secular educations, but they were good, kind people. However, there are always the exceptions. For their contribution to our misery during wartime, these few "bad eggs" deserve appropriate remembrance here.

There was Moshke with his jaundiced thoughts, one of three or four informers from our town who denounced people to the Nazis and who exposed anyone who did things forbidden by German decree. Moshke must have been paid or received some benefit for his treachery. Unfortunately, we were not careful enough to keep all our secrets because we could not imagine anything as disgraceful as Jewish collaborators.

Another bad person was Mottel Platkiewicz (not a close relative), who was having an affair with a non-Jewish prostitute. Together, they denounced Jews and Poles. The Germans ensured the anonymity of the informers—at least while they were still useful. Once their utility expired, the Germans shot them and dumped their bodies on the outskirts of town. Then rumors would circulate about who the informers were.

One day Mottel was taken to jail. His father, Leizer, a very fine man, was sitting on the steps of Galonski's shoe store in the marketplace when he learned that his son had been released. Some people asked him, "Leizer, your son is coming. He has been freed from the German prison. How welcome is your guest?" The father hung his head in shame and answered in a sad but angry voice, "You should only live so long how welcome he is!"

The Yiddish expression is the opposite of its English translation, meaning that Mottel was not welcome. The father refused to talk to or welcome his son because he had embarrassed the family. How could a person inform against his own people? Leizer was understandably bitter.

One small act of deceit I witnessed haunts me to this day. We had hidden a few rolls of bulky material behind a closet at Reb Moshe Chiel's house. When we needed to sell the fabric, I went to collect it, but the rabbi, who had been held in high regard, said he did not remember whether we had put goods there. After his first lie, he tried to convince me that I had already taken the merchandise and forgotten that I did. I knew for sure that neither I nor anyone else from my family had retrieved it. Reb Moshe Chiel never returned the fabric.

How could a trustworthy, virtuous person with a reputation for being a pious Jew act in such a way? The rabbi lied, committed theft, and cast aspersions on my family and me. If the man had said he sold the merchandise to buy food for his family, we would have understood and forgiven him, but lying and impugning our integrity was another matter altogether. Betrayals of this sort destroyed my sense of trust. I was disappointed and disillusioned. If pious people like the rabbi could exploit others and act shamelessly, what could we expect from lesser individuals?

One day during the war, my father noticed two peddlers selling suits, shawls, and kerchiefs in the marketplace that looked just like the merchandise we had hidden in Black Laya's attic. Slowly, quietly, we investigated the matter without making any accusations. The two men selling the merchandise were Hartzke and Herskowitz (who used to be called "Einlatch"). They were selling our stock gradually, two suits one day, another suit the next. We checked with the customers and established that their merchandise was definitely ours. Somehow, it had been stolen and was now being sold. We suspected that Black Laya's son was helping himself to our suits and that these two were his fences.

My parents decided to open the secret attic to check whether any of their merchandise was missing. When they tried to arrange an inspection, they were told that Black Laya's son was sick. The family had all kinds of excuses to prevent a visit: it is dangerous; the doctor forbids it; we would now need permission from the man next door, who owned the second floor leading to the attic; and so on. Lie followed lie. One *moytzei Shabes* a short time later, we learned that the Germans came to Black Laya's house with a truck, broke into the hiding place, and with the forced help of some Jews, took whatever was left of our merchandise and carted it away. By delaying our visit, Black Laya's son got word to informers, who were rewarded for the information. He had engineered a tidy little operation to get himself out of his tight spot at our expense.

Hershel Ries, an awkward, cynical loner, who was an underworld figure of sorts in our town, publicly announced that if he "had known that Zisme Tenenbaum had hidden merchandise, [he] would have gone through the roof and taken some of it [himself]." Ries was a well-known thief and used to brag about crimes he could have committed to make himself rich. "Why did they have to tell the Germans, so that the Germans would end up with the goods? Why wasn't I informed instead?" asked Ries. My parents were also aware that the guilty party could have taken some of our merchandise, sold it, and lived comfortably. Why anyone would let the Germans get their hands on it was beyond comprehension, unless it was to cover up their own thievery.

Informants also guided Nazis to our house to search for hidden valuables. I was at home, sick, when Nazis led by the *Stadtkommandant* (city commander) barged in and violently opened the book closets and searched between the pages of our holy books for paper currency. These antisemites hated Jewish books and in the process threw the books to the floor. We had been taught to treat our sacred works with such reverence that even if one fell accidentally, we picked it up and nursed it with a kiss. Watching the disrespectful treatment of our holy books was heartbreaking. Our house was searched from the attic to the basement, but the Nazis found nothing.

The days may have been hellish, but life was also heaven because of the love in our family. Mother and Father stood together as a harmonious unit. They were a loving, caring couple, and the family was closely knit. Two diametrically opposed realities coexisted: the harsh reality of the war versus the happiness that emanated from the feelings we had for each other in the inner world of our family. But I was never free to roam in the wonderland of adolescence. I was on the boundary between boyhood and manhood, between romantic yearnings and the tragic reality of the times.

THWARTED ROMANCE

When the war broke out, the Jewish community of Dzialoszyce, with about 8,000 souls, swelled to some 12,000 because of the influx of refugees from the border area. Among them were the children of Mother's cousin Yachet Platkiewicz. Yachet and her son, Israel, owned one of the town's largest fabric stores, where we sometimes bought goods for our own store. She was the matriarch of one of the finest families in town, with a good reputation and financial success.

Yachet had three daughters: Cinella, Helen, and Risele. Helen was married to Chaim Yitzchak Wolgelernter, a genius whose discourses on Torah were excellent. Cinella was married to Hershel Ehrlich and had two boys and three girls. When the war broke out, they all came to town and lived near the public school on Chmielowa Street. Cinella's oldest daughter, Helen, was a gorgeous blonde who had a scar on the back of her left leg. The middle daughter, Esther, affectionately called Estusia, was beautiful, shy, slim, and tall. She was the first girl I ever loved.

Because of the curfew, Estusia sometimes slept at her grandmother's house right across the street from us instead of going home to her parents. In the evening, her sister and others congregated in Zisme Szeniawski's garden, whose home was in the same block as the city jail. The garden, about ten houses away from us, was next to the jail and full of trees, flowers, and stone benches. I tried to get there every evening because I wanted to see Estusia and spend time in her presence, although I never dared speak to her. I talked to everyone about Estusia. I was bewildered by my feelings and the enigma of desire. Her looks, her walk, and her voice all captivated me. It was 1940, and I was 13 years old.

Estusia dominated my thoughts, soul, and spirit, day and night. She was on my mind even when I was studying Talmud. I was obsessed. I wanted to see her constantly, so I borrowed a camera from a fellow named Chaba, who somehow had managed to make the magical device himself. Chaba also lived across the road, in Mr. Wakschlag's house. When Estusia walked down the street in daytime, I surreptitiously took photographs of her. She suspected nothing. I wanted to have her picture to keep for myself and show friends. In some of the photos, Estusia carried a mop and broom, probably for cleaning her grandmother's house. In another picture, she was toting a pot of *tsholnt* to the bakery.

Chaba developed the film for me, and I paid him for the finished photographs. When Bala Dula, Estusia's close friend, moved from Dombrowa to a house a few doors away, I made her my go-between. Too shy to approach Estusia on my own, I showed the photos to Bala Dula and confessed my feelings. I left them with her, and she shared them with Estusia, who was very curious about who took the photographs. Restrained by her modesty, I never did get to embrace or kiss Estusia and had to content myself with platonic, romantic adoration at a respectful distance.

Father noted that I devoted less time to my studies, almost ignoring them. In the morning, I pored over the books with forced effort because my heart and soul were elsewhere. Father ordered me not to leave the house in the evening, not to visit the garden, not to go anywhere. This punishment struck me as too severe, so I rebelled. Between Father's restrictions and the Nazi curfew, I was boxed in. My sense of dismay and frustration mounted. I could not concentrate at all. All I could do was think and dream about Estusia. But Father warned me that if I left the house at night, he would not let me back in.

One night I sneaked out without telling anyone, and when Father noticed I was not home, he locked the two heavy doors downstairs. Around midnight, I carefully made my way through the back alley to avoid any Germans, but I could not get inside. Hurt but resourceful, I entered Cirele Galonski's house next door, went up to the second-floor balcony, and jumped the six-foot distance between her balcony and ours. I quietly let myself into the house undetected. Exhausted, I lay down and fell asleep in the first room, on the piece of furniture that was a bench holding pails of water by day and opened into a bed at night.

This pattern of deception repeated itself for quite a while. I would study in the living room during the day and spend some time with my *melamed* Shloymeleh, finishing many pages quickly. Father kept the door to this room closed because he did not want anybody to see me studying. He thus ensured that I would not be interrupted by the increased activity around the house and also kept away the evil eye. Ever since the Germans had sealed the store and the entire first floor, we were restricted to the apartment upstairs. Customers "visited" us on the second floor, and my father and Hymie secretly sold them merchandise while I studied.

Abraham Balderman, who made burlap sacks for straw mattresses, was a frequent guest. We all slept on such mattresses and every so often had to change the straw in the sacks. We sold him various qualities of burlap at different prices, and while doing business, he noticed that the door to the room from which he heard voices was always closed. Suspicious by nature, he thought his competitors were doing business there. One day, totally frustrated, he threw the door open and saw Shloymeleh and me sitting there with two large volumes of the Talmud, mulling over a difficult issue. He was stunned. He shut the door, went to my father, and said, "Zisme, if you had a large diamond on each finger of your hands, I would not envy you as much as I did when I saw Yossele sitting there studying. I have three sons, and they do not want to learn. They are not even interested in going to *heder* or praying. I really admire you."

Between 11 a.m. and 4 p.m. I studied, but afterward I had to get out to be with Estusia. Meanwhile, the Germans added restrictions to the curfew. We were no longer allowed to pray at the Gerer *shtibl* and instead assembled a *minyan* (prayer quorum of ten or more) next door at the Galonski home. By frequently attending services there, Father finally figured out that I was using their balcony to get back into the house.

He asked the Galonskis to lock their doors. I was shocked and spent the first part of the night in the garden—the garden of Eden, the garden of heaven, where I saw the beautiful face of my love and felt shivers at being in her presence—but I had no place to sleep!

It was an hour before midnight, and I did not know where to go. As I ran out of ideas, I became frustrated and depressed. Finally, it dawned on me to knock on Alchu Federman's window. Alchu was my friend because I was bigger and stronger than he was and could protect him. His parents wanted us to be friends because I was more knowledgeable than he. Alchu came to the window, let me in, and shared his bed with me for the next few nights. I did not tell my parents anything.

My parents were very upset. Father declared that I did not deserve to eat at the table with him because I did not obey him and disrespected his wish that I study at night as well as all day. Instead, I was going out and not even coming home to sleep. It was spring, and my mind was filled with Estusia. It was just before Passover, and I was being scolded while Hymie and the maid (we still had one then) were taking the books out of the closet to put them out on the balcony to air. I soon joined them in opening the books to remove any *homets* that might have fallen between the pages. (We had a habit of eating and drinking while studying so we would not waste precious study time eating.) We also put shiny moth flakes—which made me sneeze—between the pages of each book to prevent bookworms or insects from eating the volumes.

While we were doing this work on the balcony, Mother asked me, "Yossele, dear child, please tell me—I will give you some *groshn*—who is this girl?" She had heard through gossip that I was going out with a girl or was having a good time. Mother repeated her question and begged me to answer her, hugging and kissing me all the while. "Is she a shoemaker's daughter? A tailor's daughter?" (Mother was referring to the fact that it would not suit our family's status or reputation for me to associate with, or get engaged to, a girl whose parents were of lesser standing in the community.) "Who is she?" Mother continued asking, offering me the bribe again. "No, Mother, I cannot tell. I will not tell you." I was stubborn and firm in my resolve not to tell. She persisted. She doubled the size of the bribe—a lot of money to me—and that was important because I was planning to buy something for Estusia.

As the relationship between Father and me became more strained, it seemed possible that Father was coercing Mother into finding out who the girl was. I could not take any more of Mother's tears. Finally, I broke down and told her, "Mother, she is the granddaughter of Yachet Platkiewicz." When Mother heard that the girl was Yachet's granddaughter, she sighed with relief, "Yachetel Platkiewicz—mmmh. Thank God, it's not so bad. It's not so bad." Mother promised to keep the secret, not to tell Father or anyone else about the girl I liked. I had not even mentioned the name Estusia.

Because I constantly stared at her and communicated indirectly via Bala Dula, Estusia knew I was interested. Our "virtual" relationship improved with each passing day. We became bolder, looking at each other directly, exchanging glances. I paid particular attention to my attire, making sure my boots were always clean. Whenever I was near her, my behavior was always gentlemanly. Although I never said a word directly to Estusia, I was proud of our relationship.

My relationship with Father, however, was growing worse because I did not care to study as much as Father wanted me to. The store was not open, there was no cash flow, we lived in danger, and there was much work we had to do. Clandestine business dealings, curfews, and restrictions on travel only compounded our problems.

Despite all the horrible things going on around me, the feelings that awakened in me that spring and summer were wonderful. Fall came early that year and with it the High Holy Days, Rosh Hashanah and Yom Kippur. Before the war, we normally got up early to go to *shul* for confession and to ask forgiveness for our transgressions. That year, we had to pray in our houses. I remember Father watching me while I recited my prayers. He wanted me to confess and to promise that I would be more obedient, but I was stubborn. I was determined to defend my actions vigorously and to follow my heart, leading down the path of true love to Estusia.

On Yom Kippur before Kol Nidre, Father always took us into the second room and blessed us, putting his hands on the head of each child. He called us in one by one. Being the youngest, I was always last. This time, only Chaim and I were left at home. After Father blessed Chaim (whose name means "life"), he called for me. When I entered the room, Father started to cry.

"So, you're determined; you've decided not to study any more, not to learn," Father said with short breaths. "Well, okay, if that is what you want." Tears kept streaming down his face. "Father, Father, I promise to continue studying. Don't worry. I will study more than ever," I replied. "Please stop crying. I cannot bear to see you cry."

I kept my word. I became immersed in the study of Talmud, learning more about Shamai and Hillel, Chizkiyah and Abahu, Reb Meyer and Reb Yehuda, and many of the other sages inhabiting the pages of the *Mishnah* and *Gemara*. Father was pleased and repeated the expression he had used so often when convincing me to study, "Yes, my darling son, my dear Yossele. '*Shemetokh shelo lishmah, ba lishmah.*'" (The irreverent shall come to reverence, *Pesachim* 50, 2).

We also spoke about the war. "Father, I don't understand what is going on. How much longer can I take this punishment? How can I believe and pray to God with all that we are going through, while barbarous atrocities continue? It is impossible to carry on, to bear it. How can I study, how can I believe?"

Father's faith was steadfast. "No, darling, believe. Dear Yossele, pray to God. God will help. The Messiah will come. Everything will be fine. We have to live with hope."

It was a message that would sustain me through all the horrors that followed.

Part II

On whatever side we regard the history of Europe, we shall perceive it to be a tissue of crimes, follies, and misfortunes.

Oliver Goldsmith
1762 essay in
The Citizen of the World

THE EXPULSION

After three years of increasingly difficult conditions, we no longer suffered from the illusion that the war would end quickly. Our property was confiscated or stolen. Our civil liberties were drastically reduced, our movements severely curtailed. The Germans and their Polish lackeys were moving ahead with their systematic attempts to dehumanize us. And yet, we hoped. The only feeling we had left was hope. We hoped that the darkening nightmare would end. We hoped that the Messiah would come to deliver us from the mounting severity of our suffering. We fasted, we prayed, we kept repeating the Psalms over and over. We tried to maintain our faith. Faith and the love in our family were all we had to keep us going.

Then late one afternoon on the first day of September 1942, the Jews in Dzialoszyce lived through our own version of the Blitzkrieg. The Germans increased their numbers with the speed of a sudden storm, sweeping into town on motorcycles with sidecars. When Chaim-Leizer heard the commotion, he went upstairs to our third-floor *sukkah* to see what was happening. From that vantage point, peering through the small windows over the town, he saw that the *Junaki* (gangster Poles who helped the Germans and volunteered to search Jewish homes in order to loot and steal) had surrounded the city. The *Junaki*, who were equipped with spades, picks, and shovels, stood 10 to 15 feet apart, forming an impenetrable wall.

Only three days earlier, the Jews of Wolbrom, a town 50 kilometers northwest of us, were ordered to assemble at their town's Jewish cemetery in order to be "resettled." With that knowledge and the harsh reality of the sight his eyes beheld, Chaim-Leizer, who was a gentle soul, came down from the *sukkah* screaming and crying. I had never heard him yell and scream before—and with such despair! In a frantic outburst, he told us what he had seen. We were not surprised that the *Junaki* were rallying to do the dirty work for the Nazis. After absorbing the shock, we tried to calm Chaim-Leizer down. We tried to be strong.

Peering through the sheer curtains on our living-room windows, we saw Nazi officers going into Zwolinski's tavern, where they started drinking. Though the tavern was Polish owned, the Germans typically did not drink with the Poles because they considered them inferior. To the Germans, the Poles served as lackeys. The Germans, cowardly bullies, were drinking to boost their courage with alcohol before going out to murder innocent civilians.

As the Germans drank their way to courage hours before the *Aussiedlung* (expulsion), the *Ordnungsdienst* ("order police," or Jewish Militia, appointed by the *Gmina*, the management office for Jewish affairs in town) went house to house to tell everyone to abandon their homes. The Jewish militiaman was very tense and gave us his rushed orders in short, clipped sentences. We were allowed to take only ten kilograms of possessions with us. The houses were to remain open for inspection to make sure no one was left behind. Those who did not show up in the market square would be shot on sight.

We expected the Germans to treat us badly, but many of us, perhaps foolishly, could not accept—in spite of all the news that leaked in from other places—that we would be forced to leave our homes and town. Father understood the likelihood of expulsion and prepared accordingly. As rumors filtered in about whole Jewish populations being forced to abandon their towns, Father and a group of 16 neighbors built a hiding place in a basement next door. Father expected a long, forced march, like the ones the press gangs took, and knew he would not be up to it. Before the war, Father had intentionally injured his leg to avoid being drafted into the Polish army. Religious people often inflicted such wounds to avoid serving in an army without *Shabes* and dietary laws. In addition to the leg injury, he had an ingrown toenail that hurt whenever he walked too much. When the order to leave came, Father joined the group that built a double wall to camouflage the entrance to their hiding place. They thought they had stored enough barrels of water, salt, and food to sustain themselves through the remainder of the war, which they expected would last only a few more weeks or months.

Father buried our silver candlesticks and other valuables in the earth of the basement floor. The handmade candlesticks that graced our *Shabes* table were irreplaceable witness to happier times on Friday nights and at holiday dinners with the entire family. The dripping candles cried for years, and we tried to save them from the murderers' hands. Also buried in the basement was the watch Father gave me for my bar mitzvah. American dollars, other currencies, and gold coins were concealed in a brick wall in the attic. We hid these things because we were convinced we would eventually return and that everything would be the way it had been in the past. We thought we would have the chance to retrieve some of these few possessions to recall the life we had and use them to make a new start.

That night we prepared for the coming day. It was impossible to comprehend what was happening to us. We did not realize a far worse fate awaited us. As we prepared ourselves, we cried. Chaim-Leizer and I packed our rucksacks with some clothes and a little bit of food. I packed an extra *talis kotn* (*tzitzis*) and a *siddur*; Chaim-Leizer packed our *tefillin*. With a ten-kilo limit, we had to be efficient. Memories of that painful, bitter night still fill me with heartbreak and confusion. Father decided to stay behind and hide because of his bad leg and apologized to Mother for not being able to stay with her. Mother and Father spoke to each other with words of love I had seldom heard. They begged each other for forgiveness for wrongs never committed, much in the way that one would ask forgiveness of loved ones for real or imagined transgressions on the eve of Yom Kippur.

I choke with emotion when I think of what they said to each other more than 60 years ago. My father hugged us, kissed us, and blessed us as he did every Friday night. I will never forget that night of farewells. I cannot forgive the monsters who butchered my loved ones. The grief I feel is inconsolable; my hate and hurt are eternal.

After a fitful night, Father went into hiding, and we left. It was September 2, 1942. Father asked Chaim-Leizer and me to look after each other and to stay together. The last thing he said as he walked out the back door was, "I love you." We could not stop crying. We had no appetite for breakfast. I looked out our window in despair as I watched the Jews carry their bundles to the market square. Just before 7 a.m., Mother, Chaim-Leizer, and I left our house for the last time. I kissed the *mezuzah* as I walked out and left the door wide open as instructed. The street was only a hundred yards long, but the walk felt as if we had marched for kilometers. I could bear to look back at our home only for a brief instant. At the marketplace, we sat on the ground, waiting with all the others.

The scene is still vivid, seared into my memory. We sat there and experienced our own Tisha b'Av in a marketplace that once bustled with business, peasants and their goods, horses and wagons, and where Figel the buffoon made official announcements. We sat under the monument of Tadeusz Kosciuszko that still looked proudly over a square that was now crowded with old and young, men and women, boys and girls, intellectuals and simple folk, believers and non-believers, all headed toward Hell—except for the few who managed to escape or hide.

While we sat on the cobblestones surrounded by our extended family and cried, Uncle Mottel told a horrifying story. Rabbi Staszewski, the town's chief rabbi who was Mottel's next-door neighbor, refused to get out of his bed. The Nazis, informed by the Poles, lost no time in getting to the Rabbi's house and shooting him dead in his bed.

This news added to the already overwrought atmosphere, and some people began to scream in despair.

TEN THOUSAND WORLDS

It was the beginning of the end. Those who could walk were told to march to the train station. The old, the weak, and some of the women with babies were herded toward 30 or so horse-drawn wagons attended by German guards and Polish drivers. These hapless souls were offered "assistance" and told they would be driven to the train station. While we marched in rows through the narrow streets, gun-toting Germans on our flanks shouted at us. We assumed the wagons with the women and children were being driven through wider streets on a less direct route to the station.

A few weeks later we learned their final destination was a mass grave that swallowed them up in a valley near the Jewish cemetery. The *Junaki* had prepared it. Who could imagine the slaughter of such innocent, defenseless victims, shot so casually, right there, in the town in which generations of Jews, their parents and grandparents, siblings and cousins had lived in the sight of the Almighty?

The train took us, the healthy ones, down the track where I used to play, waiting for nails to be flattened by the narrow-gauge railway wheels. I used to jump on and off this very train, tens of times, hiding to avoid the ban on Jews traveling—the same train I used to take to visit my dear grandparents in Chenciny, looking out the windows at the lush landscapes. Jumping off the train was no longer an option, as *Schutzstaffel* (SS) guards were stationed between the cars. At the end of the line, we entered the gates to Hell. The train had betrayed us and led us to our doom.

The ride from Dzialoszyce, normally less than two hours, lasted six because we picked up cattle cars and roofless coal cars full of people from neighboring towns at many stops along the way. Three of the stops were at Small Ksiaz, Large Ksiaz, and Wodzislaw. I was with Mother, Chaim-Leizer, and my extended family. We were hysterical, afraid, anxious, and uncomfortable. We arrived in Miechow, the capital of the Kielce region, in late afternoon and marched a few miles to a large, swampy meadow the size of two football fields. In the distance, the *Junaki* of Miechow surrounded the town to prevent escape. There were plenty of Polish gangsters eager to volunteer for the task. A large number of Germans were closer in, ringing the field.

My extended family stayed together in a group soon spotted by Art. He had been deported from Skalbmierz with Manya and their baby, now about 18 months old. At first, we were happy to see each other, but then we were beset with worry. What next? There were almost 12,000 people gathered at Miechow, waiting on the meadow, in sufferance.

Our strong faith in the Almighty and humanity caused us to rationalize deaths like Rabbi Staszewski's. We figured the satanic Nazis had been provoked or had other reasons for their brutality. We suffered from the delusion that they would not kill randomly, irrationally, or senselessly. The Germans lulled us with the neutrality of their nomenclature. *Aussiedlung* literally meant "resettlement." Only in hindsight did it refer to our forced removal as "expulsion." Perhaps maintaining that delusion helped us keep our sanity a little while longer.

We waited in that muddy field throughout the cold, wet night, whipped by an early fall wind. Earlier that day, before we were forced to leave, Mother had asked me to dress in long pants for warmth. I used to wear Bermuda-length short pants, typical attire for young boys in Europe. I was embarrassed to put on long pants, which were called "Father's pants," and I did not want anyone to make fun of me, so I insisted on wearing short pants. Mother sewed two 500-zloty bills into the long pants so I would have money in case of emergency. The bills, called *gurals*, were the largest available and got their name from the picture of the Polish mountain dweller, a *gural*, printed on their face. Mother had also sewn gold coins into the fly of my pants. Luckily for me, Mother had packed the pants into the sack I carried with me, and I was able to put them on. The long pants also made me look taller and older, an illusion that in the coming moments proved critical to my fate.

The Germans milled through the crowd. The words *Gott mit uns* (God is with us) were engraved on their belt buckles cinching their uniforms, making it seem as if these "cultured" people were mocking us. We had not been given any food since leaving Dzialoszyce, and the only drink we were permitted was a cup of water brought to each of us by the Jewish *Gmina* of Miechow. Sitting on the ground, we consoled each other and prayed, afraid to do anything that might provoke a shooting. As the gray dawn approached, the Germans started separating us into two groups.

The selection had begun.

The SS men, behind their leader, the *Sturmbannführer* (Major), with his whip in one hand and a gun in the other, shouted, "You go right, you go left. Right, right, right, left, right." The left column seemed to be destined for labor because it consisted of young, strong men. The fate of the right group—women, children, and older people—was unknown. There was panic as my uncles were all separated from my aunts and cousins. Dressed in the long pants that Mother forced me to wear, I was standing with her when the SS officer told me to go "left." I joined Uncle Shloyme and Uncle David, and my dear mother felt reassured, entrusting me to their care. As soon as the column started moving, I ran back. "Mamasie, I want to stay with you. Mamasie, please."

"No, no," Mother answered. "You go over there. Join Uncle Shloyme now."

I started walking toward the left column but, after a few feet, stopped to look back at Mother. The SS official noticed I hesitated and said, "If you cross out of this column again, I will shoot you."

I might as well have been shot because a part of me died in the meadows of Miechow that day. I saw the hidden majesty of the Almighty's creation, my lovely mother, for the last time that day. My world was destroyed. No more tears. No more Mamasie. I, her youngest and most attached son, felt I could not live without her. I felt I had died a death without burial, without *kaddish*, without seven days of *shivah* (mourning). In Miechow, I felt as if my life was extinguished.

I plunged into the abyss.

For years, I did not know how to speak about the boy who died in Miechow. What could I say about the happy, vibrant child who lived with his Mother until she was taken away in a swampy meadow? The hand of the *Sturmbannführer* had directed me to the left while my heart and soul followed my mother to the right. The young Yossele never had a chance to grow up. The boy in him died that day in Miechow.

Fewer than 2,000 people were selected to go to the left. We did not know what happened to the others. Immediately following the war, I was under the impression that Mother had been taken to one of the three main extermination camps, either Treblinka, Belzec, or Sobibor. While writing this book, one of my children discovered what happened in Miechow. A transport of just over 10,000 people, with 8,300 from Dzialoszyce and the remainder from Skalbmierz, Proszowice, Slomniki, and Wolbrom was sent by cattle car to Belzec from Miechow on September 3 and arrived there on September 6.

Belzec was not a labor camp; there were no selections. Belzec, like Treblinka and Sobibor, was a camp built for the sole purpose of exterminating people who had the misfortune of arriving at its gates. My mother, family members, and 10,000 holy souls were probably murdered in Belzec by September 8. But there is no list of names, and so there is no absolute certainty about my family's final resting place. Remembering and retelling the story of these souls is the only lasting monument they will have.

This has haunted me through the years. When we conclude the Torah reading cycle, the last thing we read about is the death of Moses and how no one can find his final resting place. It always makes me ask, "Does this mean, Creator of the Universe, that Mother is as holy as Moses?"

The first time I asked this question, the silence that followed was deafening. I still wait for an answer. The Talmud, when it discusses the laws pertaining to ransoming Jews taken hostage, states that whoever saves one life—because of all the potential that one life holds—it is as if that person saved an entire world. That dark day in Miechow, more than 10,000 entire worlds were eradicated.

CHOSEN FOR WHAT?

As the SS prodded us with their rifle butts, I was among the 2,000 able-bodied men and women who were marched back to the cattle cars to wait at the Miechow station. We were eight in a row, 90-odd at a time, shoved into the closed boxcars. The only light and air inside came from two small windows at the top, crisscrossed by barbed wire to prevent escape. Squeezed together like sardines, people fainted, lost control of their bodily functions, and gasped for air. A trip that normally took two and a half hours lasted two days. We were starving, we were thirsty, and we were nauseous from the stench. We were being "resettled," but we were treated like vermin instead of like a workforce. We were depressed and afraid, and we were silent, unable to comfort each other. What could we say? As we traveled, the Germans added more cars to the trains. The train's rhythm indicated its movement, and the only sound we heard was the clicking of steel on steel. The tracks we were riding now were wider and heavier than the narrow-gauge tracks between Dzialoszyce and Miechow.

Throughout their odyssey, the Jewish martyrs never stopped praying. Some recited *tehillim* (psalms) and invoked the name of the Almighty. Reb Abraham Dayan clutched his holy books. The *dayan*, a saintly man who had always rendered his judgments leniently, instead of packing clothes and food for his physical survival, used his meager ten-kilogram allotment for the books he thought would provide nourishment for the spiritual survival of his people. Both he and his sacred texts disappeared in clouds of smoke. The sentence visited on Reb Abraham Dayan was harsher than any verdict he had ever rendered in his gentle-mannered way.

In the dark of night, we finally arrived at Krakow's main railroad station. After all that time, we barely had the strength to stand, let alone walk. That did not matter to the Germans who again forced us to march, eight people to a row, several miles on dusty, unpaved roads to Prokocim. We marched because we had no choice. Those who could not walk were either shot or carried on the backs of their not-much-stronger brethren.

The German guards kicked, shoved, and beat us with rifle butts. They barked "*Auf gehts, auf gehts* (move on), *einhacken, einhacken* (stay in line), *antreten, antreten* (line up)." I was so thirsty I took a drink from a sewage drain along the roadside. The German response to that was a rifle butt in my back. I was lucky I was not shot for breaking ranks, but I was so thirsty I felt as if I would die anyway. In any event, the foul water sickened me, and I vomited.

It took a few hours before we entered Prokocim, a labor camp guarded by the SS—an entirely different experience from staying at home and going out to be a slave laborer. Prokocim was fenced with barbed wire and ringed with watchtowers manned by armed guards. As we entered the camp, we were ordered to throw our valuables on the ground and had no choice but to obey. Then *Oberscharführer* (Sergeant First Class) Mueller ordered his henchmen to search several people in the front row. I heard gunshots, and two people were killed on the spot. I had not yet ripped open the seam of my fly to take out the gold coins and the two 500-zloty banknotes when I was pushed forward. I was not inspected closely, thus the Almighty allowed me to maintain both my fortune and my life.

The wooden barracks we were assigned to hold about 150 people and had no facilities except triple-decker sleeping platforms. These wooden platforms were about 6½ feet by 20 feet and held about 16 people each. That was about a foot and a quarter in width for each of us. I was in shock and thankful that, on my first day, I was assigned to the relatively easy task of sweeping the paths and area around our barrack.

On my second day at Prokocim, my brother Willie, who was a labor camp veteran with almost a year and a half of experience under his belt, arrived. I had not seen Willie since he was conscripted for forced labor in the spring of 1940, and when we spotted each other, we hugged and kissed and cried. Willie had heard that the transport from Dzialoszyce had arrived at Prokocim, and we tried to get together as many family members and friends as possible. My brother reasoned "better the devil he knew than one he did not know." He possessed a permit issued by SS Officer Kurt, manager of the Richard Strauch Hoch und Tiefbau Gesellschaft, GmbH, the construction and infrastructure firm, authorizing him to take ten people to work in Kostrze on the other side of Krakow. Willie, whom we used to call Volvele (little wolf), was not a Volvele anymore. He was a grown wolf incarnate, transformed by the harshness of existence in the labor camp. Risking his life, he changed the number on the permit from 10 to 20.

That would have sufficed to take out most of the family members who had been transported from Dzialoszyce to Miechow had we all been sent to Prokocim. I was sick with worry about what had happened to my Mother, aunts, and cousins. I could not understand what the Almighty wanted.

Within a few hours of Willie's arrival, a group of 20 people, I among them, followed him out of the camp toward Kostrze. Art and Hymie and my uncles Chaim, David, and Harry were with us. In order to avoid attracting attention, Willie, who knew the area well, took us past the outskirts of Krakow and through the surrounding fields. The route he chose was much longer than the one along main roads, but it was safer because we were less likely to be stopped.

Fearful, we marched on. I do not know what kept me going. Even at this early stage, the ordeal I had gone through from Dzialoszyce to Miechow, the muddy selection in the meadow, the trip in the boxcars, the march to Prokocim, and Prokocim itself, had already been too much without my parents. I could not get my thoughts away from them. How could I reach them? In which cattle car could I find Mother? I wanted to run to Mother, not march to Kostrze. Where was the Almighty? Where were all my aunts and my little cousins? I was too young to cope with these unanswerable questions on my own, and yet somehow, in spite of the numbing fear, the determination to move on and the will to live kept me going.

It took us about six hours to reach the fields surrounding Kostrze. We came to a flat, wet meadow near a grassy hillside. There was a fortress at the top of the hill dating from the sixteenth or seventeenth century, surrounded by a moat. To enter, we had to cross the drawbridge. The doors and windows were narrow on the inside and widened toward the outer face of the three- to four-feet-thick stone walls. The entrance was between the two levels of the fortress, which were separated by a few steps up and a few steps down. The lower level was massive, and the ceiling dripped with condensation that formed when hundreds of people were packed into a space with no ventilation. Even so, Kostrze was luxurious compared to what was to come, because it had several showers and toilets. The upper floor was for VIPs, including officers and Mr. Stiglitz, the *Lagerältester* (literally, "camp elder," but idiomatically, "camp manager"). He was a German Jew married to a non-Jewish woman, and together they managed the camp for the Strauch company.

In Kostrze, inmates woke before sunrise, some to pray and all to prepare for work. We longed for the first rays of sunshine to penetrate the darkness so that we could see what we were doing. Thousands of acres of swampy meadowland were waiting for us to drain. The Polish foreman, Bobo, and his old father supervised the project. Bobo surveyed the fields, set the benchmarks, and laid out lines so we would know where to dig. We dug deep, wide drainage trenches. The Germans seldom used excavating machines because retrieving them from the mire was too expensive. Jewish slaves were cheaper.

Using hand shovels, we excavated vast quantities of heavy mud while we stood in knee-deep water. Our Polish masters wore waist-high, rubber fishing boots, while we were essentially barefoot. We laid some track to make our carts more mobile and to expedite the work, but the process was backbreaking. With fright, revulsion, and actual blood, sweat, and tears, we slogged through the polluted plains of Kostrze, which we, the "chosen people," were forced to drain.

While I worked, I kept asking the Almighty what we were chosen for. My mind was tormented because I did not know what had happened to my parents. Where was Mother? Where was Aunt Escia and her two beautiful children, Lolek and Hanusia? Where was Aunt Frimche with Hershele and Royzele? Aunt Henna with Alter, Royzele, and Cesia? Where was Aunt Itkele, Mother's youngest sister, and her son, Lolek; Aunt Bracha with her sons, Lolek and Mark? Where was Aunt Hindele with her one-and-only Lolek? What of Uncle Yankel, Aunt Rachel, and their three children, or my grandfather and the rest of our family? Where had everybody gone? They were not in Kostrze with me. Not knowing where they were weighed more heavily on me than the mud I was forced to dig.

Each day, after working in the soggy Polish fields from the crack of dawn until it was too dark to see, we marched the two miles back to the fortress and tried to clean and dry our clothes for the next day. That was a full-time job in itself. We had very little time to sleep. We subsisted on starvation rations—a bowl of watery soup, a piece of bread, and coffee made from burnt turnips. I did not have to worry about dietary laws because there was no meat in the soup.

Some people staying in the fortress at Kostrze worked at different locations in the general vicinity, and through contact with the Polish population outside the camp or with Jews living and working elsewhere, they were able to provide some information to the rest of us. Some people had jobs in the town. I could not stand the hard work in the swamps and tried to get work at the fortress, but the *Lagerältester* would not allow it. He did, however, permit me to work at a gasworks factory in Krakow. In order to survive, I was forced to unload cars of coke and coal, and along with the others assigned there, was soon covered with soot and looked like a miner. Breathing in the coal dust without protective masks was not very healthy, and after a day of that, I let my brothers know that I would try to switch to another camp. They agreed. After we finished loading at the end of the next day, I joined the lines stationed at the Zatorska Street camp in Krakow instead of going back with the group from Kostrze.

I did not want to work in the swamps, contract malaria, or march from Kostrze to the gasworks. The switch was possible because we had not yet been given numbers, and there were still no organized roll calls. If the odd person went missing, he could get away with it as long as he appeared to be part of some group and seemed to be working.

THE ZATORSKA STREET CAMP

The Zatorska Street camp was not a typical labor camp. It was right in the heart of Krakow, in an urban setting. It was in a one-story house appropriated from some luckless Jewish family who had been forcibly removed to the Krakow ghetto. Zatorska was a dormitory, and most of the inmates worked on various projects in the neighborhood. The camp was supervised by *Lagerältester* Lieblich, who had his wife, his daughter Margo, and his brother Simcha with him. They were kind German Jews, and we liked each other. There were no other Jewish couples at Zatorska, although there were several in Kostrze.

Zatorska had approximately 120 inmates, compared to 700 at Kostrze, yet there was far less space per person. Ten of us slept in each bunk bed, and at midnight, Yurek, Margot Lieblich's fiancé, would call out to his old father, the engineer, "Father, it is midnight. Let's turn over to the other side." This would happen every two hours, and all the other inmates on the bunk would roll over as well. It was so crowded that we all had to turn in unison. Sleeping in conditions like those, the only "upside" was not being allowed to sleep for very long.

I was exhausted. We were always physically uncomfortable because of the overcrowding, the poor sanitary conditions, and the lice. We could not shower, wash properly, or change our clothes. Fortunately, the Lieblichs decided they needed someone to help them around the camp premises, a general custodian to carry water from the neighboring building, sweep, clean toilets, cook, and otherwise help in the kitchen. The job was mine, and for a while, I was not hungry.

When Mr. Lieblich realized he could rely on me, I was privileged to sleep alone in the unfinished attic. The space, beneath the roof's exposed rafters, was reached by ladder, and I invited a couple of people to share these quarters with me. One was Benjamin Mandelbaum, a fellow who lived across the street from us in Dzialoszyce; the other was Joe Rosenthal from Proszowice.

I was alone in Zatorska. From time to time, when my brothers Chaim-Leizer and Volvele went to Firma Strauch on Starowislna Street to pick up food for the Kostrze inmates, they would drop in at Zatorska and give me some bread to make sure that I was not hungry. I told them not to worry and showed them the large pots that I was supposed to clean. Mr. Lieblich always left thick soup sticking to the bottom of the pots for me to eat, and I had enough to share with others who were hungry.

Then, one day an SS officer inspected Zatorska and saw me sweeping in front of the house. The Nazi asked Mr. Lieblich what I did and wanted to know why I was not unloading coal at the gasworks in town. Mr. Lieblich apparently told him I was sick. So the SS man came over and asked me to raise my right arm. I raised it. Then he asked me to lift my left arm. I raised it. Then he told me to run. I ran.

"You are not sick," the SS officer said. I agreed because I believed illness was more dangerous for inmates than working below capacity. If guards considered you sick, you were a burden on the system and shot. "In that case," said the officer, "tomorrow you will dig trenches on Zablocie Street." The Germans were upgrading the infrastructure in Krakow because it was to be the headquarters of the General Government, the Nazi administration that would govern those parts of Poland neither incorporated into the Reich nor annexed by the Soviet Union.

The next morning I was up early and joined the group excavating the trenches on Zablocie Street. The trenches were 3 feet wide by 20 feet deep, and digging was difficult, dangerous work because the earthen side walls could collapse. We used picks and sledgehammers to break up the large stones we frequently encountered, and we built scaffolding and bridging inside each trench. One person went below, and buckets of dirt were passed from man to man, as they stood, one above the other, up to the surface. Conditions were awful, and I was always hungry because no longer were there thick soup remnants for me to eat.

I worked in a group with Heshek Markin Bleicher and others from Zatorska.

My brothers could not bring me bread anymore, and food was scarce, so on the way to work, when we passed cabbage fields that had already been harvested, I dug up cabbage roots to supplement my meager rations. Heshek bought salami from the Poles we passed on the road. I could still manage without having to eat *treyf* (nonkosher food), but I could not blame anyone else for eating anything they were not supposed to under those circumstances. I also reckoned that I would better save the money sewn into my pants for a real emergency.

Heshek was one of the lucky ones who survived. After the war, he immigrated to Toronto and raised a beautiful family. We both had sons in the same class at Associated Hebrew Day Schools, and I saw him every *Shabes* because we were both members of Shaarei Shomayim synagogue. As I was writing this book, I learned that gentle-mannered Heshek had died in his sleep—a peaceful death of the just.

While I was in Zatorska, my brothers heard that more roundups were taking place to make towns completely *Judenrein*, or "Free of Jews." Willie then figured out a way to go to Dzialoszyce to get our Father out. He got a permit from SS Kurt of Firma Strauch to bring a new labor force to Kostrze. To smooth the way, he bribed Kurt with money and jewelry. The incentive was the additional money Willie promised to pay when he recovered it from various hiding places in Dzialoszyce. Since the firm needed more people for labor, Willie proposed that Kurt lend him a truck with some henchmen to get the task done quickly. With them around for protection, Willie thought he might find our Father and possibly rescue other members of our family.

They stopped in Kazimierza Wielka, where we knew several people, including the Wolgelernters, who were Art's friends. It was about 14 kilometers closer to Krakow than Dzialoszyce. While there, Willie was told that Dzialoszyce had already been declared *Judenrein*. As he planned his next move, Willie miraculously found a group of 18 Jews hiding amid the ruins.

Willie convinced the group that they were better off getting a truck ride to the work camps he was familiar with than facing the possibility of being found and ending up shot or crushed in a cattle car transport to who knew where. Willie loaded the group onto the truck and brought them back with him to the Kostrze fortress. Some stayed there under the supervision of Herr and Frau Stiglitz, while others went to the work camp on Kobierzynska Street in Krakow proper. A few, like David Wolgelernter, went into hiding or joined the partisans.

David Wolgelernter was *shoykhet* Reb Shye Wolgelernter's son. Sometimes, Reb Shye traveled great distances on horseback to reach remote villages in order for Jews to be able to eat properly slaughtered kosher meat. David survived the Holocaust and, like his father and older brother, Abraham, before him, became a *shoykhet* in Toronto, Canada, where he lived happily with his family.

Among those Willie rescued were Helen Kleiner and her mother. One evening in 2000, I was having dinner in Florida with Mayer Goldstein, a survivor, and his wife. As we reminisced, we discovered that Mayer was related to Mother's cousin Yachet Platkiewicz. Mrs. Goldstein said she was looking for the man responsible for saving her life. As her story unfolded, I realized she was looking for Willie. She was delighted to discover that Willie was my brother and subsequently arranged a luncheon to honor Willie with gifts and speeches of thanks.

Helen described how Willie had "appeared like an angel in Kazimierza Wielka and grabbed [her] mother and [her], as if on wings, out of the Nazi fire which was about to consume them." She thanked Willie for saving their lives, asked the previously "unknown angel" to look around the room filled with her children and grandchildren, and gave him credit for their existence. Her offspring, she said, were proof of that Talmudic dictum "whoever saves one life saves a whole world."

When Willie returned to Kostrze, he told Hymie that Dzialoszyce was *Judenrein*, and they set out to learn what had happened to Father. They learned Father was in Prokocim. Those Jews who had escaped the deportation from Dzialoszyce and returned, were caught, arrested, and jailed by the Germans. The Poles who hid Jews took money in return, and those who discovered Jewish hiding places extorted money in return for secrecy but, in time, denounced their victims. The Poles denounced Father's group. The Jews caught or denounced were brought to Wodzislaw, not far from Dzialoszyce.

Father's hiding place was too small for the 16 souls crowded into it. There was only one small opening for air, and it was over the sidewalk facing the marketplace. One very cold night in mid-September, the vapor created by the heat emitted from their 16 hidden bodies condensed in the cold night air. Some Poles noticed it and thought it was smoke, so they called the fire brigade, which brought hoses and started putting out the "fire." As water poured through the opening, the small room acted as a cistern and started to fill. Those hidden in the basement began screaming and chose to give themselves up rather than drown. Caught, they were handed over by the

Polish police to the Germans, who sent them to Wodzislaw. Remarkably, they were not shot on the spot, because the Nazis wanted to extract whatever labor value they could before killing them. From Wodzislaw, they were transported to Krakow and then to Prokocim. Willie somehow managed to get Father out of Prokocim and to Kostrze, where he and Hymie could look out for him.

All the inmates from Kostrze, Kobierzynska Street, and Zatorska Street worked for the well-known Firma Strauch. Each camp was assigned to workstations in and around Krakow. Once it had been the city of famous synagogues and generations of Jewish scholars, the city where Rabbi Moshe Isserles, the Ramah, compiled *The Code of Jewish Law*. Now it was a site of hatred and slavery, a center for forced labor, a dangerous place for Jews to live, except inside the few square blocks of the ghetto.

Though it was dangerous and we were exhausted, we sometimes managed to sneak out of the smaller camps into the ghetto to meet old friends, revisit familiar places, exchange news about missing family members, and buy some clothes and food, items we took back with us. When we were in the ghetto and saw young ladies riding the streetcars, we felt as if we had fallen into a different dimension. "Today and now" was the motto of the moment. Nothing else mattered. The Krakow ghetto recalled Mordechai Gebirtig's words *"Es Brent"* (It burns). I could not understand how some people in the ghetto went about their lives, seemingly in denial.

Coming back to Zatorska to hard labor deep in the trenches was quite a contrast to life in the ghetto. Should I escape? Should I stay in the ghetto? Were my chances better if I stayed productive? Such choices were always on my mind. Father had laid the foundation for my education at a very early age. But it was only through making split-second life-and-death decisions that I learned survival was something Father could never have taught me. One has to live it—and fate is always a factor.

Moishe Shmil Goldkorn kept saying he could not tolerate the conditions at Zatorska any longer and wanted to escape. "If you come with me, Yossele, OK," he said. As badly as I wanted to escape, I decided that I just could not do it. The SS knew I had relatives working for Firma Strauch and if I went missing, my father and brothers would have certainly paid for it with their lives. Moishe Shmil just left one day and never came back. After the war, he told me how he escaped. He still tells me his stories. He fell in love with the Polish girl who hid him and saved his life. As for his wonderful family—only memories are left.

KRAKOW/PLASZOW

Although conditions at the Strauch work camps were unbearable, we thought if we worked hard and followed the basic rules, we could make it through the war, hoping that we would be reunited with our families. We got used to the hard labor, but before we got too used to our routine, life changed again.

One day toward the end of December 1942, in a coordinated and simultaneous effort, the Germans suddenly surrounded the camps at Kostrze, Kobierzynska Street, and Zatorska Street and rounded us up. We were taken by truck to Jerozolimska (Jerusalem) Street, the site of the large, old Jewish cemetery on the outskirts of Krakow in a place called Plaszow. A little way off was *Julag* One, a shortened version of *Judenlager* (Jewish Labor Camp) with several thousand prisoners. The inmates were all brought to the cemetery proper, a site the Nazis called *Julag* Two. SS *Oberscharführer* (Sergeant First Class) Mueller was the commandant in charge of both camps. He gathered us on the *Appellplatz* (roll call square) and gave us orders to build barracks under the supervision of Engineer Greenberg. Roughly 2,000 newcomers were going to expand the Plaszow concentration camp.

At least I was no longer alone. I was reunited with Father and my brothers, and that was the good part. The rest was not good at all. We were fenced in by barbed wire and patrolled by the SS with dogs and machine guns. Armed guards in towers monitored the perimeter. We were housed in a section of *Julag* Two that was built by the prisoners in *Julag* One. The barracks were long, primitive huts with only one door in the middle and small windows at either end. Most of the structures had no ceilings, and too many people were crowded into the three tiers of sleeping platforms. Soon after we arrived, we were ordered to a bathhouse where we showered in groups of 30 and put our clothes in a disinfecting machine to kill off the lice. This became a weekly routine. The latrines were about 300 meters from our barracks, but there was a nighttime curfew, which made life very difficult for some.

We continued doing what the *Julag* One prisoners before us had begun—the expansion of the camp grounds and building more barracks. To clear space, the Nazis forced us to desecrate centuries-old Jewish graves. We removed tombstones, dug out the bases, carried the heavy material to a different location, and then hammered it into small pieces for paving. The hilly terrain made our work more difficult. We picked up the heavy beams, wooden siding, and other building materials from a railroad siding a considerable distance away and had to bring them up the slopes to the various designated areas. Women, young and old, were also forced to perform the same labor.

Anyone who faltered or did not work quickly was whipped by the *Ordnungsdienst* (Jewish police) appointed by the murderous Mueller. *Ordnungsdienst* Chilowicz and his wife—a petite archetype of evil—and the brutish Finkelstein were the cruelest. Always dressed in uniforms, these *Kapos* beat, pushed, and mercilessly whipped their fellow inmates. I remember one woman was forced to lug large rocks up the hill, but was not fast enough for Finkelstein, so in a rage, he whipped her. When she cried and protested that the burden was too much for her, Finkelstein screamed, "A big, heavy man you could carry, but the stones you cannot?" After the war, this animal received the long jail term he deserved.

As cruel as the Jewish *Ordnungsdienst* were, they could not compete with the passionate abuse from the SS, especially the Vlasovtsy. The Vlasovtsy were a Ukrainian contingent of SS who derived their name from General Andrei Vlasov. He betrayed Russia when he switched sides to fight for the Germans, and he and his deserters found common cause in their hatred of Jews with the Nazis. At Plaszow, their leader was Janiec, a Ukrainian *Volksdeutsche*. These Ukrainians were willingly accepted into the SS although they could hardly speak German, and because of their rank, they were able to vent their hatred on us. They were murderous monsters who craved Jewish blood and never missed an opportunity to maim or kill. I was appalled at the vigor they demonstrated and the satisfaction they felt when they brutalized us.

In Barrack 34, my barrack, most inmates were slave laborers for Firma Strauch, while a few people worked for other companies. Pious men like Father and his friend from Dzialoszyce, Mr. Slamowich, prayed, meditated, cried, and worked. The Dzialoszycer Rebbe, Rebbe Rab Shaim, and some of his Hasidim next door in Barrack 27 did the same. The Germans wore us down, adding new rules and more work each day. We could not even go to the bathroom when necessary.

There was an elderly engineer with a prostate problem in the block. Because of the curfew, he could not get to the latrine at night and was forced to urinate in his pants. We were terrified, depressed, and could not see a way out. Our only defense was the hope we tried to give each other. Somehow, we still managed to daven every morning with *talis* and *tefillin*—not for long, but at least we prayed.

In the middle of February 1943, a new commandant, *Hauptsturmführer* (Captain) Amon Goeth, arrived with a large entourage of SS men, many with the rank of *Unterscharführer* (sergeant) or *Scharführer* (staff sergeant). SS names such as Fujar and Dziadek are names I remember here for their ignominy. But as the old Jewish curse goes, their names should be erased forever.

Goeth and Engineer Greenberg designed the camp expansion and divided it into manufacturing, storage, and residential areas. In the residential area, there were three separate barracks for women, a medical clinic, barracks for the sick and wounded, and a barrack for several doctors, nurses, dentists, and others associated with the clinic.

The work in *Barackenbau Kommando* was tough and getting worse. Under the watchful eye of the Ukrainians, Father and I fastened barbed wire to fenceposts. The work was not as life threatening as the punitive work in the Plaszow quarry, but I worried about Father because any reduction in speed was met with a beating. I tried to stay near him in case he needed my help. Father was as concerned about my well-being as I was about his. It was an exceedingly cold winter, so Father took the belt from his coat and gave it to me to close my thin coat. I insisted that Father keep the belt because I wanted him to be warm. We went back and forth for a few minutes until Father slapped me in the face in frustration and made me take it back. I felt very bad about it but could not continue to argue.

In his position as the new *Kommandant*, Goeth asserted his authority immediately. Two girls who left camp daily to work in an outside factory ran away. When they were caught, the inmates were summoned to the *Appellplatz* and forced to watch their executions. The rope on the gallows broke twice, but the girls were finally hanged as the German band cynically played *Komm Zurück* (Come Back). We were warned that anybody trying to escape would be killed. Itche Saltz, a bespectacled Jewish *Kapo* from a prominent family, was the hangman.

In mid-March 1943, Ira Lokai, another Dzialoszycer, escaped. He was alone and did not have to worry about consequences to family members, but he never fathomed the repercussions for the rest of us. After his absence was noted, there was an *Appell* (roll call), and every tenth person was shot. My family was part of this roll call, and Hymie missed being shot by one number. My friend Weinstok was not as fortunate.

Under Goeth's regime anyone not in his prime was endangered, so I tried to get Father out of *Barackenbau Kommando* by involving myself in work that would allow me some mobility without being constantly watched. Block 11 was near an area where scrap metal, barrels, and other material were stored, so I switched barracks with a man there. He wanted to get into Block 34 because he had friends there, and I wanted Block 11, a smaller, less crowded barrack near the edge of camp. I told my *Blockältester* that I was needed there to work on a roof, and he agreed to let me go if I found him a replacement.

Then I joined the tinsmith and roofing workshop, which was housed in one-third of a long industrial workshed that also held the tool-and-dye workshop, and the *Elektrische Werke*, the electrical workshop. I had to prove myself to the head of the roofing workshop, but it was easy because I had worked for Uncle Mottel in Dzialoszyce. The workshop was staffed by a network of professional roofers that included the Pantiras, the Blooms, Victor Weintraub, and Shye Miedzygurski. Two of the Markin-Bleicher brothers were in my particular group of ten.

When the carpentry was finished, we covered the roof with tar paper. We checked the roof for leaks, and this time our lives were at stake. We roofed the barracks, the prisoners' mess hall, and some administrative buildings. Most of the buildings had no ceilings, but a few of them had attics. We cut out a hatch in one of them, and made a little trap door to an attic hiding place. Whenever there was going to be a random selection, shootings, or hangings, Goeth would come to the camp from his villa. When we saw him coming, we knew there was going to be trouble, so we would climb to the roof, look like we were making repairs, and then disappear.

Whenever I suspected that there was going to be a selection that might take Father, I would hide him in the attic. But Father was afraid to climb the ladder, so I placed him in the *Bürstengemeinde* (brush factory). As a roofer, I had access to the different workshops, and I chose the most appropriate place for Father. He learned to bind brushes, and he was comfortable with the mostly religious middle-aged gentlemen with him. They discussed the Talmud as they worked, as several of them had committed whole pages of it to memory.

Alter Langarten taught Art to repair sewing machines, and he managed to bluff his way into a position in the sewing workshop, learning as he went. The sewing machines were under constant maintenance because a slowdown in the production of the military uniforms they manufactured would have severe repercussions.

I continued to work as a roofer in the expanding camp. A huge, barbed-wire-encircled area called the *Neue Gelände* (new terrain) was added to contain the industrial zone. More residential barracks were added, and there were rumors that worried us about combining *Julag* One and *Julag* Two into one large camp. The expansion and the reorganization meant the Nazis were digging in for the long haul, and our hopes of gaining our freedom anytime soon were dashed. We wondered who was going to fill the new barracks.

We soon found out. On March 13, 1943, the ghetto in Krakow was liquidated. About 8,000 of the 60,000 ghetto occupants, the strong ones, were brought to Plaszow. I do not know who was brought to Jerozolimska or to Chujowa Gorka, but hundreds of trucks carrying human cargo rolled in all day long.

A mass grave was dug at the bottom of the hill. Jewish men, women, and children were told to undress and ordered to lie down in the grave. Ukrainians in brown and black uniforms did the shooting, killing row after row of mothers and children, grandparents, and babies. Some of the victims disrobed at the top of the hill and were shot right there, then pushed down the slope into the grave. The heartless Ukrainians threw lime on each layer of bodies and then killed another layer of people. Layer was piled upon layer. A very few managed to escape; some professionals, like engineers, were given last-minute reprieves. Thousands of Jewish souls, brought to Plaszow from Krakow in hundreds of trucks, were dispatched into the next world.

Shye and Heshek Markin-Bleicher and I witnessed this slaughter from the roof, where we were working. The sight killed us emotionally and spiritually. The screams were unbearable. Some of the perverted murderers had sexual intercourse with still-warm dead bodies. We determined that our revenge would be to stay alive and struggled to maintain the will to live.

My main responsibility was to look after Father. Now that he worked in the brush factory, I tried to get him extra rations of soup. One day, the *Ordnungsdienst* in charge of the kitchen was having a tryst with his lover. He was the man responsible for distributing soup coupons to the different barracks. Shye Miedzygurski and I spied on the lovers through a hole in the roof, but when it started raining, the lovers could not carry on because of the leak in our "properly prepared" roof. I then conspicuously walked by with a big box of tools and a roll of tar paper, and when the lovers noticed me, they asked me to fix the leak immediately. As payment for services rendered, I asked the *Ordnungsdienst* for a soup permit. By adding a zero to the one on my coupon, I could get ten soups.

I had a large blue and white enamel pot salvaged from the metal scrap pile. I took it to the kitchen to get the ten soups—enough to feed Father and some friends. I also looked for other ways to sate my hunger and provide for Father. Whenever I had a chance to push the soup cart into the separate Polish camp, I would do it for the extra soup. I made containers and utensils for German soldiers' mess kits in the tinsmith workshop. On the side, I made *menashkes* (hip-fitting canteen-like soup containers) and ladles from scrap aluminum that came from downed airplanes, and I bartered or sold them for more food. We parlayed every opportunity that came along to add calories to our meager diets.

When we once saw *Kommandant* Amon Goeth riding into camp on his horse, with his two huge black and white Dobermans running alongside him, Heshek and I quickly took the cauldron we used for boiling tar and went down to Goeth's villa to help ourselves to the potatoes in his garden. It was not easy to get the potatoes without being noticed, but we managed. When the cauldron was filled with our loot, we put two two-by-fours under the rim, placed the studs on our shoulders, and carried our treasure back to camp, where we feasted on the potatoes. Stealing them was our way of taking revenge.

Plaszow was an interesting place for a Hasidic adolescent to get his sexual education. Although seeing sexual activity was new for me, what Heshek and I witnessed was in the context of a relationship, and that was something within the realm of my experience. Later on, I was sent to another part of the camp to repair the leaky roof of the Plaszow bordello, one staffed with Polish prostitutes and frequented by Ukrainian SS who paid two zloty per visit.

Sometimes I sorted clothing taken from the dead that was stored in the camp's warehouses. As we sorted, we searched the pockets for valuables. We occasionally found rings or other small pieces of jewelry, which we would use to bribe certain guards for the bread they would throw over the fence. Shye, Heshek's older brother, was in charge of making the arrangements with the guards and retrieving the bread.

Mayer Goldstein, who suffered terribly from hunger at Plaszow, told me many years later how he had managed to convince Goeth to give him extra food in exchange for a large sum of money and gold hidden in his hometown, Proszowice. When SS *Unterscharführer* Streibitz and his guards escorted Goldstein to his hometown, Goldstein managed to distract them and escape. He spent the rest of the war in hiding. We never heard about his escape back at camp, and there were no repercussions because the SS were too embarrassed to admit a prisoner could escape their direct supervision.

At one point, the Lieblichs found a way to escape and urged me to join them. They had papers for their family and two extra sets for close friends. I figured these were Turkish documents that they had acquired when they were the *Lagerältesters* in Zatorska before the roundup for Plaszow. They asked me to steal a pair of insulated wire cutters from the electrical shop, which they hid in a barrel of scrap metal near Block 11. One rainy night, they retrieved the wire cutters and snipped their way out of the camp. I did not go with them because I was afraid that my father and my brothers would be tortured or killed if my escape was discovered. I was right to be worried. After the Lieblichs escaped, the Nazis questioned me about their disappearance. I said that I had not spoken to them since we left the camp on Zatorska Street, that I was too busy as a roofer to notice much else, and that I lived in a different barrack. Three or four weeks later, I learned that the Lieblichs had been caught and shot. I also heard that by some miracle, one brother, Simche, survived, but I have no idea where he is now.

It was bad enough when we were abused by the Germans and Ukrainians, but it was too much to bear when the Jewish *Kapos* mistreated us. One day Father told me that *Ordnungsdienst* Zanger had insulted and beaten him. He had tears in his eyes when he told me the story of how Zanger caught him in *talis* and *tefillin* at the moment he called an *Appell*. Father was not able to put away his *talis* and *tefillin* fast enough for Zanger, so the *Kapo* cursed, shoved, and hit him. I saw Zanger entering the vestibule of Block 34 when I was on my way to the kitchen to get soup, and I happened to have the heavy metal pot in my hand. A split second before Zanger could spot me, I hit him in the face with the pot and ran out of there as fast as I could. There were no witnesses, and I avoided Father's block for quite some time.

Instead, I visited Father at the brush factory by pretending to be on my way to fix a roof. Sometimes I felt like asking Father about the Almighty's hand in our predicament, but usually I left it alone. When we did discuss the Almighty, he continued to persuade me in much the same way he had in Dzialoszyce.

Once I said to him, "*Tateshi* (Dad), I do not know what to do. I am going wild." I had no idea of what it meant to be an adolescent and what effect hormones were having on my behavior. Father would distract me by talking about Mother. He would say, "Yossele, think about the day you will be reunited with your mother. You are going to see her; just hold on. Everything will be fine. And you are going to meet Aunt Esther and all the others. Have patience." Warm, loving words would then pass between us and even the occasional hug. In this way, Father and I consoled each other.

I brought Father soup and bread and made sure he ate. I did not worry as much about my older brothers because they were in charge of taking large kettles of soup and bread to the inmates in the Polish camp, which was built in the middle of the general camp. Polish criminals were separated from the Jewish inmates. Willie and Chaim-Leizer poured soup from the huge, piped stationary kitchen pots to large kettles set on two-wheeled wagons. Sometimes I arranged to meet my brothers at the moment they were pouring the soup and would put my pot into the flow to get some, which helped me survive. One time I was caught taking soup by the *Ordnungsdienst*, who made me return it and then whipped me until I managed to run away.

Another day when I was cooking raw potatoes I had stolen from the kitchen, Goeth, his enforcer Janiec, and other members of Goeth's entourage walked in and caught me in the act. It was Passover, and I planned to eat cooked potatoes and raw vegetables, neither of which would have violated the laws of Passover. I was sharing my food with Father. I was sure I was going to be shot, but, thank God, instead of an execution, Goeth instructed Janiec to give me 50 lashes on my bare bottom. I let my pants down and asked Janiec to use two men so that the beating would not take too long. The first 10 lashes were the worst. Then my body became numb, and I no longer felt the pain. I screamed from the humiliation and the horror of seeing my blood all over the table. While they whipped me, I had to count the lashes, but I gave up after 20 or so. Then they counted for me. I was very lucky. Others who had stopped counting on their own were often made to count from the beginning again. My recuperation took several weeks and was no doubt prolonged because I received no treatment and returned to work the very next day.

I clearly remember Goeth and his two Doberman Pinschers, Ralf and Rolf. Whenever Goeth lusted for blood, he would shoot people in cold blood and then let his two vicious dogs rip them apart. Sometimes the inmates were still alive, and their agony was beyond description.

We worked to maintain our faith in the Almighty, and we hoped for our liberation. We just wanted to survive another day. Who knew then how many camps, how much forced labor, how many near-death experiences we would have to live through to survive.

SEPARATED AGAIN ... AND AGAIN

The hard work, the permeating fear, the hunger, abuse, and drudgery were relentlessly constant, but concentration camp life was hardly predictable.

In the summer of 1943, Willie; Chaim-Leizer; my uncles Shloyme, Chaim, and Harry; and a few hundred other people were rounded up and placed in the Polish prison camp. People were nabbed off the streets and taken from their barracks, including Father's. He was not there at the time, so he was not in the group. I spoke to my brothers through the eight-foot width of double barbed-wire fence separating us. They heard that they were being relocated and asked me to bring Father to go with them. Willie and Chaim-Leizer felt they could look after Father best. "I am afraid to let Father go with you because you do not even know where you're going," I stammered. "What will happen to you? Life is difficult here, but at least Father is well placed in the brush factory, working with his kind of people, with friends. Art and I are here, and we can look after Father."

My brothers pleaded with me, but I refused to get Father and vehemently defended my position. At Plaszow, Father blended in and had a relatively easy job that made him productive, the only criterion the Germans used to keep anyone alive. I was mobile, able to get around and keep an eye on him, but I was scared to take a chance that Father would be forced into hard labor and would end up separated from my brothers. Rumors of concentration camps where the conditions were even worse than those at Plaszow were trickling in from escapees and Polish engineers who took the trains to those places. This news hung over our heads as we debated back and forth in bitter tears.

Once the decision was made, I found a hidden spot and ripped apart the seam in the fly of my pants. I took out one of the two 500-zloty banknotes Mother had sewn in, rolled it up tight, wound some string around it as if it were a spool of thread, and threw it over the fence. (I always kept some string on me, in case something tore. I had stolen the string from the brush factory.)

This was the fourth time our family was being separated; it was painful and we were terrified. Who knew where my loved ones were going? The Almighty, the eternal witness, was silent—as usual. Standing there, I relived the scene in the Miechow meadow, but in Plaszow the barbed wire separated us.

Once my brothers were gone, I seemed to lose my bearings. I could not think clearly and my mind wandered. I was forced to think only of the present and the future, to remind myself that survival was revenge. Each new decree knocked the wind out of us, but somehow we found the strength to reinforce our dedication to life. Every plunge into darkness renewed the struggle toward light. I awoke each day at 4:30 a.m. to the trumpet sounds of Willie Rosner, the scion of a famous musical family from Krakow, and pushed myself through another day. All the while, as I fixed the roofs in the camps, I witnessed things I would never forget.

Then one day, as I worked near the entrance to the camp, a group returning from a day outside was searched. The groups that worked outside the camp proper often had the opportunity to obtain and smuggle food into the camp, food they shared with others. One of the people in this group of 50 was my friend Norman Kamelgard. Everyone in the *Kommando* was ordered to toss all items in their possession on the ground as Goeth and his 30 henchmen watched. This operation was the brainchild of SS *Scharführer* Dostoyevsky, who wanted to demonstrate his exceptional diligence. A lone chicken lay on the ground. Goeth took a rifle from one of the guards and shot one prisoner, then another. "To whom does this chicken belong? If you do not confess immediately, I am going to kill all of you!" he declared.

Kamelgard came forward and pointed to the dead man on the ground, "Herr *Kommandant*, he bought the chicken, and I begged him so not to buy it." Goeth replied, "He has already received his punishment." The surviving members of the group were each given 50 lashes; clearly, Norman's quick thinking saved them all. This incident was later portrayed in Steven Spielberg's film *Schindler's List*.

This was not Norman's only close call. He was with 25 men taken to the *Appellplatz* for execution, but when the *Kapo* was distracted, Norman ran to

Uncle David's group working nearby. My uncle immediately handed him a shovel, enabling him to blend in with the group installing concrete sewer pipes, and thereby saved his life. In the end, the Nazis murdered Norman's parents, five brothers, and two sisters; he is the sole survivor.

Mundek Reich, the inveterate bully, was the *Ordnungsdienst* assigned to the barrack containing the tinsmithing and roofing workshop. When I commented to fellow prisoner Shloime Lefkovich that Jewish *Kapos* were terrible, he tried to curry favor by repeating my opinions to Mundek, who punched me in the face several times. Reich had been a professional boxer, and my face was swollen for days. After the war, Reich was tried in Poland for committing atrocities, convicted, and sentenced to two years in the penitentiary, a lenient punishment in my opinion.

Engineer Greenberg, the man in charge of maintaining and expanding the camp, was more bruised than the rest of us. This elderly, gray-haired intellectual was productive and hard working, but if there was the slightest imperfection in the work or a delay in the schedule, Goeth never missed the opportunity to whip and humiliate him. Part of Goeth's hold over Greenberg was that the engineer had a wife and daughter in the women's section, and Goeth would use them to taunt him. Eventually, Goeth shot him. Shootings in Plaszow took place often, whereas hangings were relatively rare; whippings were the punishment of choice.

When friends gathered in the barracks and talked about home—their families, their towns, and the lives they once led—the stories were heartbreaking. When enough time had passed since I took that swing at the *Kapo* in Barrack 34, I went to visit Father. One of his barrack-mates was Sam Federman from Kielce, a cousin of Moishe Shmil Goldkorn, who had escaped from the Zatorska Street labor camp. When the war broke out, Sam sought refuge in Dzialoszyce only to be deported. Now he used his beautiful voice to fill the barrack with "*Mayn Yidishe Mame*" (My Jewish Mother) and other soul-touching, melancholy melodies.

In March 1944, a bow-legged SS man whom we called *Dziadek* (grandfather) caught me. I use the word "caught" because when they needed bodies for a particular purpose, the Nazis would just nab whoever was around. I was headed to the latrine when *Dziadek*, assisted by Gos, a Ukrainian, took me, my Uncle David, and others to the Polish camp. We were taken by train ten kilometers to Wieliczka, but it might as well have been another planet because Father and Art were still in Plaszow. With more than 300 kilometers of underground caverns, Wieliczka was—and still is—the largest salt mine in Poland and the oldest such mine in all of Europe.

At the labor camp, I met the Reifler brothers, Yoil and Mottie, who had been stalwarts of their community in Drohobycz, a Galician town in southeastern Poland (now Drogobych, Ukraine). Now they were reduced to slavery. Mottie was strong and handsome, but withdrawn. Yoil was Father's age and became a mentor to me. We discussed political events, the war, Zionism, and Jewish suffering through the ages. He would also talk to me about his beautiful daughter and show me the pictures he had managed to keep.

The salt mine was more than 100 meters deep, dark and damp. We felt like we were working in a tomb, and it could easily have been our own because there had been cave-ins just before we arrived. I pushed carts filled with salt and stone a few hundred feet along rails to the elevator, ten hours a day. I was alone, except for Uncle David, so with no immediate family members who could be held hostage, I seriously entertained the thought of escaping. One morning, I simply walked away and spent the day roaming the streets, looking at market stands, trying to plan my next move, but I returned to the salt mine that evening because it was too risky. I had no place to go and did not know anyone on the outside. I would have had to depend on unsympathetic Poles.

I saw how Poles watched as we were marched through the streets. The smiles on their faces and their occasional epithets indicated their deep hatred of us. I could be denounced for a kilo of sugar—the going price per Jew—and end up dead anyway. Wieliczka, lightly guarded by *Luftwaffe* (German Air Force) personnel, had no SS presence and was relatively easy to reenter. I told the guards at the gate that I had been looking for a set of misplaced tools and had gotten lost. They had no idea I was lying and assumed that if I was coming back to camp on my own, I was probably telling the truth.

My work in the mines had nothing to do with mining salt. We were preparing large bunkers deep underground to accommodate heavy machinery. We removed material, leveled the substrate, and poured concrete. The two primitive elevator cabs had to be used at the same time because they were counterweights to each other. The humid, briny air was good for asthma sufferers, but was too heavy for me. (As a result of working in those mines as a teen, I have lost my taste for salty foods.) To get out of going underground, I volunteered as a roofer, citing my Plaszow experience. Every few days, I repaired the roofs, and in April, I was sent to Mielec, a camp 100 kilometers away. I was now, for the first time, totally on my own.

Before the war, Mielec had been a major Polish airplane manufacturing plant. The Germans took it over and renamed it the *Henkelwerke* after their Henkel airplane. The camp was four to five kilometers from the village and had only three SS *Oberscharführer*, who were strict, mean, and eager to execute inmates. As soon as we arrived, the SS and Ukrainian guards tattooed the letters *KL*, for *Konzentrationslager* (concentration camp), on our upper right forearms, just above the wrist. The prisoners said that *KL* stood for *Kodesh L'Shem*, (sanctified to God), a biblical term that describes certain animal sacrifices in ancient Israelite practice. The altar for the human sacrifices in 1944 was a single kilometer from the camp, hidden in a small forest.

The SS "high priests" took 12 prisoners and returned with four who had been forced to bury the sacrifices. In Mielec, the Almighty demanded the tranquillity of the woods, so there were many daily sacrifices in the Tabernacle of the Forest.

The *Lagerältester* was Freedman, an *Ordnungsdienst* with a quirk—all his speeches, rebukes, and other expressions were punctuated with the word "effect." His son, Lolek, was a fine young man, and we pitied him for having such a father. Mr. Segal was the camp secretary, and there were several other *Ordnungsdienste*—Hashke and Jack Kleiner among them. Hashke came from a Hasidic family and did not have the personality for the job. He was uncomfortable with his role and kinder than many others.

After the war, there were many former *Kapos* who tried to portray themselves as kinder than they were. In 1946, Jack Kleiner came to me in the Feldafing displaced persons (DP) camp and asked me to sign an affidavit testifying that he had been a kindly *Ordnungsdienst*. While we were all trying to build new communities, Kleiner lived alone near a lake in Starnberg and stayed away from former inmates. When he asked for the affidavit, I asked him to name one person he helped. My response to him was honest and direct, "Many inmates complained that you whipped and abused them. The best I can do to help you is to do nothing. I do not even want to remember you."

In 1970 in Toronto, a former camp foreman asked me to testify that he was "wonderful" in Mielec. Today, he atones for his sins by working for United Jewish Appeal (UJA) and other worthwhile causes. He was not as bad as some of the others, so he will remain unnamed here. Unfortunately, however, a number of Jews, some of whom came from the very best families, felt compelled to collaborate with the Nazis, compromising their integrity to save their own skins.

In contrast, others with no official power used and did whatever they could to help others. Chaim-Leizer and Willie saved many people in Czestochowa by organizing extra food for the sick, who were always put on half rations. It was important that they recover and get back to work because anything short of a speedy recovery was permanently cured by death. Uncle Shloyme, also in Czestochowa, protected his co-workers by taking the blame—and the whippings—for any faulty workmanship in his workshop. I can only hope that if I had been faced with the same temptations of power, I would have maintained my integrity and declined to collaborate—and I am certainly proud of those in my family who did not.

I was assigned to Airplane Assembly Hall No. 3, a large hangar. It was not difficult for me to adapt what I already knew as a roofer to the drilling, capping, and leveling procedures required to assemble an airplane. I took extra care to make sure I drilled the aluminum accurately and set the sheets for the aircraft skin so that the butt joints were absolutely flush. I had to—any noticeable defect would bring a charge of sabotage. My life was on the line.

Still, it was difficult to please Herr Schultz, the nitpicking master mechanic. Schultz was a miserable, tall, acne-scarred German screamer. No matter how diligent my efforts or excellent my work, nothing was good enough for him. Once when he criticized me, I politely asked him to show me how it should be done. Schultz picked up the tools, started to demonstrate the correct procedure, and damaged the entire plate he was working on. In fact, he ruined the fuselage, and we had to take it off line. To conceal his incompetence, Schultz took the damaged aluminum to the laboratory. Then he claimed the material was a tougher density and that the composition of the alloy in that plate was different than all the others—a poor excuse for poor workmanship.

Schultz was also very strict about taking care of the tools. In Hall No. 3, we worked around the clock in two 12-hour shifts, and at midnight on the night shift, we were given an hour break. Walking the two kilometers back and forth to camp left us with only 10 or 15 minutes to rest and eat our watered-down soup, so sometimes I would skip the meager meal and take a much-needed nap in the fuselage. Once, I left the tools out while I was napping, and Schultz, seeing the tools unattended, locked the electric drill in the "on" position and threw it into the fuselage, knowing full well I was in there. The drill hit me in the head and the bit penetrated my skull, got stuck there, and then broke off. I was bleeding but waited until morning to see the doctor.

The doctor was more of a shoemaker than a physician. He either fixed your injury on the spot or sent you to heaven for "divine" treatment via the "altar" in the Forest Temple. He put a bandage over the hole in my head and told me he had removed a piece of metal from my skull. I went back to work as if nothing had happened and considered myself lucky that the wound was not infected. Eighteen months later, after I was liberated, I took care of myself properly. I went to see Dr. Peisachovich, chief surgeon of the Milbauer Hospital in Munich in January 1946, who, with his assistant, Dr. Kurzweil, removed the remainder of the broken drill bit still lodged in my head.

Cockpits and fuselages continued to be produced at full speed. Aluminum arrived in sheets, plates, and bars—flat and curved. We assembled the parts and fastened them with bolts and sheet-metal screws, using new "electric" power tools to maximize efficiency. "Just produce, do not talk. The enemy listens," read the slogans ubiquitously displayed on the walls. They were directed at the salaried, Polish master mechanics who stayed on at the plant to work for the Germans and returned to their homes each evening.

We Jews were marched into the hangar under heavy guard, so there was little chance of anything we said or heard being of any consequence. From time to time, though, we received hints of what was going on in the outside world from Polish workers. "The war will not last too long," they were saying. They would never talk about specific events. Though scraps of news were sometimes more consoling than scraps of bread, the information the Poles gave us was like the Nazi soup—extremely watered down. They threw us dry, meatless bones and said very little.

The Poles, however, were not averse to smuggling food into the hangars—for a steep price. Though I had been tattooed, I was still wearing my own clothes, the same ones I had been wearing when I was first deported. Miraculously, I still had some of the gold coins Mother had sewn into the seams. Her foresight allowed me to survive. If I was caught trying to "organize" some food, as a Jew I would be shot immediately, whereas the Pole would be fired or, at worst, imprisoned.

One evening, prisoners arrived from Budzyn, a labor camp about 40 kilometers southwest of Lublin, Poland. They, too, had been tattooed, and they told us things that shocked and depressed us. For the first time, I heard about the death camps at Belzec, Treblinka, and Majdanek and learned about the assembly-line mass extermination of Jews.

I was alone, unable to determine if anyone else from our family was still alive. I went into a tailspin as steep as the tailspins I wished on the planes we were assembling. Was this the highest development of German culture—to hoodwink us in such an evil manner? My sense of isolation was exacerbated because I also felt that the Jews had been abandoned by the world's democracies.

Why was there such acquiescence in Washington, Ottawa, London, Paris, and the Vatican? Why were they not stopping this? Did they, too, want the world to be *Judenrein*?

The news from the Budzyn inmates opened up a whole new level of worry about Mother. I had no idea where she was, and now I could only imagine the worst. I still do not know with certainty where Mother was murdered. Mother, may she rest in peace, was the whole world to me.

Since Mother and Father were taken like that, my life has not been whole. Even the greatest optimists among us never imagined that Germany's mighty military machine would ever collapse. Brainwashed, systematically degraded, physically tortured, and emotionally starved, we thought of death as a narcotic to ease our pain. The upside to annihilation was that it promised relief. We flitted in and out of a mentality that was seduced by death one moment and by life the next. I decided to choose life.

My sole comfort was the possibility that, against all odds, I still might be reunited with my loved ones. The SS officer Schomberger, who ran the camp in Mielec, stopped short of murdering us because they needed us in order to keep their jobs as our supervisors—otherwise they would have been sent to the eastern front, where they risked being shot or taken prisoner. They were so terrified of the Russians that they even postponed killing their Jews.

TO APPEASE A LONELY GOD

Sometime in the beginning of August 1944, we returned to Mielec, where we were immediately ordered to an *Appell* and told to leave our possessions behind. It was laughable because we had almost no belongings and certainly not anything of worth to the Nazis. To us, however, the few items we kept in the wooden boxes we had made for ourselves and stored underneath our bunk beds were most valuable. A stale piece of bread held back for an emergency, a picture from home, or a dirty, old, lice-infested undergarment was a treasure—we had nothing else. Yet we were not allowed even that. The SS lashed out with their whips and rounded up 2,000 of us in no time. We were marched to the train station under heavy guard and shoved into boxcars.

"*Auf gehts, auf gehts,*" the guards yelled. We were treated like cattle instead of an essential human resource necessary for building airplanes that were vital to the *Luftwaffe*.

Crammed into closed cattle cars for hours, we wondered where the train was taking us this time. Inexplicably, we stopped at Wieliczka. Why would we be taken there? What industry in Wieliczka could be as important in wartime as airplane manufacturing? Were they going to liquidate us? Was the *Henkelwerke* being transferred to Germany, as was all the gold and silver in Poland? Maybe the Germans were taking us to the salt mines to be buried alive—just blow up the entrance and they would not have to waste any bullets or gas on our deaths.

I discovered that Uncle David and the Reifler brothers were still alive.

We were taken to the mines and ordered to dismantle drilling and mining machinery and load it onto trucks for shipping to the Reich. We finished in five or six days at most. As soon as we had finished, we were taken to the main railroad station in Krakow and jammed back into boxcars. I expected we were being sent back to Plaszow, but we were on a motionless train, and no one knew why.

After several hours, columns of people were marched in our direction and forced into the already crowded cars. We watched this scene through the small, wired windows high on the cattle car walls, and still we hoped, looking for that glimmer of light, a sign that soon redemption would come—in an hour, two hours, in a day or two. If we waited, surely it would come. It must. The Russians would catch up with the Germans. The Germans were tired. Discouraged, they would retreat. Everything would be fine, we reasoned, if we had just a little more patience. We offered the Almighty our prayers, and He answered, as always, with silence.

Finally the train moved out, and after five hellish days we arrived in Mauthausen, Austria—bewildered, hungry, and exhausted. When the heavy sliding doors of the boxcars opened, a burst of light and air entered, relieving the darkness and stench in the wagon. As our eyes grew accustomed to the light, we saw that this camp was very different. I quickly learned that Mauthausen was a *mord-hausen*—a house of murder. Mauthausen had a gas chamber, a crematorium, and an "ash dump," the Nazi's crude euphemism for our martyrs' final resting place. The camp was notorious for its medical experiments and its infamous Torture Bunker. Interestingly, Mauthausen seemed to have a larger percentage of non-Jews in the inmate population than the other camps I had been in.

When we arrived, we were sent into a room, ordered to strip, and stayed naked while our clothing was confiscated and we were disinfected. Any photos, bits of gold, or money sewn into our clothing was now gone as part of the German attempt to eradicate our personae and obliterate anything that might serve as evidence against them in the future. "Experts," German and Austrian criminals, inspected us to ensure that we did not have anything hidden in our mouths or other bodily orifices. They shaved off all our hair—from our heads, our faces, our armpits, our genitals, everywhere. The "rich" camp diet we had been fed had probably retarded certain aspects of my development. I did not have any facial hair yet, so I was spared that humiliation. They left us with nothing but our souls, which they could not take unless they killed us.

Before, it was sometimes possible to negotiate with or bribe a *Kapo* to get some leeway, but not in Mauthausen. Here, the *Kapos* were not Jews, and they hated us as much as the SS did. After disinfection, we entered a clothing hall and were handed thin, blue-and-white striped, unlined cotton jackets and matching trousers. (After the war, when my children wore blue and white wide-striped rugby shirts, I could not help but think of our uniforms.) The sizes were all mixed up. "Just take it and move on," barked the foreman. If we did not walk quickly, the *Kapos* whipped our naked bodies. We were also issued banded fabric caps and wooden clogs. After all the clothing was assigned, we inmates traded around until we had uniforms that "fit."

Before they assigned us to a barrack, the Nazis registered each one of us. I wondered why they bothered until I realized that we were no longer humans; we were numbers. Until we arrived in Mauthausen, we had been called by our names, signifying, more or less, that we were still human beings. Even pets had names. Now we were stripped of our names and given numbers—an ultimate degradation. My registration number was, and still is, 86043. We were like items in an auction with no one in the world who cared to bid on us. We were considered completely worthless, dead inventory in a warehouse called Mauthausen.

I was handed a small strip of white fabric with my number clearly marked on it and a red triangle. I was given needle and thread and ordered to sew the number strip and triangle to my chest. The triangle, narrow end pointing down, designated me as a Jewish inmate. Political prisoners and criminals wore triangles pointing upward like pyramids, and they displayed their badges with pride.

I was assigned to a barrack where the Block *Kapo* was a middle-aged German criminal with a twisted jaw. His method of communication with new arrivals was via beatings. New prisoners at Mauthausen were put in separate blocks in a kind of quarantine and holding pen for two or three weeks before being moved into places left by those who had been gassed, shot, starved, or worked to death.

I was assigned to the Wienergraben stone quarry, where I carried large rocks from deep in the quarry up man-made stairs to the top of a mountain. The inmates had weakened constitutions, and many could not climb the 186 steps under such heavy loads. If the weak ones did not slip on their own, they were often pushed off by criminal *Kapos* or SS men. The drop was more than 100 feet, and prisoners were killed when they banged against the rocks as they tumbled down the gorge. Those who survived a day's work returned to the barracks and dropped onto their bunks, most of them too exhausted to stand in line for watery soup or a few grams of bread.

Mauthausen was unbearable—so many around me died of starvation and exhaustion, and I came close to dying myself. I was in some other world and yet I felt "the Lord has indeed punished me but did not leave me to die" (Psalm 118).

Mauthausen was a central camp with a network of satellite camps. It functioned as a registration site for new inmates, where the weak were culled in the Wienergraben quarry, and the survivors of this cruel initiation were then sent off to one of the subcamps. When the SS command decided to make room for new arrivals by shipping approximately 1,500 of us to Melk, I thought I was lucky. Melk was about 100 kilometers east of Mauthausen, along the Danube River, and named for the Benedictine Abbey that dominated it. For the first time, we traveled in regular passenger cars, and it seemed to bode well. I could not imagine that any place could be worse than Mauthausen.

Like Mauthausen, Melk was a heavily guarded camp surrounded by double rows of barbed wire. The camp was located in a military garrison in the town. Some of us were assigned to huts in the courtyard and others to the original buildings. New quarters, for me and 120 others, were on the second floor of a small, concrete barrack. Four inmates shared a bunk that normally held one person. Similar numbers of people were crammed onto each of the first and third floors. The camp probably held about 14,000 inmates during my time there.

Some old family friends from Dzialoszyce were on the third floor. One was Isaac Mandelbaum, who survived the war and now lives with his family in Montreal, Canada. Another was Itche Meyer, who owned a fabric store and had been one of the richest businessmen in Dzialoszyce. I had studied Hebrew at Professor Joseph Landau's school with Itche Meyer's daughter, Pola. Itche Meyer had once been a giant of a man who weighed about 114 kilos and proudly stood six feet three inches tall. Now, he was down to less than half of his former weight and, when climbing the stairs to his room in Melk, he had to stop midway because he was out of breath. He complained about his poor health and the difficulty of enduring the inhumane treatment. I tried to lift his spirits and begged him to persevere just a little longer.

Unfortunately, Itche Meyer did not survive—he died of dehydration.

There were times a little word of encouragement from a friend could make the difference between giving up and hanging on just a little bit longer—especially because there were reasons for despair around every corner. Right after I helped Itche Meyer to his room, I walked back downstairs and saw the German *Blockältester*, Otto, forcing an inmate's head into a bucket of water, one of his favorite forms of murder. The sadist held his foot on top of the prisoner's head until the poor man drowned. The reason for the murder could have been as absurd as the victim having tracked a little bit of dirt into the barrack.

A German gypsy we called the *Zigeunerkapo* had a dark, wide-boned face and probably worked as a professional boxer, wrestler, or bouncer before the war. When he got hold of an inmate, he usually finished him off, and we were terrified of him.

The *Blockältester* on my floor was a small Pole, a criminal with a shaven head, the face of a pig, and the name Stach. He always checked to see that the rooms were neat, the floor was spotless, and everything was in order. He deprived us of much-needed sleep because he conducted inspections in the middle of the night and demanded we clean anything that was not up to his standards.

Food in Melk was held to a bare minimum. Anyone who lined up for a second helping of watery soup was hit over the head with a metal ladle by the *Blockältester*, who wanted to discourage inmates from taking extra food. There were times when our starved bodies craved food so badly we would eat the bark off the trees.

Uncle David was my only relative in Melk. He worked in the railroad track repair gang supervised by Ludwig, a German *Kapo*. Uncle David had lost lots of weight and was afflicted with a rash and boils. When I was assigned to wash the terrazzo floor in the corridor of Block Two, I received two bowls of soup as a reward for doing the extra work and gave one of them to Uncle David, leaving it on his bunk so he could eat it after his work shift. When I could, I visited Block Six, which was under the supervision of a Jewish *Blockältester* named Einhorn. I knew many people from other camps in that Block, including Norman Kamelgard and some other Dzialoszycers.

While we were in Melk, a powerful, healthy labor contingent of captured Russians was brought in as prisoners of war (POWs). They were still wearing their military uniforms, but exchanging clothing or trading and bartering with them or anyone else was strictly forbidden. If you were caught, you would receive 50 lashes on your naked bottom or your food would be withheld until you starved. Hunger and hard labor had already weakened the Jews because they had been in the labor/concentration/death camp system for a long time. By the time we got to Melk, we were susceptible to disease and plagued by typhus. Starvation pushed us over the edge. The Russians, fresh off the front, were relatively vigorous and strong and had no scruples about taking what they wanted, especially from the weakened Jews. When they saw someone hiding bread, they stole it.

There were two rooms on the second floor, with a separate area for the *Blockältester*, the *Schreiber* (secretary), and *Kapos*. About 90 inmates lived in our room, half of them Russian, the other half French, Greek, Hungarian, Polish, Spanish, and Jewish.

The *Schreiber*, a French bookkeeper, was the assistant to *Blockältester* Stach. The two men had four helpers, two Frenchmen and two Spaniards, who did menial tasks like fetching and distributing food. The Spaniards—one was older and one was younger—spoke only their own dialect of Spanish so communicating with either of them was difficult. Survival required us to learn the language of the person in charge; otherwise, we were in trouble. So it was with my *Kapo*, Uncle Zelik, a middle-aged Hungarian Jew. He did not speak any language other than Hungarian. During roll call, to avoid getting beaten by him, I would shout out *"Nultz ven hot null nadvanharem"* (86043) as he checked my number off his list. Any other response meant standing, waiting, and getting whipped. We learned fast. The Russian prisoners of war with their habitual thievery were no better. One had to learn quickly to communicate in Russian—with a liberal dose of profanity.

I was troubled by the attitude of the antisemitic French inmates. I thought of France as a tolerant nation ready to fight for liberal causes. These were the people who had stormed the Bastille, whose anthem was *"La Marseillaise."* We were together in the same camp, also hungry and persecuted, yet they despised us.

A Hungarian Jew, Mr. Weiss, and his son, Imre (who was even younger than I was), were in the bunk next to mine. This fine gentleman, who took sick and died at Melk, is someone I will never forget. Weiss told me stories about his home, his business, his family, and his daughter. He promised me that after the war, if we survived, he would give me his daughter in marriage. In an effort to cure his father once he became ill, Imre and I brought him charcoal, which was thought to control diarrhea. Weiss's mouth and lips were blackened from eating ash, but in the end, we could not save him.

After his father's death, a Russian POW stole Imre's clogs from beneath his pillow, where they were stored for safekeeping. I woke up to see tears coursing down his face. When I heard the reason, I looked around and saw an extra pair of shoes on Nikolai Ivanowicz's bunk. I snapped at him, "Return the shoes!" Nikolai refused. He was a big man, about 40 years old. I asked nicely, "Please give me the shoes. They belong to Imre." But Nikolai would not listen. I mustered all my nerve, pulled him from his bunk to the floor, and started punching him. I was outraged. Being shoeless would have led to Imre's death. I could not stand by and let two generations of that family die in less than a week without trying to do something about it.

Everyone in the barrack watched Nikolai stand up and fight back, and no one interfered. A few bruises later, I won Imre's clogs back, and from then on, Nikolai and the other Russians never bothered the Jews in our barrack again.

I wish I knew whether Imre survived the war and, if so, where he lives now. His father was incinerated in the crematorium at Melk and is now keeping the Almighty company. Why else would he and so many millions of others have gone up as sacrifices rising to heaven in smoke, if not to appease a lonely God? The Lord seemed to have chosen a better, kinder people as His retinue, accompanied by innocent infants whose sobs contribute to the heavenly music. In his classic essay, *The Lonely Man of Faith*, Rabbi Joseph B. Soloveitchik wrote: "The role of the man of faith oscillates between ecstasy in the Almighty's companionship and despair when he feels abandoned by God … I am lonely because at times I feel rejected and thrust away by everybody." We were lonely. The Almighty was not, not anymore.

The train that took us to work left from a wooden platform built on a steep hill. Waiting for the train when it was cold was intolerable. The height of the open platform exposed us to penetrating winds, and in our thin clothing and wooden shoes, we literally froze. I often prayed for the bridge to fall so that we might be allowed to board the train from a more sheltered position. To get our blood circulating, we would rub each other's backs, but soon even this was forbidden. An Austrian SS man, "The Shoemaker," would pass among us as we stood four or five deep and, holding his pistol by its muzzle, would bang the steel butt against the inmates' noses. He hit the prisoners hard and stopped only when blood poured down our faces. The Shoemaker had a crooked, ugly nose himself. This protuberance must have been the reason that he viciously attacked other noses.

When the train of boxcars arrived, we would run toward the sliding doors, stepping over each other to get out of the cold wind. Inside, 60 of us would huddle together for warmth during the ten-minute ride to Roggendorf, three miles east of the camp. An SS guard sat in an outside booth between the cars, protected from the cold, and *Kapos* always accompanied us inside. After arriving at our destination, we walked for five minutes from the unloading platform to the front of the tunnels. Cliffs towered over acres of flatland, and the landscape was dotted with machinery. Trucks and metal containers were perched beside narrow-gauge railroad tracks. The mountain was pocked with tunnels labeled from A to F, the entrances to which were approximately 50 feet wide by 40 feet high with semicircular arched ceilings. These tunnels, or *Stollen*, were being dug into the sides of the Austrian mountains to house munitions factories and warehouses that would be protected from Allied bombing. When we got to the tunnels, we split up and entered *Stollen* A or B, each about a kilometer in depth. We did not know it at the time, but the underground network of tunnels in all the satellites of Mauthausen totaled some 300 kilometers.

DIE STOLLEN—THE TUNNELS

I started my apprenticeship at Melk by doing the most basic manual labor. First, following the instructions of the German foremen, I used a pick and shovel to remove earth, load it into a wheelbarrow, and haul it to the dump area. I also mixed concrete and learned that each task had its advantages and disadvantages. Outside, I was exposed to the wind and cold, but after emptying the cement from paper bags, I used the packaging as crude undershirts to cut the wind. In the tunnels, the work was more dangerous, but at least I was out of the wind.

As we dug deeper into the tunnels, we installed conveyor belts to remove the dirt. When we hit hard ground or rock, we used pneumatic jackhammers. After we got to a certain depth, we installed thick, iron "H" beams to support the ceiling and walls. To reach the upper parts of the tunnels in order to install the beams and to do our digging, we built wooden scaffolds, which served a dual purpose. To eliminate the old and the weak, or to inflict punishment, the SS and the *Kapos* would order several Jews to shovel dirt onto the conveyor belt while they climbed the scaffold to demonstrate the proper method for removing material. Inevitably, when they jackhammered material out of the ceiling, a huge mass of rocky earth would fall from the heights and kill the people working next to the conveyor belt. Whenever the Nazis did this, they would report 10 to 20 inmates dead from "work accidents" at roll call, in addition to the five or six who would normally expire during the course of a work day.

Not a word was spoken during these "accidents." The Nazis' transparent plots tore us up inside, but we stifled our feelings. While we choked on our emotions, the brutal killings continued. Those killed near the entrance to the *Stollen* were brought back to the camp to be cremated, but most were buried in the tunnels, and we were forced to pave the floors right over their graves. This killing method also saved bullets—so thousands of Jews were killed this way, and by the world's silence. That was no accident either.

I eventually "graduated" to building the steel rings that were part of the concrete formwork. I did not get the *Ringbau* (ring building) job because I was big and strong—I was not—but because I spoke the *Obersteiger*'s (supervisor's) language. One way or another, he had to produce four ring sections per night, but it was impossible for a single crew to install more than two rings per shift. To meet his quota, the *Obersteiger*, a German mining engineer, taught me to assemble the rings so that while he supervised one crew, I could complete two sections in a different location. I was not unhappy with this, especially when the supervisor assigned eight powerful Russians to my work gang. The crew pulled the heavy steel "H" sections up on the scaffold with a constant rhythm from their chant, "hey, gee, a jolly." After they brought the beam up high, I stood on a ladder and bolted it to its mate with a heavy wrench.

The ring sections had to be flush and the whole assembly had to be properly placed relative to the excavations and the wooden frames that braced them. Because of my accuracy, the *Obersteiger* secretly rewarded me with two cigarettes, making me a "rich" man in the world of Melk. At mealtimes, on either the day or night shift, the *Obersteiger* purposely did not finish whatever he happened to be eating. He would never hand me his leftover food directly, but he would point out something that needed "fixing" and would hint at where he had left the food. His extra scraps saved me from starvation.

The rest of the crew did not speak German and could not communicate with the *Obersteiger*, but I always gave them one cigarette to share and each would take a deep puff. Tobacco was "manna to some, dementia to others." The Russians craved cigarettes no less than I hungered for bread. With a little bit of each, we were all happy.

I would give the second cigarette to Uncle David or exchange it for one-sixteenth of a piece of bread that I shared with Uncle David. I once saved four cigarettes and traded them for a fur hat from a newly arrived Russian POW. My head stayed warm, the flaps covered my ears and I customized it by removing some of the cotton from the lining and replacing it with cement—that way, when I stood in line for second helpings of soup, the *Kapo*'s heavy, metal ladle did not hurt when the *Kapo* hit me in the head with it.

That fur hat saved me in some ways, but it almost cost me my life.

It began on the train to the *Stollen*. *Oberkapo* Ernst, a German criminal, noticed my hat and said he could use it because he was often outdoors. Since I worked inside, to his mind, I could get by with a thinner hat, and he offered me his *Kapo* hat in exchange for mine. It was an honor for some inmates to have a *Kapo*'s hat; it gave the wearer certain privileges associated with *Kapos*—protection, soup from the bottom of the pot, and generally opened doors, as much as doors could be opened for Jewish slave laborers. However, this was one deal I was willing to forgo. I wanted to keep the fur hat that had cost me four cigarettes and was now lined with cement.

"I do not do business in camp," I explained. "It is forbidden."

Ernst did not like my answer, especially since I had obviously traded for the hat in the first place. I saw his face redden in anger, but what could I do? The next day I tried to dodge Ernst, but he found me and asked which *Stollen* I was working in. I told him C, even though I actually worked in B, and I knew that there was going to be trouble. I told my *Obersteiger* the story about the hat because I was afraid that *Oberkapo* Ernst was going to put me in the worst *Stollen*, *Stollen* F. There I would have to work up to my knees in muddy water and operate heavy equipment and air-hammers that outweighed me. The tunnel walls were not supported during digging, so there was always the danger of collapse and being buried alive. No one could survive longer than a week or two in *Stollen* F. The only consolation of that *Stollen*, if one can call extra food for one's last meals a consolation, was that for every yard and a half of ground excavated, laborers received an additional soup coupon.

The courier, who brought used steel air-hammer points to the machine shop to exchange for their sharpened replacements, told me that the *Oberkapo* was looking for me everywhere. I thought my end was near and recited *Vidui*, the confessional prayer a Jew recites on his deathbed. "To hell with Hell," I reasoned, I was there already. I prayed to the Almighty for help. "You saved me before, although you did not save many. Should you not balance the scales a little?" I asked the Almighty. "Don't you need a witness to testify on Your behalf, to be proof to the higher court in Heaven that You did not wipe out Your entire people? Don't you want somebody left to tell the story, someone to defend Your name? Please, do it for Yourself, not for me. Who am I? What am I? I am nothing and less than nothing." I continued working and praying; the Lord would decide my fate.

Oberkapo Ernst did not find me in *Stollen* C at the *Ringbau Kommando* that day. He saw me during roll call at the end of the shift and again in the boxcar. He gave me an order, "Wait for me tomorrow, and I will assign you to work." In the morning, *Oberkapo* Ernst had me follow him to *Stollen* F. Every step in that direction was a step closer to death. I could not refuse because he was the *Oberkapo* and had a right to assign work to inmates.

He led me to the end of *Stollen* F where I waded in the mud. There was little light, even less ventilation, and lots of smoky exhaust from the machinery. I listened to every word Ernst said.

"Here is the hammer, and you have to dig at least one meter deep," Ernst said. I took the pneumatic jackhammer, its weight almost breaking my back, and started working. Luckily, there was a solid wall of hard earth in front of me. I could rest the hammer on it instead of lifting it for repositioning. The loud noise it made was deafening, but I worked as hard as I could and did not turn around because I suspected that the *Oberkapo* was right behind me. I stared at the different strata of earth, lying there, tranquil, until my attacking hammer disturbed them.

At lunchtime we were given a 15-minute break to eat our watered-down soup. Other workers told me that Ernst had been watching me. I asked if he said anything, but he had not. "How many times was he here?" I asked. They said twice. Then, close to the end of the shift, the *Oberkapo* came to see me. I wanted him to measure the depth of my hole and hoped he had soup coupons because I had gone over the norm to receive a bonus. He lied and said I was ten centimeters short.

The next day the same thing happened. As I dug through the mountain, I saw *Oberkapo* Ernst approaching me menacingly through a cloud of dust. What could I do but hope for a miracle? Maybe he would have an accident. Maybe he would die. Just then, the *Obersteiger* came into *Stollen* F, saw me hammering, and told me to stop. At first, I pretended not to hear him and kept working, but he pulled my arm and asked in an official tone, "Who put you here?"

"*Oberkapo* Ernst," I answered, and the *Obersteiger* left. I thought my death sentence was confirmed by his silence. My whole body was numb from the jackhammer vibrations. The next day the routine was the same but with one difference. At the end of the shift, the kind *Obersteiger* appeared in an SS *Hauptsturmführer*'s uniform, looking spiffy from head to toe. I had never seen him in any kind of uniform. I had no idea he was SS. Was this the same person? At roll call, my *Obersteiger* glanced at me from time to time. When we went into the boxcars from the train platform, he entered a regular passenger car, and the train headed for the camp. Once there, we had to reassemble and were not permitted to enter our barracks. We lined up in rows, and they started counting, noting the fate of all those killed in "accidents."

Obersturmbannführer Julius Ludolf, the *Lagerkommandant*, exchanged salutes with my *Hauptsturmführer Obersteiger*. After a few minutes that felt like hours, I heard over the loudspeaker: "86043, step out!" That was my number. Trembling, I moved toward the group of guards. As I stood in front of them, my muscles spasmed in agony and torment as I imagined the worst.

Lagerkommandant Ludolf asked me why I left my *Ringbau Kommando* job. I explained that *Oberkapo* Ernst had ordered me to go to *Stollen* F. Ludolf ordered Ernst to come closer. The *Lagerkommandant* yelled, "You sabotaged the *Ringbau*, the construction of the rings. Why? How could you do that?" With a whip, the *Lagerkommandant* struck Ernst on his face and head again and again. Then he ordered him to stand next to the electrified fence. I never knew what happened to *Oberkapo* Ernst. I do know that I never saw him again. Years later, I heard *Lagerkommandant* Ludolf was tried and hanged.

Since that time, whenever I see the wind blowing a hat off someone's head, if the person runs out into traffic after it, I always yell out, "Stop! Use your head. You do not want to get hit by a car and lose your head over a hat. If you have a head, you will have a hat."

I went back to work in the *Ringbau Kommando*. The eight-voice chant from my Russian work gang, as they lifted the heavy, steel beams, was heavenly music to my ears. I was still deep in the mountain, still in the smoke and dust and cold and darkness, yet in my mind's eye, there was a rainbow of hope, and my heart was warmed by the fire of God's wrath.

I had experienced a miracle. While standing on the top rung of the ladder installing the steel rings deep inside the mountain, complex emotions overwhelmed me. My dried lips murmured, "I extol Thee, O Lord, for Thou hast lifted me up and hast not let my foes rejoice over me" (Psalms 30:1).

EBENSEE

Sometimes I took a few precious moments to stand at a window in the corridor of Block 2 and catch a glimpse of the free world outside the walls. The town of Melk was set in a beautiful, serene landscape surrounded by mountains, topped off by the enormous abbey on the hill, overlooking the gurgling sounds of the Danube. It seemed inconceivable that the people of Melk could allow this inhumanity to go on right under their noses. I was sure that many of the supervisors in the *Stollen*, certainly the engineering professionals, lived in the town. There was no way, as they later claimed, that the burghers could not have known what was going on in their midst. Their complicity in the perpetration of atrocities places Melk in the Hall of Infamy, along with Belzec, Majdanek, Oswiecim (Auschwitz), and many other European towns.

Early in the second week of April 1945, I was staring out the window with mixed emotions. I was furious with the people of Melk for intruding on the peaceful feelings elicited by the landscape, when suddenly the war burst upon us. Sirens wailed, rousing the sleepy city. The camp guards left their towers and ran for cover. High in the sky above us were airplanes engaged in dogfights. One of the planes was hit, burst into flames, and fell to the ground. We did not know whose plane it was or whether there were any survivors, but we hoped it was a German plane, and we laughed with joy as we watched it burn. With no access to newspapers, radio, or other sources for news, here, at last, was some action.

"How much longer would the war last?" was the question in our hearts.

Would we live to see the end of the cruel wars—the one raging outside, the one we fought daily inside the camp, and the ones in our hearts and heads?

Then Schreiber, the French bookkeeper, sent us to our rooms. "Don't you see? It's the end." "The end of what?" I asked. The end had already come for so many. In the one year Melk was in operation, thousands perished there. In January 1945, 1,100 inmates, more than ten percent of the remaining camp population, died. On March 12 alone, another 245 souls left for heaven. For us, it was not the end; it was just the end of our stay at Melk. The next day, after we put in a full shift at the *Stollen*, we were taken as we were to the Danube. I could not even get to my stash of three cigarettes—valuable currency for bread.

Was our routine being broken because the Red army was approaching? What was going to happen next? The Nazis were not marching us to the Danube for swimming lessons—of that we were sure. Were they going to drown us en masse? We were apprehensive when they ordered us to board barges docked on the riverbank.

The barges took us along the Danube in a westerly direction. One of them stopped near Mauthausen, while the rest, mine included, continued on to Linz. From Linz, they trucked us a short distance and assembled us for what turned out to be a death march. I decided that the reason for trucking us out in our debilitated condition as walking skeletons was that the Germans wanted to get us far away from the civilian population as quickly as possible. We began a marathon march through the Austrian Alps—7,500 of us. I do not know how many died along the way, but I do know the journey was the most difficult I have ever undertaken.

I had so little strength left that, as I marched, all I could do was pray and think about the words of the prophet, "When you pass through water, I will be with you; and streams will not overwhelm you. When you walk through fire, you will not be scorched and no flame shall burn you" (Isaiah 43:2). I kept thinking of the questions posed by the *Unesaneh Tokef*, the solemn prayer we recited with awe on Rosh Hashanah in the Gerer *shtibl*: "Who [shall perish] by fire and who by water?" We trudged along without knowing where we were being led. Finally, at the end of that second week in April, after hiking 64 kilometers, we arrived in Ebensee, another Mauthausen satellite camp.

As soon as I saw the watchtowers and passed through the gates to another place surrounded by an electrified fence, my heart filled with despair. I was entering another hell, but this time the sudden influx of 7,500 of us doubled the camp population, and conditions were the worst I had ever experienced. In the words of Dante's *Divine Comedy*: *"Lasciate ogni speranza, voi ch'entrate—* Abandon all hope, ye who enter here."

In Ebensee, I called out to the Almighty again, "How much longer?"

The watchtowers were unnecessary. We were so completely exhausted and weak by the time we arrived, the Germans did not bother to worry about our escape attempts. The mountains surrounding Ebensee were steep rock walls that even mountain climbers would have found challenging. Emaciated, we had no strength to save ourselves, and vultures would have passed us over for better fare. Despair, depression, hopelessness, melancholy, and fear became our constant companions. "How could I be alive and dead at the same time?" I asked myself.

I was herded into Block 26, where the crowding was unbearable. The effect on the sanitary conditions in the camp was indescribable, and our meager rations were smaller and of worse quality than those at any of the other camps. Our energy came from our anger, and I had plenty of it. Fury saved me from madness. So did meditation. Hunger put me into an altered state, and I turned to spirituality. Other times I was able to beat despair by concentrating on hope. One day I would be rich, the sole owner of a full loaf of bread.

I could fantasize all I wanted, but the horror around me inevitably brought me back to stark reality. That April, 4,500 of 16,000 prisoners died. The crematorium was so overtaxed that bodies waiting for incineration had to be buried. The work routine was similar to that in Melk except that at Ebensee I did not have a choice job, nor did I have the *Obersteiger* to protect me or reward me with food scraps and cigarettes. I had absolutely no one.

The Germans were going full tilt, building tunnels to hide their assets. The difference was that in Ebensee the mountains were solid rock and using the pneumatic jackhammers was significantly more difficult than it was at Melk. My heart cried out, "Rock of Israel, arise to help Israel and fulfill Your promise of redemption." The answer to my prayer came with each burst of the jackhammer, vibrations that numbed my body and mind, shaking my weightless body to its core. I could chip away at the wall of rock, but the Almighty seemed impenetrable.

After about three weeks of working in conditions where each hour of survival was a miracle and victory, we heard music to our ears. The *Luftwaffe* and

Wermacht guards dropped hints in three-word sentences, *"Hitler ist kaput"* (Hitler is finished). If there was no food to nourish us, this was at least a form of sustenance that helped us hang on despite our near-death condition.

On Saturday, May 4, 1945, SS *Lagerkommandant* Ganz and his henchmen contrived to take us to the *Stollen* to "protect" us from Allied bombing sorties. Employing their usual insidious tactics to deceive us, the Germans used interpreters to make sure we thought it was important to go to the tunnels. We were suspicious when Ganz, speaking in an atypically mild tone, announced that even those who worked in camp buildings had to go. Since the guards and SS were missing, we stayed put. First we stayed on the *Appellplatz*, and then we spread through the camp. No one gathered for the roll call. The revolt was spontaneous and a new phenomenon. It had never happened before in the camps that I was in. It was unprecedented, and it filled us with pride. We just said "No."

On May 5, Ganz announced that we would not have to work that day, but he ordered us to go to the *Stollen* for our own protection. By that time, we had formed a committee with representatives of different nationalities who advised the inmates not to follow any orders given by the Germans. We worried about how Ganz would react to our disobedience, but we had nothing left to lose. We were ready to fight to avoid being murdered. The *Lagerkommandant* was pale and speechless and turned to confer with a group of SS. The tension grew. When he turned back to us, he said that his request was really in our best interest and that he just wanted to save us, but he was dropping the orders to send us to the *Stollen*.

We dispersed to our barracks, and I thanked the Almighty for this miracle. Although we still did not know what to expect, we were elated. Our victory filled us with self-confidence. A scant hour later, the Germans were gone. They left while our committee discussed what to do next. With the Germans gone, pandemonium broke loose. The Germans had shed their weapons and uniforms so that they could blend in with the civilian population. A group of Russian POWs armed themselves with the weapons the Germans had left behind. The Russians were hell-bent on revenge, and those of us who could muster the strength joined them. The first *Kapo* we caught was the despicable gypsy who had tortured and killed so many of us. The gang beat him badly and kicked him to the ground. We urinated on him, and then the Russians unloaded their weapons into him. I was not proud of what happened, but under the circumstances, the *Zigeunerkapo* got what he deserved.

That same day, Ebensee was liberated by the 80th Infantry Division of the U.S. Army. Shortly thereafter, American tanks from the 761st Tank Battalion, an all-black fighting unit attached to General George Patton's Third Army, which had liberated the nearby camp of Gunskirchen, arrived at Ebensee. It was an event of cosmic proportions, and I swore never to forget it. The sight of the first tank in front of the camp gate is branded on my brain. Weak as I was, I gathered what strength I had and climbed onto the tank. In tears, I embraced and kissed the black American soldier in his dusty camouflage uniform who rode on top of it. I will never forget his face until my dying day. I love, honor, and respect this soldier because he had come to liberate me and because he, like many of his compatriots, was a messenger of justice. The convoys arrived late, but at last they had arrived—and for that I will forever remain grateful and indebted to the Americans.

In July 2002, as I read the *Canadian Jewish News*, I noticed an article accompanied by a photograph of a man who brought back memories. I read the caption and learned he was Johnnie Stevens, one of the men who had liberated Ebensee. My heart skipped a beat when I realized that he was the same man I had embraced on that tank so long ago. We have since been in touch, and I am grateful he sent me pictures of himself that were taken on the day of our liberation. I want to publicly thank this brave soul for the *hesed* (kindness) he bestowed on me and my fellow inmates when he and his fellow Americans liberated us from the Inferno.

It turned out that we were not wrong to suspect *Lagerkommandant* Ganz's motives. The Americans found a locomotive filled with explosives at the entrance to the *Stollen*. The SS intended to get us all into the tunnel and blow it up to eliminate the evidence of Ebensee—our end was that close. The Almighty had sent us an answer on that fateful day. So while He remained silent, He did indeed answer some of our prayers.

On May 5, 1945, a new world was created for me, a new genesis. My life was renewed, and since then, each year I commemorate two birthdays. February 9 is the date on which I was likely born in 1927, and that is the day my family chooses to celebrate. I attach more significance to May 5. On that day every year, I put on a fine suit, go out for an excellent lunch, and rejoice in the Almighty's special gift—my second chance at life.

Part III

The tree of Liberty must be refreshed from time to time with the blood of patriots and tyrants. It is its natural manure.

Thomas Jefferson to William Smith
Paris, November 13, 1787

LIBERATION

The rush of freedom was one thing, but the hunger in my stomach still ripped through me. What I wanted more than revenge, at that moment, was food. Wearing my striped inmate's uniform, I walked into town. At the station, there was a train with sealed boxcars standing on the tracks, and I broke the seal on one of them. It was filled with wooden crates of lard that weighed 25 kilograms each. I removed a foil-wrapped pack of lard and bartered it for a loaf of bread. I then traded the contents of another crate for a pound of sugar, and a third for a pound of butter. Before long, a quarter of the shipment was gone. When the Russian boys got wind of the boxcars, the contents of the whole train disappeared in a flash. Instinct told me to take it easy with foods I had not eaten in so long. However, many ex-inmates gorged themselves, got sick, and died. Their bodies could not handle rich diets after so many years of deprivation.

Stores belonging to Austrian shopkeepers were fair game. We walked around with guns and any "deal" we proposed was accepted. How could they not accept? They had been complicit in our degradation, and we looked like ghosts returned from a netherworld. We were entitled to whatever we wanted, much in the way that the Children of Israel were entitled to the booty they took from the Egyptians after their long enslavement. The shops had some food but almost no clothing, so Bertchie, one of the older survivors, outfitted himself with clothes that had been drying on a line in some Ebenseer's backyard. We went "shopping" during the day and returned to camp to sleep. The looting raged for a few days, and in the ensuing chaos, even American food supplies vanished—from trucks, warehouses, and kitchens. Once that happened, the American military police restored order, and we all settled down.

The Americans instituted a coupon system for rations, got us some clothing, and forced the Austrians to house us in their homes. My accommodations, shared with four other ex-inmates, were in the upper unit of a two-family hilltop home abandoned by a fleeing SS family. For the first time in years, we slept in soft beds on clean linens, and we slept alone, that is, except for Skaviner. Skaviner, who was three or four years older than I, went missing. We looked for him in town and back at the camp. He was nowhere to be found, and we were getting worried when suddenly he showed up with a wide grin on his face. He had "organized" food and was "shacked up" with one of the local girls. He said the Austrian women were sex-starved because most of the local able-bodied men were not back from the front. Inviting us to join him, Skaviner went back to his frolicking and did not come up for air for another few days. I declined; I was younger, and with my Gerer background, I had no idea how to approach such matters.

Our Austrian landlord was very accommodating, whether he wanted to be or not. I borrowed his bike to ride into town, and someone asked me for a ride. He sat on the frame for the steep, downhill ride, and as the bicycle picked up speed, it hit a rock, and the front wheel collapsed. Instead of fixing the wheel, we took a bike from another Austrian and continued on our way. Later that day, I returned the second bicycle to my landlord, and he complained it was not his. "Your bike is in the garbage," I answered. "Be happy that you got a bike back at all!" Yes, things had quieted down, but we still took liberties.

The American rationing plan had a twofold purpose. When we registered for coupons, the Americans could ensure that everyone—not just the talented "organizers"—received the basic nourishment that rations provided. Registration also gave the Americans basic information about each ex-inmate so that they could decide what to do with us.

After spending years under tyranny, I trusted no authority, not even one as benevolent as the Americans. I did not really feel like registering, yet I stood in line to get an identity card for food coupons. I never had a passport before the war and, because I lived in a culture where regular birthdays were not celebrated, I did not know exactly when I was born and still do not. Like most of my friends, I never needed a passport because we never went anywhere. We stuck close to Dzialoszyce, where everyone knew everyone else, and even an out-of-place cobblestone would have been noticed. Father kept all the records inside the cover of his *Yoreh Dayah*—one of his books on *halacha*. All the names and birth dates of his children were listed there.

The Americans, in their naïveté, asked ex-inmates for documents. They did not realize that we had passed through seven gates of Hell, nor did they understand that the Germans had purposely stripped us of our identities by assigning us numbers instead of names. Had we tried to keep any documents, where would we have hidden them? Every inch of our bodies was subject to scrutiny during strip searches. If it all were not so tragic, it would have been funny.

As I stood in line, my mind raced as I wondered what I should say. Non-Jewish Poles were going to be repatriated to Poland, willingly or not. Jews who did not want to go back to Poland were going to be sent to DP camps. I surely did not want to go back to Poland, but I was not very enthusiastic about the uncertain prospects of a DP camp either. I was skeptical of the process and was worried that if I told the truth, I might be forced to go back to Poland. As the line grew shorter, every identity card given out seemed to hit me over the head like a sledgehammer. I needed a solution.

When my turn finally came an officer asked, "What is your name?" I answered, "Josef Tenenbaum." Originally, our last name was spelled Tanenbaum, but I spelled it Tenenbaum because I thought it made the name sound less German. I inadvertently used the Polish spelling of Josef. The next question was about my birthplace. I replied, "Jerusalem, Palestine." The man lifted his eyes from the desk, looked at me with raised eyebrows, and murmured a skeptical "Hmmm." His doubt was obvious, so I added, "In Palestine there are places such as P'kiyin, where the Jews never left the land."

My anguish was indescribable, but I figured if I was going to be repatriated, let it be to Palestine, the only place left in the world that felt like a homeland to me. I detested Poland because of its complicity in the atrocities. My intuition directed me like a magnet toward the *Yishuv*, as if I had been born and raised there. When the officer asked me my age, I thought of Norman Kamelgard, who believed he was born in August 1927. I wanted to "be older" than Norman out of boyish competitiveness, so I gave February 9, 1927, as my birth date. I was probably born in the winter of 1927 anyway, if the date was close to the day in 1940 on which Father buried my bar mitzvah watch.

The card that the Americans gave me that day, was the only identification paper I had until the youngest of the Spielman brothers, Jutche, asked me to do him a favor. I had known the Spielmans in Plaszow, and they had once been Bobover Hasidim from a fine family. The oldest was the kind *Ordnungsdienst* mentioned earlier in this book. After liberation, the middle brother, Chaim, ran errands and washed dishes for the Americans and helped me get extra food from time to time.

About three weeks after liberation, people started to move around and travel across borders to do "business"—smuggling goods from the Russian zone to the American zone and vice versa. Jutche wanted to go to Poland to look for family and find his prewar business connections to bring leather and salt back to Austria. Jutche was three years older than I was and would have been drafted into the Polish army on his return. He begged me to lend him my identification card because it had no photograph on it. I showed him that the card said I was born in Jerusalem, so it would not help him prove his Polish citizenry and get him into Poland.

Jutche asked me to register again under the name of Josef Tenenbaum, born in Dzialoszyce on February 9, 1928. I did it and gave him the card, but he never returned it to me. I spent lots of time with Chaim, who taught me the beautiful, melancholy song "By the rivers of Babylon, there we sat and wept, remembering Zion." This ballad spoke to our hearts. Recalling our lost youth, we wept bitter tears. The Bobover melody still rings in my ears. The last time I saw Chaim was in New York, where he and Mottel Markin-Bleicher were partners in Global Knitting & Manufacturing, Inc. In the 1950s, I did good business with them.

Many liberated inmates were so sick and emaciated that the American medics could not save them. My beloved Uncle Mottel, from whom I had learned so much, was such a case. Though I had yet to recuperate from years of Nazi abuse, I was well enough to travel and did not want to hang around Ebensee. My main concern was to rebuild my life. To do it, I tried to eclipse my memories, inadvertently obliterating the good with the bad. I attempted to brighten the darkness, to suppress recollection—even those thoughts that had sustained me through hard times.

Our dear ones had begged us, in our dreams, to keep them alive. If I could not escape my mind, at least I could leave Ebensee behind. About three weeks after liberation, I climbed aboard an American army truck bound for a large transit camp in Salzburg.

That spring all Europe was in motion as people sought to return to their countries of origin. Frenchmen went back to France, Greeks returned to Greece, and even the Italian POWs, who fought alongside the Germans, returned to Italy. The only groups who did not go home were SS murderers, who fled to South America and Arab countries, and the Vlasovtsy—the Ukrainian turncoats who took SS positions in the concentration camps. Ukrainians, who would have been executed for treason or sent to Siberia, were rightfully afraid to go home and managed to flee to the West, often falsely claiming to be victims.

The camp at Salzburg was the transit hub for the DPs from Ebensee, Mauthausen, Gusen, Linz, and other camps in Austria. I tried to get information about my family members from former inmates, but could not find out anything. Equally fruitless was asking people who went back and forth to the Soviet zone and Poland. I have to admit that I did not try all that hard because the rumors were that my parents were dead, and if I did not have to face that reality, I could keep some faint hope alive. In the meantime, the authorities transferred the sick to hospitals or convalescent homes, and the majority of Jews were transferred to DP camps run by the United Nations Relief and Rehabilitation Administration (UNRRA).

The idea of any kind of camp, even a charitable one, did not sit well with me, so I threw in my lot with a group of soldiers from the Jewish Brigade. You cannot imagine the pride and happiness I felt the first time I saw soldiers in uniforms with the Star of David displayed on their shoulders—the proud badge of a unit of soldiers from the *Yishuv* who fought bravely for the Allies against Germany. They eased our transition back to living, and seeing them lifted my spirits so high that I felt I floated on a cloud. Brandes, one of the Brigade members, was originally from Dzialoszyce and had immigrated to the *Yishuv* before the war. Knowing that one of my townsmen was part of the Brigade filled me with hope. Maybe there was a way for me to get to Palestine, so I immediately volunteered to help the Brigade any way I could.

After the rehabilitation of the Jews, our most important task was to convince as many politicians as possible that a Jewish state was the only solution to the "Jewish Problem." But even after the Holocaust, there were those who felt differently. The *Bundists* were strong supporters of Jewish identity but felt Jews should fight for equal rights wherever they lived. These idealists did not necessarily believe a Jewish state would be a panacea, but I needed no convincing. The world taught me, the hard way, that the best place for my Jewish heart and soul was eternally in Zion.

Zionism itself came in many flavors, and *shlikhim* (representatives) and *madrikhim* (group leaders) from different parties competed for members in the transit and DP camps. Most people supported the centrist *Ihud* (United Zionist Party). There were also a good number of right-wingers and left-wingers—there was no shortage of ideologies.

Because of what I had lived through, I became an adherent of Vladimir (Ze'ev) Jabotinsky's philosophy and joined the Zionist Revisionist Party through *Betar*, its youth movement. Jabotinsky believed in active Jewish defense and was instrumental in the establishment of an underground Jewish military force to counter British-instigated Arab uprisings. Because of this involvement, the British barred him from entering Palestine. From 1929 until his death, he never saw the country again. In 1935, at a founding congress in Vienna, the Revisionists decided to establish the New Zionist Organization. Jabotinsky, its leader, was fed up with the "minimalism and whole atmosphere of constant compromise and surrender" that plagued the Zionist party. There was also a split in the Palestine *Haganah* (Defense) between the advocates of the official policy of *havlagah* (self-restraint) and those who, in the face of growing Arab pogroms, demanded that Jews actively retaliate. The Activist wing, whose spiritual leader was Jabotinsky, emerged as the *Irgun Zva'i Le'umi* (National Military Organization).

What struck me to my core was learning about Jabotinsky's appeals and warnings to European Jewry in the years immediately preceding the war. He foresaw the catastrophe that was imminent in the wake of Hitler's rise to power and pressed for the mass evacuation of Jews. His famous dictum was, "Either you liquidate the Diaspora or the Diaspora will liquidate you."

Now I took into account Socrates' dictum, spoken before a court in Athens in 399 BCE, "The unexamined life is not worth living." In the *Irgun*, we examined our lives, how we lived, and what attitudes allowed Jabotinsky's prophetic words to come to pass. The impetus to organize and take our fate into our own hands was very strong. At the back of our minds, there was the lingering thought, "What if the Germans managed to regroup and try again?"

We formed a *snif* (branch) of *Betar* and prepared ourselves for the *Yishuv*. We printed identification cards that were four inches by six inches when folded, with a picture of Jabotinsky on the inside. The cards were printed entirely in Hebrew, except for the name of the bearer. I already spoke some Hebrew because of those long-ago lessons with Professor Landau. I could converse with *shlikhim* and with members of the Jewish Brigade and that further improved my Hebrew putting me at an advantage. I quickly learned what I needed to do to assume an active role.

Groups of 30 to 50 refugees were formed to learn about the *Yishuv*, to study Hebrew, and to exercise their crippled bodies in an effort to rebuild them. The setting of goals helped fill our emotional voids. Quite a few of us were eager for some kind of arms training, but we did not get any because the Brigade, whose presence may have been unofficial, had to be politically cautious. Sometimes Brigadiers sympathetic to Jabotinsky's philosophy came and talked to us, but for the most part, they offered logistical support to get us to *Eretz Yisrael*.

TO PALESTINE

I became involved in smuggling groups across borders. Moving in and out of the transit camps or DP camps was no problem, but moving between Allied zones and across national borders was somewhat more difficult. When groups were ready to go, we took them across the Austrian border, down through Italy, from town to town, and boarded them onto ships bound for Palestine. This operation, known as the *Brihah*, the illegal immigration, was vital to the establishment of the future Jewish state. The British Jewish Brigade supplied canvas-covered military trucks and drivers. They could not actively smuggle people, so we took care of the rest, and that is where I fit in. Like many of my fellow KL-niks (ex-inmates), I felt the world belonged to me. We walked tall, no matter how broken and thin our bodies were. The Germans and their Axis partners, the Italians, the Austrians, and, for that matter, the whole world, owed us a lot. Yes, they did. With this attitude, I was emboldened to be a front man for the people-moving operation.

UNRRA was useful, too. Those who were registered received rations, food, and clothing or even money, depending on where they stayed. If you lived in a city on your own, instead of living communally in a DP camp, you could get money to purchase your own necessities. I recommended this path to those on their way to Palestine because it gave them the most flexibility. UNRRA workers were everywhere and worked hard to help former inmates.

Our first transports passed through checkpoints with hardly any scrutiny. The Brigade-supplied military trucks seemed "official." We would drop our charges in Bolzano and hand them to those who continued south with them.

Then we returned to Salzburg to get another group ready. On one return trip, on the Austrian side, we were driving slowly over a stretch of road that had been bombed out. Suddenly I noticed an SS sergeant from Mauthausen walking toward us. In my excitement, I shouted, "Get that Nazi bastard!"

The driver, a hardened combat soldier, took me literally, instantly swerved the truck, and ran over the Nazi. We did not stop, and we felt no remorse. No one else was around, and we drove back to Salzburg as if nothing had happened.

Once the borders were more tightly controlled, we gave up trucking people from country to country and walked them across the borders in the dark of night—risky and dangerous work. A truck carried us to a spot near our crossing point, where a guide would meet us and lead us over the mountainous terrain. On the other side, another truck would be waiting. After organizing a few of these crossings, the powers that be decided that I, as a *farbrenter* (fired up) Revisionist, should stay with the groups in Italy because other factions were "stealing" our members while they waited for further travel arrangements. We wanted as many people as possible in the Revisionist framework because we believed that only action would bring us statehood. We wanted as many young, able bodies as we could get into the *Irgun*. Soon I became one of the few people in charge of the *Irgun*'s *Brihah* in Italy.

Transferring the groups farther south was challenging because many railroad tracks were bombed out, and it could take days to travel a few hundred miles. The trains were packed with Italians returning home, ex-soldiers, POWs, and former concentration and labor camp inmates. The trains were so crowded that people rode on the roofs, hung from the steps, or clung to the outside car handles. We made sure we kept heading south, even if it was just a station or two at a time. In the beginning the rides were free, but when the crowds thinned out, and conductors could make their way through the cars, they asked for "tickets, please." We were traveling in groups of 50 to 60 people and occupied two cars. None of us had tickets, so we watched for the conductors. When I was alerted that one was approaching, I would pretend to sleep. My "bodyguards" would not let the man wake me. "The commander is sleeping," they would say.

Once, the conductor noticed I was awake and asked for tickets. I looked in my pockets, pretending to search, and came across my identification card from *Betar*, printed in Hebrew and with the picture of Jabotinsky on it. When I showed it to the conductor, the man took the card, turned it in all directions, and tried to decipher it in front of the passengers. Then he returned it to me. "Many thanks," he said with a smile. Happily, I no longer needed to feign sleep, and my people did organizational work instead of watching for conductors.

I was convinced that I was acting in a national cause during revolutionary times and that my behavior was appropriate, because we felt that the world owed us, and anyone associated with Axis forces, as the Italians were, owed us even more. Half an hour later, the conductor returned and humbly inquired, "Excuse me, *Signore*. I know the traveling ticket is valid, but who is the person in the picture?" Without a moment's hesitation, feigning exasperation, I answered, "That is President Truman." The conductor apologized and promised not to bother me again. We were wild, we took risks, and we did not let anything stand in our way.

At last, in October 1945, it was my turn to go to Palestine. My friends and I had already boarded the British ship HMS *Princess Kepley* and were waiting to sail from Bari when I received an order from the *Irgun* to disembark and continue my work in Italy. I was to bring another group south because I was experienced, spoke several languages, and knew the routes. I was torn. My heart yearned for Palestine. I was sick of being on soil soaked with Jewish blood. My mind told me to go along with the *Irgun* request and to wait, hoping that my parents would be among the transportees headed south from Poland. I wrote several poems in Hebrew at the time that reflected my feelings. Here is a rough English translation of one of them:

> We should not be wasting our time,
> What can you find or see here?
> Soil fully planted with mass graves,
> Stop crying because no one will ever understand our misfortune.

Later, when I learned that Theodore Adorno, a philosopher, had said, "To write a poem after Auschwitz is barbaric," I took his dictum literally and stopped writing.

I made my way back up to Bolzano and brought a group to Modena, where we took over the Accademia Militare. The Italians were happy we didn't treat them like the Germans. Why didn't we treat them like the Germans? Perhaps because the Italians were not the same kind of murderers as the Germans.

As we traveled from Modena to Bari, we stopped several times at various locations to register with UNRRA under different names. No wonder, then, that UNRRA officials thought more people survived the Holocaust than actually did. We needed food and money to go to Palestine, and UNRRA arranged for us to have access to several large villas in different areas along the route. We organized them into transit camps in and around Bari, Taranto, Foggia, Lecce, Nardo, Santa Croce, Santa Catarina, and Santa Maria di Leuca, among others.

Because of the British immigration policy at the time, some of the transit camps became more like DP camps. Bevin's White Paper of 1939 reinterpreted Britain's Mandate for Palestine to restrict Jewish immigration to 75,000 Jews between 1939 and 1944. Now, after the war, the British still refused to let up on their restrictive policy. When I was 18, I escorted a group and ended up with fewer than the requisite number of certificates. I could not do what I had done back in Plaszow—adding a zero to a one on a soup coupon to make it into a ten-soup coupon. I had to take my disappointed charges back to DP camps, where they were held until the next opportunity to reach the Promised Land arrived.

On my many trips through Italy, I would ask refugees, especially those from Eastern Europe, if they had heard anything about my family. After a while, I found my uncles, Chaim Platkiewicz and Shloyme Freiman. Chaim was Mother's brother, and Shloyme was Mother's brother-in-law. They joined Uncle David and me in Santa Croce. Before the war, all three uncles had belonged to *Brit Chayal* (Soldier's Covenant), a branch of the Jabotinsky Revisionist movement, and their children were in *Betar* (*Brit Yosef Trumpeldor*). I remember their pictures—particularly one of Lolek—in their *Betar* uniforms.

The uncles and I spent a few weeks together, until we had a major disagreement. Uncle Chaim said to Uncle Shloyme, "When the child dies, there is no need for a guardian anymore." Chaim was referring to Esther, Uncle Shloyme's wife, who had not survived the Holocaust. The point being made was that, consequently, the uncles were no longer related.

I found this statement offensive and punched Uncle Chaim. "If a guardian is not needed anymore, then it is also finished between you and me," I said before I left with Uncle Shloyme, a fine, gentle person. Uncle Shloyme, who was single, was able to leave for Palestine soon thereafter. He met a fine woman in Jerusalem and married her, and they went on to have three children. Uncle Chaim and Uncle David met their wives in the DP camps and were married in Italy. As a result, the British stopped them from immigrating, and they were forced to stay in Italy for two and a half more years. When the *Irgun sheliah* attached to the Santa Croce DP camp was exposed to the British, he was forced to leave, and Uncle David took his place.

Eventually David and his wife left for Palestine on one of the secret transports, but they were intercepted by the British and held in a detention camp in Cyprus for nine months. They did finally get to the *Yishuv*, but between 1946 and February 1948, the British intercepted 47 shiploads of immigrants and interned 65,307 people, most of them Holocaust survivors, in detention camps. Once in the *Yishuv*, David and Shloyme fought in the War of Independence. Shloyme also fought in the Sinai Campaign in 1956. All three of my uncles raised their families in Israel and died there.

The first time I traveled in Italy, I was with a *sheliah* who knew the country well and took us to see the sights while we waited, sometimes days, for train connections. Later, when I took groups through Italy, I did the same. It was more interesting to go sightseeing than it was to hang around a crowded train station. We looked at the Leaning Tower of Pisa near Livorno, the Duomo in Florence, and the museums in Bologna. In Rome, I pointed out the triumphal Arch of Titus with its carving of the menorah and other spoils from the Temple in Jerusalem being carried in a victory march in ancient Rome. We visited the catacombs of Rome, and I tried to explain the significance of what we were seeing in terms of Jewish history.

One Sunday morning, I escorted 18 people to the Vatican. The Italians were dressed in their Sunday best, and thousands were assembled, waiting their turn to pass the Pope and receive his blessing. The Chief Pastor of the Catholic Church was seated on a throne. As each person reached him, he knelt, kissed the Pope's ring, and then moved on to give the next person in line a turn.

As I stood there with my group, discussing Zionism as a way to fulfill Judaism, I became uncomfortable looking at His Holiness. Here I was, Gerer upbringing and all, in front of Roman Catholicism's world leader, amid a motley group of people who were badly groomed, unshaven, in need of washing, wearing poorly fitting threadbare clothes, and burdened by large knapsacks. When my turn came to greet the Holy Father, he nodded, signaling me to speak. I announced in Italian, "We are Jews on our way to the Holy Land." We did not kneel or kiss his ring, and the Pope understood. He answered in Hebrew, "May God bless you."

People around us wondered who we were. "Are they messengers of God? Are they the Apostles? What kind of emissaries has the Pope thought to honor, holding up the throngs to speak with them?"

After we left the Audience Hall, crowds surrounded us, tried to touch us, and even offered money that we refused to accept. We explained we were *Ebrei* who had been through the fires of Hell and were now on our way to Palestine. With tears in their eyes, they wished us well.

The time spent in Italy was not all work; there was plenty of play, too. Those of us whose youth had been stolen by the Nazis were intent on making up for lost years. Despite what we had been through, many of us were still able to have a good time. There were many young, orphaned older teenagers like myself. We formed social groups where boys met girls. At one point I was in Santa Croce for several weeks, and in addition to discussing the practical and ideological aspects of our work, taking Hebrew enrichment lessons, and exercising, we were taught to dance.

The girl who was my partner taught me how to hold her and how to move. Later, I understood what she meant with these lessons. I was naive, or perhaps I did not want to understand. When those "certain" feelings stirred in me and I had gone to Father back in Plaszow for advice, he told me to "think about your mother, worry about where she is, and you will get rid of these thoughts." I was taught to believe in mind over matter. Nevertheless, "certain" matters did prevail on occasion.

Not far from Santa Croce, there were fig-tree orchards and orange groves. I would jump a stone fence, pick some fruit, and a tall, beautiful Italian girl would chase me, but I never let her catch me. Once, I looked back, saw her gorgeous face, and decided to slow down. When she caught me, she hit me hard with both hands, but I could not stop laughing. She asked why I was picking her family's figs and oranges, and I promised to stop if she would sit with me and talk. She did, and a romance developed.

This southern Italian girl, Julia, was a good, warm-hearted person who invited me to her grandparents' summerhouse, where she spent her vacations. My Italian was pretty good by then, so I was able to converse fairly fluently.

The family, of course, asked about my intentions for Julia, and I explained that I was Jewish. *"Io sono Ebreo,"* I said, "and since Julia is Catholic, marriage would not work." Hearing that I was *"Ebreo,"* the family was willing to compromise and accept me. Julia's eyes filled with tears of joy. But I was getting in deeper by the minute, so I told them I was being transferred and would be leaving for Palestine shortly. Julia was heartbroken and started to cry. I felt bad hurting this warm, beautiful person, but what could I do? I had had no experience with relationships, and I had no real concept of my effect on another person. It was unfortunate that learning this lesson came at her expense. As I left, Julia hit me, but the blows felt like kisses. The Almighty had created her a very gentle soul.

DERAILED

As I was doing my usual routine in the *kibbutz* (collective farm) at Santa Croce one morning, I saw my brother Willie, walking toward one of the buildings. I could not believe my eyes. "Willie, is that you? Is this a dream?" I shouted. As soon as I got closer, I asked, "Have you heard anything about Father and Mother?"

After the first moments of a joyous reunion filled with hugs and tears, we both started crying when my questions about our folks met with deadly silence. I could not face the truth. I still hoped that someday I would find my parents and that we would all be together again. Willie told me that Avrum and Chaim-Leizer were in southern Germany, in Feldafing, and that he had come to find me so that we could be reunited. I listened to the words that came from his heart, but the idea of living in the former Nazi state filled me with revulsion.

"Willie, you cannot be serious," I objected. "Do not go back to Germany. Come with me to Palestine," I said. "I am determined to move on to Palestine." Willie insisted that our first duty was to reunite the family, and I insisted that we should go to Palestine where our brothers could eventually join us. I sensed that Willie was not convinced and that, in his exasperation, he would leave and go back to Germany, and I would not even know it. Because Willie was not officially at Santa Croce, he shared my bed for the night. After Willie fell asleep, I tied one of his legs to mine so that his slightest stirring would alert me, then I fell asleep. At about 3:30 in the morning, Willie got up to leave, and his movement pulled on my leg and woke me.

"Where are you going?" I asked. That day started early for both of us, with more arguments, as each of us tried to persuade the other. Finally, we agreed to go north temporarily. Before we left, I rid myself of accumulated things that I did not need and went to the flea market in Lecce to sell three pairs of shoes that did not fit me, six shirts that were too small or too large, two blankets, and other such items and made 60,000 lire. At that time, 600 lire were worth one U.S. dollar. When I came back, Willie and I packed my few things into a valise. (Now we were traveling in style, not with knapsacks!) We stopped at UNRRA so I could collect my money.

It took a few days for us to get to Munich. Then from Starnberger Bahnhof, we took the train to the DP camp in Feldafing, a former German military complex that stretched for blocks. General Eisenhower had visited the concentration camps and had seen what the Germans had done to the innocent Jews. When he came to Feldafing and saw how overcrowded it was, he ordered the Germans to vacate large dwellings in the vicinity and turn them over to displaced persons. Chaim-Leizer, his wife Rose (he met her in Czenstochowa and had married her right away), Art, and Willie were privileged to share one of those vacated premises—a three-story house called the Villa Buda. Other families at the villa were the Markowitzes (a family of eight), the Borenkrauts (five members), and the Kashmars (Amadeo, a Greek Jew, and his non-Jewish, Polish wife).

We spent hours sharing our experiences. Tears of joy and pain mingled freely. I handed over 40 U.S. dollars to Art for safekeeping. He put them in the table stand together with my other brothers' currency. Willie and Chaim told me about going back to Dzialoszyce to find family. All they found was hate. The same hate that was there before the war had survived the war and was as strong as ever. One of Willie's ex-schoolmates actually kicked him and said, "Jew! Why are you still alive?" The Poles moved in and plundered as soon as the Jews were expelled—often before the Germans had a chance to loot. The father of my friend Tzvi Piekarz (who took the name Topaz when he came to Israel) was among those murdered in a Polish pogrom after the war. The Poles were worried the Jews might come back to reclaim their stolen property. Novakova, the wife of a Polish landed nobleman, sheltered Chaim-Leizer and Rose and gave Rose my Mother's monogrammed linens that had been entrusted to her. My brothers retrieved some of the hidden money and a few possessions of sentimental value, but they did not find any family. They feared for their lives, left Poland quickly, and never went back.

How disturbing that the Holocaust is, these days, a tourist industry in Poland, a country where a good many citizens remain antisemites.

KADDISH

I was not yet prepared to accept my parents' death without an extensive investigation. My brothers, however, simply accepted their deaths as reality. I went to Germany because I had not yet given up hope of finding one or both of them. I began looking for people who knew Father and were in Plaszow at Jerozolimska when the Germans started liquidating the camp. Several survivors told me the same sad news.

The first person I asked was Shye Markin-Bleicher. We had worked on the roofs at Plaszow, and he knew my father well. He and Father were in the same transport to Mauthausen and then to a subcamp in Gusen. (Gusen I and Gusen II were separate satellite camps from Mauthausen.) The transport to Gusen I consisted of about 300 people. The Germans disinfected most of them by telling the prisoners to enter the bath, undress, and take showers. Then they were led, wet and naked, to the *Appellplatz* and forced to stand in freezing temperatures in the middle of January in the Austrian Alps. The SS poured cold water on the inmates, who literally froze to death. Shye witnessed this atrocity from elsewhere on the *Appellplatz*. Among the victims was *shoykhet* Leibish Lubelski from Dzialoszyce, a good friend to my father and the Gerer Hasidim.

When I heard that the inmates were deliberately frozen to death, I still did not want to believe it. I continued searching for more witnesses to Father's fate. I heard the same account from Luser Wolfowitz's son Yossel, who had seen the same thing. Luser, the biggest hat dealer in Dzialoszyce, used to visit our store before the war. He told me how capable Mother was and what a hard-working businesswoman she had been.

Other witnesses were Cantor Martin Rosenblum (the son of *"schwartzen Yoyl"*), who had played soccer with me at the Stawisko when we were children, and Hershel Epstein, son of one of the rabbis. They both told me the same unbelievable story about Father and the other *kedoshim* (holy martyrs). It is hard for me to describe the picture that was drawn for me. A group of men in their 50s and 60s were left standing without their clothing or *talisim* or *tefillin*, and they asked the Almighty to end their suffering quickly.

We, the children of Tuviah Zysman, decided that the date of our Father's *yahrzeit* (memorial day for a death) would be the fifth day of *Shevat*, the same date as the *yahrzeit* of the *Sfat Emet*, the great Gerer leader, because that date corresponded approximately to the date of Father's death, and because Father would have been pleased to have this association with the Gerer Rebbe. The words *sfat emet* mean "language of truth," but the truth was that Father was no longer alive and had been put to death in a brutal, cruel, and merciless way that was very hard for me to accept. In the beginning, I refused to say *kaddish*. I could not bring myself to praise the Almighty because in my heart I wanted Father to be alive. Then there was the question why. Multiply that simple one-word question six million times: Why and why and why and why?

This part of my story is being written on the very eve of my father's *yahrzeit* as a kind of *kaddish*. This evening I will go to *shul* and say *Kaddish leylui nishmato*, for the elevation of Father's soul. Tomorrow is the fifth day of *Shevat*, yet tomorrow and every tomorrow of my life, I am going to pray, bless, glorify and exalt, adore and honor, extol and laud the name of the Almighty for what He did. I have to light a candle, a light for someone whose light within me was never extinguished. I have to keep that candle burning throughout my life, in me and in my children and grandchildren.

I had even more difficulty coming to grips with Mother's death. I have never been able to get any information about where and how she perished. Was it at Belzec or Treblinka? Where was she taken? What monstrous place devoured her? All sorts of rumors circulated, but who really knew? I did not really want to know. By not knowing, I could keep searching and wondering.

Nevertheless, I wanted to commemorate the loss of both my parents, so I ordered small slabs of white marble and spent time engraving in Hebrew the following inscription:

> In everlasting memory of our dear father, Tuviah Zysman, son of Eliyahu and our dear mother, Chaya Gryna, daughter of Eliezer, who were murdered and butchered at the hands of the barbaric Germans, may their names be blotted out, on the fifth day of *Shevat*, 1944, and on the 24th day of *Elul,* 1942. May they rest in Eden, and may their memories be blessed.
> *Tav nun tsadik beit he.*

The final initials stand for the phrase: "May their souls be bound up with the living." I gave these memorials to my brothers and kept one for myself.

These marble slabs were the monuments that served in lieu of proper gravestones, because we had no idea where the remains of our parents lay. In all probability, they went up in smoke, like the sacrifices in the Forest Temple. And if sacrifices they were, then we would carry these marble slabs with us wherever we went, just as the children of Israel carried their altar in their wanderings. We set Father's date as described earlier and Mother's date to correspond to a week after the last time I saw her during the selection in Miechow.

In Mother's case, the date corresponded to the *yahrzeit* of the saintly Rabbi Israel Meyer Hakohen Kagan, whose major concern was guarding one's tongue from uttering evil. He was known as the Hafets Haym, from the verse penned by King David, "Who is the man who desires life, loves days, and sees goodness? Guard your tongue from evil and your lips from speaking falsehood; shun evil and do good; seek peace and pursue it."

This seemed appropriate for my soft-spoken Mother. These dates were our best estimates of the times of our parents' untimely exits from this world, when their souls went to Heaven for everlasting rest. Since then, we have always kept these days as their *yahrzeits*. When we, the four brothers, gathered and said *kaddish* on that first *yahrzeit* in Feldafing, no words came out, though we each knew the prayer by heart. We were too choked with emotion.

Whenever we were together during a *yahrzeit*, we talked about our parents and reminisced about how much they cared for our well-being and education. We talked about their charitable ways, their contribution to the Jewish community in Dzialoszyce, their devotion to religion and tradition. The question "Why?" always remained with us. That question is still alive and is becoming more persistent. It will remain with me forever.

GOING UNDERGROUND

In Feldafing I joined *Betar*, but after my work in Italy, *Irgun* leadership felt secure enough to recruit me. Even while I was in Italy, I suspected I was really working for the *Irgun*. I had minimum contact with one small cell of four or five men, though I imagined others in *Betar* belonged to other cells. Now I was given more responsibility.

My secret initiation ceremony took place in the spring of 1946, about a year after liberation. I was committed to the cause and had learned what was required of me. Late one night, I was led, blindfolded, for a kilometer through the woods to a dark, excavated place covered with branches. When the blindfold was removed, a spotlight was directed into my face so that I was not able to see those interrogating me. To my side, the glint of oiled steel shone off weapons lying on a crate. The scenario was designed to scare off the gutless. I stuck with it and swore an oath of loyalty. I promised not to divulge secrets and to be devoted to the ideals of the *Irgun*. After the ceremony, I was still not permitted to see who the people behind the lights were. Then and there, in the cool white light of the moon, I was given weapons training. Then, blindfolded again, I was led back to Feldafing—the fewer people who knew of an arms cache, the better.

Officially, I was still in *Betar*, leading discussions about Zionism, Jewish history, and the ideology of Vladimir Jabotinsky. I was once part of a panel talking to a group of about 60 people when a gentleman came and listened to our presentation. At the end the discussion, he asked me why I used certain Hebrew words instead of more familiar terms. I sprinkled my lectures with choice language to see if people were paying attention. When several *Betarim* asked me the meaning of some my expressions, I knew they were listening. The man smiled at my response and introduced himself as Reuven. When we knew each other better, he told me that he was also in the *Irgun*.

A few months later, I took a crash course on the philosophy of leadership and military training in Heidenheim, where Reuven was one of the chief instructors. The seminar was conducted in memory of David Raziel, fallen hero of the *Irgun*. When Menachem Begin was elected prime minister of Israel, his right-hand man and chief adviser was Reuven who, by that time, had reclaimed his real name—Yechiel Kadishai.

My mentor was Moshe Zilberberg, a knowledgeable person and marvelous speaker who could hold the interest of large audiences for hours. He and his wife, Shoshana, were wonderful, and I spent much time in their company, talking and listening. Both were professional educators, and I was fortunate they took an interest in me. I learned from them and still had a great deal to learn. Moshe wrote articles for Jewish newspapers in Feldafing and gave many passionate lectures on Zionism. Before the war, his brother was a leader of the Revisionist Party in Lublin. When they came looking for me one time because I had not shown up for days, they found me in my bed, sick. These good people ran home and brought me back some cure-all chicken soup.

But things were not always so simple in Feldafing. The president of the camp, David Borochowski, was a Communist. Despite his ideological leanings, he worked hard for the camp and did his best for all. He even organized a well-equipped print shop and issued a popular and widely circulated weekly Yiddish newspaper, *Die Freie Zeit* (The Free Times). When the British in Palestine confiscated all the printing presses of the underground that issued anti-British flyers and of the paper *Rak Kach*, we received their SOS. But Borochowski would never agree to part with his presses. For him, Jewish life in the Diaspora came before the birth of the state.

One night at 11 p.m., a few members of the *Irgun* entered the Communist print shop in the basement of Borochowski's Feldafing administrative offices. The camp police were housed on the second floor. We dismantled the press and filled about 15 burlap sacks with the parts and as much lead type as we could carry. As we removed the iron grates from one of the windows to get the heavy sacks out, one of the sacks fell and made a loud noise. Two camp policemen, hearing the commotion in their upstairs office, came out on the balcony to see what was happening. We called up to them, "Come down. We have nice girls here. You will have a good time." They both came down and we jumped them, tied them up, taped their eyes, and warned them not to make a sound. They complied because we were carrying weapons.

We planted a red herring by scattering nonessential type along the route to the train station. Then we headed to Lake Starnberg, loaded the sacks into waiting boats, and took them across the lake to a drop-off point. The goods reached their destination without further mishap. The next morning, I got up early and hung around with friends who did not belong to the *Irgun* and had no knowledge of my activities. Borochowski approached us and started screaming, "You *Betarim* stole the presses and the type from the print shop!" Ignorant of what had transpired during the night, my friends became indignant and were ready to hit him for being falsely accused in such a hostile manner. I defended myself by positing that if I had been awake all night, I would not be up so early in the morning and out on the street. The American military police were of little help in solving the mystery. They followed the telltale type to the station and fruitlessly posted a guard there for a week to see if anyone tried to load printing equipment on a train.

Our activities flipped back and forth between practical underground work and more (or less) overt political activity. Borochowski's good friend was Eliezer Zborowski, who was an intelligent, soft-spoken individual. He was the leader of *Ha-Shomer ha-Tsa'ir* (Young Guard), a left-oriented Zionist youth movement. Eliezer and I were at opposite poles politically; he pulled the young people to the left, and I pulled them to the right.

Eliezer and I did, however, have one thing in common; we liked the same girl, Pola Kreizer. Pola had beautiful, blue eyes, a pretty face, and she knew how to play her suitors one against the other. In the end, Pola preferred my friend Josef Klausner to me, but he liked someone else. In order to make a good impression on girls such as Pola and her friend Feigele Kaufman, a boy had to be properly dressed. I once borrowed Chaim-Leizer's salt-and-pepper tweed jacket and loaned it to Josef Klausner, who had a date with Pola. A few days later, I borrowed the jacket and Pola saw it on me. "Both you and your friend have the same jacket," she observed. "You two dress alike."

Then and there, I decided that I needed to get my own suit. I was starting to date and needed to care about my appearance. The clothes from the American Jewish Joint Distribution Committee (AJDC) were not very appealing, but the clothes I did have were worn out from my underground activities and from the beating they took from my other pastime—motorcycle racing on a dirt track.

I went to Art and explained that I needed a suit to wear when I went out to attend meetings and to make a good impression on girls. Art decided I did not need one because I was the youngest, and he suggested that we continue doing what we had done at home before the war—leaving me with the hand-me-downs. It was hard enough to accept this as a child. As an adult, it was even harder to bear Art's attempt to infantilize me. I demanded the money that our parents had buried in Dzialoszyce, which he, Chaim, and Willie had retrieved after the war. Art resisted, and because I did not want to fight over money with him, all I took was the 40 U.S. dollars I had given him for safekeeping when I arrived from Italy. That money allowed me to buy my first new suit ever.

I was amazed that we had just lived through the most life-altering experience imaginable, and yet we had carried through it, untouched, a pattern of relationships that had existed in our home from as early as I can remember. I have to admit that this infantile regression was my fault whenever I behaved as the pesky youngest brother. I was very interested in filling in the educational and cultural gaps created by the war, so I saved money for a violin and took music lessons. We shared a single room at Villa Buda, and when I practiced, it drove my brothers crazy. Willie was especially disturbed because he was a DP policeman who worked the night shift and slept during the day.

Beginner's violin practice is not conducive to sleep. One day when Willie was totally exhausted and my squeaking was too much for him to take, he got out of his bed, grabbed the violin out of my hands, and smashed it to pieces. I responded to his outburst with my own and scratched his face. I profoundly regret my behavior to this day and now apologize to Willie again, first for being inconsiderate and then for physically hurting him.

In Willie's case I felt especially guilty because I was beholden to him; all of us were. Willie was the first one selected for hard labor and consequently spent more time than any of us in labor and concentration camps. Because he learned the ropes before we arrived, he helped all of us adjust. Though we knew that no one in our family was to blame for what happened to Willie, the fact that he suffered longer than we did pained us all.

Eliezer Zborowski competed with me for recruits and women. He also had political aspirations, and he ran in the elections for president of the DP camp at Feldafing, which was not good for *Betar*. It was against our rightist party's interest to have the left-oriented *Ha-Shomer ha-Tsa'ir* party win. To run for office, one had to be 21. When Zborowski applied to run for office, he misrepresented his date of birth to qualify. One of our sympathizers working in the camp office obtained Eliezer's original registration papers. We confronted him with the truth, forcing him to pull out of the race. He has come a long way from his leftist youth and is now an Orthodox Jew who works to support Yad Vashem and other forms of Holocaust remembrance.

I had enough of the DP camp at Feldafing and moved into a private, third-floor apartment at 11 Parkstrasse in Munich. To support myself, I dealt in currency and anything else. I bought jewelry from Germans and sold it to Jews, who bought it as a commodity. As busy as I was, I worked day and night for the future Jewish state and never accepted a single cent for the hard work and time that I devoted to Zionist organizations. When I later earned money from my business, I freely gave whenever funds were needed.

The Zionists were in a large apartment in a villa at 39 Petenkoverstrasse, which was where I worked. It was used as an office and gathering place for the Revisionists and *Betarim*. The *Wohnungsamt* (Housing Bureau) catered to the Jews under orders of the military government, and anyone who was a Nazi had no rights—and if they did, in fact, have any, they were too afraid to assert them. We had the Nazi occupants evicted and took over the ground and second floors of the villa. The artist Yankel Perkel, who could transform ideas into visual images, took months to paint Revisionist mottos and murals on the walls, including portraits of Zionist martyrs. (The paintings were so magnificent it was a pity they were not on canvas so that we could have taken them with us when we moved.)

The villa was used for meetings, drills, and lectures. I was in charge of calisthenics and gave physical instruction to people who, for the most part, were middle aged. I taught a scaled-down version of the *Irgun*'s drill—marching and other exercises to prepare them for what lay ahead.

Fundraising was important. We collected security tax and iron tax. Security tax aided the general population in Palestine, and both the left and the right supported it. Iron tax supported the *Irgun* and was shunned, for the most part, by the left. A person who paid one tax was not obligated to pay the other; the choice was left to the individual. This arrangement was not always honored. In the Foehrenwald DP camp, the chief of police repeatedly harassed members of the Revisionist Party for not paying security tax when they had already paid iron tax. When people in the camp complained, the local Revisionist representatives sent a delegation to Munich to complain to the *Irgun* leadership.

In Munich, we tried to resolve the problem peacefully, but alas, our efforts were to no avail. Four members of the *Irgun*, including me, went to Foehrenwald. I sent word to the chief of police asking for a meeting, without weapons, of course. We were to talk in the street and, if our discussion became protracted, we could continue our negotiations in his residence. The discussions did drag on, and as we walked to his house, he threatened me. I did not respond. After he unlocked the front door and we entered his home, he showed me his gun. I reminded him that we had an agreement that no weapons would be involved. He said he did not trust the *Irgun*. I asked if I could examine his pistol, but he would not part with it. I then called his attention to a fight taking place outside. As the man stood to look out the window, the closet door swung open, and one of my armed backup men stepped into the room.

"Freeze!" said my accomplice. I removed the bullets from the chief's gun, returned the weapon, and warned him that in case of further trouble, there were several other fellows with us, including one right outside his front door. The chief did not believe me, opened the door, and was confronted with a bear of a man who stood well over six feet. We went back inside, and I calmly explained that whoever raised a hand against a member or supporter of the *Irgun* was a traitor to the Jewish people and would be dealt with accordingly. We refused to tolerate any further harassment from the likes of him. I stood up to leave and said one word, *"Shalom."*

Afterward, we went back to his office and I returned the bullets that I had taken from his gun. The only other time I ever saw this man was at *Kinus Betar*, an international gathering I organized in Foehrenwald. Aaron Propes from the United States, Gideon Abramowicz from Palestine, and other important members attended. The police chief began to realize that there must be something to this movement, and he cooperated fully, making sure that order was maintained. All of what we did, the risks we took and the long hours we put in, came from the wellspring of our abiding belief in the justness of our cause.

HEADACHES

In the spring of 1946, I developed severe headaches. My head swelled until my eyes and ears were invisible. I went to the best neurosurgeon I could find, a German professor named Dr. Lepsche, whose clinic was on Bavariaring No. 40 in Munich. He and another prominent doctor examined me, took X-rays, and came to the conclusion that I needed emergency surgery because the remnants from the drill bit in my head had become infected. I did not want a German operating on me, even one as famous as Dr. Lepsche, so I was taken to the Jewish Hospital on Mühlbauerstrasse 15. Art, who lived in Munich, and Chaim and Willie, who were in Feldafing, came to see me. From their worried faces and tearful eyes, I inferred that the situation was more serious than I thought. Two other patients who had undergone skull surgery had not survived.

Drs. Peisachowicz and Kurzweil cut open my head, and the last of the drill bit lodged in my skull by the brutal Schultz in Mielec was removed. When the doctors came to examine me after surgery and touched my head, the pain was so excruciating that I screamed uncontrollably. Nurses helped the doctors hold me down because I was ready to jump out the window. After a few days, however, I felt better. Wolf Peisachowicz, the surgeon's brother, ran the facility, and I decided to help the hospital as a gesture of thanks. After I recovered, I brought food to the hospital once or twice a month. At the time, most commodities were rationed and hard to get. I brought cartons of butter and sugar for the patients, and consequently, I met interesting people—rabbis, cantors, and writers—some of them famous. I also got to know Max Deutschmeister, an amputee. Unfortunately, there were many cases like his.

When I regained my health, I went into business with Art, partially because I needed the money and partially to disguise my activities for the *Irgun*. I dealt in foreign currency, scrip issued to the American armed forces, and gold coins, but it was illegal to trade in currency at the time. I was doing very well and making a fine profit until the day the scrip suddenly became void.

Every dollar of scrip I had purchased for 80 to 82 cents was now worthless. I lost thousands of dollars; at the time, that was a lot of money. The military government recalled its currency more than once to restrain black-market activity, and any of us who were caught with the wrong currency at the wrong time suffered losses. Most of these transactions took place in Cafe Grünwald, located in the hotel of the same name not far from the Starnberger train station, at the side of the Grand Central station.

Despite being able to overcome physical and financial headaches, the one headache I found most difficult to bear was the emotional one caused by Art. There were occasional setbacks, but considering the times and circumstances, our business in Munich was profitable. Granted, some aspects of the job were difficult, but everything would have been bearable if we had both shared the burden. One part of the business involved traveling to Berlin with foreign currency hidden in the double soles of my shoes. The shoes were so heavily loaded that I could barely walk. On the way back, sacks full of money had to be carried between the American and Soviet zones of occupation.

Art and I agreed we would alternate these trips between us, but, when it was Art's turn, he suggested that we wait until the next trip to start alternating. I went along with his request; but when his turn came, he refused to go. I felt Art was taking advantage of me.

Later, I needed some money for a car. When I asked Art, who acted as banker for the two of us, for some cash, he answered that we did not have any. "What do you mean by that?" I asked. "Where is our profit?" "We have no profit," said Art. "As a matter of fact, all we have are losses." I knew that it was not true. Art's attitude affected me deeply, and I became physically ill from the hurt I felt. While in bed, I listed each transaction we had conducted and the profits we should have made.

I told Art that I would call him to an arbitration court, and the judge, Dr. Rivkind, would decide the case. A summons was sent to Art to appear and submit his list. There were some items on his list that I had forgotten, so I added them to my list. In reviewing Art's list, it became apparent that there were transactions he had conducted for his benefit alone. I, on the other hand, reported every single transaction I undertook and considered all of my activities to be on behalf of our joint enterprise. After the preliminary discovery, Art decided to settle rather than have the matter turn into a full-blown hearing. Though I did not get all that was owed to me, I decided not to push the matter. I felt that if the incident taught Art that he could not take advantage of me, our relationship would improve.

In the meantime, another brother was causing me heartache, if not a headache. Willie, who saw no future in Germany, was aware that our uncles had been intercepted by the British on their way to Palestine and were being held in Cypriot detention camps. He was registered for expedited immigration to a number of countries—Australia, New Zealand, Canada, and the United States. Before long, he was called to the Canadian consulate and then to the *Funkkaserne,* the transit camp. Willie packed and prepared for his departure. We all felt bad about the move because the four Tenenbaum brothers would be split up again, and Willie was not going to Palestine. That added an element of finality because both Art and I harbored Zionist dreams.

We were heavy of heart and angry at the same time, but we had no choice but to accept Willie's decision. The last time the four of us were together on Europe's blood-soaked soil was on December 16, 1947, the day we saw Willie off at the Munich railway station, when he began the first leg of his journey. We worried about him, especially after he wrote to tell us that he was working as a lumberjack in the winter wilderness of northern Ontario.

Most of Munich—and much of Germany for that matter—was in ruins. Around the corner from Cafe Grünwald on Marsstrasse No. 3 was a bombed-out little store owned and operated by a German couple named Reisinger. The woman was very kind and hid parcels for me, no matter what was in them. I reciprocated her kindnesses by giving her real coffee beans to replace the ersatz she was used to drinking. I also brought her chocolate and cigarettes as a reward for safeguarding my packages. Soon, I convinced the Reisingers to fix up their store and go into partnership with me, selling wholesale butter, sugar, canned foods, alcohol, and other products.

We sold most of the food to the DP camps, especially at Feldafing, where concentration camp victims wanted to supplement the rations they received and enrich their diets to compensate for years of starvation. I preferred to provide the scarce goods to survivors instead of selling to Germans, and I donated the better part of my profits to the hospital and Jewish organizations.

Hans Reisinger was a gentle soul and an intellectual. I spent hours discussing politics with him, and he told me how he got sucked into the war. He had been in the Wehrmacht, but not the SS, and showed me pictures taken of Jews during raids in Lithuania. Before the war, he had taught natural science and collected beetles. Many glass cases, holding hundreds of different species of dried bugs, were among his possessions. In time, a respectful relationship developed between us. Soon we opened a second store on Paul-Heiserstrasse No. 17 that specialized in liquors and wines. Our business was going well, and the Reisingers enjoyed the profits from selling the hard-to-find products I managed to supply.

This went on for some time until one evening, in the middle of a discussion, Hans turned to me and said, "Joseph, I cannot go on like this anymore. I can understand that you, as a Jew who suffered at the hands of the Nazis in labor camps, want revenge on the German people by diverting all the rationed food from them and supplying it to the DP camps. But I, as a German, cannot continue doing it. My conscience does not permit it."

I did not know if it was conscience or fear behind his declaration, but I responded, "How much did your German brothers do for you, Herr Reisinger? How did they protect you? They forced you into a mess that you wanted no part of. Why don't you look out for yourself?" I suggested that Art, whom the Reisingers knew well, buy a third of the business. With the Reisingers becoming minority shareholders, my brother and I would be legally responsible for the business, and Hans would not have to worry if the German authorities questioned him or if he was subjected to other types of pressure. I thought Art had learned his lesson in dealing with me, and I was willing to forgive and forget. I was concerned because the authorities were clamping down on the activities Art was involved in. (Even selling apples privately was considered dealing in the black market.) Those caught were denied the right to immigrate to their choice of countries. By joining an officially recognized business, Art would not face that risk. The Reisingers agreed to the deal and received a nice lump sum for the share they sold. I did not ask Art to be compensated for my part of the business; I simply expected him to carry his share of the workload. The business prospered, and for a while everything ran smoothly to the satisfaction of all concerned.

Even though my brother and I devoted much time to the business, I still worked vigorously for the *Irgun* and *Betar*, as he did for the Revisionist Party. We were very busy on all fronts. When elections came for president of Munich's Jewish community, Art and I both did our best to bring voters to the polling station. Mr. Schwimmer, the Revisionist candidate, won the race and became head of the Jewish community. Art was in charge of administering the distribution of clothing from the AJDC to the Jewish community. I tried to get whatever "special items" the *Irgun* required. For instance, we badly needed Hebrew typewriters and copy machines at one point. The postwar shortage of such equipment made it available only to official institutions. The *Irgun* was hardly official, so in order to get office equipment, I arranged to receive it through the auspices of a DP convalescent hospital in St. Pelten. Then I would pick it up and bring it back to Munich. I was constantly called on to find "alternative" solutions to daily problems.

One day, placards went up in Feldafing to announce that Golda Myerson was coming to give a seminar on "Zionism and Its Political Future." This put the *Irgun* on alert because we worried that her talk might defend Socialism. We did not protest because we expected to hear a mostly informative lecture about Palestine, Zionism, and the Jewish people. I mobilized all the *Betarim*, Revisionists, and party sympathizers to fill the hall. We briefed our people on how to react to the speech, if and when necessary, and I was chosen as spokesman for the evening. About ten minutes into the speech, Mrs. Myerson, who represented the Jewish Agency for Palestine, began discussing topics not mentioned on the posters nor mutually agreed on beforehand. She used the opportunity to express her own myopic political stance. Politely hinting that the address was off course, I asked, "Mrs. Myerson, is Zionism a political solution for the Jewish people in Palestine or a solution for the Socialist labor movement in the world?"

"In any event, it is not Fascism," she snapped back. I felt bad that I had to resort to raising my arm, signaling the *Betarim* behind me to start booing and shouting, "Why don't you answer the question?" The woman who later became prime minister of the Jewish state (Golda Meir) did not continue speaking that night, and I think we both learned a lesson from the incident. It could have been a wonderful evening, and perhaps a few more people might have made *aliyah* (immigrated to Israel) if we had allowed her to complete her talk.

Shuttling between Munich and Feldafing, whether by train or car, did not take too long. We always had work in both places. In Feldafing, we kept in touch with Commander Misha and *Betar* Commander Twerski about preparations for memorials, lectures, and eventual *aliyah*. In Munich, on Maria-Theresienstrasse 11, people who ran the office and party included Mordechai Cederbaum, secretary of the Revisionist Party; Mottel Karnowski, co-publisher of the newspaper; Motek Sandberg, a writer for the paper and party worker; and Eliezer Blankenfeld, head of the youth section. These men worked for the Revisionist movement throughout Germany, and we were devoted to the ideology of Jabotinsky and the liberation of Palestine.

Once, a delegation from Feldafing contacted me in Munich because a conflict had developed between members of the Revisionist Party. Herbert Volpert was running for election against Meyer Gawronski, and the two were killing each other in heated competition. Volpert had engaged Moshe Halperin to be his spokesman for that speech. Halperin, who was editor of the newspaper *Unzer Velt* (Our World), had connections to UNRRA and was an excellent orator. Volpert might win because of Halperin's backing, but that might lead to disaster within the organization because of his newness to the party and his dispassionate Germanic approach. It felt like civil war. I knew that Gawronski was "one of us" in his approach. He was born in Lithuania and was a *farbrenter* who was passionately staunch in his support of the *Irgun* and the Revisionist Party as well as an intellectual.

Initially, I declined to get involved between brothers in arms, especially since Volpert was dating a good friend of mine, Lola Markowitz, whose family lived on the ground floor of Villa Buda. Prodded to at least research the issue, I went to Feldafing. After I spoke with a few people, Moshe Zilberberg among them, I decided that, personal connections to Volpert notwithstanding, it would be in the best interests of the movement if I helped Gawronski. The powers that be wanted me to speak on his behalf. It did cross my mind that pitting my informally educated self against a professional orator like Moshe Halperin was like a confrontation between David and Goliath—with me, of course, in the diminutive role.

I returned to Feldafing the day before the elections. I sized up the hall and spoke to my people about organizing a last-minute campaign for Gawronski. The following evening, an hour before the voting was to start, Moshe Halperin appeared. The hall was almost full. I knew it would be unwise to engage this man in a debate I might lose. If he spoke before I did, the outcome would be bad. I *had* to speak first! The chairman of the election committee introduced me and informed the crowd that I would speak on Gawronski's behalf.

On wobbly legs, I walked to the head table and announced at the microphone that I did not come to speak for Gawronski. I was there to help choose the right man, the one who could represent the Revisionist Party with conviction, the man who was devoted to our organization.

"The Talmud teaches that for ten generations one should not remind a convert of his ancestry (*Sanhedrin* 94A) because we, too, were strangers in the land of Egypt. At the same time, we should not make a *Maharal* [Rabbi Judah, the great leader of Prague in the 16th century] out of a recent convert. Herbert Volpert used to be a Communist." I held up photographs of Volpert marching in a parade with the red flag in his hand. "We welcome Volpert and appreciate his joining our party. We embrace him. He is a valuable addition, but making him president would not be the right thing to do. Furthermore, if South Africa were to become Israel and Johannesburg, Jerusalem, I would vote for Mr. Volpert because he requested and received a visa to go to South Africa. How can he represent us unless we seek to make our homeland in South Africa?"

Moshe Halperin was one of the first to shake my hand and congratulate me. He told his people that, unless they could prove me wrong, he would not speak. A few days later on the Möhlstrasse in Munich, the street on which the Jewish community center was located, I met Halperin again. He told me a story about Rabbi Yochanan and Reish Lakish. Halperin said, "*Tanya demsayeh lah*" ("A *braita* [uncodified Mishnaic source] has been taught that supports you.") (*Bava Metzia* 84:1). It was Halperin's very elegant way of saying that he agreed with me.

As we were walking, a Jewish stranger came up to us and asked for the location of the Hebrew Immigrant Aid Society (HAIS). I asked him to follow us, since we were going in that direction. At one point, Halperin noted that we had just passed the HIAS building. I politely suggested to Halperin that he please be still and bear with me. We traversed the full length of Möhlstrasse until we came to Maria-Theresienstrasse and turned left. We passed a few villas and then arrived at one with a large sign in front that read: "Jewish Agency for Palestine." I pointed to the sign and said to the man, "Here is the *Jewish* HIAS."

Moshe started laughing. The man looked at us quizzically, and I began explaining the importance of going to Palestine. In the meantime, Moshe went to the *Centrale*, headquarters of the Revisionist Party at Maria-Theresienstrasse 11, where he edited the party newspaper. An hour later, I showed him the stranger's registration to go to Palestine, the fruit of the time I had spent with the man. Moshe was sitting at his desk, his glasses perched on his forehead. "Erez," he said, using my *Irgun* code name, "only you could do this."

I answered, "Moshe, it was your doing. Your talk inspired me to act this way."

At that time, I knew Moshe primarily from his newspaper articles, lectures, and speeches. He was a logical, determined person who held strong convictions and was solid in his ideology. Among his accomplishments were many books he wrote on education. He also served in the Jewish Brigade and told me the story of how he met his wife, Pesia, while delivering a speech at the DP camp in Bergen-Belsen. The hall had been packed, and Pesia, one of the *Betarim* in uniform, was holding the Jewish flag. Impressed by the lecture, Pesia walked over to him and praised his words. Moshe responded with a proposal, "Would you like to be my wife?"

"Yes!" she immediately answered. Pesia and Moshe made a wonderful, happy couple, fulfilling and complementing one another. They shared a deep devotion to each other and to the creation of a Jewish homeland.

Between the time devoted to the cause and our business, there was little time for anything else. Still, I managed to squeeze some study time into my schedule because I felt an intense need to further my education. Although I resisted my studies as a youngster, as I matured I began to recognize the importance of learning. As one reads the great authors, one gains insight to their minds and invites their wisdom into one's personal world.

Father had instilled this appreciation of learning deep in my psyche, and it surfaced when it was too late for him to see that his hard work bore fruit. I hired professors from the University of Munich to tutor me at home. Most of them asked about the framed photographs of Jabotinsky, Shlomo ben Yosef, Dov Gruner, and other Zionist heroes hanging on the walls of my apartment. Telling my professors about these Jewish giants was a job in itself! I do not know whether the German teachers liked my political philosophy, but when I gave them butter, sugar, and coffee beans, they kept coming back for more.

Friends also played a role in my informal education. Moshe Zilberberg, about 15 years older than I, inspired me greatly. He finished his formal education before the war, worked hard at maintaining it, and transmitted his vast knowledge to others. He made this transmission of knowledge his career and pursued it with pleasure. The recipients of his wisdom always wanted more because spending time with Zilberberg was uplifting. His beautiful wife, a gentle woman, was also highly educated, and while he was energetic and spontaneous, she was calm and thoughtful. They made a lovely couple, working together, each playing off the other in a kind of educational tag team.

Another good friend and mentor at that time in my life was Levi Shalitan (later Shalit). Whenever he spoke, his words became visual images. Levi was a dreamer, a poet who let his imagination soar. Despite his artistic proclivities, he was a doer who would not sit idle. His powerful, expressive personality was reflected in his deeds as a member of the Central Committee and as a writer for *Darkheynu—Unzer Veg* (Our Way). Shalitan tried to convey the message of the *churban* (a Hebrew word referring to the destruction of the Temples that also came to refer to the Holocaust). His first book, *Azoi Zenen Mir Gestorben* (This Is the Way We Died), was published in 1946 in Munich. Levi and I first met at a literary evening in the Cafe Bristol, where he gave a reading and discussed chapters of his book. It was the first of many volumes he was to write. Another inspiring person in my milieu was Chaim Lazar, whom I met during *Kinus Betar* (the *Betar* Convention). Chaim had lost his hand fighting with the partisans during the war and worked for the *Irgun* and *Betar*.

Palestine was the central theme that united us. Getting there and establishing a Jewish state was our main goal. Yet disputes broke out over political control, resource allocation, and the modus operandi—even among those who shared the same Revisionist ideology. Gideon Abramowicz, better known as Baruch Giladi, was the Governor of *Betar* in Germany. One evening in the Petenkoverstrasse Hall, during a meeting of the top brass of the *Irgun* and *Betar* in Germany, a fiery argument broke out between the two closely-knit factions. Both groups issued contradicting directives, effectively paralyzing the "troops." The dispute culminated in screaming and fighting. Eli Blankenfeld, head of *Betar*, began to weep and questioned what was happening to us. It was unbelievable that such a thing could occur between brothers. We swore loyalty to both the *Irgun* and *Betar*, and here we were, stymied by our own infighting.

Overwhelmed by tension added to an already excessive workload, I decided to go to a well-known ski resort in Bavaria, Garmisch-Partenkirchen, for a few days of rest. A *Betari* named Mordechai Goldberg lived in Garmisch. I visited with him and asked if he would like to go skiing and climb the Zugspitze (the highest mountain in Germany) with me.

Goldberg answered, "I have lived in Garmisch for some time but have never been to the Zugspitze. You came only yesterday, and already you want to go to the top of the mountain? We have more important work to do, especially since you are here. We could use some help."

That was my fate. I could not get away from Revisionist work. Goldberg introduced me to other members, and together we laid out strategic plans for the organization and its educational mission.

As statehood became more imminent, the internecine fighting diminished. On May 14, 1948, David Ben-Gurion declared the State of Israel. On May 15, I was in Garmisch again to attend a celebratory gathering in a packed hall. Mr. Spector, the president of the Revisionist chapter in Garmisch, introduced Rabbi Leibish Borenstein, the rabbi of Garmisch, and when he finished his talk, I was called on to speak. I was not dressed properly, in my shorts and a short-sleeved shirt, and I was totally unprepared, having had no idea I would be asked to speak. Still, I could not refuse because of the importance of the day, so I approached the podium and said, "The Torah says of the people of Israel, '*V'ayisu v'ayachanu*' (they moved and they rested). Once upon a time, we were wanderers. Today, we have finally become an independent nation. '*V'ayachanu*'—we rest, we stay put. We are not going anywhere, anymore."

I continued to speak about nationhood and its principles and ended with a parable of appreciation for the *Irgun*. "On this day, we must wonder what forces brought us to the position of statehood." I cited a story that I had heard from Rabbi Bernstein, the head of *Brit Yeshurun*, the religious faction of the Revisionist Party.

The story was about a boat caught in an ocean storm amid treacherous waves. The sailors and captain became frightened and started to jump ship. On the lower deck, a few bare-chested men were busy shoveling coal into the furnaces and did not give up, despite warnings to save their lives. Finally and miraculously, the boat reached the port. Who was responsible for bringing the boat to shore? Rabbi Bernstein pointed to the unseen people below, the people in the underground who did not abandon their positions. They did not let the furnaces cool. The people in the *Irgun* kept shoveling coal and brought us to the shore of our dreams. We now have an independent State of Israel.

I do not know if it was what I said or if it was the emotion attached to the day, but I never again received applause of the kind that followed that speech I made on the day after the State of Israel was declared.

LIFE IN MUNICH

While the creation of the State of Israel was a celebration of import to the Jewish people at large, our family had its own little celebration. About one month after the declaration of independence, Rose gave birth to a boy and my brother Chaim held our family's first postwar *bris* (rite of circumcision). The *bris* was conducted at Villa Buda in Feldafing by Mr. Hoffman, who would years later and on another continent, conduct the *britot* of my sons. (That first nephew is now a respected teaching physician at the University of Toronto Faculty of Medicine.) The reaffirmation of life was wrought with emotion and, like so many of our postwar experiences, was bittersweet. Soon after the *bris*, Willie succeeded in getting immigration papers to Canada for Chaim's family. Willie, ever the pioneer, left the lumber camp and went to work as a presser in Toronto. He scraped together the funds to bring them over, and soon, they too were gone. I, in the meantime, went about creating my own life-affirming experiences.

In the *Irgun*, one of the guiding principles was to be "one who sees but is not seen" while effecting an "event that happened." That principle applied equally to certain aspects of our social lives. In Germany, it was common for Jewish men to date non-Jewish girls, but I was never seen in public with one—not in a restaurant, not in a theater, not in an opera house (I acquired a taste for opera at La Scala in Milano), nor in a sports arena. On my commute on streetcar no. 19, I frequently saw a beautiful, shapely brunette who got off at the same station as I did. One day I walked up to her and asked her name. Pauline refused a number of my invitations but finally agreed to have coffee with me. Gradually, we developed a relationship, and we talked about everything, though I knew the friendship had no future because she was German. In time, I told her we had to break up, and I never saw her again, not even on the streetcar. I thought that she might have moved away because of me.

The night the *Irgun* and *Betar* executives confronted each other, Pauline followed me without my knowledge. She waited on a dark street and trailed me through the fields from Petenkoverstrasse to Parkstrasse. When I got close to home, Pauline jumped out of the shadows and, with a happy smile, embraced me. "Joseph, I love you," she said. I could not reciprocate.

The next day, Gideon Abramowitz teased me, "Erez, she was not bad looking. As a matter of fact, she had a beautiful figure, but I could not see her face in the dark."

I could no longer say I was "one who sees but is not seen"; I had been seen with Pauline. It was enough to convince me that I had to be more careful—at least until the next opportunity.

Moshe Turkentaub (or Turek, as he was later called) was born in Stopnice, Poland, the same town as Rose, my brother Chaim's wife. He came from a good family and was always considered a smart and capable young man. During the war, he survived on Aryan papers and lived in Austria; at one time, he even impersonated a German officer. After the war, Moshe studied at university, received a degree in dentistry, and achieved great success.

He once approached me on Möhlstrasse near the community center and asked me to join him in a prank. He pointed to two beautiful young women who looked like models standing with a short man. When I asked Moshe if he knew who the man was, he identified him as Yagdele (which means berry). I still do not know this individual's real name, but I knew back then that the entire Jewish community of Munich was afraid of him. Yagdele was a Mafioso type who extorted protection money. Turek suggested we lure the two women away from him, a scheme that seemed dangerous, but the women were tantalizing enough for me to agree.

I went to Mandelbaum's Restaurant on Möhlstrasse—better known as "The Barracks" because it was housed in a long industrial shed. The place was a bourse of sorts, and one could obtain almost anything on the black market there. I bought some nylon stockings at nine dollars for three pairs. Nylons were a novelty in those days, especially in Germany, and they were in great demand by females of any age. I went back to Moshe and asked, "If I manage to get the women away from Yagdele, what will you do next? I cannot be seen walking on the street with these women in broad daylight."

Moshe answered, "Joseph, do not worry. I will take them to my place. I have a beautiful apartment." I walked over to the women, excused myself, and asked if they would be interested in buying nylon stockings at 50 cents a pair. Of course, they were interested and paid me $1.50 for the stockings. The girls thanked me and then followed me, explaining that they would like to purchase more stockings at that price. "Right now I am sold out, but my friend has more," I said, pointing to Moshe. The women spoke to Moshe for a few minutes, and then they entered the front compartment of a two-sectioned bus. I got into the rear compartment and watched the front to ensure that when the women got off, I also got off at the right stop. Then I followed them, unseen, to Moshe's apartment, near the English garden on Kurfürstenstrasse.

When we were all inside the apartment, we talked, had a few drinks, and listened to music. After a while, Moshe took one of the girls into his bedroom, and I remained in the living room with the nicer one. (With two girls, there is always a nicer one.) We talked and had a good time. After a couple of hours, Moshe came out of the bedroom alone and said to me, "Joseph, it's no good. It's a *Yom Tov*" (literally "holiday," but he meant "time of month"). We looked at each other. The food and drinks were almost gone. I moved away from the couch and sat down on the chair. Moshe took my place on the couch and tried to embrace the other girl. I heard a slap followed by an angry outburst. "What do you take me for? Don't you see that I was sitting with this nice young man, Joseph? How dare you even approach me?!"

I pretended to be upset and insulted by Moshe's behavior. We finished drinking the wine and eating the white bread, oranges, and whatever else was left on the table. I offered to go for more food as an excuse to get out of there. A few hours of hedonism were enough for me. After all, I was a survivor, and I was unused to so much enjoyment in such a short period of time. When I left, I bumped into my friend Josef Silberman, a student of economics. When I told him about my adventure, he volunteered to take my place or at least deliver the food so he could see for himself. I told him neither he nor I would go back to Moshe's. The game had gone far enough. We had to stop.

The following Sunday at about noon, Moshe again ran into me at the same place near the Jewish community center. I expected him to be angry with me because I had left him with both girls in a difficult situation. However, he was not upset at all. He was happy that I had not come back, and he had the opportunity to have both women to himself. In fact, he was going to go skiing with them at Mittenwald. I wished him good luck. About four weeks later, I met Moshe again at Möhlstrasse.

"Joseph, I came here today especially to see you. It is very important. I have to talk to you," said Moshe. He wanted me to go to the police and testify on his behalf. Moshe told me that the girls had stolen all the gold he had, the gold he needed for his dentistry practice. They had cleaned him out completely. Because I had been to his place and could identify both girls, Moshe asked me to serve as a witness. I declined to go to the police. I did not want to get involved and have my name associated with such a sordid affair.

Years later in Canada, when I told my sister-in-law Rose this story about her friend Dr. Turek, she had trouble believing such a thing could happen to such a smart person. When Moshe, who lived in Chicago, came to Toronto on a visit, he was invited to my brother's house for the first seder night. Moshe told the story of my abandoning him in a delicate situation and not returning. Rose admitted that, in light of Moshe's confirmation, she finally believed my account.

After getting out of situations that would have done little to add favorably to my curriculum vitae, I directed my social life more carefully. I paid serious attention to Jewish girls. The problem I always had was extricating myself from a relationship after I determined there was no long-term interest on my part. One girl I liked, Halina, was not so shapely, but she was beautiful. I liked her Lithuanian Jewish accent, and when she spoke, her choice of words revealed intelligence and education. Eventually, I decided that I was not going to fall in love with her and stopped seeing her. When my friend Josef Klausner came to Munich, he said Halina told him I dated non-Jewish girls. I was upset. The next time I went to Feldafing on business, I made a point of seeing Halina. She was happy about our meeting and hoped I had changed my mind about her. When she asked how I was doing, I answered, "You seem to know more about how and what I'm doing than I do!"

"What do you mean?" she asked. I said, "You know I am going out with non-Jewish girls and I do not know about it. Maybe I'm 'going in,' but I'm definitely not 'going out.'" Halina confessed she'd started the rumor to attract my attention, and her plan worked—but not in the way she had hoped. I liked

Halina, so I introduced her to one of my friends, and they eventually married.

In Munich, the survivors went dancing at the Cafe Tel-Aviv, with its large dance floor and good music. I improvised on the dancing skills I had picked up in Italy with lessons from my new Aunt Lotke at Feldafing. Lotke taught me the English waltz, and I became a fairly good dancer.

One night at the Cafe Tel-Aviv, I met a pretty, shapely girl who attracted me until the day she announced that she did not blame Jewish guys for refusing to date Jewish girls "because Jewish girls have wide behinds." That kind of vulgar remark spelled the end of my interest in her, but I had trouble figuring out how to break off the relationship without hurting her feelings. After the war, many of us lived social lives that would not have been acceptable in the worlds of our destroyed childhoods. Yet, the values we were taught as youngsters—about modesty and respect for our bodies and other things—were buried deep in our psyches and surfaced when we evaluated lasting relationships. More than we may have realized, those fundamentals were safe inside us.

Meeting Jewish girls was part of my work for *Betar* and the *Irgun*; I was supposed to win them over to the cause and convince them to join the organization. I received plenty of tempting offers, but if I did not really see the prospect of a future with a girl, I declined them. I dated one girl—let's call her Rita—a few times for the purpose of recruiting her. New members had to be interviewed thoroughly to check their attitude, character, loyalty, and intelligence. These things could not be evaluated in just one or two meetings. Invariably, the girls mistook my dedication to my job for something else. The younger ones especially seemed to think I was a good catch—handsome, young, and the owner of my own business. I received invitations from parents to come visit.

Rita's parents soon asked me to their home. When I arrived, I noticed lit candles in a five-branched silver candelabrum. Rita's parents and relatives were gathered around the table, which was beautifully set and laden with delicious food. Then the father made a startling announcement, wherein he offered me partial ownership of and full managerial responsibility for a leather factory in Palestine. He proposed that his daughter and I become engaged right then and there. I looked at the parents and then at the door. I said, "You are all gathered here, parents, uncles, cousins, and I am alone. I have an older brother, and it would not be right that he should be absent on such an important occasion in my life. Let me find him and talk to him." With that, I left and stopped trying to recruit Rita.

Art dated blonds and redheads. Maybe his preference was a subconscious avoidance of what could have been a painful reminder of his beloved, raven-haired Manya, who perished with their infant. Girls were always asking to be introduced to him.

Willie also had his share of romances, including one with Ellen, a stunning, blond Lithuanian actress. He did not marry her because he was overwhelmed by her expansive presence, even off stage. Chaim-Leizer was the only exception; he never dated or slept with another woman in his life before or after marrying Rose. There are not many men in this world like Chaim. In this respect, he was unique and a very good person. When Chaim passed away in the early 1990s, we engraved his tombstone with the words from Proverbs 6:22 that refers to the Torah: "When you walk, it shall guide you; when you lie down, it shall guard you; and when you awake, it shall speak on your behalf."

Although some of what I have written here is slightly embarrassing to me and might be to my brothers or friends, that is not my intention. I do not seek to hurt a soul. My only wish is to transmit an accurate picture of what our lives were like in those postwar years. Our life in Germany was very fast paced and passed with astonishing speed. Somehow, we connected a traumatic past to an unknown future. We were caught in the middle, trying to meld several worlds that did not quite mesh. Germany was a transient place. We met people, we were with them for a while, and then they were gone. We expected never to see most of them again. Life was in flux, and it was exciting.

THE PRINCESS IN THE WOODS

As a young boy, Mother used to say, "Yossele, when will you be settled? Will I live to see it?" I had resuscitated my life—I had friends, a cause, a business, a fancy Adler sports car (convertible, of course), and stylish clothing—but I was not settled. Perhaps it was precisely because Mother did not live to see me settled that I refused to settle down during those first years after the war. Though a hint of sadness was attached to it, I lived life with a kind of abandon I never would have experienced in the Gerer environment of my youth. As I matured emotionally, Mother's words came back to me. I concentrated on finding more-meaningful relationships.

One Saturday while visiting Feldafing, I introduced myself to a young lady named Mila and invited her to join me for a movie in Munich. Mila would not ride in my car because she did not want to be seen violating *Shabes*, something that did not faze me, given my postwar anger. I drove to a spot a short way outside the DP camp where Mila met me, and we continued on to Munich. Later, I drove her back to the outskirts of the camp, and we walked from there to her parents' place. I liked them, and they liked me.

Her father offered us some wine in large water glasses because they did not have wine glasses. Mila and I continued to spend time together, and we often included her close friend Bela on our dates. It was spring, Passover time. Trees and flowers bloomed, birdsong filled the air, and the atmosphere was conducive to romance, but I was not convinced that Mila was the right girl for me. That relationship, too, ended.

In my role as a recruiter for *Betar* and the *Irgun*, I made the acquaintance of Dr. Altman, principal of the Hebrew Gymnasium (high school) in Munich, who invited me to a student performance at the Schauspielhaus on Maximilianstrasse. A shapely brunette in the performance caught my fancy as I watched her graceful body and the way she moved her arms and legs. I thought she was a professional dancer, but the people sitting near me told me she was indeed a student like the others. I thought about her long after she left the stage. In fact, I thought about her for many months, and whenever I happened upon her accidentally, I paid close attention, watching the way she walked and carried herself. I wanted to learn as much about her as I could from observing her.

For someone who had no qualms about meeting people—even possessed of a healthy talent for doing so—I was stuck in a situation where I wondered why I made no move to speak to her. I concluded that I could not afford to take a chance and risk rejection. In serious matters, I did not like to gamble, so all I did was watch from a distance. At the same time, I was concerned that I would lose the chance to meet her. People did not stay put for very long in postwar Germany; everyone was on the way to someplace else, and time was flying. I was almost 20 years old!

I finally decided to take the chance and approach her. She was with her friend Maryla, who happened to be a friend of mine, too, so I walked over with some excuse to talk to Maryla. I expected her friend to join us in conversation. Alas, the graceful stranger said not a word. I was hoping Maryla would introduce us, but that did not happen either. Another time, while I was campaigning during the election for president of the Jewish community, I saw the girl standing with Rita Shor, another student I knew.

Rita lived with her uncle in the western part of Munich, and the girl in whom I was interested lived with her parents in the Borstei, in the eastern part of town. Both girls had finished classes and were ready to go home on the streetcar. I walked over and offered them a lift to the eastern part of town in my car. I hoped Rita's friend would jump in and say, "I'm going east. I live in the Borstei. Can you give me a ride, please?" Instead, Rita said, "Erez, you know that I live in the west." Her friend remained silent.

I could not figure out how to meet the dancer properly. Whenever I rode the streetcar, she always seemed to be there, right next to me, as though fate were throwing us together. If I did not see her, I would catch sight of her younger sister, Anda. I did not know how to act. My frustration mounted, and I found it hard to concentrate on study, business, and the *Irgun*. Thoughts of this girl overpowered everything else.

One day, Esther Sniatowski, a young woman who used her official job in the Jewish Community Center as a cover for her work in the *Irgun*, had an argument with me on the third floor. She accused me of favoring one member, Chayele, above others and giving her better *Irgun* assignments. Esther thought I was in love with Chayele. I was not, but I did admire Chayele for her intelligence and efficiency, and that is why I gave her choice assignments.

In self-defense, I pulled Esther over to the window and pointed to three girls standing in the Hebrew Gymnasium schoolyard. "Do you see the girl in the navy blue coat with the gray fur collar and blue knitted hat? I'm in love with that girl, and I'm going to marry her."

"But Erez," said Esther, "I never saw you with her."

"You are right," I answered.

"Did you ever speak to her?"

Esther could not fathom how I could be in love with someone I had never spoken to. She was astounded. My conversation with Esther ended right there, but unfortunately my torture did not. I did not know what to do next.

To distance myself from the girl and my obsessive thoughts about her, I decided to take another vacation in Garmisch-Partenkirchen. I checked into Haus Roseneck, a very elegant, clean, and cozy inn. I took a shower, went to bed, got up early, dressed, had a good breakfast, and left for a walk. Who was before my eyes? The girl of my dreams was with a group of students; I could not escape her. I thought, "What is going on?" I knew most of the people in the group she was with, including her cousin, Josef Meisels.

I invited the whole group to my room and offered them oranges and other delicacies that were rare in Germany. It was fun watching these kids, with tremendous appetites, enjoying the spread I laid out for them. I even proposed a contest to see who could eat the most. Despite my efforts, I did not get a chance to really talk with the object of my affection. One fellow sat on her right, another on her left, which left no room for me. It seemed she was always surrounded and difficult to approach. I was not getting anywhere.

I did not want to include the group on my next attempt to speak to her and would have preferred a party of just two, but I was willing to settle for a party of three. I approached our mutual friend Maryla with a proposition. I knew a man who owned three horses, and he was willing to let us take them for half a day. We three could go riding in the beautiful meadows surrounding Garmisch. "Who would you like to have join us?" I asked Maryla.

"Gena Meisels," replied Maryla, to my delight.

"Whatever you say is fine with me," I answered nonchalantly.

We arranged to meet the following morning. I was so happy that I could barely contain myself. The rest of the day I walked around on a cloud. The evening dragged on forever; at night, I could not fall asleep, and I prayed for morning to hasten. Finally, morning arrived. I got up early, dressed, and without breakfast, rushed to wait at our appointed meeting place. I hoped that the long-awaited opportunity for Gena and me to meet officially was finally at hand. Then I noticed Maryla walking toward me alone. Before Maryla could say anything, I explained that I had tried to reach her and let her know that something had happened and that I was not able to get the horses.

"Erez, Gena could not make it," said Maryla.

Pretending that I did not hear what she said or that it did not matter, I continued telling her that the horses had been sent to a show, but perhaps the three of us could go riding another time.

The students were touring the Tegernsee, a beautiful lake in exceptionally picturesque surroundings. At first, I was reluctant to join them because chances were poor that I would be able to speak to Gena when she was surrounded by friends. Maryla, her sister Mala, and their friend Giza talked me into going anyway. (Mala was in love with a friend of mine, Josef Silberman.) Since I had nothing to lose, I joined the students.

The countryside at Tegernsee was magnificent, with undulating green fields, a sparkling azure lake, and perfect weather. We hiked, played sports, and had lively discussions. Privately, I felt like I was just going through the motions because I had other things on my mind. The interminable group activity got to me, so I walked into a meadow ablaze with blooms and picked a white flower, admiring it for its delicate beauty. After a while, I rejoined the group, which at that point was engaged in a game that involved running in single files, passing one another.

Suddenly, my dream girl ran by, pulled the flower out of my hand, and stuck it into her beautiful black hair. I was delighted that my precious flower had found its proper home. The incident gave me some hope—a springboard from which to dive.

The games ended, and the day was coming to a close. We all went back to

Garmisch and decided to finish the outing properly by dining at the *Weisse Roessel* (White Horse) restaurant. At dinner, Gena and I sat next to each other. The whole group went "Dutch," but I insisted on paying for the four people at my table. While we were eating, the waitress came over with a note for Gena from a gentleman seated a couple tables away with three young women. He kept looking at our table, but not at Schwalb, Olek Pariser, or me. "What *chutzpah*!" I thought.

It was obvious that he was interested in Gena and that she was responding positively to his overtures. I was trying to control my jealousy when I looked in her eyes and saw them respond to him. Gena's looks were penetrating. The gentleman must have been an experienced *maven* (expert) with women and picked up Gena's signals. After I paid the bill, Gena told me that the note contained his telephone number and that he wanted her to call him.

"By all means do it, Gena. You have nothing to lose," I said.

I made it my business to find the fellow and get to know him better. I went to see Karl at his farm and bought sacks of flour from his mill. He was a wealthy, single man who had inherited a fortune from his parents. He always asked me about Gena and said he would like to meet her. I told him Gena was busy with her studies. I traveled back and forth between Munich and Garmisch, and this fellow kept insisting on meeting Gena. I repeated our conversations to Gena and stressed how eager the man was. Gena said she would like to meet him, too. But when I suggested that she come to Garmisch so she and Karl could get together, she always offered an excuse and refused.

After my next trip to Garmisch, Karl returned to Munich with me to see Gena. After a two-hour drive through the picturesque mountains, we arrived in the Borstei, where Gena lived on the Voigtstrasse. When I rang the bell, Gena came to the window, saw us leaning against Karl's fancy red convertible, and said that she was too busy to see us.

In Polish, I told Gena that unless she came down immediately, Karl and I would come up to the apartment. Gena came down, and Karl was very happy. We walked to the Borstei's beautiful flower garden, and Gena and Karl discussed how time-consuming school studies were. I began to feel like a fifth wheel, so when I saw that Gena seemed happy and was smiling, I said I was leaving to look after some business.

"If you leave me alone with him, I will kill you," Gena said in Polish in a panicky voice. "Don't you dare!" When Gena announced she had to go to the library to get a book for an exam, the disappointed fellow headed back to Garmisch.

Next day, I visited Gena to hear her comments about the previous day's events, but she did not say a word. It was as though nothing had happened. I did learn, however, that Gena was planning to go to Paris with Maryla. Joseph Axen, a friend of the family with whom Gena's father did business, took it upon himself to chaperone the young ladies. This news did not please me, but there was nothing I could do about it. I took it as a good omen when I received a few postcards from Paris and Gena brought me back a gift. My hopes picked up after we went for a walk to Dante Stadium and sat on a log on the grass.

During our conversation, Gena told me that, because she had a sister and no brother, she wanted me to be her brother. I told her that I had three brothers, but that I needed more than a sister. She looked at me, and then we hugged. It was the very best hug I was ever given. While I built up my hopes and made imaginary plans for a relationship, Gena saw other men. I did not know what stand to take. She dated Sigmund Rosenblatt, a journalism student who left for America when sponsored by his relative Helena Rubinstein of the cosmetic empire. Gena's other suitors may have been more eligible than I was—after all, these men were attending universities and would one day be professionals with secure positions. There I was, with no formal education, asking myself why Gena would choose me if she had better prospects.

I decided to act gently, yet persistently. The man I considered my number one competitor was Henry Libicki, a handsome engineering student. I had lunch with him, and we talked about his feelings for Gena. I advised him to propose right away so she would have to make up her mind one way or the other. Henry took my advice and gave Gena an ultimatum, to which she said no.

Rubin Abramowicz, another journalist and one of Gena's admirers, had a visa to leave Germany, and thus did not present a real threat. I knew it would be tougher to get rid of Sigmund Rosenblatt, although he was already in America. Gena and Sigmund's relationship was longer lasting and stronger. The amount of time Gena spent answering the many-paged letters he sent her made me take him seriously. But Sigmund was on the other side of the ocean, and time and distance might help the relationship cool off. Absence could also make the heart grow fonder. As I tormented myself with these musings, I needed to decide whether to ignore my rivals and continue my quest.

When Gena needed surgery on her foot and the only good orthopedic hospital was in Bad-Tölz, I drove her to the hospital, and with her mother, visited Gena once or twice a week. An hour on the beautiful, winding road gave me time to discuss Gena's future with Mrs. Meisels. On the way back, her mother asked me when I planned to go back to Bad-Tölz, and I said, "Maybe by the end of this week or next." That was not really the case. I visited Gena every day, but I did not want to take her mother along every time.

On one of our drives, Gena's mother told me that the Israeli consul in Germany wanted to meet Gena and that a rich businessman named Weiss hoped to marry her. Mr. Weiss himself approached Gena's father with this proposition. A third man, a university graduate, was also interested in Gena. Mrs. Meisels asked my opinion regarding these suitors, and I helpfully replied that Gena deserved the best. "Each of these men sounds nice, but Gena deserves somebody even better," I said. "Besides, in my opinion, Gena is too young to marry. Don't you agree, Mrs. Meisels?"

"Yes, Erez, truly you are a good friend," came the reply. Mrs. Meisels told me a story from her childhood about a princess sitting in the woods, waiting for someone to find her. A lucky man would marry her. I agreed wholeheartedly, but we could not put Gena in the woods in her present condition, when she was unable to walk. She needed someone to look after her.

The day before Rosh Hashanah, I went to Gena's house to wish the family a happy New Year. Gena's father, a fine and noble man, expressed his fervent wish that Gena could be with her family for the holidays and seemed ready to give anything to bring the family together. Saying not a word, I drove straight to Bad-Tölz, checked Gena out of the hospital, moved the front seat forward so she could arrange herself in the back with her foot in a cast, and brought her home for the holidays. After she recuperated, Gena continued having a good time with her friends, going to movies, the theater, and the opera. I did not seem to be her main concern.

My friend Levi Shalitan and I were talking about some of his writings in *Unzer Veg*, and I asked his advice about Gena. Levi, an educator, had met Gena at a summer camp run by her school. Levi's opinion of her, in general, was excellent, but he had misgivings about the kind of wife she would make. "Gena is like a white suit; any little spot will show," he said.

"What does that mean, Levi?"

"She is good to have as a girlfriend, but as a wife, I do not know," he replied. I looked beneath his bushy eyebrows into his expressive eyes and tried to read more into them than what he had said. Levi was going out with a nice Lithuanian girl named Hanele and was much older than us, so I did not have to worry that his advice was "strategic." Another of my confidants was Fela Rechnietz. I shared my thoughts about Gena with her, describing Gena's personality and my love for her, and Fela offered a woman's perspective. Later, I happily attended Fela's marriage to Marian Goldberg. They were both fine people who came from good Jewish homes and were well suited for one another.

Although my campaign to win Gena was not advancing perceptibly, our business progressed quite nicely and prospered. At the same time, Art's personal life was undergoing a positive change. We introduced him to a friend's sister, and they started courting. With the business doing well, Art learned to drive and bought a brand-new car so he could take his girlfriend on long drives. I was happy to look after the business while Art pursued his relationship with Shirley. Unfortunately, on one of these drives, Art had a serious accident. He may have been concentrating more on Shirley than on driving. Thank God, they both came out alive, though their recuperation did take some time, and I continued to look after the business alone.

When Art returned to work, he announced that he and Shirley were getting married. The wedding was very nice. Shirley's sister-in-law, Fira Rosen, helped with the arrangements. When we had to seat Mr. and Mrs. Reisinger, our German partners, Fira said she would sit with them and explain Jewish wedding rituals. Just before dinner was to be served and everybody was seated, I directed the Reisingers to Fira's table, but she got angry and started crying, conveniently forgetting she had promised to host them.

After the wedding, Art and Shirley honeymooned in Bad Reichenhall, where Shirley used to live. Then Art came back to work at the store, and there were other changes. The Reisingers were uncomfortable with their 33 percent minority share, and we concluded that we would split. We were very generous with our payout, letting them keep their original store on Marsstrasse without paying for it. Art and I ended up with the Paul-Heiserstrasse shop to share equally between us.

With our business stable and with Art back at work, I could again concentrate on my relationship with Gena. I attended gatherings the Meisels hosted in their apartment, where once a week, about a dozen students and an occasional older person would gather for readings and discussions on a wide range of topics. Emil Wolfe, an intelligent, well-educated man from Switzerland, was among those I met there. He did some business with Mr. Meisels and had lived in the United States. He was an American citizen living in Munich when we met.

One evening, I was in particularly good spirits and presented a controversial issue that prompted heated discussion. Afterward, I approached Mrs. Meisels and asked if we could speak privately about a serious matter. She followed me into another room, and I politely asked her to sit down. Then I said, "As you know, I am a good friend of Gena's. I'm also in love with her. Therefore, I am respectfully asking you for Gena's hand in marriage." Mrs. Meisels looked at me in surprise, as though something had fallen out of the sky on her.

"You talk to me about something so important in the middle of a gathering when I have other guests in the house?"

"Mrs. Meisels, is the discussion in your living room more important than the future well-being of your daughter?" I asked.

"Not now. Now is not the proper time," said Mrs. Meisels, and we both returned to the living room. I went to the vestibule, took my coat, and left the apartment. I did not visit the Meisels' home again, although I saw Gena often and occasionally met Mr. Meisels on Möhlstrasse.

Thinking I should open myself up to other possibilities, I took out Mindzia, a nice blond who also lived in the Borstei, on the same street as Gena. I sometimes took Mindzia to the movies or to the theater, but my heart was not really in it. Instead of concentrating on Mindzia, I would be peeking at what was going on in the Meisels' apartment, because you could see into it from the windows in Mindzia's third-floor apartment. The surveillance techniques I had learned in the *Irgun* came in handy. I was asking Mindzia more about Gena than I was about her. Once, Mindzia even asked me if the sole purpose of my seeing her was to learn more about Gena. I was forced to face myself and acknowledge that I was still "stuck" on Gena and honestly answered yes.

I realized it was not fair to see Mindzia any more and, with less grace than the situation warranted, offered up the lame excuse that my car was in the garage for repairs to break off our next date. Mindzia's father was anxious for us to continue our association and offered to let us borrow his car, but I declined. It was time to get back to my true feelings and work on a relationship with Gena.

I continued to meet Gena outside her home. In time, Gena assured me that visiting her at her parents' apartment was fine, but I was reluctant to do so.

Gena tried to convince me that things had changed. I wanted to know exactly what she meant, since her mother was undecided about my appropriateness for her daughter. I asked Gena directly, "Will you marry me without her permission?" Gena said no, but insisted that, in the end, her mother would agree to the suit. I could not accept this answer, but I eventually relented and visited Gena at home.

On January 22, 1950, I visited the Meisels' apartment when the whole family was present. I did not say a word, and Gena's father started a discourse on the importance of being *ba'ale batish* (respectable) in life. We drank a "*l'hayim*" (a toast "to life"), wished each other *mazel tov* (good luck), and hugged and kissed. Gena's sister embraced me and said, "Ereziku, now you are going to be my brother. How wonderful, finally I will have one."

Though I had hoped and prayed for this moment, I could not believe it was happening; I wanted the elation to last forever.

HONEYMOON

The next day, I picked Gena up, and we went for a long drive without any particular destination in mind. We just wanted to be together. Now that we were engaged, we had to start thinking about our future in Israel. Mr. Meisels was in a partnership with two other people and invested in manufacturing electric light bulbs in Israel. The factory was to be shipped to Israel and reassembled. We started to plan the wedding and honeymoon, which included visiting Israel. We took out new passports and visas and went through all the formalities and paperwork.

My brother Art did not like our proposed honeymoon trip. He went to see Mr. and Mrs. Meisels and tried to convince them to object. One of his reasons was that he did not believe in squandering money on frivolous travel. I think the real reason was that Art, also a Revisionist, had not gone to Israel on his own honeymoon. Notwithstanding Art's protests, we refused to change our plans. Preparations continued, including getting Gena a new wardrobe designed by Frau Villanova (a well-known dressmaker in Munich). The Meisels bought me a gold Schaffhausen watch as an engagement gift and, near the wedding date, Mr. Meisels gave me a new *talis* and *tefillin* that I still use. Wedding invitations were printed and sent, the hall was rented, musicians were hired, and the best caterers were retained—in short, we did everything to make the wedding festivities memorable.

But the real truth was that Gena and I did not really want to get married … yet. We were both too young. So, though we loved each other very much, we decided to stay together only until either of us would find a better, more suitable mate. (More than 50 years later, we are still looking for those mates—in the meantime, we are still together.) We also did not want the official record of our nuptials to be a German marriage license issued by a German judge. We decided to have a religious wedding. Just prior to the wedding I went to the *mikveh* because Mr. Meisels wanted to make sure I was ritually cleansed of my wild, postwar exploits.

On June 4, 1950, we had a great banquet. The hall looked like a veritable flower garden, and many people attended. Rabbi Baruch Leizerowski officiated at the ceremony. My dear friends Moshe Halperin (now Dr. Tsemach Tsamrion) and his wife Pnina stood in as my accompaniers, and filled the role of my parents when they led me to the *hupah* (wedding canopy). I wore a white *kitl*. Our tradition tells us that on their wedding day, a bride and groom receive complete atonement, a clean slate. After going through the war, I wondered if I would ever have a clean slate.

As I walked toward the *hupah*, my thoughts were of my parents. I missed them so much and wished they were walking me to the *hupah* and witnessing this important day. There, on what was certainly one of the happiest days of my life, a day on which I recognized the Almighty's beneficence, feelings of loneliness and abandonment crept in, and I thought, "My God, my God, why hast Thou forsaken me?" (Psalm 22:1). These thoughts broke my heart, and I could not hold back my tears. Despite my embarrassment, the salty rivulets ran freely down my cheeks. The sad reality hit me with full force: for the first time in my life, I accepted the fact that my parents were no longer with me. And yet, my acceptance could not have been very complete. I fantasized that maybe a miracle would happen one day and my parents would be found. Emotionally, I was trying to force the square peg of the past into the circular hole in my heart. Because I was so attached to my parents, always driven and motivated by them—Father in his quest to teach me Talmud and Mother's admonitions that I settle down—I could not stop thinking of them. My parents' absence on the most solemn day of my life caused me to vacillate between acceptance and denial—my other survival tool.

No one, however, could deny that Gena was a gorgeous bride, inside and out. She was my princess. After the ceremony, we danced in the beautiful, festively decorated hall and basked in the warm wishes of our finely attired guests. The earlier sadness dissipated and I floated. We all had a good time and danced until the early hours of the morning. Then the guests slowly drifted out.

The custom in those days was to give crystal, silver candlesticks, or some other elaborate gift—never cash. We received many duplicates—like four identical silver Hanukkah lamps. We gave away three later. The one we kept showed each gift-giver that we enjoyed that individual's generosity.) We packed our gifts into a large carton and loaded it into the trunk of a vintage Mercedes taxi—as spotless as a newly minted coin—and proceeded to my apartment. We paid the driver and went upstairs, so tired and anxious to get to bed that we completely forgot about the box of gifts. Not until the next morning did we realize that we had left the carton in the trunk of the cab.

This loss was the first negative experience of our married life. After a little bit of hand-wringing, I went to the police to report our loss. The officers did not offer much help, and nothing was found. Then we typed up several notices in German, "We know the taxi and driver who drove a newlywed couple to Paul-Heiserstrasse 17 in the early morning of June 5. If the driver does not come to this address within 24 hours, he will lose his license and be charged by the police." Within hours of posting the notices at various taxi stands, the driver showed up with the carton and apologized for "forgetting" to take it out for us. He also claimed he forgot the address and therefore had not been able to deliver the box. I accepted the carton and the excuse, happy to have our wedding gifts back in our possession.

The following day, we left for our honeymoon. We traveled through Germany and Austria and stopped in Italy for a longer stay, with Israel as our final destination. At our first stop in Venice, we stayed at the Canaletto Hotel, facing the Venetian canals near the Piazza San Marco. We visited the old Jewish Ghetto and the International Biennale of Art on the Lido di Venezia. In Rome, we visited the Vatican, the Colosseum, the Arch of Titus, the museums, and architectural sites that were saturated with history. We visited Pompeii, Naples, Sorrento, and Amalfi. Riding along the precipitous Amalfi coast was scary, and we hovered thousands of feet above the ocean without the slightest guardrail or embankment to stop cars from plunging over the edge. The view was literally breathtaking. We drove to the tip of the peninsula and took a boat to Capri to visit the Grotta Azzurra. We had the most wonderful time. I spoke the language, was familiar with all those places, and was glad to act as Gena's exclusive guide. Our experience was unforgettable.

We intended to continue to Bari and take a boat to Israel, but we heard that war had broken out in Korea. When the United States entered the fray on

June 27, 1950, rumors circulated about World War III beginning. Gena and I were completely shocked. After what we had lived through, we had hoped that World War II, with its devastation and millions of human sacrifices, would have acted as a deterrent to war. Our wounds were still not completely healed from the last war, so we decided to return to Munich.

The trip was long, hot, and tiring because there was no air-conditioning in railroad cars in those days. Gena went to one of the washrooms to freshen up, and when she came back, she noticed that the gold watch I had given her as a present was not on her wrist. While washing, she had taken it off and left it in the washroom. We went back as soon as we noticed, but the watch was gone. I told the train conductor what had happened and that the watch had great sentimental value. On hearing our story, the man reached into his pocket, pulled out the watch, and told us to be more careful in the future.

The following day we arrived at the *Hauptbahnhof* (central train station) in Munich and went to claim the trunk that contained almost all of our earthly possessions. It was missing, and we assumed it had been stolen. We called everywhere, but there was no trace of it. Gena lamented that everything was going badly for us: first the carton with the wedding gifts went missing, then the watch was taken on the train, and now the trunk with all our new clothing had disappeared. Gena thought it was a very bad omen. I tried to calm her down and reminded her that we had recovered our first two losses and that in good time, we would recover the rest. We just had to be patient.

We went to see Gena's parents, who unhelpfully reminded us, "We told you not to take so many things with you." I did not understand the use of telling us that when what we needed was reassurance. Now I had to deal with a whole family who exacerbated Gena's bad mood.

The next day, a Tuesday, I returned to the *Hauptbahnhof* office to claim our luggage, but there was still no trace. Wednesday morning I saw the general manager and told him a "secret." I said that what really had me worried was not the luggage, but the bottle of dangerous chemicals that had been packed among our possessions. If it were to overheat or be tossed about too vigorously, it could explode and cause a fire. If our trunk was with other luggage, a whole train or station might be in danger. The manager immediately put his staff on alert. I left for home after giving him our address and telephone number. Soon, I was advised that every border crossing from Italy to Austria, Switzerland, and Germany had been notified. Everyone was warned of the potential danger and the need to find the trunk immediately.

On Friday evening that same week, my father-in-law asked me to join him in *shul*. Everyone liked it when he led prayers because he had a pleasant singing voice. As I stood and prayed behind him, my sister-in-law Anda came running in to let me know that train guards were looking for me. The trunk had been mistakenly sent to Switzerland, and they wanted me to pick it up at the station immediately. Now that the trunk was recovered and safe, I told the authorities that by now the dangerous liquid had probably evaporated and that I would claim it Saturday night.

On Saturday evening I drove to the central train station, parked my car close to the baggage area, and presented my claim check to the supervisor. He pointed to the trunk, which bore two large red stickers reading "Danger! Explosives!" No one would touch the trunk or help me with it; I dragged it out of the station myself. Outside, I found someone who helped me load it into the car's trunk—and three-quarters of it was sticking out.

Gena and I happily unpacked. Our clothes needed washing, so I left them at the laundry, a few doors away from where we lived. A couple of days later, when I went back to get our laundry, the clerk said I had already picked up our clothing. Disregarding the claim ticket I presented to him, he began screaming at me. I went to the police immediately and filed criminal charges against him and his company. This was yet another loss, but then fortunately, our laundry was found within 48 hours. A mistake had been made, and someone else had picked up our wash.

STILL THE YOUNGEST

A few days after we returned from our honeymoon, I went back to work. While Art was courting, getting married, and going away on his honeymoon, I had diligently looked after the business. Normally, we took inventory and pulled out monthly profits, and I had done this with Art just before he left and soon after his return. I expected that he would do the same for me. When I entered our store, I was shocked to see that the shelves were bare. I immediately demanded that Art take inventory with me, but he wanted to postpone it to the end of the month. When the end of the month came, Art wanted to postpone it again. I started taking stock on my own. About two or three hours into the process, Art said that he had taken his money out of the business. When I asked him what had happened to my money, he answered, "You have no money."

I was still sharing an apartment with the Reisingers above the Paul-Heiserstrasse store. Gena and I occupied one of the large rooms—though we were no longer partners, we were still on good terms with the Reisingers. I came home late one evening when Gena was out, and to my surprise, I saw Art's car out front. There were no lights on in the store, so I continued upstairs to the apartment. As I was about to enter, I overheard my brother talking to the Reisingers about a plan to take over my interest in the business. I could not believe what I was hearing, so I quietly opened the door and stood in the vestibule. There, in the reflection of the hall mirror, I saw the three of them discussing a takeover. What I saw and heard hit me with such force that I sighed. Mr. Reisinger heard my sigh and signaled his wife to stop talking.

She did not notice him until he called her name. My brother kept going. I was bursting and decided that my best course of action was to leave immediately. I was worried about what I might do if I stayed.

This is not easy to write about, but I feel that I need to describe those events. They forced me to grow up. I was already disillusioned about humanity in general, and I should have known better because Art and I had a nasty side to our history that went back to when I was seven years old. Still, I had hoped that my brother, ten years my senior, would have some sort of protective instinct toward his youngest brother. Art had more schooling than any of us and therefore had the tools to acquire knowledge easily. I looked up to him as a role model. And in that period right after the war, when we were all still licking our wounds, fraternal love should have made us look out for one another more than ever.

Instead, my brother chipped away at that love, bit by bit, deed by deed. Maybe that is why I was as deeply hurt as I was. For a while, we did not speak to each other. Art said he wanted his own textile or haberdashery business similar to the one his friends the Gleitman brothers had opened. He needed money to do that and wanted to liberate his capital from the business.

Although I did nothing to warrant such treatment, there may have been several underlying reasons for the way Art acted. Perhaps he never accepted me as an equal. In his mind, I was the little brother, and consequently, he may have felt he was at liberty to do business as he wished. Art was the only one of us who had also lost a wife and child to the Holocaust. The inability to protect his loved ones may have impaired his capacity to feel protective toward me.

The strained relationship began in our childhood when he took the money I had saved for so long out of its hiding place in the wall clock. Ostensibly, he had taken my money because I had broken the lightbulb in his flashlight, but was that a good enough reason for a 17-year-old to take the pitiful savings of his 7-year-old brother? When I was a young boy, Art taught me to play chess, and sometimes, for want of a better partner, Art challenged me to play with him. While I enjoyed these occasions, Art turned the game into a contest of wits and forgot that I was so much younger than he. He never helped me out or allowed me to win. Perhaps his intentions were good, but I was hurt despite the benefit of having my wits sharpened.

Certain family patterns are very difficult to break, and I have to point to early family patterns that existed before the war to help explain our complicated relationship. As the oldest of four sons, Art was led to believe that he was privileged and entitled. Our parents reserved the best for Art—the best food, books, and clothing—and they constantly reinforced that attitude. The result of such preferential treatment was to make the rest of us jealous. We had wonderful parents, but as the Bible illustrates in story after story in Genesis, favoring one child over others leads to problems that can last for generations. My parents meant well; their intentions were the best for all of us. They simply did not know any better.

All of that is now water under the bridge; I forgave Art a long time ago, and I love him dearly. Believe it or not, when Art was planning to move from Columbus, Ohio, to Southfield, Michigan, I suggested he move to Toronto instead, and I offered him a sweetheart of a deal with the intention of getting all four of us brothers to live in the same city.

At the time, I owned lots for single-family homes and offered Art ten lots with no need for a deposit, to help him get into a new line of work. A building boom was under way, but had there been losses, I undertook to absorb them. Art would have had to pay for the land only after he sold the houses and made a profit.

Art and Shirley decided to proceed with their move to Southfield, and an opportunity was lost. Of course, when the four brothers did get together for bar mitzvahs and weddings, we mentally landed right back in our hometown. Once we were having lunch in Willie's house, reminiscing about life in Dzialoszyce, as usual. It was ironic how Art's perceptions differed from those of the rest of us. We, on the one hand, remembered his preferential treatment; he, on the other hand, insisted that because he was the oldest, our parents demanded more of him and expected him to be a role model—and that put him under tremendous pressure. We laughed at Art's pronouncement: "I am my brother's keeper." At least we can look back and laugh. I wish him well and hope he lives to a ripe old age together with Shirley, his children, and grandchildren.

In any event, I did not continue my partnership with Art. We made an arrangement, and I took over the store. Soon I started to prosper again. It was liberating to be on my own—I sold wholesale liquor, poultry, and frozen fish that I stored in large freezers I rented in the *Reichenhalle,* an industrial park that once served the Third Reich.

MONKEY BUSINESS

During the postwar years, many frauds were perpetrated in Munich. For example, dishonest individuals sought out rich women and tried to sell them diamonds. When samples of the diamonds were taken to appraisers, they turned out to be genuine, but before delivery, the real gems were exchanged for fake diamonds of the same shape, cut, and weight.

One day, a middle-aged Russian man wearing an eye patch approached me. He walked into my store and bought a few items. The man paid for his purchases and then asked in a hushed voice if I knew anybody interested in buying gold and if I could give him directions to Möhlstrasse, the street on which the black market was located. I asked a few questions, and the man took out an old English coin partially covered with dirt for which I offered 30 deutsche marks (DM). The value of such a coin at the time was at least DM 40, if not more. The man accepted my offer, and I paid him.

As he was leaving the store, he turned back and said that he had about a thousand coins, but I would have to prove I had enough money to pay for them if I wanted to buy more. I asked where he had acquired the coins and where he kept them. The man explained that he was working with a large excavating machine at different sites around the city, and he had made many finds. One site was a bombed-out bank where he claimed to have found a vault. I told him to bring the coins to me.

The Russian "gold digger" left my store with his bag of groceries and told me he was going home on the streetcar to get the other coins. My intuition told me something was off, so after he left, I followed him. He entered a car parked around the corner, where three additional men were waiting, and they all drove off. If my suspicions were correct, the Russian had offered me a bargain price so I would bring enough money to buy the other coins, and then his accomplices would rob me. The police chief for this district—who owed me a few favors because I was always generous in filling his orders, despite his ration card—lived in my building. I returned to the store and called him.

The chief arranged for some plainclothesmen to stake out the area, and he hid in the back of the store. Half an hour later, the con men drove by the store. Five minutes passed, ten minutes, but no one came in. Looking through my display window, I noticed two of the men on the opposite sidewalk, pacing up and down. They had obviously identified the police and were now afraid to come into the store. I wanted the police to arrest them as suspects in schemes to defraud innocent people, but walking was not a crime.

I continued to operate the store to build up a stake so that Gena and I could move to Israel. Life in Israel, as we heard from relatives, was very hard at the time. Everything was rationed there as it was in Germany, except there was even less in Israel. Arabs were continuing their border incursions. My in-laws, by then middle-aged, were afraid to start over again and face the hardships associated with becoming pioneers in a new country. The Holocaust had been enough. Long before Gena and I married, the Meisels had registered to go to the United States. My mother-in-law had two older brothers who moved to New York at the beginning of the twentieth century to avoid conscription by the Austro-Hungarian Empire during World War I. Mrs. Meisels lost most of her family in the Holocaust and was eager to see her two remaining brothers. The Meisels received one visa for the whole family, but I had not the slightest interest in going to the United States, and I did not know how to handle the situation. I had no right to stop the Meisels, just as I could not prevent my two brothers from immigrating to Canada.

The only solution was a compromise: Gena would accompany her parents and sister, so as not to invalidate her family's joint visa, and she would come right back. The Meisels did not like the idea of Gena traveling to Germany on her own, so they proposed that I come to the United States, undergo a civil marriage, and then we could move directly to Israel. Since the final destination was Israel, even if getting there entailed a major detour, I agreed. I registered as a plumber who wanted to move to the United States. The Meisels had already been called to the *Funkkaserne*, the assembly point from which they would leave for Bremerhaven and board a ship for America.

I was fortunate to sell my profitable business to two men from Foehrenwald. The prospective buyers did their due diligence for a few days, watching me in the store and accompanying me on errands. They observed the turnover, the supply sources, and clientele to see if they matched my description. The wife of one of the partners was German and knew the business well. When customers came in, she asked them about the quality of goods they received from the store and how they had been treated as customers. Everyone was pleased with the merchandise and service. The men from Foehrenwald were satisfied; after we took inventory, they paid me the agreed-upon price, and I handed them the keys. I sold my car to Benjamin Lapin, a Lithuanian friend who lived with his sister, Sarah Levitan. He and his two partners, Moshe Leizer Einhorn and David Firestone, were big importers of Swiss watches. Firestone is now a successful entrepreneur in South America.

It took me about three weeks to finish my arrangements, and I left for Bremerhaven to follow Gena. I was sure that by that time, if the Meisels were not already in the States, they were at least on the way, somewhere in the middle of the ocean. To my surprise, when I arrived in Bremerhaven, the Meisels were still there because of a series of delays—they had to be vaccinated, they had to be quarantined, and their ship had not yet arrived. I tried to book passage on the same ship but was not able to manage it. Though we all stayed together in the same quarters, we left on separate ships about two weeks apart. In the meantime, we passed the time by reading, walking, and playing cards and chess; food was provided by the immigrant aid societies.

One day, two German policemen came to the transit camp and asked for me. Since I had no reason to hide, I came forward and identified myself. Without giving me a reason, they arrested me and led me away. After some prodding, they told me that I was being charged with fraud. I could not imagine who was behind such an allegation. We traveled by train a whole night; never before had I slept so well under German guard. When we arrived in Munich, I immediately asked for an American judge since I was a displaced person and under the jurisdiction of the American courts. At 10 a.m., I appeared in a Bavarian court and was charged with selling a store that did not belong to me. The prosecutor read the charge, making sure I understood it clearly, and the judge asked me to respond. With the help of an English interpreter, I proceeded to tell my story.

"Your Honor, the Reisingers had a bombed-out little store on Marsstrasse, containing no merchandise other than a few candles and some matches. They were a nice couple, and I loaned them money to fix up their store. In time, they needed additional funds to buy merchandise and offered me a 50 percent partnership in the business, which I accepted. A few months later, we took in my brother Art as a third partner; then we bought and renovated a second store on Paul-Heiserstrasse 17. Each one of us had a 33 percent interest in the two stores."

I related the facts chronologically. "After some time, the Reisingers wanted to be on their own, so we all came to an agreement whereby they retained the store on Moehlstrasse while Art and I kept the one on Paul-Heiserstrasse. Subsequently, my brother sold his share to me, and I became the sole owner of 100 percent of the store. Therefore, I had the right and authority to sell it. I also shared an apartment with the Reisingers; that unit was in the same building as the store, directly above it. If the Reisingers had any problem with my selling the store and leaving the country, why didn't they raise the issue during the weeks I was packing and making preparations to leave? Being in the same building, they knew exactly what was going on in the store. Why would they wait four weeks before going into the store and informing the new owners the store was theirs?"

Just retelling the story enraged me, but I controlled my voice. "Your Honor, Mr. Reisinger wanted to do what the Nazis did—rob innocent people. The Reisingers thought that by now, four weeks after I 'left' town, I would have been well on my way to America. I would not have been able to defend the new owners, who in turn would have been unable to defend themselves. The Reisingers hoped to steal the store from them. Actually, the new owners could have sent me a telegram since *they* knew I was still in Germany, and I would have come back immediately."

Without letting me conclude my defense, the judge, who was angry with the Reisingers, said, "Case dismissed!" But that was not good enough for me. As far as I was concerned, the matter was not yet closed. I contemplated the next step. First, I postponed my departure to the United States and borrowed my old car from my friend Benjamin. I deliberately walked around Möhlstrasse so that everyone would see me, especially the new owners of my store. The new owners were not doing as well as I had done with the store and were looking for an excuse to get their money back. When the storeowners caught sight of me, they requested that I accompany them to a *din Torah*, hoping, through some twisted logic, to force me to take back the store. At first I refused the *din Torah* because I wanted to be asked twice so that it would seem that the new owners had forced me into court, but in fact, I looked forward to an opportunity to clear my name and collect damages. In the end I agreed to go to the *beys din*, and we came before Chief Rabbi Samuel Abba Snieg, who was almost blind; Rabbi Ross, who sported a red beard; and Rabbi Leizerowski.

The rabbis stared at both parties, trying to assess the situation. They took out a large, red handkerchief for being *mikabel kinyan* (symbolically taking hold of a physical object of determinate value to signify accepting the authority of a contract or a ruling) and asked each of us, in turn, to take hold of it. I agreed right away to this formal, binding commitment, but also demanded that the new owners put up DM 25,000 to guarantee that they would abide by the court ruling. The rabbis looked perplexed and asked, "Who is the plaintiff here, and who is the defendant?"

"It does not matter right now," I replied. "What is important is to render a verdict."

The rabbis looked at each other and then asked me, since I was the one who was called to the *din Torah*, why was I demanding collateral from the plaintiffs. I saw we were getting nowhere, so I proposed a compromise. If either of the two plaintiffs understood the meaning of the words *mikabel kinyan*, I would not request collateral. One of the rabbis asked the men the question, and neither knew, adding, "Rabbi, you gave us a red kerchief to wipe our hands, and we did as you asked." They obviously did not understand the legal significance of what they had done.

"Well, Rabbis, what do we do now? I am leaving!" I said and pretended to be uninterested in the *din Torah*. The rabbis advised the other parties to hire an arbitrator. Lo and behold, a man by the name of Jacob Katz walked into the room. Jacob Katz was widely known for being very knowledgeable in *halacha* and Talmud, and had acted as an international arbitrator in the most complicated disputes. Even though one of his legs had been amputated, he carried himself with aplomb. As soon as he sat down, he asked me why I demanded collateral.

"You will find out later," I replied.

Katz had a little conference with his new clients, and the men agreed to put up DM 15,000 in collateral. Katz was the first to speak and made all kinds of spurious accusations, mainly related to his clients' anticipated sales. In the end, he demanded that I take back the store and return the money I received from his clients. I listened and waited for my turn to speak.

I began by explaining the harm the others had caused by besmirching my reputation and by delaying my departure. I was, therefore, the real plaintiff, or claimant. I demanded DM 30,000 compensation for actual and punitive damages. It was not hard to defend my position, especially since one of the owners had stayed in the store with me for several days to watch me do business. They had done their due diligence, and I had concealed nothing from them. I could not, and should not, be held accountable for their mismanagement. Jacob Katz called for a break and held a little conference with his clients. Then, he summoned me outside, alone, and suggested that we settle amicably on our own, without the rabbis. When I asked him how much his clients were offering me in damages, he said, "Nothing." I laughed and started walking back to the rabbis' office.

Katz said, "Listen, Tenenbaum, you are my friend. You are Mr. Meisels' son-in-law. I would like to settle this matter with you."

I answered, "My status is the same as it was before the *din Torah* started; I was Mr. Meisels' son-in-law then just as much as I am now. Why did you not propose to settle the matter then? Why did you insist on collateral from me, too? At that time, there was more reason to ask for a settlement because then it was I who was demanding at least DM 30,000 for having been slandered and for having unfounded charges filed against me with the police."

After my little speech, Katz proposed trying to convince his party to pay me DM 5,000 as a show of good will. I got angry and told him to go back to his clients and let them know that I was willing to accept DM 20,000. "And please remember that this offer is being made outside the courtroom. Once inside, I will not be bound by a sum negotiated privately between the two of us."

Katz could not get his clients to accept. He called one of the partners outside, and when they came back after only two minutes, they declared they wanted a different arbitrator. The case was postponed again, and that upset me greatly because I wanted to resolve the whole mess and leave for the United States. Unfortunately, I had no say in the matter, and the new owners were entitled to change arbitrators if they were unhappy with their first choice. The next day, the men announced that they had found a better-versed arbitrator than Mr. Katz. I wondered who this person might be.

On the day we agreed to meet again in the rabbis' office, the new owners brought along a tall, sturdy man who seemed familiar to me. He started speaking aggressively in simple language and stared at me throughout. Suddenly, I realized where I knew him from and asked Rabbi Snieg if I could use the phone in the next room. The new arbitrator excused himself and said he had to leave immediately. The following day, the same scenario repeated itself; each time he started to argue the case, I pretended I had to make a call, and as if I were performing magic, the arbitrator disappeared. The next session did not take long at all. This time the arbitrator wanted to know where the store was located, and I offered to take him there. I led the man to my old car, which I was using courtesy of my friend, and drove to Paul-Heiserstrasse. I parked near the store, linked my arm in his, and started marching back and forth across the street from what used to be my store.

"Do you remember now?" I asked him. "A few months ago, you walked up and down this sidewalk observing my store. You must be smarter than the police because you got away before they had a chance to arrest you."

With a sly smile, the man declared, "You are OK." He got my message.

The next morning I returned to the rabbis' office, where my opponents were already waiting. However, the arbitrator did not show up. In front of those assembled, I told them what had transpired the previous day. Though I did not know which criminal gang the arbitrator belonged to, I was sure my opponents understood my point. Since I did not want to wait for the arbitrator to show up, or for the storeowners to find a new substitute, and because I was unwilling to keep postponing the case and waste the rabbis' valuable time, I pushed for an immediate ruling. I demanded the DM 15,000, already held in escrow by the rabbis, plus an additional DM 15,000 as partial compensation for damage to my reputation, for anguish, and for costs incurred.

The following morning, the rabbis gave me DM 15,000. The verdict was that if a larger sum had been kept in escrow, the whole amount would have been justly mine, but I never received the additional money. By this time, I was anxious to leave Germany. I spent a few more days in Munich to buy presents for Gena: a Persian rug, a sterling silver coffee and tea set, Rosenthal dishes, some porcelain figurines, and a black alligator bag. Then I left for Bremen. When I arrived at the train station, I saw Gena waiting for me in the pouring rain, her trench coat and hair completely soaked. Never will I forget that scene. We hugged and kissed, and then I hailed a taxi to the transit camp.

I told Mr. and Mrs. Meisels everything that had happened, including the *din Torah* and my vindication through the dismissal of all charges. Rabbi Snieg sent warm regards and a message to Mr. Meisels. "Please tell Mr. Meisels that now, after meeting his son-in-law, I fully approve of the match." When I asked my father-in-law the meaning of this message, I learned that before the engagement Mr. Meisels had gone to Rabbi Snieg to request references concerning my character, but the rabbi was not much help. Although Rabbi Snieg had heard of me, he had not known me personally. After the *din Torah,* he was in a position to comment.

A few days later, Mr. and Mrs. Meisels, my sister-in-law Anda, and my Gena boarded a ship and left for the United States. We were separated once again.

PART IV

Nature that framed us of four elements,
Warring within our breasts for regiment,
Doth teach us all to have aspiring minds.

Christopher Marlowe (1564–1593)
Tamburlaine the Great, Part I

ONE FOOT IN THE NEW WORLD

HIAS arranged passage for refugees by having them work on board ship. The HIAS escort officer had us organize the kosher kitchen and take charge of daily prayers. Jews who kept kosher provided for themselves and, with the cooperation of the supply officers on board, made satisfactory arrangements. We were assigned a special cooking and eating area, and engaged a number of Jews to help. If they had not worked in the kosher kitchen, these people would have been swabbing the decks or scrubbing toilets. For *Shabes*, we prepared a huge pot of *tsholnt* (a slowly simmered stew of beans, barley, potatoes, onions, garlic, and meat).

In our free time, we sat on deck for the fresh air and to people-watch. The farther into the North Atlantic we went, the rougher the ride became. The waves were so high they seemed ready to swallow us. The ship swayed to and fro, and seasickness took its toll. As we embarrassedly watched each other getting sick, we relieved our misery with humor. There was one elegant young lady whose model-like looks made her stand out of the crowd, but her composure did not help her as she, too, leaned over the railing and heaved her stomach contents over the side. We lost our appetites and could not hold down any food. As a result, the ton of *tsholnt* we prepared was spoiled, and it, too, was tossed over the side.

The next job assignment was to clean the large, walk-in refrigerator, which was a blessing in disguise. The low temperature made us feel better, as did the food inside. There were plenty of grapefruits and tropical fruits—a rare and healthy treat.

We stopped in Halifax, Canada, then continued to New York to disembark on Pier 26 on Manhattan's West Side. We did not go through the immigration ordeal on Ellis Island because we had been precleared in Bremerhaven. It was January 20, 1951. I was among 140,000 Jewish refugees who came to the United States between 1946 and 1953. To my great joy, my darling Gena was waiting for me at the pier. She was fashionably dressed in a black wraparound coat with a large Persian lamb collar and a beautiful hat decorated with an unusual pin. She looked exquisite, and we were thrilled to see each other after our long separation.

After I went through U.S. Customs, I put most of my luggage into storage and took a taxi to 355 Schenck Avenue in Brooklyn, where Gena had rented two rooms for us from the Cohen family. We shared the kitchen but bought and prepared our own food.

Our landlords were an elderly couple who still had vim and vigor. When I first arrived, Gena and I hardly left our rooms because we needed to catch up. Occasionally, the Cohens engaged us in conversation because they wanted to hear stories from the Old Country, and we obliged, but they imagined that Europe was the world of the *shtetl*, the world they had left many years earlier. The Cohens never experienced the vibrant culture and abundant luxuries of large European cities. Their memories enshrined villages of overcrowded cottages filled with ragged children. They fled that kind of poverty to chase the *goldene medina* (golden land)—an American dream, where mythic streets were paved with gold. In New York, conditions improved for the Cohens, but the couple never acquired riches. Gena and I were careful with these nice but simple people because we did not want to hurt their feelings.

I registered for English classes, and Mrs. Cohen insisted on accompanying me to school because she wanted to help. We got my application forms in the school office, but Mrs. Cohen was at a complete loss and looked for someone who could speak Yiddish. After 50 years in America, she still could not communicate in English!

I gained a rudimentary knowledge of English and tried to improve by reading the newspaper. Mrs. Cohen tried to teach me proper pronunciation. She had a heavy Brooklyn accent with Yiddish-inflected mispronunciation and insisted that I say the words her way and not in the proper fashion taught in school. The Cohens' children and grandchildren visited on weekends. Once, Mrs. Cohen started "correcting" my geography (a subject I had liked since childhood) in front of the children, so I decided to defend myself and set the record straight. Mrs. Cohen became very upset. How could I, who just came from the Old Country, dare to tell her, who had been in America for more than five decades, how to speak properly!

For the next few weeks, Mrs. Cohen did not try to fix my English. One day I walked into her kitchen, carrying a bag of grapefruit.

"Do you like grapefruit?" she asked.

I politely answered, "Yes."

"Did you see grapefruit in the Old Country?"

"Yes."

"Does grapefruit grow in the Old Country?"

"No."

"So, Yossele, how could you see grapefruit in the Old Country?"

I explained that grapefruit was imported and sold in European fruit stores.

Mrs. Cohen, as warm-hearted as she was, and others of her generation, never seemed to understand that Europe was not the backwater they remembered, so they often engaged in discussions that were typically like the one about grapefruit.

ODD JOBS AND ODD BEHAVIOR

Being in America did not sit comfortably with me. I had ended up there because of Gena's family visa and Mrs. Meisels' wish to join her two brothers. Unfortunately, after our arrival, we discovered that one of Mrs. Meisels' brothers had died. HIAS helped us and generally did a magnificent job of assisting Jews who immigrated to countries other than Israel, but not those who wanted to make *aliyah*. I resented the agency for that. From a humanistic perspective, I respected HIAS for reuniting families and providing health care. But I believed HIAS should have concentrated on settling more DPs in Israel from 1945 to 1955.

The HIAS office was on Astor Place and East 8th Street in Greenwich Village. The staff wanted me to leave immediately for Chicago, Illinois, where my sponsor had a plumbing job for me. I said, "Chicago? I haven't heard good things about Chicago, and I am afraid to go there."

"What did you hear about it?" she asked.

At first I was reluctant to say, but I continued, "I heard that Chicago is full of dangerous gangsters, and I do not think I belong there. I would rather stay in New York." The woman at HIAS let me know that she had no jobs for me in New York, but one was assured for me in Chicago. I explained that I would assume responsibility for finding a job on my own. Even though I had no prospects right then, I expected to find a job in the near future. I was young and resourceful, and New York City was full of possibilities.

That was the extent of the help I received from HIAS and the end of my association with the organization. I was now on my own although I did not know the language and was not yet familiar with the city. One day, I found myself in Times Square and stopped to ask a man for directions. From the few words I knew, I guessed he was directing me to a subway station. Vehemently I cried out, "No, no subway, no underground. I spent enough time underground. I want to be able to see the city from above ground."

The man smiled and walked away, leaving me standing there. When I would ask someone in Rome for directions, the person took time to explain accurately and usually accompanied me part of the way to make sure I did not get lost. No such courtesy was shown in New York, where everyone is always in a hurry.

My mother-in-law's surviving brother, Uncle Phillip, and his wife, Tillie, had a fur store on West 29th Street. The store was centrally located, so we often used it as a rendezvous point. Auntie Tillie was a smart lady, so I asked her about the problem with my visa and told her why I refused to go to Chicago. I explained my family background and my business experience and asked if she knew anyone who would give me a job. Perhaps she could recommend a place I could look?

She went to the back room and returned with two pages torn from the Yellow Pages of the Manhattan telephone directory listing haberdashery stores in Manhattan. I was disheartened because I had expected to be given the name of an acquaintance with a job offer. At least she took the time to explain where the stores were located. I thanked her and used those pages to learn the city's streets.

There were no jobs, and if I had been offered a dollar for each rejection, I would have been rich. I began to focus on the Lower East Side because of its high concentration of small stores. I went door to door, from Orchard to Canal, and from Irvington to Eldridge. The proprietors sized me up and told me they could not hire people who did not belong to the union. Weeks passed. I continued going door to door, sounding like a broken record, "Can you use me?" (That was all I could ask in English.) When they answered in English, I was in trouble because, most of the time, I could not understand them. At those moments I remembered Mrs. Cohen's plaintive question in the school office, "Doesn't anybody here speak Yiddish?"

I went to the union offices on 16 Astor Place and sat there for hours, waiting for someone to see me. Finally, I understood that the union was almost impossible to join: it was a closed shop. I later learned that admission to this particular union, Local 65, was extremely unlikely unless you were a Communist.

I tried a new strategy. I approached the stores with a fistful of $20 bills and asked the same question, "Can you use me?" It was a Friday afternoon, and there were a few stores on Allen Street that I had not yet covered. I reached 33A Allen Street, walked up to the owner (my money in hand), and boldly said, "Here, I will pay you. Can you use me?" The owner looked at me as if I was crazy. "I need the job desperately. Please, I will pay *you*," I repeated.

Mr. Beaver, a short, dark-haired man, asked me, "How much will you pay?" I explained that any sum he suggested would be fine. "I will accept $35," he said. I agreed, and he asked me to come to work on Sunday at 7:30 a.m. On Sunday at 7 a.m., I stood in front of the store, waiting for my new boss to arrive. When he showed up, I helped him remove the iron bars from the front door and went inside. I listened carefully to his instructions and his warning to watch for shoplifters. I arranged the merchandise, cleaned the shop, and prepared for the customers. I worked and until very late, but it was rewarding. Work was all I wanted. On my first Friday afternoon, the owner took out $35 and was ready to pay me, but I took $35 from my pocket and gave it to him. "This was the agreement we made. Either you accept this money, or there is no deal."

"I thought you were joking," my boss said.

"I do not joke in business. A deal is a deal. The money is yours."

"What about next week?" he asked.

"Well, next week *you* will pay *me* $35."

I came to work again the following Sunday, sold merchandise, and did everything that had to be done. On Monday morning my boss took me down to the basement and showed me hundreds of medium-sized boxes, yellowed with age, that were stacked on the shelves. He opened one of the boxes to reveal white rubber bathing caps and then picked up a clean box to use as a sample. "All this merchandise has to be unloaded," he said. I promised to do my best.

I went from store to store. The first day I sold a gross and the following day a little more. Within two weeks, I had sold all the bathing caps. When Friday came, the owner paid me $35. After he gave me the money, I told him my wages for the next week would be a $100. He offered me $50 and then went to $75, but I was firm in my demand. I told him that union wages were $125, and he was saving $25 a week by employing me. Besides, a union man would not work late hours or sell bathing caps as quickly as I did. Mr. Beaver agreed.

After working there a while, I realized that Mr. Beaver's business margins were much smaller than the ones we had back in Europe and that so much competition in the immediate vicinity made it even tougher. I saw there was no great future in his business, so after I collected all the payments for the caps and turned them in to Mr. Beaver, I left.

My in-laws had a friend from Europe, a Mr. Lublin, who was in a supposedly lucrative waste material business. I was interested but could not approach the people I knew to find out more about the business. They would not have shared accurate information with me because they did not want competition. I wanted to figure out how to get into it. The Yellow Pages were no help. I did not want a job; I wanted my own business.

On Sunday morning, I went to the HIAS office in Manhattan, which served as a gathering place for newcomers. I approached Shmulowitz, a fellow I had met in Bremerhaven and gotten to know on the boat coming over. He seemed honest and was also looking for something to do. I proposed a partnership, but in the beginning I was hesitant to disclose what kind of business I had in mind, lest he take the idea and run with it. Once I decided he could be trusted, I told him that the first thing we had to do was buy a truck. We purchased a one-ton truck, printed business cards, and named the company "Allied Waste Material," using the word "Allied" for sentimental reasons. The name "Allied" also ensured that we would be listed at the beginning of the appropriate listings in the Yellow Pages.

So, we were in business: we owned equipment and business cards, but we knew nothing about prices or stock. We went to Greene Street, where all the companies dealing with waste materials had warehouses and the streets were strewn with swatches of fabric that had fallen from burlap-wrapped bales of cuttings while they were being loaded and unloaded. We picked up handfuls of these cuttings as samples and approached different dealers, offering them 2,000 pounds of one kind, 500 pounds of another, or 3,500 pounds of a third. Whatever rates the dealers quoted, I replied with an offer to sell at half a cent more per pound. Had anyone agreed to our price, we would have been in real trouble because we could not deliver merchandise we did not have; but that was how we learned about pricing the different fabrics.

Taking the samples with us, we then drove our truck to the garment district in Manhattan. We parked, rode the elevator to the top of one building, and went from door to door making inquiries. In four hours, we bought a truckload of goods. Paying in cash and offering a little more than the going rate helped us. We were satisfied and rented a place to store the material. We temporarily shared a loft with someone who was no longer active in business but did not want to give up his place. Using a metal sorting net, we separated the various cuttings according to color and quality. Shmulowitz stood on one side and I on the other, racing to see who was faster at filling up barrels.

After a while, I had to blow my nose, and two black beads of soot came out of my nostrils. I realized that dirt was settling in my lungs, which could affect my health adversely, even in a matter of weeks. I could not breathe properly through a mask, and after what I had been through in the German mines and tunnels, I did not feel like playing around with my health. Right then and there, I concluded that the scrap business was not for me. I immediately told my partner, and because the profit on a day's investment was pretty good, Shmulowitz decided to keep the company. We worked out the financial details and parted amicably.

One rule I honored without exception was never to pursue a business that would jeopardize my health. A side issue in the scrap business was that I did not like lifting the huge bales of fabric with the S-shaped hooks that reminded me of the SS.

Next, I imagined that the mail-order business was clean, reputable, safe, and profitable. I researched the advantages and disadvantages by reading newspapers, magazines, and ads. Usually, advertisers printed only post-box numbers, but I managed to visit a few establishments that included their addresses, arriving without an appointment because my imperfect English made me self-conscious. I thought I would have a better chance if I faced people in person when applying for a job. A cute ad with a picture of a utility briefcase attracted my attention; the address also seemed right, as did the name of the company: Allied Briefcase Company.

I entered a building on the corner of 23rd Street and Fifth Avenue and took the elevator to the fifth floor. At the office, a nice gentleman greeted me, and I said I was looking for work. Mr. Schwartz listened to my broken English and asked exactly what I would like to do. My answer was quick and firm, "Everything the job requires." Seeing that I was neatly dressed, he may have doubted that I could do the required work. I reassured him again.

"Call me Bernie," he said in a friendly, charming way.

I explained that where I came from, we addressed people respectfully by their last names. I was impressed by Mr. Schwartz and determined to get the job, so I asked him to show me what the position entailed. I was dressed in a light, made-to-order, double-breasted beige suit that I had bought for my honeymoon, with a matching gold and white striped shirt with cufflinks. I took off my jacket, rolled up my sleeves, and said I was ready to start. He said, "No, not now. I will show you around, but then you will have to go home, change into work clothes, and come back whenever you want."

Back at the apartment, Gena was already home from work. She was employed not far from Allied Briefcase in the vicinity of Fifth Avenue and 19th Street at the Hoover Uniform Company, another mail-order business. Gena was in the advertising department and was responsible for catalogue layout.

The next day, I reported for work, eager to start. Mr. Schwartz spoke in a gentle, unassuming voice. Yet his deportment was that of a chairman of a large corporation or the president of a bank. He managed the company for the owner, who seldom came to the office. Mr. Schwartz packed briefcases, labeled cartons, and shipped them off. On the rare occasions the owner did show up, he always criticized Mr. Schwartz and caused dissension.

My job resembled Mr. Schwartz's, and besides labeling and packing, I stacked cartons on a two-wheeled dolly that, when loaded, often exceeded my height. I had difficulty getting through the doors to the elevator. When I left the building, I joined other young men pushing carts on the way to the post office on the east side of Gramercy Park. Mr. Schwartz accompanied me to the post office on my first two trips and showed me what to do. We specialized in briefcases for doctors, priests, and executives, so our ads were placed in different trade journals, magazines, and newspapers.

After perhaps two months, my enthusiasm waned, though my feelings for Mr. Schwartz had not changed. I decided that being a shipping clerk was not the American dream—it certainly was not mine. After I resigned, I visited Mr. Schwartz whenever I could to keep him informed about my life. Bernie Schwartz was sincerely interested in and proud of my progress, and he took me under his wing and assumed some responsibility for my well-being. I really appreciated his teaching and advice; his small acts of kindness gave this immigrant a leg up on American ways. Any good news I brought him made him happy. I miss Bernie. Seldom in life does one encounter such a noble man.

When Gena and I lived in Brooklyn, we attended services at Rabbi Schmidman's *shul*—a large Orthodox synagogue. Rabbi Schmidman liked my father-in-law and was especially appreciative when he led prayers. We all enjoyed services there, but then my in-laws moved to the Bronx, and unless we visited them, we were usually on our own for *Shabes*.

One day, I received a draft card from the Selective Service Commission requesting my appearance for a physical examination. Some of my friends had already been drafted. Those who did not want to serve in the army went back to Europe or left for other countries. Gena and I did not plan to stay in the United States after my in-laws were settled. We considered ourselves en route to Israel. With the war in Korea, the prospect of becoming an American soldier and endangering my life in Eastern Asia, after what I had been through in the German extermination camps, did not appeal to me. I admired the American people and their policy of fighting for freedom. Indeed, American troops had saved my life when they liberated Ebensee. But I was not ready to sacrifice my life on the altar of another war.

I decided to go for the physical, but first I wanted to be legally married in the United States. After receiving a marriage license in court, Gena and I went through an American civil marriage ceremony administered by Rabbi Schmidman with only our closest family members in attendance. It was a moving moment, because again we were not sure what the future might hold. Just the thought of fighting in far-off jungles was enough to mar the occasion. In the meantime, Gena and I found a nice apartment in the Bronx at 1950 Andrews Avenue, thanks to Mr. Egert, a friend of Mr. Meisels who had come to America before World War II. From our corner apartment on the top floor, we had a magnificent view of the George Washington and Henry Hudson Bridges.

When the time came for my army physical, I reported to Whitehall Street. It was a hot July day, and there was a long line of perhaps a thousand men, standing stripped to the waist, waiting to be examined. As the line moved forward, we shed more clothing until we were down to our undershorts. With the help of several nurses, a panel of doctors processed the new recruits and accepted almost all of them. The line moved slowly, but finally my turn came. I stayed in my long underwear despite the sweltering heat. When I reached the first physician, he asked me to take off my underwear, but I refused, claiming to be cold. The attendants weighed me; looked into my eyes, ears, and mouth; took blood; and classified me as 1A. The last doctor who examined me was a major—I think a psychiatrist—and in a low voice he asked me several questions, including one concerning the whereabouts of my parents.

I answered, "They were killed by the Nazis. I only wish I were dead, too, so I could be with them."

"By all rights, you should have been dead, too," he said. I could not tell if he meant what he said as an antisemitic comment or if he meant it sympathetically. I decided, either way, to keep acting eccentrically, so I embraced him and patted his back while saying, "I see you are my friend. You understand me." At that point, he took the card back from me and replaced it with one marked F. I figured he wanted me out either because he hated me and thought that I had a few screws loose or because he felt sorry for an orphaned concentration camp survivor. I had mixed feelings about being rejected by the army. On the one hand, I was happy not to be going to Korea; on the other hand, I felt bad about not being grouped with the other healthy men who had been accepted. Only one other person was rejected that day, and he was brought in on a stretcher. Gena was waiting impatiently for my return and worrying about the outcome. When I got home and told her about my rejection, she was overjoyed.

DAVY CROCKETT AND THE BANDITS

Gena's company, Hoover Uniforms, needed a file clerk. A college student named Marsha Perlman came looking for summer employment and applied for the job, but company policy was not to hire students because it was not worth training temporary workers. Gena had taken a liking to Marsha and advised her not to mention that she was a student. Consequently, Marsha was hired. She was studying to be an English teacher and was married to Leo, an optometrist. Pretty soon, the four of us became great friends. Though they lived in Brooklyn and we were in the Bronx, we visited often. We also went to the movies and the theater and planned small trips together. Once we even went camping on Candlewood Lake in Connecticut.

To improve my English, I forced myself to struggle through the *New York Times* or *New York Herald Tribune*. When I made mistakes in my spoken English, Marsha would apologize and correct my pronunciation and usage. I was grateful for the opportunity to learn and insisted that her corrections were a demonstration of true friendship.

Uncle Phillip's store on 29th Street remained a convenient gathering place. I met his children there—his oldest daughter, Rhoda, and her husband, Willie; his daughter Gloria and her husband, Eddie; and his only son, Stanley, an artist. Stanley received a fellowship to continue his education in France, and two of his paintings were accepted at the Metropolitan Museum of Art in New York. Gena and I went to see his work and were delighted that many of the artistic treasures in that glorious museum compared to those in Europe.

Uncle Phillip and Auntie Tillie were not very worldly; they were homebodies.

They were shocked when soon after we arrived, I bought a car and announced that Gena and I intended to visit my brothers in Toronto.

"Are you crazy? We've been here over 35 years, and we have never been to Canada. You've only been here a short time, and already you want to undertake such a long trip?" Uncle Phillip wanted to know how I would find my way. Gently I let him know that a map would help me locate Canada and my brothers. He was still worried and made me promise to call him from the road. Early the next morning, we were on our way; by evening, we called Uncle Phillip to let him know we were fine.

"Are you already in Monticello?" Uncle Phillip asked. To his surprise, we were already in Toronto. We called Chaim to let him know we had arrived. When we got to his house on Shaw Street and rang the bell, a little boy in a checked flannel robe appeared at the top of the stairs and yelled for his mother. After warm greetings from Rose and little Jerry, I learned that my brothers had gone to get us at Union Station, because they assumed we were coming in by train.

When there were no passengers left on the train, Chaim and Willie came home and, amid hugs and kisses, tried to catch up on all that had happened since we had parted. Eventually, the talk turned to Art. I shared only part of my dismal experience with him, but Chaim refused to believe me. Gena was angry that my word was doubted and, despite her gentle nature, was compelled to confirm the veracity of my statements. Gena was meeting my two brothers and their wives for the first time; I was glad to have an ally at my side to defend my honor. The visit did not start off on the right foot, but at least we let our viewpoints be known.

Both of my brothers were employed as steam pressers in factories in the Spadina garment district of Toronto. After he worked in northern Ontario as a lumberjack, Willie came to Toronto and met his wife, Dina, a war orphan who had survived Auschwitz/Birkenau in the "Canada" section. My brothers labored in sweatshops and were not paid a regular salary; they were paid for piecework and received nothing if they were not at work producing. We did not want to hold them back from their work, so after only two days, we returned to New York.

When we told Gena's parents about our trip to Toronto, my father-in-law told me that one of his friends, Alex Tantzman, manufactured novelties made of fur and asked if I would be interested in working for him. I agreed to see if I liked him and the job because there were no better prospects on the horizon.

The next day we went to Tantzman's factory, where they manufactured Davy Crockett hats from raccoon tails. The television shows, books, and comics were telling the story of this American frontier hero, and the item was a good moneymaker. The factory was full of people, all of them very busy. When I asked Mr. Tantzman what he expected me to do, he said I would be in charge of shipping, receiving, and overall production. I was pleased; this position was not bad for a newcomer with little experience. When I asked about the salary, he replied, "If you are what your father-in-law described, I am willing to pay you $100 per week." I gladly accepted because I really needed the money. All the funds I had brought with me from Germany came to $7,777, and we had spent it buying good furniture and filling up our new apartment.

Mr. Tantzman's factory was busy. He supervised the cutting, sewing, and lining of the hats. Because of the great demand, large numbers of our hats were produced by outside contractors. Monitoring the incoming and outgoing goods was vital. After half a day on the job, I sent the receiving clerk out to do other work on the floor, locked up the room, and took over the job. Two large cartons came in with the first shipment and a packing slip showed that there were 500 hats in each carton. I called in the clerk and asked him what to do. He took the packing slip and signed for receipt of 1,000 hats. The contractor argued that he was in a hurry, but I insisted that we inspect the merchandise. We opened the cartons, and the three of us started counting. Each carton was short 100 hats. We counted again and again—the total was always the same. The same "error" was repeated when we checked shipments from the second and third contractors, except that the numbers of missing hats were slightly different. Evidently, the deception had been going on for quite some time and with great loss to the company.

I brought this problem to Mr. Tantzman's attention and showed him 12 delivery slips that did not correspond to the actual number of hats received. There were about 1,500 hats missing. I had uncovered this fraud after working at the factory for only three days, and when Mr. Tantzman realized what was going on in his shop, he almost hit the ceiling.

"Now I understand why, even though I work like a horse day and night, I do not see the results of my labor. It's no wonder, being surrounded by such thieves!" I dismissed the receiver, hired another one, and told the new man why his predecessor had been fired, thereby issuing a warning that dishonesty would not be tolerated and contractors must be watched. Similar "errors" were evident in production when operators were paid by piecework and claimed more items than they produced. I was promoted and replaced the foreman on the floor.

Unfortunately, I was allergic to raccoon fur, and between that and all the dust swirling around, I could not stop sneezing. With regret, I gave Mr. Tantzman notice that I would be leaving, but I promised to stay until the shop was well organized and running properly. Mr. Tantzman did not want me to go and offered me $300 a week, hoping I would change my mind. When I declined, he proposed a 50 percent partnership in the business. I assured him that I held him in the highest regard and were my health not in jeopardy, I would be pleased to stay.

In the meantime, my father-in-law became a partner in Uncle Phillip's fur business, and after he invested a few thousand dollars in it, the company prospered. Although my father-in-law had never been a furrier, he was a keen businessman and was well liked by everyone for his honesty and fairness. It did not take him long to familiarize himself with the fur business. Before the war, Mr. Meisels had been in a large-scale grain and seed business. His company was listed on the Lemberg stock exchange, and he had been in the import/export business with Germany, Italy, and Hungary, exporting grains and seeds and importing tropical fruits.

THE DYNAMICS OF DYNAMIC ELECTRONICS

It was time to look for a venture that would not make me sneeze—literally. Television was a fairly new phenomenon, and the potential market was huge. News, entertainment, sports, and education could all be enjoyed in the privacy of one's home. This novelty did not come cheap, but a huge advertising apparatus had been set in motion to entice people to purchase TV sets with minimal down payments and small monthly installments. Free demonstrations were provided. A prospective customer simply made a phone call, and within an hour a man with a TV set would arrive at the interested party's home. A customer could keep the set for a week and then decide whether to keep it or return it. Television commercials and promotions that ran in newspapers and on radio heralded the competing companies: Davega Stores, Vim Stores, Dynamic Electronics, and so forth. I listened carefully to these ads and decided to get on the bandwagon. Maybe TV would be the right thing for me.

I checked out a couple of stores but decided against being an inside salesman because I would not be free to come and go, and the commissions were not as high as those for people on the road. I was drawn to the name Dynamic Electronics—it seemed to imply modernity and movement—and drove out to their main office on Woodhaven Boulevard in the industrial section of Queens. Once there, I asked for an employment application form and filled it out as best I could, inflating the details of my experience a little. Otherwise, I would have no chance of getting such a job. I looked around to see what kind of people were associated with the company and was pleased that most were presentable and well dressed. At my other positions in America, I had to wear casual clothes, but I aspired to a white-collar job. Although I hoped to be selected, I had doubts about my ability. Still, I owed it to myself to try. I submitted the form and was told by the receptionist to return the next day for an interview.

Back home, I described the operation to Gena. In anticipation of the next day's meeting, I was too excited to sleep. By now, I was certain I wanted the job. The words "free home demonstration, free home ... free" kept ringing in my ears. The following morning at Dynamic Electronics, I was ushered into the office of the general manager, a nice man in his 40s. He asked me many questions, and with my imperfect English—never mind the heavy accent—I answered as best I could. I kept talking, asking for a chance to prove myself and assuring the man that, if he hired me, he would not be sorry. At this point, the general manager tried to discourage me, suggesting this type of work might be too difficult for a person of my background.

The more hesitant he was, the more I wanted the job. This tactic had always worked in reverse for me. Realizing that I was determined and that he could not dissuade me from trying, the manager started to explain, "Point one: we advertise on the radio, and each call costs us $50, which is a lot of money. Do you understand?"

"Yes, it is a lot of money."

"Point two: if you go to a prospective customer and leave the television set, you will be personally responsible for the set. No matter what, do not leave the TV as a demonstrator. Do you understand?"

"Yes, Mr. Levine, I understand." (By that time, I had noticed his engraved nameplate on the desk.)

"Point three: if a prospective customer complains to the radio station, or any publication, about misrepresentation, you will be fired. Do you understand?"

"Yes, sir, I understand what you're saying."

"Do you have a car?"

"Yes, I do." I had put that information on the application, but Mr. Levine wanted to make sure.

He went on to tell me I would be lucky if he hired me because he already had 436 salesmen working for Dynamic Electronics, a very reputable corporation. "Do you understand?"

"Yes, Mr. Levine."

All of a sudden, a man barged into the office (later I learned his name was Irving Tepper) and said to Mr. Levine, "Mickey, what the hell are you doing? Now you're hiring refugees right off the boat? What's the matter with you, Mickey!" The partition wall that divided the offices was less than five feet high, and everybody could hear whatever was discussed in Mr. Levine's office. Irving Tepper had probably listened to the whole exchange between us. Levine was angry and let Irving know it was none of his business whom he hired.

"It is my business if we're forced off the air!" Tepper replied.

"Let me worry about that," said Mr. Levine. But I started worrying instead and had second thoughts about the job. Mr. Levine came from behind the desk and suggested that he and I take a little walk. On the way out, he passed his secretary, picked up a bunch of cards—"leads"—and pulled out two for me. Outside in the yard, Mickey put his arm around my shoulder. "Joey, do not disappoint me. I would like to teach this bastard a lesson, so please try your best."

I looked into his shining eyes and said, "Mickey, I promise you."

Mr. Levine asked me to drive with him to the loading dock at the back of the building. After we both signed for a new television set, I put the set I had in the trunk of my car. "Joe, if you sell one of the two leads I gave you, I will be satisfied."

I assured him that my aim was to sell both leads. We shook hands, and I drove off with my ammunition: catalogues, antennas, prices, contracts, applications, and the heavy artillery—one TV. While driving, I was praying for help, "God, lead me, help me. I confess that I need your help." As overly dramatic as it seems in hindsight, I started reciting parts of the *Hazzan's* prayer before the *Musaf* of Yom Kippur—*Hinneni, he'ani mi'ma'as*—in which he declares that, although he is personally unqualified to represent the congregation, he asks the Almighty to accept his prayers on their behalf. I, too, hoped that He would speed me along in my mission on behalf of Dynamic Electronics.

I drove to one of the tenement blocks in Manhattan, walked up four flights of stairs, and knocked on the door. I introduced myself, the residents let me in, and they asked me to sit on the couch in the living room. I opened my briefcase and showed them pictures of television sets in the catalogue. We discussed the differences between the various models, and I tossed some questions in their direction: Where did they work? How much did they make? In the meantime, I filled out an application and told them there was no problem with their credit rating. I kept talking, explaining that the monthly payments would be $30, and asked them which television set they had decided to purchase.

"The better one, the Philharmonic," they said promptly, and offered to pay $100 down, with the balance on delivery, because they did not like to buy on credit. I promised them a free antenna, worth about $30, plus a two-year warranty instead of the standard one-year type. I also told them that if they found me another customer so that I could reach my quota, I would give them an additional gift. "Yes, yes, my sister wants to get one, too, and they did not deliver on time as they promised, so she might be interested." I immediately closed the transaction and walked two blocks to the sister's apartment.

The sister was expecting me because my customer had called her on the phone, so I received a nice welcome and an offer of some coffee. I declined the coffee but asked for a glass of water. Back to business: obtain the credit information, fill out the application, praise the choice of a Philharmonic, and assure her that as soon as the credit was approved, the television would be delivered. I told her she would be treated well, and she was. I also asked if she knew anyone else interested in buying a television set, in exchange for which we would either refund her down payment or cover her first installment. That was not company policy, but I was willing to take a cut on my end to get more customers and reckoned I would make more in the long run while also proving my value to the company. She was very happy with that offer and promised to find me some new customers because she had many friends.

I rushed to cover the second lead because it was already 9 p.m. I apologized for being late by explaining that there were so many customers buying television sets. I showed my new prospects the signed contracts in my possession and said I would be happy to accommodate them as soon as they told me what kind of television they wanted. "We asked for a free home demonstration, and you are showing us pictures. Where is it?"

"Yes, you will get a free home demonstration once you decide what kind of television set you would like to have demonstrated." I sat down and pulled out most of the catalogues I had with me. I showed them photographs of the RCA, Magnavox, Philco, Dumont, and other brand names. "We have all kinds of televisions, but you have to decide." Slowly, I explained the differences between consoles, table models, or combinations with record players or radios. By the time I had closed a deal with them, it was past 11 p.m. The only problem I had was coming home so late and explaining where I had been. Gena could not understand who would let me into their home at such an hour. This was not the first or last time I had to justify coming home late. The work did not end when I got home. I sat down at my desk and reviewed the three contracts to make sure I had not made any mistakes. Some I had to correct, and then I was unable to sleep, anticipating the next day at the office.

In the morning I drove to Dynamic Electronics and entered my sales on the scoreboard with my sales and identification number, 437. We also had to list the number of the model sold, the date of sale, and the date of delivery. When I brought the three deals into the office, Mr. Levine was ecstatic. He was happy I had not let him down and felt vindicated for trusting me, in spite of Irving Tepper's nasty remarks. "Joey, now that you have proven yourself to be a good man for the organization, let me introduce you to the credit manager, Marvin Greenberg."

We walked to Mr. Greenberg's office, which was completely private—no partitions there. Mr. Levine knocked on the door but did not wait for an answer before entering. We were asked to sit down, and Mr. Greenberg looked at the two contracts. The one that was a cash deal Mr. Levine retained in his hand. He asked Mr. Greenberg to process the contracts right away because "Joe Tenenbaum needs the dough." Then we left. On the way to the shipping department, I was introduced to the head accountant, Eli Glitzenstein. We exchanged a few words, then Mr. Levine and I proceeded to shipping, where I was again presented to the department head and told to bring cash deals to this man, who would look after me and make sure the merchandise was delivered on time. When Mickey went back to his own office, I stayed behind to get acquainted with the people from the other departments.

I will never forget when Norman Bender, a hulk of a fellow about 35 years old, invited me to the cafeteria. "Joey, I overheard what Tepper said to Mickey about you. I have been with this company for many years—my number is 52. Listen, my parents also died in the Holocaust. When you go to sell, in one pocket you have to carry with you a knife and in the other pocket a grenade. The people you will meet will take your heart out and throw it away. They will roll it, pinch it, puncture it, bleed it, squeeze it, break it, and then give it back to you." To make sure I did not forget this lecture, Bender repeated it. I had sympathy for this man; evidently, he had been hurt badly.

I also met John Chow, a very nice Chinese American. Although he did not talk much, he was the top salesman in the company. His number was 96. From John Chow and Eli Glitzenstein, I learned that besides the commission, the company held a monthly sales contest with a top prize of a $1,000 U.S. savings bond, and a second prize of a $500 bond. All the salesmen had to attend general meetings every Monday morning, and the one who made the most sales had to deliver a speech and explain the techniques of superior salesmanship—the tricks of the trade that led to his success. In my second month with the company, I won the $500 bond, and after the third month, no one beat me for first prize for several months running. I developed a good rapport with the credit manager, shipping manager, and people in all the different departments.

When Mickey Levine asked me to deliver a speech, I declined, telling him I was not comfortable because I was not a public speaker. He would not accept my refusal and insisted that I do him the favor of speaking. Irving Tepper was present and was most curious about my selling style. I reluctantly went up to the podium. When I overheard Tepper making derogatory remarks about me again, I stood there in silence, unable to say a word. Tepper yelled out, "Tenenbaum, speak! Tell us how you make the sales."

My answer was, "Me no speak English. Me have an accent, not like Irving Tepper who speaks so nicely." Everybody started to applaud, and Tepper got the message. I stepped down from the podium and said nothing else.

Dynamic Electronics pushed the Philharmonic television. It was just an average box, but they had their name on it, and it was made exclusively for them. To encourage Philharmonic sales, we were given 200 points for each Philharmonic sold. It was hard to sell an unknown brand, but some people succeeded in selling a few. Ninety-five percent of my sales were Philharmonic sets. Sales leads were distributed according to different areas of the city, and salesmen naturally wanted the better sections of town. They did not care how far they had to travel. It was important to make a sale, but one had to be careful that customers did not complain to the radio station about misrepresentation. We also did not want to waste too much time with customers or give them a chance to change their minds about a purchase.

There were some leads that no one wanted to touch. Experienced salesmen knew which areas of town and customers to avoid, yet undesirable leads had to be followed up, too. One such lead was a Dr. Buchbinder on East 54th Street between Fifth Avenue and Madison. The advertisement on the radio kept repeating, "Within one hour, the television set will be delivered to your home. Just pick up the phone and call for a free demonstration." Dr. Buchbinder called and rightfully expected a television set to be delivered. No one wanted to accept this lead. Mickey took me aside and practically begged me to take the assignment. Otherwise, we might have a problem with the customer. I was afraid to take the card because no matter what I did, in the long run I expected to be the loser. Yet I did not want to let Mickey down. Finally, I decided to do Mickey this favor; after all, I owed him for taking a chance on me in the first place. I took the card and prepared psychologically for combat.

While crossing the 59th Street Bridge into Manhattan, I imagined different scenarios for meeting Dr. Buchbinder. The appointment was for 3 p.m. I pushed down the accelerator so as not to be late and arrived at the customer's door at 3:10. I rang the bell once, and there was no answer. I rang two more times, still no answer. "Thank God," I thought. "Fine! It's wonderful. Problem solved. Now I am safe. Nobody is home." I was about to enter the elevator when I heard somebody calling, "Mister, Mister." I turned around and saw a man standing in the hallway. "Did you ring my bell?"

I told him I had rung three times.

"Yes, but I expected you at three o'clock, not now," he answered, looking at his watch.

"I'm sorry, Dr. Buchbinder, but the traffic was heavy, and that's why I am five minutes late."

"Twelve minutes," he corrected me. I told him again how sorry I was and offered to come back at a more convenient time. "Since you're already here, why waste more time?"

I walked into a beautiful, classy apartment, and he called for his wife, Gertrude, telling her that the television set had arrived. She entered the living room, and the doctor introduced me as the television man. "Where is the television?" he asked.

I told him that before we brought up a television set, we liked to make sure it would meet the requirements of the caller. Then I opened my briefcase and started removing the catalogues. He stopped me and said I should not waste my time because they already knew what they wanted. He pulled out a thick folder with a bunch of papers, each with different models and prices marked. By this time I knew all the statistics, but Dr. Buchbinder appeared to be an expert.

He must have shopped around all over the city and wasted the time of many salesmen. There I was, his next victim. Upset, I prepared myself for war. They wanted a free home demonstration on a Dumont model 1350, if possible.

"Dr. Buchbinder, that's fine. If you've decided on this particular model, you can have it."

He asked me the price, and I told him $599, quoting a figure that was about $60 below our own cost. I knew I had no choice but to gamble that way, hoping for a miracle. By now, Dr. Buchbinder was convinced that he was getting an excellent deal, cheaper than at any other place, $150 less than in the Davega store, and $175 less than Vim. He asked me to write out the contract and gave me a $200 deposit; the balance would be paid on delivery. I offered him the television on installments, but, thanking me, he declined, preferring to pay cash. Everything was signed and sealed, and slowly I started to collect my materials when he asked me if he had gotten a good deal.

"Dr. and Mrs. Buchbinder, you have gotten a very good deal, but I could have given you a better deal." My hand was already on the door handle when he stopped me.

"Herr Tenenbaum, please sit down." I sat, and he asked what a better deal would be.

"A better television for less money," I replied. "A Philharmonic." I had a beautiful color photo of the new Philharmonic and a good description of it. I showed it to the Buchbinders, adding that if color television came out in the future, all they would have to do was add a "califati" switch and this set would be converted into a color TV. To this day, I do not know what a "califati" switch does, nor does anybody else. With other brands, this "change" was not possible. Buchbinder started to ask his wife what they should do, and, of course, she gave him the right advice: cancel the Dumont and order a Philharmonic for $450. The Buchbinders were so happy they would not let me leave without offering me coffee and *kuchen* (cake). As we talked about *Die Walküre, Der Ring des Niebelungen, Tristan und Isolde*, and other Wagnerian operas, they became so friendly that they gave me two tickets to the Metropolitan Opera so that Gena and I could attend. They wanted to meet again so that the four of us could go out together for dinner.

It was late in the evening already, and I was too tired to cover the other leads I was supposed to follow up that day. I called the people from the Buchbinder apartment and rescheduled the appointments for the following day. Refusing to let me go, Gertrude Buchbinder brought in another pot of freshly brewed coffee. The evening passed quickly, but I finally got away. When I arrived home, Gena noticed that something was wrong. I told her the whole story and said I felt bad about selling the Buchbinders a Philharmonic. They wanted us to be friends, go out together for dinner and to the opera, and here I had cooked up such a soup. I did not know what to do. Needless to say, I could not sleep the sleep of the innocent that night. For hours, I lay in bed thinking about the problem and trying to figure out how to undo what I had done.

First thing in the morning, I drove out to Dynamic Electronics. Mickey Levine was already waiting for me, curious about how I had made out with Dr. Buchbinder. I pulled out the contract with the $200 deposit for the "best television on the market," the Philharmonic. He looked at me and started laughing.

"Mickey, this is not a laughing matter. I have a problem." I said.

"Joey, you know that sometimes you can make an exception and *not* sell a Philharmonic."

I told Mickey that Dr. Buchbinder knew all the models and prices from different stores better than we both did. The only one he did not know about and could not compare with others was the "famous Philharmonic." Then I told Mickey about the entire visit with the Buchbinders and the "friendship" that had developed. Mickey said to go back and sell them a brand name.

"Mickey, I cannot go. You do it. You wanted me to push the Philharmonic; I did. If you are worried about any future problems that might develop, you go talk to them." The supersalesman who had trained hundreds of salesmen for Dynamic Electronics asked me for Dr. Buchbinder's telephone number and called him. I listened in on the extension without interfering.

Mickey Levine introduced himself, and before he had a chance to say another word, Dr. Buchbinder started praising me, telling him what a wonderful man I was. "The company should be proud to have Mr. Tenenbaum working for it." The doctor said how much he and his wife liked me and appreciated what I did for them. Mickey offered Dr. Buchbinder a better television, but the doctor insisted that he and his wife were not going to change their minds because they trusted Mr. Tenenbaum. If Mickey changed the order, he was warned, he would have a court case on his hands. The doctor hung up the phone.

"Joey, you sold him."

What were we to do now? Eventually, I would have to face the music. I continued with the same song and dance. When Dr. Buchbinder phoned and told me about the call he had received from Mr. Levine, the general manager who tried to make him switch from Philharmonic to another brand, I said, "You are 100 percent right, Dr. Buchbinder. We will stick with our deal—no changes." A few days passed and then a couple weeks, and I called Dr. Buchbinder to inform him that the new models coming off the production line lacked the quality of the previous ones, and I could no longer recommend the Philharmonic. Since I did not want him to have an old model, I suggested that he wait a while and, in the meantime, I would deliver another set on a temporary basis. I sat down with Mickey Levine to pick the best television and antenna for Dr. Buchbinder. When the deliveryman called to say that the television had been delivered, I drove to the Buchbinders' home to make sure it was properly installed and that they had good reception. In the end, I made good on what I had initially offered Dr. Buchbinder—the best TV set. All this did not please me. I was not comfortable with this kind of business; something was wrong.

Sometimes, other salesmen came to me to complain about how slowly the credit department processed their deals, contracts, and credit. I had not encountered that problem with him to any great extent, and the fact that he and one of the office workers were having an affair was no concern of mine. But one day when I entered his office with three signed contracts, the credit manager asked me to wait outside while he was busy with her. It was one thing to be kept waiting a few minutes, but when it became 45 minutes, I did not like the situation one bit. I told him to his face that if he did not keep his personal life outside the office, he would have problems with all of us. He responded by insulting me and threatening my job. Of course, I did not want to lose my job, which I really enjoyed, because I was making $400 a week, plus bonuses and benefits.

Life in New York, especially for business, had been good to me. The job took me all over the city and gave me the opportunity to meet folks from different ethnic groups, rich and poor, intellectuals and simple souls. I found them all interesting. Now, I realized that the manager was threatening my entire livelihood. He did not listen when I asked him to keep his monkey business out of the office and to behave in a fashion befitting his position. I called a meeting of the top salesmen with Mr. Wiener, the owner and chairman of Dynamic Electronics. Mickey Levine supported us on the sidelines but officially remained neutral because he could not be perceived as being against management. If he openly supported us, he could be accused of a conflict of interest because his commissions were based on our sales. At the meeting everybody came forward with their complaints. One salesman complained that the credit manager did not process orders fast enough, which resulted in cancellations. Another complained that he required too large a down payment. A third complained that the credit manager's attitude quashed the salesmen's enthusiasm before they went out on sales calls. He said staff left the office depressed, which was not conducive to making sales.

When my turn came, I said to Mr. Wiener, "All these complaints are valid, but I will show you yet another way that the credit manager has sabotaged Dynamic Electronics. The company is losing money because of him. Here are five contracts that are four months old. The television sets have been in the customers' houses for 90 days, but the bank has not processed the contracts and the money has never been paid to Dynamic Electronics because the agreements are collecting dust in his lower drawer. The customers have not even made the first installment on the amount they owe."

This evidence of gross neglect and the credit manager's other counterproductive practices horrified Wiener. I never raised the issue of the manager's lover, although the other salesmen expected me to do that. It was not necessary. Besides, someone else's sex life was none of my business. Not long after the meeting, the credit manager resigned, making the sales staff at Dynamic Electronics very happy.

I enjoyed my job and was doing well enough not to have to worry too much about my livelihood being threatened by new salesmen. My stability afforded me the chance to be magnanimous toward other refugees, so I asked Mendel and Hershel Tenenbaum, two brothers whom I knew in Germany, if they would like to join the company. They thought the job was too hard, and they declined my offer, but they were not the only friends to whom I reached out. I wanted to bring in Sam Rosenzweig, who had just arrived from Germany and was looking for employment. I promised to teach him the ropes, telling him that if I could do it, he could, too. When he asked how much I was making, I said $400 and let him think it was per month (rather than per week) in case he did not believe me. I also did not want to boast, because in those days, the average weekly wage was $50 to $60. I managed to bring a few people into the company, including Emil Wolfe, a Swiss fellow I had met at my in-laws in Munich, and Benjamin Lapin, who did well but did not stay long.

I was doing so well that I needed the services of an accountant. Dynamic's chief financial officer, Eli Glitzenstein, whom I liked because of his gentleness and honesty, introduced me to his brother Irving, an accountant and lawyer in Brooklyn who provided me with accounting and legal services. His wife, Trudy, was nice, and we all became friends, taking short car trips together to places like Jacob Riis Park, Bayshore, and Fire Island. Though I was doing well, I was not totally comfortable with the style of high-pressure sales, and I aspired to something higher.

Benjamin Lapin had a cousin who studied at New York University. When she heard from Benjamin that I was interested in law, she advised me to go with her and register for university courses at the Washington Square campus in Greenwich Village with the notion of eventually attending law school. I figured it would take me a few years to become a lawyer, so I was very happy and agreed to try. She and I met with the dean, who gave us 15 minutes of his time. I explained that I had studied in Munich and eventually wanted to enroll in law school. He said that I would need a high school diploma from an American institution. I offered a compromise, respectfully suggesting that I take all the exams required for a high school diploma. If I passed, he would accept me at the university; if I failed, I would attend an American high school. The dean was adamant, insisting I had to attend high school first. I thanked him and left. Feeling bad about being rejected, my enthusiasm waned.

When I told Irving Glitzenstein what had transpired, he said he would gladly exchange both his professions in order to make what I earned. I was a bit consoled but not altogether happy. I failed to understand why Irving's accounting and legal practice barely brought him a living. After he prepared my income tax returns, he contemplated giving up his practice to sell appliances for Dynamic Electronics. With a little prodding from his brother Eli, Irving joined me in another Dynamic Electronics venture—renting out washing machines for one dollar down and one dollar a week. Irving bought my car to take on a route, and I bought a new one.

Washing machines were just becoming popular, particularly because the postwar baby boom made for lots of dirty diapers. Ads screamed from the radio and newspapers, "Pay one dollar down and one dollar a week, and you can rent a washing machine to do the diapers. You get a package of diapers free, and the whole deal will cost you less than a diaper service." We received leads from maternity hospitals and other sources.

Together, we started on our route, visiting the mothers of newborn babies and trying to "lease" them washing machines for one dollar down and "one when you catch me." Although the ads all promoted rentals, the real purpose behind the campaign was to sell instead. If you rented out too many machines, you risked being fired, so you had to "rent" but *not* rent. Going about this process took some doing. We had to convince the prospective purchasers that buying was more economical than renting, and in a way, it was; in two years, the machine would be theirs. At the same time, they could get a better model in terms of durability and load capacity. The machine was guaranteed for five years, and the only place that offered such a good deal was Dynamic Electronics.

Irving saw that in half a day I had converted six prospective rentals into sales. Initially, he spent time observing how I operated, and I split my commission with him. In the end, he declared that he could not do what I was doing, working late hours with only a briefcase as an office. Irving was used to a desk job. I used to leave the house at 10 o'clock in the morning. My neighbors once asked what I did for a living that allowed me to start work so late. I would say, jokingly, that I worked in a bank, and the neighbors took my answer seriously. I certainly did not keep bankers' hours at the other end of the day.

When Mike Newman, one of the top Dynamic Electronics people and a Spanish speaker, opened an appliance store in a Cuban area of the Bronx, he offered five of the best Dynamic salesmen a very good salary plus commission and bonuses to join him. Dynamic Electronics only paid commissions and sometimes gave bonuses. I had to decide what to do. On the one hand, I had been at Dynamic for a year and a half and was very happy there. On the other hand, I knew Mike and his wife, Rita, very well and found their lucrative offer very enticing. The prospect of being in on the beginning of something and helping it grow also appealed to me.

As a child, when I studied the Torah, I learned that one of the ways textual problems were resolved by the rabbis was through *gematria*, the numerology system where letters have equivalent number values and meaning is inferred by finding words or events with equivalent numerical values. In the Torah, many events took place based on the number seven; the Creation, perhaps the most significant event of all, ended with the start of the seventh day. It may seem superstitious, but if something included the number seven, I gravitated toward it because the number seven was always lucky for me. The seven days of the week I spent with my parents were very good. In the Mauthausen concentration camp, my number was 86043, and I had survived. Adding the digits together equals 21—three times seven. When I came to the United States, I brought $7,777 with me. At Dynamic Electronics, my assigned number was 437, which adds up to 14 or two times seven, or, with four and three being seven, 77.

Mike's new company, Public Service Appliances, Inc., was located on 147th Street in the Bronx. Playing with *gematria,* I could extract three times seven ($14 = 2 \times 7$ and another 7 equaled 3×7)—a good omen—so, I left the security of Dynamic Electronics for a new opportunity. Although the product line and the racket were the same, the scale and volume of business were much smaller. Mike did not advertise nearly as much as Dynamic did, and therefore sales leads were not produced. Before long, Mike and Rita separated (the breakup was not Rita's fault). When Rita left the company, the operation faltered, and the business went down the drain. Public Service Appliances ceased to exist. This was one case where the numbers did not add up.

TRUTH IN ADVERTISING AND EVERYDAY LIFE

While Mike Newman's business went down the tubes, a blessing came to us in another form. Our first son, Sidney Tobias—Zisman Tuviah—was born on March 28, 1954. We named him after Father, but we reversed the name to symbolically reverse the bad luck that had befallen Father at the hands of the Nazis. The *bris* took place in our apartment on Andrews Avenue in the Bronx. I still do not know how in the world, despite the fact we moved all our furniture into the hall, we were able to pack almost 60 people into the apartment. The mohel was a survivor and a Hasid from Brooklyn, the same man who had circumcised my oldest nephew, Jerry, back in the DP camp at Feldafing. We served as much food and drink as at a wedding, and everything was beautifully prepared. I will be forever grateful to Sara Levitan, Benjamin Lapin's sister, for cooking the fish for that joyous occasion. We have since performed other *britot* in the family, including those of my second son, Gary, and my grandchildren, Ari-Lev, Elie, Avi-Chai, Josh, and Daniel, yet I must admit that Sidney's was special. He was the first of the new generation to signify the future of the Meisels and Tenenbaum families.

Sam and Frieda Rosenzweig, friends from Germany, also lived in the Bronx. Sam and Frieda came to visit us often because Gena did not know how to change diapers or bathe the baby, and Frieda was already an experienced mother. When we sat down in the living room to relax, Sidney was in the crib in our bedroom (when he was not crying). Over coffee and cake, we discussed life in the United States and how it differed from Europe. At one point, Frieda said that in America, the husband—the breadwinner—takes out life insurance, especially if there are children. Sam did not like hearing that and said, "Frydziuniu, did you make a contract with God about who will go first?" I was embarrassed to listen to this conversation. Unfortunately, it turned out that Frieda was right: men usually do go first, and Sam passed away before Frieda did. Of course, it works out that way because men do not want their wives going first and leaving them with a mess; they would rather go first themselves so that their wives can clean up after them.

Our apartment was beautifully decorated, and we did not want the baby to mess up our good couches, so we decided to make slipcovers. Because I was not working then, I offered to undertake the slipcover project. Gena laughed because she did not believe I was capable of such a task, but I proved her wrong. I made slipcovers, with piping and zippers, and the drapes and curtains for the entire apartment. When I finished, it was time to get back to looking for employment.

The television business was by now too competitive, and only so many mothers of firstborn babies needed washing machines. I thought that the fur business, with ladies as customers, might be a good business to try. I bought a white cotton coat and went to see customers who had bought television sets or washing machines from me before, asking if they had fur coats that needed fixing. As soon as I walked in, they thought I was a doctor. I explained that I was a furrier and that my whole family, including my father-in-law, uncle, and cousins, was in the fur business. I would ask the lady of the house to show me her old coat, which she would then bring out. Most of these coats were made of muskrat or mouton skins and were 20 years old. I pointed out that the worn-out sleeve elbows would require two skins at $10 a piece to be fixed. The seat was usually rubbed out, requiring two more skins to replace that part (another $20), and the collar needed at least one skin ($10). The lining was generally gone, and the replacement would run $25. After new skins were added in, the whole coat would require cleaning to make the skins match. The entire job would come to $95, but the customer would have a coat that looked brand-new.

I would take the old coat, make out an invoice, and take a $30 deposit, with a $65 balance to be paid on delivery, or a special with two installment payments. Then I went a couple of blocks away, tore out the sleeves and collar, and threw the coat into a garbage bin. Next, I went to 27th Street in the fur district, where I bought about 20 brand-new coats at $15 to $20 each. Fourteen days later, I delivered a brand-new coat to the customer, who was so pleased that she called in her neighbors to show off the "refurbished" coat. Everyone was amazed that an old coat could look just like a brand-new one. I made many customers happy in this way. In spite of the customer satisfaction, when I started to think about the reality of what I was doing, I did not feel good about it. Even if people enjoyed the product and I provided good service, I was not comfortable with the ethics of doing business this way. I had not spent my childhood studying Talmud so that I could deceive people.

I did more research and this time decided to go into the credit business. That required both a lot of office work and purchasing and selling merchandise, so I took a partner, Emil Wolfe. This distinguished gentleman from Switzerland once told me he had come over from Europe before the war to look for a business and saw a newspaper ad offering a 25 percent interest in a successful restaurant. Emil went to Sixth Avenue and 40th Street near Times Square, walked into the establishment in question, and saw it was packed with customers. There were no empty seats; people were lining up. Emil asked the owner if he wanted to sell the 25 percent interest, as advertised.

"Are you crazy? This is a goldmine! Why should I sell it?" the man replied.

"So why did you advertise if you do not intend to sell?" asked Emil.

"Maybe one of my partners, Tom or John, wants to sell."

Emil finally found Tom, who told Emil the same story: he did not want to sell, but maybe Harry did. Emil approached Harry, the fourth and last partner. "Harry, do you want to sell your share of the restaurant?"

"I really do not want to sell, but have a look." Harry pulled up his trousers and showed Emil his swollen leg wrapped in a towel. Harry complained that he could hardly stand, let alone run around with heavy food trays or clean tables. His partners were not compassionate enough to give him even one day off to recover because the restaurant was busy all the time. If not for the leg, Harry said he would never consider selling his share in the restaurant.

Emil sat down with Harry and negotiated a deal. There was a lot of cash involved, and after reaching an agreement, Emil paid Harry. A happy Emil went home to his wife, Edith, to tell her about their good fortune. On Monday, Emil started work at the restaurant, but it was not as full as he expected. Emil hoped that by lunchtime more people would arrive. When Emil asked his partners why so few people came for breakfast, he was told that folks around

Times Square were not in the habit of eating breakfast. When lunchtime rolled around, Emil waited for the rush. It was noon, then 12:30, and very few people showed up. Emil became upset and started screaming at the partners, demanding an explanation. They yelled at him in return, "What do you want from us? We did not sell to you. It was Harry, and Harry is gone."

Finally, the partners sat down with Emil and explained about the restaurant business. Every Thursday, they sent out coupons to all the offices for 50 percent off the regular prices, valid only on Friday. "Naturally, all the customers come. Why shouldn't they? It is true we lose money, but this is also the reason why you bought 25 percent of the business. Now, if you are really unhappy and want to sell your shares, we each have to get $5,000 to reduce our losses, and this time we will advertise a 50 percent sale of the restaurant, but you will have to bandage your leg in a towel."

Emil had tears in his eyes when he told me how fast he learned about the restaurant business. I said, "Mr. Wolfe, you did not learn about the restaurant business but about crooked business and dishonest people." The business I proposed to Emil was hard, legitimate work with tremendous potential. We registered under the name Wolten Credit Company, Inc. Wolten stood for Wolfe and Tenenbaum, the first three letters of each name, and we rented an office at Broadway and 96th Street in Manhattan. We bought stock and sold every possible item that was needed in a household: pots and pans, bedspreads, curtains, dishes, cutlery, clocks, and so on. We hired four good salesmen and later added a fifth. Emil and I also loaded up both of our cars with merchandise. Our policy was to sell something for five or ten dollars down with a balance of one to two dollars to be paid per week. We parked our cars next to each other so that only one of us had to watch them, and we could supply the salesmen with new merchandise when they came back from their customers. Each salesman took two tenement houses and started on the ground floor. After reaching the top floor, he went up to the roof and climbed over to the next building, then worked his way downstairs, going from door to door.

In the television and appliance business, I had worked from leads. When people called and wanted to see us, we made appointments. Now, the approach was just the opposite; prospective customers did not expect you or want you. When a person opened the door, his face told the story. The salesman had to be able to read it instantaneously and find the proper approach or the door would be slammed in his face. I do not want to be philosophical here or compete with Dale Carnegie, but there are many steps to climb and fences to jump and gates to unlock in order to succeed. Unfortunately, I had to learn the hard way, but I learned from everybody—even children.

When I went out to sell, I always accepted the notion that people are basically good and basically honest. Everything depended on a customer's mood, so one had to step up or step down to meet the prospect on an equal level and establish a line of communication. The salesman had to gain the person's trust. To do this kind of face-to-face cold calling, one had to be an actor and impersonate different people. The role also depended on the salesman's mood. Sometimes I pretended to be a deliveryman and knocked on the door, yelling "Knickerbockers," which was a brand of beer that was popular in Harlem. Once people heard that word, they could not resist letting me in. Other times, I played the part of a surveyor and asked questions, which eventually led to sales. I always made sure my foot was in the door before my head was in. Now and then, I used a pencil and a pad. When the potential customer would not open the door wider, my pencil always managed to fall inside the apartment. The homeowner had to step back, I went inside to pick up what I had dropped, and they could no longer slam the door in my face. I mention these techniques not as a sales course, but to describe what I had to do to make a living.

Emil and I built up a successful business of a few hundred accounts. Money came into the office every day in the self-addressed envelopes we provided to the customers, but we pursued two opposite philosophies. Emil started at 9 a.m., and after he made two or three sales, he was satisfied and wanted to go home. If he made no sales by 10:30 a.m., he would declare it a bad day, say there was no use knocking himself out, and go home. I, however, felt that if I made one or two sales in the morning, I did not want to break the streak; I hoped to achieve more sales. If, after two or three hours, I could not make a sale, I was still unwilling to give up. I would keep at it until I broke the trend and made at least two or three sales.

Emil and I had a problem between us: one pulled right and the other pulled left, and our differences in approach affected the morale of the salesmen who worked for us. They were demoralized by Emil's behavior, but if he left, I would have to watch the car and all the merchandise, which would cut into sales drastically.

I tried to talk to Emil in order to resolve the conflict amicably. When I asked what he wanted to do, he said he did not care to be involved in the selling end and would rather stay in the office. For the office work, I could hire a secretary to open envelopes and make deposits; I did not need a partner. I told Emil that his talent would be wasted this way, and if he insisted, I'd have no choice but to part company with him. Emil and his wife were friendly with my in-laws and used to visit them in the Bronx. One summer afternoon, the salesmen and I decided to quit working early, around 3:30 p.m., because of the heat. I knew my wife and the baby had gone to visit her parents, so I drove to their place near Mosholu Parkway and found Gena, the baby, my in-laws, and Mr. and Mrs. Wolfe in the park. I walked over to where they were sitting on the benches and overheard my mother-in-law saying to Mrs. Wolfe, "And do you think my daughter Gena likes her husband working so hard, staying out so late at night? She would also like him to be home earlier."

This was the first time I had heard Mrs. Meisels speak up for me. (Well, maybe it was for Gena.) I had tried again and again to convince Emil to stay on and not break up the business, but when I realized his wife was adamant about his not putting in the same kind of hours I did, I knew that continuing to talk was a waste of time. I arranged to meet with Emil the next morning and dissolved our partnership by dividing the accounts, stock, and cash. As the business still required a partner, I turned to my friend Sam Rosenzweig. Although he did not have much official schooling, he was smarter than many educated men. A Holocaust survivor, he had lost both his parents while he was still a young boy and received his training in the trenches. He was street-smart, and we understood each other.

While Sam and I were negotiating the terms of partnership, we were supposed to meet to inspect a storefront on Audubon Avenue to use as an office. The deadline was on a Tuesday at 7 p.m. Sam called me at 6:45, assuring me that he would be over right away. At 7:30, he phoned to say he was having problems with his car. At 8 p.m. he was waiting in the garage, and at 8:30 he had a new problem. At 9 p.m., he let me know he was on his way. At 9:30, I left after signing the lease on my own. A few days later, I mentioned the incident to his wife, Frieda, and she exclaimed, "Now I understand why during the movie he left every few minutes to go to the washroom. He was actually calling you!"

These things happened with Sam from time to time. Years later, Sam; his partner, Anolek; and I had an important meeting that was supposed to take place at 2 p.m. I was coming into Manhattan from New Jersey and arrived at 1:40 p.m. I always liked to be punctual, did not mind being 20 minutes early, and used the time to take a walk. At 2 p.m. I went back to the office to wait, but at 2:30 there was still no sign of either of them. At about 2:40, Anolek walked in with an excuse, "Joe, I drove around and around and could not find a parking place. A policeman was standing in front of the building, so I could not double park. Please forgive me." Then Anolek asked if Sam had arrived, since Sam had promised to be in the office at 2 p.m. The two of us sat down and waited; 3 p.m. came, and there was still no sign of Sam.

At 3:20, in walked Sam full of apologies. "Forgive me, Joe. I drove around and around and could not find a parking place. A policeman was standing in front of the building, and I could not double park." Anolek looked up and said, "Sam, how many times did I tell you to use your own excuse. I already used this one today. How does it look?"

I mention these incidents not only because they are funny but also because they describe my milieu. I know that Sam would forgive me for repeating them because I loved him very much. In spite of Sam's inability to manage time or tell the truth when it came to appointments, he was a fine, honest man and a good friend on whom one could depend. When we moved to Canada, Gena went ahead with the children and I was left on my own to do the packing. Sam came over to our apartment to help load the van until 2:30 in the morning. He would not let me do it all myself. In sum, the good outweighed the bad, and I truly miss him. Sam is buried in Jerusalem, not far from the grave of the Hebrew poet Uri Zvi Greenberg.

So on that night so long ago, when Sam did not show up at 307 Audubon Avenue, I took the space on my own and immediately informed all my customers about the move. The office was near the Henry Hudson Bridge and not too far from the George Washington Bridge. It was close to Yeshiva University and near our apartment. I also changed the name of the business from Wolten Credit Company to Josten Credit Company, Inc.

As a sole proprietor I worked doubly hard, and the business prospered. Still, it was hard, so I took on a new partner, Henry Jurysta, a fine man from a good family in Dzialoszyce. I liked Henry very much, but he was always sad because of the suffering he and his family had endured during the war. Henry's father, Simcha, had been Father's close friend. Both men had prayed in the Gerer *shtibl*. Simcha was the first war victim in our town. While he was digging trenches on September 3, 1939, a Sunday morning, the *Luftwaffe* strafed the trenches, killing Simcha on the spot. Henry's mother was taken to Treblinka or Belzec with my friend Abie, her youngest son, and they both perished there. Henry's brother Chaim, the second-oldest son, survived the war. After liberation, he returned to Dzialoszyce where he and many other Jews who had survived the war were murdered in a pogrom by local Poles.

Henry worked hard and drove himself even harder than I did. Together, we built up a good business, but after a while we got tired of running up and down the stairs, selling and collecting. Sales were not an easy way to make a living, so we decided to sell our business, and Henry and I parted company as partners.

SELLING HOUSES

Each time I changed jobs, I would take a vacation to relax and build up the energy for my next venture. This time I drove around Manhattan, Long Island, Staten Island, and New Jersey to see what was happening. After I did research, I looked into real estate. I thought the business would be good—if I could get into it. Nobody I knew could help me, so I decided to start small, as a real estate salesman. I drove out to a real estate company on Hillside Boulevard in Queens. The owner, who was also a lawyer, was very sharp, and I registered as an agent. I bought a license and began selling real estate.

I made quite a few sales in a short time and earned nice commissions until the broker changed the rules midstream. We had originally agreed to split the profits equally, but after a few months when he saw how well we were doing, he demanded that I pay him for the advertising, his overhead, and other charges. I decided to leave, but not before I made one very important sale—one for which I accepted not a single cent in commission.

This transaction involved our friends Larry and Anda Zellner and their two boys, who lived in a house in Jamaica Estates North. The home belonged to Anda's parents, and they all lived there together. Her parents had decided to move to Mexico, and I spoke to them about selling their house to their only daughter, which they were reluctant to do. Chances were slim that her parents would find a customer willing to pay as much as they wanted for the house, but I listed the house for the price her parents asked and started showing it—to regular customers and "special" people—those with five or six children, or husbands without jobs, who had great need for such a house but insufficient means to buy it.

I knew that Mr. and Mrs. Tauber, Anda's parents, liked to sleep in the morning and take an afternoon siesta. Why not? After all, they were retired people. And those were precisely the times I would bring the prospective customers by to look at the house. The Taubers kept a very clean house, so I made sure customers viewed the house on rainy days, when their children would run around the house in muddy shoes. I also discussed the price with prospective customers in the living room, so that everyone in the house could hear how much they were willing to pay. I assured the people beforehand that they could get the house for much less than the asking price, and I named the amount.

In time, the Taubers realized they would not get the price they were seeking. I sat down with the Taubers, showed them the three offers that were made on the house, and told them I could have shown these customers other homes, closed the deals, and made the commissions. In this situation, I was just wasting my time. When I asked Mr. Tauber what he intended to do, he gave me the answer that I had been waiting for, "Well, Joe, I'm very sorry, but for this kind of money, I would rather sell the house to my daughter." Mr. Tauber was well off and did not need the money, whereas his children were struggling. I said that it was not for me to tell him what to do, and whatever he decided to do was fine.

A few years later when Gena and I went to Mexico on vacation, we visited the Taubers in Mexico City on Calle Leone. They invited us to their lovely apartment for dinner, and I considered that evening my commission for the sale of their house. No money in the world could have given me more pleasure than knowing that Anda, Larry, and their children had their own home. Their appreciation for what I did was enough of a reward for me. Though it might not seem that what I did was totally above board—acting the part of a real estate Robin Hood—it all worked out for the best.

EVERY BIT OF IT

My mother, a Platkiewicz, had a second cousin named Meyer. Before the war, Meyer lived in Proszowice, Poland. His wife died and left him with three children, who were raised by their grandparents. After Meyer remarried, his children sometimes came to Dzialoszyce to visit their father, which is how I met Alex and his brother David, my friend before the war. The Nazis killed David and his other brothers; Alex was the only survivor. I had not seen Alex since the war, but one day I ran into him on Broadway. I gave Alex my telephone number and invited him to visit, and we became close friends. Alex liked all our children, especially Sidney. Alex, still a bachelor, babysat for Sidney many times and would rock our little screamer for hours, trying to put him to sleep.

Gena and I were tired of Sidney's constant crying. He already had great hopes and wanted to change night into day. To accomplish this goal, he did not let us sleep. When Emil and I had divided the stock from the Wolten Credit Company, I was left with three Universal sewing machines I could not sell. To try to quiet Sidney down, I took the motor off one of the sewing machines, attached it to the wheels of the baby carriage, and took the control pedal to bed with me. That way I was able to rock Sidney without getting up. Sometimes this contraption helped and sometimes it did not. Without it, I had to pick Sidney up and carry him around, which gave me a chance for exercise that I really did not need.

It was not easy to carry Sidney, who was a miniature Sumo wrestler. I did it lovingly and we managed because we were young, but it was harder for my in-laws to babysit, and we used to leave Sidney with them quite often. When they were not trying to sleep, they enjoyed taking care of him, especially when we went on vacation. We visited with them often, especially on Jewish holidays, when we all wanted to be together, and they had special seats reserved for us in their synagogue.

My father-in-law was very active in Rabbi Twerski's synagogue, and I enjoyed going there. I liked the rabbi personally. He was a fine man who never discussed money, even when it related to the *shul*. Luckily, there were others who looked after the physical survival of that house of worship. Sometimes they asked me to speak or make an appeal on the holidays. I also organized auctions to raise funds for the synagogue by going to my regular suppliers and asking them to donate merchandise. In return, I gave them receipts for tax purposes, and I was seldom refused. The reserve bid was very low, but I usually got top prices and collected quite a substantial sum. If I did not get the right bid, I bought the merchandise myself and resold it at farmers markets—my next business venture.

The entrepreneurial spirit in me was never afraid to embark on new projects. I tried to form a company with Sam Rosenzweig and Alex Stanford (he changed his last name from Platkiewicz) to build houses in Long Island, but it did not work out. I was willing to try anything that made sense, but my potential partners felt that our lack of experience in the field doomed us to failure. Although I was willing to take on the challenge, I did not have enough capital to do it on my own. Instead, Sam and I decided to go into a business that handled a variety of merchandise. The business kept us busy but also allowed for a lot of free time, so it was ideal for someone with a family of young children. Sam and I traveled to different farmers markets, open only on certain days of the week. Sam dealt in children's clothes, and I handled ladies' knitted goods.

To test the business, I drove to the nearest farmers market in Lodi, New Jersey, where I rented a 12-by-18-foot stall and sold knitted goods. When I bought merchandise, I followed the lesson my Aunt Tillie taught me when I first arrived in the United States. Look in the Yellow Pages. I kept those two pages she had torn out as a souvenir for a long time. Eventually, I misplaced them, but I never forgot the lesson I had learned. I searched for manufacturers of knitted goods and learned quite a number of them were in the industrial area of Brooklyn.

I assumed factories used the same kind of flat, eight-foot knitting machines

I saw when I picked up sweaters from Zilberberg back in Dzialoszyce, but the equipment in America was different. Even the smallest factory had six circular and four Scott and Williams knitting machines running on electric motors. Rolls of paper with punched holes programmed the machines for the different designs. Of course, big factories such as Oscar Schlossberg & Son Knitting Mills or Gombie Knitting Manufacturing, Inc., had many knitting machines. I got good deals, especially on closeouts, because I paid cash. Sometimes the items were all the same color or size, but I had no shortage of merchandise. The problem was that the farmers market in Lodi was open only once or twice a week. To increase business, I also rented a stall in Sommerville, New Jersey. Lodi was just over the George Washington Bridge not far from where we lived, but Sommerville was 35 miles away. All the merchandise had to be packed into the car, unpacked and displayed in the stall, packed up again after 10 p.m., and loaded back into the car. Sometimes I got home at one o'clock in the morning. To put it simply, the whole process was a schlep (a drag), but I did it in order to be independent, to support my family, and to afford the necessities of daily life.

Two days of such work were not enough for me, and since Lodi and Sommerville were in the west, I added two more farmers markets in the east, out on Long Island—Bethpage, Amityville, and sometimes Massapequa. I was busy all week, but I was short on days because some of these places insisted on renting stalls for two days a week, not one. Occasionally, Sam Rosenzweig and I traveled together, but if we wanted to have some fun, we packed all the goods into a large van and took along a fellow named Goldstein, a veteran of farmers markets.

Once, Goldstein wanted us to stop in Jersey City, but we got lost on the way. He asked a man on the road, "Mister, where is New Jersey?"

The man answered, "You are in New Jersey."

"But Mister, you do not understand, I want New Jersey."

Again the man answered, "You are in New Jersey."

Impatiently, Goldstein repeated, "I am asking for New Jersey."

The man got angry. "Goddamn it, every bit of it is New Jersey. You damned refugees can drive a person crazy!"

Sam and I were doubled up with laughter. For years, we joked whenever we met, "Where is New Jersey?" Goldstein, the expert driver, always managed to provide us with entertainment.

Growing up in Europe and trying to fit into North American culture had its moments. I had a learned friend, Chaim Einhorn, who was older than I was and extremely well versed in Talmud. Chaim was raised in a very Orthodox home and attended a Hungarian yeshiva, where he was considered brilliant. He owned a delicatessen on Mount Eden Avenue, near the Grand Concourse, not far from where we lived. Because I enjoyed Chaim's company and our discussions, I sometimes stopped by in the mornings.

Chaim used to say, "Yossele, it's hard for people like us to understand life here." To illustrate, he gave me an example. "You see these dried prunes?" He pointed to two burlap sacks, one three-quarters full of prunes and the other just a quarter full. On the former, a sign read $.99 per pound and on the latter, there was a sign for $1.99. "Every Yente in the neighborhood comes in and buys the more expensive prunes. If they want to do that, fine, but even my own wife only wants the $1.99 prunes. They are all the exact same prunes!" This was America! Eventually, Chaim sold the store and became a successful diamond dealer on 47th Street. In America, even prunes can lead to diamonds.

Although trying to adjust to American culture was often funny, there were times when we worried. Senator Joe McCarthy dominated American politics and media in those years, and I was glued to the television set to see who was targeted and what the process did to the country. We were witnessing a veritable witch hunt. As Holocaust survivors, we were concerned about an antisemitic backlash because so many targets were Hollywood Jews. Sometimes it felt like we were taking two steps forward and one step back, but at least the sum of our steps equaled some kind of advancement. We went to movies, theater, and opera. We spent time with friends and took vacations in the Catskills.

Adjusting to life in America, for me, was like being at a Jewish wedding—everyone is happy, but there is always that sad yearning for a never-forgotten Jerusalem. I felt guilty for not being in Israel. I felt I had betrayed the cause. Occasionally, I went to Zionist meetings, yet somehow these gatherings did not motivate me; the group lacked fire and enthusiasm. Perhaps I did not allow myself to be motivated because I felt stuck in the Diaspora of Diasporas, without any immediate hope for change. We had a small baby, and my in-laws were getting older, so we kept postponing the move. We kept saying, "Let's wait a little bit longer."

I was excited, however, when Menachem Begin came to New York in 1954. I met with him, and we spoke for quite some time about the *Irgun*, the Altalena affair, and his vehement opposition to German war reparations. At that time, I agreed with him on the issue, but after a while I changed my mind because I saw no sense in letting the Germans make money from murder. Better to take the funds and give them to charity. I applied for restitution, a word I hate, because in reality there can be no restitution for exterminating millions of people.

Every once in a while, something would come up that would draw us back into dealing with Europe. In my father-in-law's case, it was some unfinished business. He had done some business with a man in Germany named Moksel, who needed money to finance a salami factory. Moksel had a good reputation and the business was solid, so my father-in-law loaned him $10,000. When the Meisels were getting ready to leave Germany, my father-in-law went to him and requested repayment of the loan, but Moksel did not have the money and instead gave him a receipt for 10,000 "*lokshen*" (noodles) because it was illegal at that time to possess dollars. Moksel assured my father-in-law that he would forward the money to the United States within a month. A month passed, then six months, two years, and then three, and still there was no word from Moksel. My father-in-law wrote many letters, but none was ever answered. When Mr. Meisels heard that some people he trusted were traveling to Germany, he asked them to see Moksel about returning the money. One of them was my friend Dr. Jacob Stern. When the two men met, Moksel laughed in Dr. Stern's face and denied owing my father-in-law anything.

When I heard about this fraud, I could not abide the injustice. I asked my father-in-law for his power of attorney so I could handle the matter on his behalf. Mr. Meisels was skeptical and advised me not to waste my time. He believed I would get nowhere because evidently the man was a thief. However, I persisted, and finally my father-in-law agreed. I wrote to the German-American Chamber of Commerce and sent a copy of the letter to Moksel with an accompanying note to let him know I would sue him in Germany and freeze his bank account in Munich. Moksel's brother-in-law in Buffalo, New York, was a Mr. Laufer, who soon called me and said he would like to meet with Mr. Joseph Meisels. When I replied that I was Joseph Meisels, Laufer expressed a desire to settle the matter amicably without going to court. Laufer offered $5,000, but I insisted upon the full $10,000, plus interest—$15,000. If the case were litigated, Moksel would have to pay legal fees plus court costs, which would be considerably more than I was asking.

Laufer kept saying he wanted to meet Mr. Meisels, which I feared could be a setup. Having met Meisels in person, Laufer might claim in court that he had already returned the money. Nevertheless, I told Laufer that if he came to New York with the money, I would meet with him. I warned my father-in-law not to come to my house that evening. When Laufer arrived, he asked questions about my wife "Anna" and "two daughters." I said my wife was still suffering from migraine headaches, one of my daughters was married, and the other was studying at university. I needed money for her tuition and added that I had made arrangements to meet with a lawyer in Germany if we did not settle the matter.

After a very long negotiation, Laufer and I agreed to $10,000 without interest. He handed me the money, and I gave him a receipt for 10,000 *"lokshen."* By the time we parted, it was 2:30 a.m., but despite the late hour and being unable to contain my satisfaction, I drove to Mosholu Parkway, knocked on my in-laws' door, and handed my father-in-law the $10,000 that was rightfully his.

THE MANHATTAN STORE

I was not doing badly at the farmers markets, but the distance I had to drive almost every day, plus the constant packing and unpacking of merchandise, was draining. To alleviate some of the strain, I began renting booths instead of stalls. Although they cost more money, booths allowed me to leave items locked up until the next market day and saved me from the constant packing and unpacking. I still needed more merchandise to keep the various locations properly stocked. Traveling late at night was not pleasant, however, especially with Gena pregnant with our second child, so I looked for a new venture. Six months of farmers markets were enough for me.

In the meantime, I spent more time with Gena to make life easier for her. One hot day, we went to Orbach's Department Store on 14th Street. We had quite a few parcels, so I asked Gena to wait near the entrance while I went to get the car from the parking lot. When I came around the corner, I signaled for Gena to approach, but she did not respond. She was leaning against a wall and slowly sliding to the ground. I stopped the car in the middle of traffic, ran out, and carried her to the car. She had fainted because of the heat and her condition. I opened the windows and tried to revive her. I was scared. I took her to Ratner's, a kosher dairy restaurant on Delancey Street, where she regained some strength after eating potato pierogies with sour cream, her favorite food.

To stock my booths at the farmers markets, I attended auctions that were interesting, exciting, and sometimes profitable. One day there was a large auction of ladies wear. In those days, petticoats were in style, and most women wore petticoats or crinolines, as one particular type was called. One company, with several stores all over the city, went bankrupt, and its entire stock was being sold at auction. This was a great opportunity because the cost was reasonable and there were very few buyers. I could not resist purchasing most of the petticoats. With so much stock, I rented a store that was less expensive than storage space would have been and made a large sign that read: "Fashion Bargain Center." I brought in all the merchandise sitting in my booths at the farmers markets, and that was how I made the transition into my next business.

The storefront had a large display window, and with Gena's artistic touch, we made it attractive to passersby. Located on 38th Street and Fifth Avenue near Lord & Taylor, our store had prices about 50 percent less than those in neighboring stores. We competed with department stores by carrying brand names at lower prices. We could afford to do that because I bought my merchandise in job lots and not from the manufacturers. I carried a wide selection of ladies wear, including undergarments by Peter Pan and Maidenform; Rose Marie Reid and Catalina swimsuits; and sweaters and knit suits by Helen Harper, Mademoiselle, and Vogue.

We were near a subway station that provided commuter traffic, especially in the afternoons, when people shopped on their way home. When I could no longer handle sales by myself during peak times, Gena helped me out and behaved as though she were just another saleslady, a good policy for the business. I never told anyone she was my wife, especially when ladies came in and wanted to be waited on only by me. Some women asked for invoices that were larger than the amounts of the sale. When I asked why, they'd respond, "Let the sucker pay for it. He has enough money."

One time a lady came in and, after spending a few hundred dollars, asked me to join her in the Catskills for a few days. I said I could not afford it, but she offered to pay for me. When I asked about her husband, she explained that she and her husband would be staying at the Brown's Hotel, so I should check into the nearby Brickman; she would pay for my room and visit me there for our rendezvous. The woman assured me that I would have a good time. I protested that I could not leave the store, so she suggested that my saleslady, Gena, whom the woman found very capable, take over for me in my absence. Gena replied that she only worked afternoons.

I bought merchandise on weekends, which was convenient for the factory owners, too. I sold the best three-piece bouclé suits on the market. For the low price I paid, they were all size 14, but because they were bouclé knit, they stretched, and I could fit any woman from a size 10 to a size 16. The same was true of cardigan sets and other knit novelties. I bought hundreds of beautiful sweaters, including designer samples that never went into production. Sometimes I purchased larger quantities than I needed and sold goods to other stores.

Norman Kamelgard used to come to the store and buy knit suits from me at wholesale prices and resell them to stores in New Jersey. Norman was my only surviving peer. One day, Norman told me I had "ruined" him. I was shocked and asked him what he meant, because Norman was my best friend, and there was nothing in the world I would not do for him.

Norman said, "Well, Yossele, when I first arrived by boat, you came to the harbor to pick me up. My two cousins, Chaim and Morris Zelmanowicz, were also there to greet me. You hugged me and said, 'Nachum, do not worry; I have a job for you. Dynamic Electronics is the best place to work.' Well, Yossele, you should never do favors for anybody when you are not asked. Do not do that anymore. If my cousins had not overheard you offering me that opportunity, they probably would have invited me to work for them [which they later did anyway], I would have eventually become a partner in one of their businesses, and ultimately I would have been a rich man. But now, because of you, I have to sell sweaters to make a living. Do you understand now what you did?" Life had taught me many lessons, but understanding this piece of logic was not among them.

People came from near and far to buy knit goods from us because we advertised in newspapers, including the Zionist paper *Herut*. I wanted to support the organization and could contribute by placing ads in the paper that would benefit me, too. I advertised the three-piece bouclé knit and beaded suits, which regularly sold for $299, at only $49. Once, a very nice lady who was at least a size 20 came in. Usually, I directed the amply endowed customers to Lane Bryant, a store that specialized in plus-sizes, and they were usually thankful that I had not wasted their time trying to sell them something that would not fit them. This woman, however, was insulted that I would direct her to a store for larger women. She then looked at me carefully and called to her husband, who was waiting outside, "Leibish, come in. Leibish, listen to him. Doesn't he sound just like William [her formal appellation of Willie]?"

When I heard her mention Willie, I almost collapsed from embarrassment. I then noticed that she was holding my ad clipped from the *Herut* newspaper. I realized I was in an awkward situation and did not quite know how to handle the matter. I started to explain that I was only trying to help her out, but the two left abruptly. Immediately, I made a long-distance call to my brother Willie in Toronto to tell him what had happened. He got upset and asked me to get in touch with the couple right away and apologize. I had not done anything wrong, but Willie begged me to apologize anyway. He told me the name of the hotel where these people were staying, and I bought a bouquet of flowers and went there. By the time I arrived, the couple had already left for Canada. (The flowers were not wasted; they went to my darling Gena.) Who were these people, and why was Willie so concerned?

Father, were he alive, would have been the happiest man in the world over the match Willie made when he chose his bride, Dina, because of the distinguished family from which she came. Dina was descended from a dynasty of spiritual leaders that went back generations. The men in her family were all rabbis—her grandfather was the learned Baidechiner Rebbe, his father was the renowned Avigdor Ezra of Radomsk, and the family's lineage had been traced directly back to King David. Dina had been in Auschwitz-Birkenau. Three sisters from her family survived the Holocaust, and after liberation, they landed in Sweden with help from the Red Cross. The couple visiting my store, Mr. and Mrs. Shields, were the Uncle Leibish and Aunt Edith of these three sisters, and the Shields sent papers to the sisters in Sweden and brought them to Canada. These were people of valor.

The Shields took the girls into their home, supported them, and married them off as though they were their own daughters. One of them happened to marry my dear brother Willie. After the sisters married, the Shields were instrumental in placing the sisters' husbands in the building business. Indirectly, I too have the Shields to thank for becoming a builder in Canada, because I was attracted to the business and entered it a few years later, initially with Willie and his partners. Later when Gena and I were invited to Canada for joyous family occasions, we always met the Shields. Staunch Zionists, the Shields were also business partners with Nathan and Lily Silver. Nathan Silver, my friend, was head of the Revisionist movement in Canada and Menachem Begin's good friend.

Another series of related coincidences took place years later in Toronto. On a *Shabes* in late May of 1974, Willie's future son-in-law celebrated his *aufruf* (calling up to the Torah) just before his wedding to Linda. The event took place in the "Junction" Synagogue (so named because it was near the junction of two railway lines), a small, intimate synagogue whose atmosphere reminded me of the *shul* in prewar Dzialoszyce. The walls were beautifully painted with biblical scenes and quotations, the reader's desk was on a central *bimah* (elevated podium), the vaulted ceiling was painted to resemble the sky, the women's section was in a second-floor gallery ringed with balusters, and the light coming through the stained-glass windows was otherworldly. I was overwhelmed as a wave of nostalgia for what I had lost washed over me.

After services, there was a *kiddush* downstairs. I was so moved and curious that I explored some of the other rooms in the basement. Piled in the corner of a service room was a scorched, ash-covered, damp pile of religious books that seemed to be waiting for burial. I picked through the pile, hoping to be able to save some from their fate, all the while thinking of the Nazi book burnings. Without paying particular attention to the titles or contents but to the physical condition, I selected a few books that looked like they could be restored, brought them home, and spent hours dusting, damp-wiping, and drying the books, page by page. While I worked on the books and thought of what they had been through, I compared them to myself—literally plucked from the fire and given another chance at life.

Among the books was one that I had never heard of before, *Korban Shmuel* (The Sacrifice of Samuel). I had heard of the sacrifice of Isaac, but never the sacrifice of Shmuel. It turned out that the book was an in-depth study and compilation of opinions about Temple sacrifices and was authored by Rabbi Zvi Shmuel Silverstein, hence its name. Rabbi Silverstein left Europe before the war, started the book in Jerusalem, and came to Toronto where he completed and published it in the mid-1940s.

Coincidence number one: Rabbi Silverstein was none other than the Baidechiner Rebbe, my sister-in-law Dina's grandfather and Mrs. Shields' father. The book even had an inscription acknowledging the Shields family, among others, for support in its publication.

Coincidence number two: My son Sidney coauthored and shot all the pictures for a book on synagogue architecture titled *Treasures of a People: The Synagogues of Canada*. The cover photo was none other than the interior of the "Junction" Synagogue. The space that had "brought me back home" had obviously made a strong enough impression on him to be featured prominently in his book.

Coincidence number three: It is a tradition among scholarly writers of religious texts to seek the endorsements of the great scholars of their time. Of the seven rabbis who endorsed *Korban Shmuel,* the first listed was Harav Yosef Chaim Sonenfeld, the Chief Rabbi of Jerusalem. Years later, in 1996, my daughter, Tamara, married Uli Friedman, the great-grandson of this saintly man. And it was Tammy's wedding in Jerusalem that provided the catalyst for the Baidechiner Rebbe's granddaughter Dina to make her first trip to Israel.

Mr. and Mrs. Shields were not the only customers from Canada to come into our store. A handsome man used to visit from time to time and buy beautiful sweaters for his wife. He was in the millinery business in Canada, and our store was located near the hub of the millinery industry in Manhattan. Once he visited the store with a very nice-looking lady and bought something for her. Jokingly, I said to him, "Aren't you going to buy something today for your wife?" He said the woman was his wife. When I asked her about the fit of the red sweater he had bought for her last time, she looked at him strangely and asked, "What red sweater? What else did he buy here?" The wife was convinced that her husband was seeing another woman. That joke got me into a lot of trouble, and it took me a long time to persuade her that I was only kidding. Luckily, I managed to undo the damage, and years later, I bumped into the couple at Beth Shalom Synagogue in Toronto looking quite happy.

The store was more than just a place of business; I met all sorts of interesting people there. We had international customers because 38th Street was not too far from the United Nations complex, and many tourists visited our shop. A man with a British accent once came in with his wife and purchased a large selection of merchandise. He appreciated the savings we offered and told me that he was the British ambassador to the United Nations. I told him I respected the British people but wanted to convey a message to their government from a survivor of the inhumane Nazi regime. I told him that the British mistreated Jews during and after the war, wearing white gloves so the world would not think ill of them. While I spoke to the ambassador, I did not wait on other customers and asked them to come back another time.

The man insisted I tell him then and there why I made such derogatory statements about his country. I said, "Imagine that the dead bodies of my brothers and sisters are floating like monuments around the British Isles. The bodies are from the *Patria* and the *Struma,* Jewish immigrant ships that the British sank, with women and children aboard. The British hanged Dov Gruner, Josef and Mordechai Schwartz, Mordechai Alkashi, Eliezer Kashnai, Yehiel Drezner,

Avshalom Haviv, Meir Nakar, Yaakov Weiss, and others who tried to secure a Jewish homeland in Palestine. Do you know about the Russian Compound in Jerusalem and Acre prison? The British are guilty of murder. How many Jews could have been saved from the clutches of the Germans if not for the British White Paper that restricted Jewish immigration to the Holy Land?"

I lectured the ambassador about the British obligations undertaken in the Balfour Declaration of 1917, the Palestine Mandate of 1922, and the Peel Commission of 1927. In spite of all this legislation, the British did everything to block Jewish immigration, causing many unnecessary deaths. Conveying these facts to the British ambassador meant more to me than any business losses that afternoon. The ambassador was shocked—a little Jewish storekeeper was standing there and berating him. He did not apologize, but neither did he walk out. He completed his purchases and cordially left.

Our apartment in the Bronx was in a great location, but there was restricted parking in the area, and alternate side of the street parking regulations were very inconvenient. After the police towed my car twice, I sold it for $100 to the gas station on the corner of University and Burnside. I did not need the car during the day when I was in the store, and using the subway was far more efficient than driving and paying for expensive parking downtown.

At night, I was too tired to go anyplace. But when the weekend came, Gena demanded that we visit her parents and friends or go to the beach or on other outings. She was not happy sitting home all the time. I told her that taxis were more economical and convenient than maintaining a car. But what does one not do to please the mother of two young children?

Our second son, Gary Jay, like Sidney, was born in Dr. Loew's Maternity Hospital on the Grand Concourse. It was difficult to schlep two children around, so I gave in to Gena and bought back our car for $150. After the car was towed again, I sold it back for $175. About six weeks passed, and I was still under pressure from a "higher authority," so I bought back the car for $225! Did I do badly? Six weeks of parking for $50 was better than the going rate!

My cousin Alex used to visit and bring us fresh eggs from his cousin Harry Stamford's chicken farm in Vineland, New Jersey. Businesses were contagious among Holocaust survivors. When one newcomer went into a certain line of work and others thought he was doing well, they followed in his footsteps. Many survivors went into chicken farming in Vineland. A good percentage of the Jewish builders in Toronto came from chicken farms in New Jersey, but I was never attracted to chickens or farms.

Alex, a hardworking man, worked as a leather cutter in a Brooklyn factory and was always welcome in our home. Once, he made a beautiful, baby blue leather James Dean–style motorcycle jacket for Sidney, who, at age three, looked like a miniature biker whenever he wore it.

Always willing to lend a hand, Alex once helped me arrange the display window at the store, which was changed every four to six weeks. I warned him several times to be careful not to cut the alarm tape on the window. At 4:30 a.m., after working all night to place the mannequins and merchandise in their proper places, we decided to leave and clean up the next day because we were exhausted. As we closed up, the alarm went off. When I asked Alex what he had done, he innocently replied that he was just testing the tape to see if it would come off. We had to take everything out of the window, fix the tape, and start all over again.

The competition ratcheted up the tension in the business. Manufacturers complained that I was underselling them, especially on merchandise covered by pricing agreements that retailers and authorized distributors were forced to sign. With no such agreements, I did not have to subscribe to cartel pricing. I continued to sell in my own "free market" and soon received threatening letters from lawyers. I collected all the letters, pasted them on a sheet of plywood, and placed them in the display window so that the public would know that we offered real bargains. As a result, customers flocked to the store, and I made even more money. Once, a Viennese artist visited the store and asked me to sell his paintings. It was not something I could do, and I also doubted whether the work was his. He was a nice fellow in need who begged for my help, so with misgivings, I advised him to advertise in the neighborhood, and I would allow him to display the paintings in my store for one day. Dressed in a white smock stained with paint to make it seem as if he had just finished painting, he touched up a small patch in the corner of a painting in view of prospective customers. He sold quite a few paintings for $200 to $300 each. Of the 30 paintings he had brought to the store, he left with only 4.

CLOSING A CHAPTER

Despite the store's success, a part of me still hankered to get into the construction business. Originally, I thought selling real estate would somehow lead to building houses, but it did not. I kept talking to Sam Rosenzweig, Alex, and a couple of others about building, but they had legs of lead. I could not convince any of them to join me, and I still did not have enough capital to do it on my own. In the meantime, Dina, Willie, his partner Jack Silverstein, and Jack's wife, Dolly, came to New York to visit. They thought the store was very successful, but I told them that I would rather be in construction. They came to our apartment for dinner, and we had a nice meal, a few drinks, and a good time. Then they proposed that Gena and I move to Canada.

Such a move would pose no problems. I could sell the store. They were skeptical about the amount of time it would take to make such a sale, but I was not worried. We had a good conversation, and I left the final decision to them. A few days later, Willie called and said they had drawn up papers for a company with me as one of the partners, and we would build eight houses in Oakville, a town near Toronto. A deposit on the lots was given to Dave Shier, the developer who had subdivided the land. I promised to be ready to join them soon.

In preparation for the move to Canada, I sold off merchandise at greatly reduced prices. Bouclé knit suits that used to sell at $49 went on sale for $39, then $29, and finally $19—and I was still making a profit. When Marian Goldberg stopped by and I told him I was thinking of selling the store—he smiled and said it would take a long time. His friend Herschkopf had a textile store he had been trying to sell, without success, for quite some time. Goldberg could not imagine how I could sell my store in four to six weeks, the time I had allotted myself to accomplish this task. Goldberg spoke to me on Thursday morning, and that same afternoon I noticed a Viennese man who owned a millinery factory on 38th Street, looking at my display window. I went outside and asked if I could help him, thinking he might be looking for a gift. "You have a goldmine here," the man said to me. "Yes, it is a goldmine," I repeated. "Would you like to buy it?"

The Viennese man could not believe I was serious, so I challenged him to find out whether I meant what I said. He asked me my price, and my answer was very reasonable. I gave him a figure for the value of the merchandise, and the store could be his in no time. The man left and returned in an hour with his brother and his brother's wife. While I was busy with customers, they asked me again if I really wanted to sell, and as soon as I was finished serving my customers, I assured them I was. Upon receipt of a $1,000 deposit and the rest paid in cash, dollar for dollar, to take care of the stock, I offered them the store without even charging for the fixtures. We wrote out a contract by hand and arranged to meet the following day after closing time to go through the inventory, to count the merchandise carefully, and to write down every detail. Taking inventory took the whole night and the following day. We secured the store with two locks so that neither of us could enter without the other, and on Sunday, we added up the inventory lists. They gave me the money; I handed over the key to the other lock and wished them the best of luck.

On Tuesday, Goldberg called me in disbelief. He had gone to the store on Monday only to discover that it was no longer mine. He could not understand why I would sell such a profitable business. I reminded him that he had asked in the past why I kept changing businesses, and I told him I had always intended to build them and sell them when I found the right purchaser. In the meantime, I would keep searching, step by step, for what I really desired. I also warned him to watch out for the Chrysler shares he was stuck with, because the fluctuating stock market was making him nervous. He promised that the minute the stock went up, he would sell and go into business with me. I am still waiting.

I went around to the people I knew to say my farewells. Rabbi Mordechowicz, who studied Talmud with me on Sunday mornings, felt bad, but gave me his blessing and wished me well. He also added a strange warning: should I ever meet a Rabbi Kirshenblatt in Canada, I was to stay away from him. Rabbi Mordechowicz said, "He became an apostate." The two had studied together at the Lomzier Yeshiva and had been close friends, but Rabbi Mordechowicz had heard that as soon as Kirshenblatt had arrived in Canada, he had become a Reform rabbi. To Rabbi Mordechowicz, that was tantamount to conversion. Canada was geographically even larger than the United States, so I was not too concerned about staying away from Rabbi Kirshenblatt.

I used the two weeks I had before I actually left to spend time with my family, who would be left behind initially. The time I spent at home playing with my children was a true pleasure. Gary was not even one year old when I had to leave for Canada. A day after Passover, I left for Toronto and drove alone, wondering whether I would like my newly chosen endeavor and country.

I stayed with my brother Willie, and my sister-in-law Dina was very kind to me. They lived on Fairholme Avenue in a nice house Willie had built for his family. Compared to the homes in Levittown and other places on Long Island, his house was a palace.

CONSTRUCTION

Willie and I took a ride in his green pickup truck to Oakville. It was there that they started building the eight houses in which I had invested $40,000, the proceeds from my store. On the side of the truck, printed in large letters, was the name of the company, Dominion Builders. My brother and his partner, Jack Silverstein, also owned another company, Fairholme Builders. We started to negotiate the option to extend my participation beyond the first eight houses by forming a new, permanent company.

Jack did not like the idea because he was worried that the two Tenenbaum brothers would outvote him. He insisted that I, the younger Tenenbaum brother, form a partnership with Gordon Silverstein of Chicago, the eldest of the three Silverstein brothers. First, I wanted to meet Gordon, who was supposed to be my future partner, so Jack arranged for him to come to Toronto.

As soon as I saw Gordon, I thought of David Ben-Gurion. His size, build, long white hair, and bald spot were very similar. As we discussed the investment, lots, location, and what salary I would get for doing the actual work, my future partner asked if I could guarantee his return. At that point, I lost interest in doing business with him. To me, a partner, if he was not participating hands-on, was at least someone who shared in the risk, and Gordon did not want to assume any of the risk. For no amount of money would I consider anyone with Gordon's attitude as a partner, but I did not react on the spot. We decided to take more time to think about the matter and to meet in the future for further discussions.

In the meantime, I put my time to good use by going to the job site every day, studying the plans, staying until late at night, and doing my best to learn the business. While I worked, Jack and Dolly Silverstein sat in the trailer drinking coffee and playing cards. Dolly was a very nice lady, and she accompanied Jack to Oakville almost every day because she had no children and was bored at home. Jack showed me around and assigned me insignificant tasks such as picking up nails the carpenters had dropped or filling in joints the bricklayers had missed. I decided to put my time to better use; I went to the lumber truck when it arrived and proved to Jack that King's Lumber Company had short-shipped our order by many planks. Jack did not think I was spending my time efficiently, but after I checked the second and third loads, I convinced him that was where money was being lost, not in a few nails scattered on the ground.

Willie, Jack, and I went to the lumber company's office to speak to the manager. His lame excuse was, "It was probably a mistake." Then, instead of taking the company to task and holding it responsible for compensation, Jack and Willie settled for an apology and a few pieces of lumber. I saw in their dealings no business astuteness, no backbone, or prudence. Their attitude bothered me, but I did not say anything because, after all, what could a guy from the New York *shmate* business know about construction?

Jack insisted I would need two to three years to learn how to read the house plans Jack had given me. To make me feel good, he added that, normally, it took three to five years. Dolly always complimented me on being the best-dressed builder; I did not want to admit that I wore what I did only because I did not possess work clothes.

Harry, Jack's younger brother, tried to teach me the business from his perspective. He was the "smart one" in the family, and putting his arm around my shoulder, he would say, "When people in Canada say 'Joe is a nice guy,' you'll be in big trouble. That means you're a failure, but if they say you're a bad man, that means you're a success. This principle should guide your life in Canada. I should know because I'm an experienced man from Chicago."

Pointing to the land around us, Harry added, "You see, Joey, all this land, as far as you can see and beyond, belongs to me, which is the reason I know what I'm talking about." More than anything else, Harry's "lesson" taught me what type of person he was. Jack had quite a different personality. He never raised his voice, he spoke without fanfare or boasting, and he liked to settle matters amicably.

While we constructed the eight houses, I went to look for other lots in the city. At the time, some friends from New York came to Toronto and put up apartment buildings of 18, 28, or 36 suites. I went to see them and got interested. My friends were doing very well, so I suggested to my brother Willie that, with the profit from the eight houses, we should build a small apartment house to give us an income stream. An agent offered me the land for a building of 18 suites, and I wanted to buy it. Willie could not act on his own without his partner, and when Jack heard about my proposal, he said, "Joe, you have to walk before you can run. You should continue building houses for at least five to eight years. Then maybe you'll be able to start on apartments, but now? It's too risky and dangerous."

I came up with several other business ideas that I thought were promising, and the people who eventually bought the lands made a good profit. However, every time I suggested something, I got a negative response from my partners. Finally, I realized that a partnership with them just could not work. Faced with an ongoing stalemate, I proposed forming a partnership with Willie, just the two of us, on the condition that he sever his partnership with Jack. Willie and my sister-in-law Dina did not accept my offer because they did not want to jeopardize what they considered a good business. They expressed regret but were unwilling to change the status quo.

I went ahead and, on my own, bought 12 lots for $3,200 each directly from Dave Shier and his son-in-law, Barney Loftus. Now I needed a partner. My brother Chaim wanted me to go in with his brother-in-law Harvey Norden and offered me a substantial loan. Jack Silverstein asked me to do business with his brother Gordon, but I needed somebody who would be actively involved in construction on a daily basis.

I knew Joe Wolfe from Dzialoszyce. When we used to play together as children, if he did not return the hoop we played with, I would beat him up. Now Joe was an expert fur manufacturer. I offered him participation in building the 12 houses for which I had already purchased the land. He expressed interest, and I had a lawyer draw up a partnership agreement. That was September 1958, and Joe promised that by March of the following year he would give up the fur business and start working full-time at the construction site. Until then, I was to do the job for the both of us. However, I had a sneaking suspicion that Joe Wolfe might not give up his successful fur business so easily.

At the same time, I traveled back and forth between the United States and Canada because Gena and the boys were still in New York. I had been alone in Toronto all summer. In New York, I visited my friends Marian and Fay Goldberg in their Washington Heights apartment. I showed Marian the signed contract with Joe Wolfe and explained that I had reservations about whether or not Joe would get actively involved. I had three days left to make up my mind about accepting the partnership conditions, so I made Marian the same offer I had extended to Joe. Jokingly, I asked Marian if his money was still tied up in shares of the Chrysler Corporation, but he would not give me a definite answer. I waited two days, and when Marian failed to contact me, I went back to Toronto and accepted Joe Wolfe as my partner. We went to a very good lawyer, who concluded the agreement and formed Wolten Builders Ltd. Again, the first part of the name was "Wol" for Wolfe, and the second part was "Ten" for Tenenbaum.

Driving back and forth from Toronto to New York was not easy because the trip took ten hours. If I had the opportunity to give someone a lift, I gladly did so for the sake of doing a favor and to have company on the road. Once Joe Wolfe and his wife, Dina, came along. They wanted to meet Gena and visit relatives in Brooklyn. I did not know exactly where the relatives lived, so Dina, whose English was better than mine or her husband's, asked a passerby for directions, but the man had never heard of the street. Dina asked several other people, but the answer was always the same, so I told Dina to let me try. I yelled out to the next person who passed by, putting on the thick Brooklynese accent Mrs. Cohen, my former landlady, had taught me on my arrival in the United States. I was immediately understood and given directions. Both Dina and Joe burst into laughter.

After a week in New York, we prepared for our return trip to Canada. While in New York, Joe had purchased some chinchilla skins, which were rare in Canada. He put them in the trunk of my car, along with the rest of the luggage, without telling me about it. On the way to Canada, we also picked up my cousin Alex Stanford from New Jersey, who wanted to visit his uncle, Simcha Meyer, in Toronto. When we got to the border, it was about one o'clock in the morning. We were all very tired, and Joe Wolfe, who did not want to have to deal with the tedious filling out of forms for his skins, told us all to be quiet and not joke around with the customs and immigration officers. Neither Alex nor I knew what Joe was really thinking, but "border caution" was something that had stayed with me as a result of my wartime experience and my involvement in the Zionist underground, so Joe's advice seemed reasonable to me. Alex, an eternal kibitzer, took mock offense, announcing in a loud voice overheard by the officer in the Canadian border booth, "I'm not afraid. Why don't you want me to talk? Why can't I joke if I want to?" Alex's comments immediately perked up the ears of the border guard, who asked us to pull over to the customs building. At that point, Joe Wolfe figured that he had better declare his skins, but there was no one to handle commercial goods at that hour, so we had to drive back to Buffalo and come through again the following morning.

YAHRZEIT

On Mother's *yahrzeit*, I rushed back from Oakville to make it to synagogue in time for the service so I could say *kaddish*. Because I was running late, I went straight to the Beth Shalom Synagogue on Eglinton Avenue without stopping to change out of my work clothes. The sexton of the synagogue would not let me in because I had no tie, but I just walked past him, telling him that it was only a regular Thursday evening service and that I had to say *kaddish* for Mother. The next morning, my two older brothers joined me, all of us dressed in suits and ties. Chaim-Leizer was asked to lead the prayers, much to the pleasure of the congregation.

One gentleman, Louis Mayzel, was particularly taken by Chaim-Leizer's voice and invited us to breakfast. Though we met just that morning, our host was hospitable and warmhearted. Afterward, I told Mr. Mayzel what had happened the previous evening. Mayzel called over the sexton and suggested he use common sense in the future.

We were not the only guests; two other gentlemen had been invited as well. Mrs. Mayzel was awakened by news of our presence and served her unexpected guests a breakfast fit for royalty (with help from her housekeeper, Kozakowa). Rabbi Shimon says in the Talmud that if three people dine without discussing Torah, "It is as if they have eaten of sacrifices offered to a dead idol." So we discussed Torah, because one of the invited guests was none other than the verboten Rabbi Jacob Mendel Kirshenblatt. Could I ever have imagined I would meet, on my very first visit to a *shul* in Toronto, the man my rabbi had told me to avoid?

Initially, I said little, asking him only what yeshiva he had attended. "Lomzier," he responded. When asked if he remembered the names of fellow students, he recalled a genius in Talmud, Rabbi Mordechowicz, who would no longer speak to him after he took a pulpit in a Conservative synagogue. Rabbi Kirshenblatt could never convince Rabbi Mordechowicz that there was a difference between the Conservative and Reform movements. I told Rabbi Kirshenblatt that I used to study with Rabbi Mordechowicz and that I had heard the story. Rabbi Kirshenblatt was happy to meet me. Even if he could not communicate directly with Rabbi Mordechowicz, the rabbi who "defected" became a close friend of mine, and I met him often for *Shabes* meals at the Mayzel house.

Although Beth Shalom was a modern synagogue, conveniently located close to my brothers' homes, when the High Holidays came, we felt the need to daven in a more intimate setting. My brothers and I wanted the davening to feel more like the old days with our parents, and we wanted to find a place where the davening was a bit more fervent and emotional. We chose the Kielcer Synagogue in downtown Toronto because it was as close as we could get to the atmosphere of Dzialoszyce's *shtiblach* and because it emulated the spiritual fervor of our youth.

We slept in a hotel downtown so we would not violate the religious prohibition against driving on holidays. *Erev* Yom Kippur, as we assembled in the synagogue and were about to say *Kol Nidre,* I noticed a man wrapped in a long prayer shawl who closely resembled my grandfather. The only difference was that this gentleman was clean shaven, whereas my grandfather had had a long beard and *peyes*. I thought that I was dreaming. Trying to think clearly, I attributed the impression to the ambience of the synagogue on this holy night and decided that I was imagining visions of the past.

I asked my brothers if we had any relatives living in Canada. They knew of none; all our relatives were in Heaven. Then I pointed to the figure praying right across from us and declared that he was our relative. My brothers thought I was crazy. As the cantor chanted the awesome melody of the *Kol Nidre,* I had a vision of my tall, handsome grandfather. As soon as the cantor finished, I insisted that my brothers accompany me. I asked the man his name, and he said, "Tenenbaum." My brothers and I looked at each other in shock.

"Are you from Chenciny?" I asked.

"Yes, I am from Chenciny."

I told the man we were also from Chenciny, our name was Tenenbaum, and

I was the grandson of Eliyahu Tenenbaum.

"So you must be Zysman," said the stranger.

I told him we were the sons of Zysman. The man explained that he was the son of Shye, my grandfather's brother, and Father's first cousin. My brothers could not understand how in the world I recognized my grandfather in this man. I explained that all I did was imagine this man with the addition of a beard and *peyes*, and I saw the face of our grandfather, exactly as he was in 1939 when I visited him in Chenciny when I was 12. I never learned Father's cousin's first name, nor did I ever see him again. He chose to live in a state of oblivion, as did many others like him, who feared the obligation of assisting refugee relatives, financially or otherwise. Thank God, we did not need his help.

(About 20 years later, Marian Goldberg came up from New York to visit us in Toronto. We took him to Hershel's Restaurant for dinner, where we sat across from a man who bore a strong resemblance to the elusive Mr. Tenenbaum, Father's cousin. I spoke with him and discovered that he was the son of the man I met that first Yom Kippur in Toronto, but he did not seem interested in maintaining contact either.)

In the winter of 1959, I moved Gena and the boys to Toronto. Willie sold the house on Fairholme Avenue to the Highway Department of Metropolitan Toronto. (It was demolished later to make way for the Spadina Expressway.) We rented our house from Metro Toronto, and we, in turn, rented out the basement apartment. We had many fine neighbors, including the two Bens. Ben Sunshine, a survivor and a homebuilder, had two sons, Eddie and Joey, who played with our boys. (Eddie eventually became a prominent lawyer, builder, and chairman of Council Trust Corporation.) Ben Zuckerman of Ben's Electric did all the wiring for our properties. We never had any disagreements nor did we ever have a contract. In the end, we lived in the house for three and a half happy years.

DIGGING FOR TRUTH

I continued to build houses, 12 of them on Vilma Road in Oakville. I bought two additional lots from a neighbor who could not get a building permit and managed to get one by revising the lot configuration. I always cooperated with tradesmen and contractors and paid them a bit ahead of time to help them out as much as I could. Nevertheless, there were some contractors guilty of inferior workmanship.

Once, a group of bricklayers botched up a wall, and after they left, I decided to push it down, as the mortar was not yet dry. In the morning, they asked me why I had done that. I said that the Almighty had sent a wind to knock over the poorly built wall. I told them the biblical story of Abraham who blamed the smashed idols in his father's shop on the largest idol there. The superstitious men screamed they were quitting, that they were afraid to continue their jobs. They calmed down only after the master bricklayer looked at me and said, "Giuseppe, if God sent the wind, the bricks would have fallen to the inside of the house. Since the bricks fell to the outside, it was not the wind that knocked down the wall. You did."

Another time, the bricklayers refused to pick up leftover bricks and blocks and carry them to the next lot, where they were about to begin work. With the help of a couple of laborers, I loaded their truck with the masonry. When the bricklayers wanted to go home, they found their trucks loaded to the limit. They were angry, but they had not listened to reason, so I was forced to discipline them and other tradesmen who tried to shirk their responsibilities.

I had similar experiences with plumbers. A woman who purchased one of our houses asked me to come by for tea, and I said I would stop by the first chance I had. When the Italian bricklayers overheard the invitation, they started teasing, "Giuseppe has a girlfriend." I continued to postpone my visit, but after a couple weeks, her husband asked me to visit because he had something to show me. When I arrived, he led me straight to the bathroom and asked me to sit down on the toilet. I told him that I had no need to use the facilities at that particular moment, so he pressed the flusher and hot water gushed into the toilet. We laughed at the unusual sight of steam rising from the commode. Since I had used only two plumbers on the job, one or the other had hooked up the hot water by mistake, but neither would admit to it.

The trades taught me all I ever needed to know about shifting blame. An incident with a painter who did inferior work is illustrative. When I said the job was sloppy, the painter blamed the plasterer. The plasterer, in turn, blamed the gyprock (sheetrock) man. The gyprock man blamed the carpenter for uneven framing, the carpenter blamed the shoddy work on uneven foundations and footings, and the foundations and footing people blamed the poor quality of the soil.

The moral of the story is that one has to dig deep to get to the truth.

My third building project was to buy land and do the same thing that Dave Shier and his son-in-law, Barney Loftus, were doing—developing and subdividing. Joe Wolfe was about to join me as a full-time partner, or so he said. We went looking for land, and a real estate agent showed us several parcels, none of them suitable for development. On our own, we found a lovely apple orchard owned by a farmer. I had learned from my previous project that if a lot had a tree or two on it, the house sold much faster. The orchard held promise. The day we closed the deal, my partner and I, and all of Canada for that matter, received a shocking surprise. Prime Minister John Diefenbaker had scrapped the multimillion-dollar development of the Avro airplane, and there were mass layoffs that affected the communities in the vicinity of the Avro plant as well as the price of land. Our plot and the planned houses were close to the airport and still had great potential for increased value, but immediate loss seemed inevitable. The 50 acres were put on hold.

I expected Joe to join me for full-time work, so I continued building the houses on Vilma Road in Oakville and started others on Milvan Avenue in Bronte, close to Lake Ontario. The area was picturesque, and I thought the houses would sell quickly. Our company office was on Spadina Avenue in Joe Wolfe's factory, Top Furs. Dina was our secretary and bookkeeper. Both

Joe and Dina saw how hard I worked. The project was a good investment for them, but Dina, an honest person, warned me that her husband would never give up his fur business. "Why should he?" she asked.

"Why shouldn't he?" I replied. "We signed an agreement."

"But this is his baby," Dina answered.

I relied on Joe's promise, the signed agreement, and his constant reassurances. In the end, Dina was right. She was also right when a contractor came to the office and threatened to take me to court for failing to pay him money to which he was not entitled. Dina turned to the contractor and, pointing at me, said, "This man already has answers to questions you have not even asked him, so stop blustering. Go finish the work, and I guarantee you will be paid."

We developed such a good name with contractors and suppliers that some of them left uncollected the last few hundred dollars coming to them. When I would send the check, they would not cash it. I wanted to clear the accounts and asked why they did not deposit the checks. They said they preferred that we owe them money so that we would not forget each other when the next job came along.

In 1960, most of our friends were immigrants and Holocaust survivors like us. Joe and Dina were more than business partners. On hot summer weekends we visited them at their cottage in Jackson's Point on Lake Simcoe, and our children played with theirs. One time, we took the kids for pony-cart rides, and the ponies went wild, overturning the two-wheeled carts and injuring many of the passengers. Gary's jaw was completely dislocated, and he was covered with cuts and bruises. Gena's bleeding earlobe hung loose, and her face was completely covered in fine, brown, trail dust. We rushed back to the Hospital for Sick Children in Toronto where Gena's ear was reattached and Gary's jaw was repositioned. Everyone healed, and Gary turned into a handsome young man.

We once took Dina and Joe to the Lower East Side of Manhattan and were walking along Orchard Street when a man in front of a store yelled out, "Mister, Mister." He wanted to know if I had any more bathing caps! I told him I was all sold out.

"I still have the ten dozen bathing caps you sold to me seven years ago. They're on my top shelf, and you can have them for half price if you need any. By now, they've dried out like crackers."

"Well, your mistake was that you kept them. They were to be sold, not kept," I said.

"But nobody wanted to buy them," he explained.

"You bought them, didn't you?" I asked.

Selling the 12 houses in Oakville was not going to be as easy as getting rid of those bathing caps had been. The Canadian economy was growing worse, and two real estate brokers controlled Oakville's entire housing market, with eight local builders dependent on their services. My brothers' companies each built about 30 houses a year, a large number at that time. In order to move on and have the capital for my next project, I was desperate to sell the 12 houses. One of the brokers told me that Harry Silverstein offered him $50 on top of his regular commission to push his houses first.

I went to the Canada Mortgage and Housing Corporation (CMHC) for some help or at least some advice and ideas. They had committed to $10,000 first mortgages on the houses, but the only advice I got was a print of a house with the face of a clock superimposed on it. In place of the numbers were images and inscriptions of what houses meant to different people. To the seller, the house was a castle; to the fire department, it was a firetrap; to the insurance company, it was a risk; and to the purchaser, it was a doghouse because that was the price he wanted to pay for it. I looked at those images and got the message; I had to do something drastic.

The next day I drove home from Oakville through small towns along the lake instead of taking the highway. The scenic route gave me a chance to think. As I drove through Port Credit, I noticed a lawyer's shingle that read "Gogek." I went up to his office—above a store—to speak with him.

"Mr. Gogek, I have secure second mortgages for sale. Would you be interested in buying them?" He asked how much they were, and I told him that he would receive a 30 percent discount off the face amount—whatever it was. We discussed the matter further, and he decided that it was an offer he could not refuse. Once our deal was in place, I started off to Toronto, but I stopped at the Brethouer & Morris Real Estate Office, also in Port Credit. I spoke to the general manager and showed him a way to sell all my houses in one weekend with a down payment of only $100. We shook hands, and he prepared a nice ad for the weekend newspaper. The ad read, "You can move into your own home with only $100 down." At the time, the terms were a tremendous incentive to buyers.

To get my money out with a small profit, I needed to get $15,000 for each house. I was not drawing a regular salary and all my money was tied up in real estate. CMHC had $10,000 in each house. By arranging $8,000 second mortgages with Gogek and discounting them 30 percent, I was left with $5,600 from the second mortgages. That and the CMHC mortgages gave me more than the $15,000 I needed per house.

On Monday morning, my brothers and their partners came to the job site in Oakville and saw that all of my houses, even the ones that were not fully built, were plastered with "SOLD" signs. Willie took me aside and said, "Joe, you are making a mistake by putting sold signs on all the houses. It would be enough to put a sign on one or two houses, or maybe three maximum, but not on all of the houses. If you put signs on all of them, it means you have nothing left to sell. You will not get inquiries from potential customers."

"But Willie, they are all sold," I said. He did not believe me. Harry Silverstein did not believe me either; he said I was playing one of my New York tricks. A few days later when they saw furniture being unloaded from moving vans in front of some of the houses, they knew I was telling the truth and that there were ways of selling houses with which they might not have been familiar. All I told them was that I did not bribe any real estate agents with $50 bonuses to sell my houses first. When all of my houses closed, the project was complete. Later, I told my brothers how I promoted the houses to sell in a single weekend.

BACK TO THE USA

By mid-1961, the construction business in Toronto and the general economic situation had deteriorated. Selling houses was difficult because it was hard to get mortgages. I looked for other kinds of opportunities and came close to a deal in the knitting business with Mr. Davidovicz, a sweater manufacturer on Spadina Avenue, Toronto's *shmate* district. However, that, and whatever else I looked at, did not seem to work out. One solution would be to return to the United States and try construction there. Gena felt a little tug back to New York because her parents still lived there. I sat down with Joe Wolfe and proposed that we look for land in the United States.

I scouted on my own before moving my family. Sometimes I went with fellow Torontonians who were already doing business in New York or were looking for opportunities themselves. One was Motek Fishtein, a prominent Toronto builder who was a partner in the Union Maritime building on West 13th Street and Seventh Avenue in Manhattan. Motek knew the other partners, Roman Blum and Sam Edelstein, from Frankfurt, Germany. Roman, a New Yorker, had a lease on the Hotel Chelafonte, which is where we Torontonians usually stayed. One time I had to share a bed with Sam Edelstein because there were no other accommodations available.

Several deals for high-rise apartments in the Bronx did not make sense, so we looked for development land in New Jersey. One deal involved an entire mountain in Verona, New Jersey. We drove up the mountain as far as we could, parked the car, and climbed to the top. We were absorbed in our deliberations until two armed guards approached us and asked what we were doing. We said we were builders interested in buying the land. "Do you realize that you are trespassing on the grounds of a penitentiary and could be arrested? How did you get in?" they asked.

We explained that we just walked up the mountain, unimpeded. It turned out that Fishtein and his partners were interested in large-scale, high-risk projects for which I had little taste, so I went looking for projects more appropriate for me.

I concentrated on Passaic, New Jersey, an area relatively close to my in-laws' apartment in the Bronx. Passaic had the potential to be a neighborhood where I could raise our children, who were still in Toronto with Gena. After a while, I rented an office in Passaic that was so large it served as my temporary residence, saving a daily commute in congested traffic and money that would have been spent on hotels.

Other survivor-builders from Toronto tried the construction business in the United States, but only a few started projects. Most stayed in Canada. When Ike Rosenblum arrived in Passaic, I had already bought land for an apartment building from a Dr. Randazzo and bought development land to rezone for residential use in Caldwell, New Jersey. I offered Ike a share, and we agreed to a partnership, shaking hands on the deal. The next day, Ike told me that he had changed his mind. I understood, and such a decision was his prerogative. That was the second time he had agreed to a deal in the evening and changed his mind by the next morning. After questioning him, I concluded that his wife, who was still in Toronto, was behind it all.

I proceeded with the apartment project on my own and prepared plans with architect Nathan Gurtman, an uncle to survivor friends of mine. After I had construction plans, I arranged for financing. Banks in Passaic, as well as other institutions in New Jersey, were not eager to lend large amounts of money for apartment buildings. Conventional mortgage companies also were not ready to lend money to me on reasonable terms. I had no choice but to turn to the Federal Housing Authority in Newark, New Jersey. I submitted all the documentation—surveys, plans, specifications, and financial statements—and after a long time and many trips to Newark, I received a construction loan commitment.

The day I got the commitment, I threw a party in the cafeteria right across from my office on Howe Avenue. All my friends were invited, including Ike Rosenblum, Alex Stanford, and Yoyne Tylchyn. That cafeteria was a blessing for us because it served all our needs away from home and was the nerve center for our little community of survivor-builders. We ate there, held business meetings there, and sometimes just went there to see a friendly face, because some of our our families were still back in Toronto. My office also got lots of traffic since I was the only one with a tub in his office bathroom. Yoyne Tylchyn practically lived in my office because he liked to take hot baths.

Now that things were progressing in New Jersey, it was time to move the family. Back in Canada, Joe and Dina Wolfe threw a farewell party for us at their Jackson Point cottage, and many of our friends and relatives attended. Mixed feelings permeated the party. We celebrated a new opportunity, yet our departure was sad. The following week, there was another, more intimate party for us at the Barclay Hotel on Front Street. Seated at the table next to ours were Norman Goodhead and Max Tannenbaum, the philanthropist-owner of York Steel. I knew Max and had done business with him, so I went over to say hello and told Max that my main reason for leaving Canada was problems I had with the name "Tenenbaum." Wherever I went, people asked, "Are you Max Tannenbaum's son?" or "Are you his brother?" "Which Joe Tenenbaum are you?"

I noticed that Uncle Max (which is how I used to address him, though we were not related) was getting a little agitated. He stood up and said, probably more for the Reeve's benefit than mine, "Joey, there are seven continents in the world, and this one is the best; and on this continent there are many countries, and Canada is the best one. There are many provinces in Canada, and Ontario tops them all, and Toronto is the best city in the province, and the name Tannenbaum is the best in the city. Do not leave Toronto because you cannot go wrong with a name like Tannenbaum here. I'm not drunk, and I know what I'm saying." Then Uncle Max declared that he was going to adopt me. A couple of weeks later I bumped into Uncle Max and his wife, Anne, at a bar mitzvah. I reminded Max of his promise to adopt me and even offered to pay for the legal work involved. I watched Max, ever the businessman, as the wheels turned in his head. Then I told him not to forget to include me in his will along with his other children. Uncle Max laughed and replied that he would think it over.

I moved the family to Passaic in the summer of 1962. Before the move, I rented a beautiful one-family house at 11 Cornelia Court in a neighborhood full of young families. The house was perfect for our family, with a huge backyard full of flowers and a big sour cherry tree in which our boys built a tree house.

I helped found a Young Israel synagogue in the neighborhood, and instead of embarking on a costly building campaign, a group of us rented an old, burnt-out print shop and cleaned it up. I was happy to have an Orthodox synagogue within walking distance of our home so that my father-in-law would feel comfortable attending services when he visited us for *Shabes*.

Mr. Meisels always enjoyed leading prayers, and this gave him an opportunity to do so. The synagogue took up quite a bit of my time, but it was Sandy Stern, a real estate and insurance broker, who worked the hardest to found the synagogue. Rabbi Lehrer, who had come from Israel with his family, volunteered his services. Everything was done on a volunteer basis; we did not have the funds to do it any other way. Everybody thought that because of my involvement, I wanted to become president of the *shul*, yet when we drew up a constitution, I proposed, as the first motion, that members who were not strict Sabbath observers could not be elected to that position. Because my interpretation of Sabbath observance was more liberal than what I expected from a community leader, my lack of presidential ambition soon became clear.

Hillel Academy, the local Hebrew school under the administration of the capable Rabbi Brenner, was religiously to the right of the Associated Hebrew Day Schools in Toronto. I did not mind that Sidney tied *tzitzit* for his teachers and refused to kiss his mother in public because it said not to do so in the *Shulhan Arukh*, but I did mind that Hebrew was taught with the Ashkenazi *shtetl* pronunciation of my childhood instead of the Sephardic modern Hebrew pronunciation spoken in Israel. I wanted my children to be able to go to Israel and be understood.

VISITING THE LUBAVITCHER REBBE

Now that we were back in the United States, Gena and I resumed our relationships with old friends from New York City, Long Island, Brooklyn, and New Jersey. Friends from Canada, including Joe and Dina Wolfe and Marilyn and Jack Kostman, visited us on occasion, always trying to convince us to move back to Toronto. With promising business prospects in the works, we were staying put, at least for the time being. Among the people who visited from Toronto were Louis Mayzel and Cecil Rotenberg. Mayzel had introduced Rotenberg to the Lubavitch movement and brought him to New York to visit the Lubavitcher Rebbe, Rabbi Menachem Mendel Schneerson in Crown Heights. Louis insisted that I accompany them. At the time, I thought I had a heart problem, so I agreed, because I figured that a blessing from the Rebbe could not hurt.

My "heart problem" had developed over the High Holidays. On Yom Kippur there had been no one to blow the shofar at the Young Israel Synagogue, so I had volunteered. I had not practiced before, and since I was not used to blowing the shofar, it took some effort. I wanted to make sure that the congregation would wake up and that the Almighty Himself would hear my pleas. So with all my strength, I blew the shofar as a messenger for the congregation for the first time in my life. Right after *Yom Tov,* I suffered excruciating pain in the middle of the night and woke up drenched in sweat. When Gena asked me what was wrong, I started trembling and she called an ambulance. The medics carried me downstairs from our second-floor bedroom on a stretcher, and all I asked of Gena, who was pregnant at the time, was that she name the baby after me.

At the hospital the doctor declared there was nothing wrong with me and sent me home. When I asked if I should go by ambulance or taxi, he told me to walk. The doctor gave me some pills, but I was not convinced that everything was fine. If I was OK, why did he prescribe medication? The pain persisted, allowing me no peace of mind.

Harry Botnick knew a good heart specialist in Toronto, and I decided to go see him, but when I called to make an appointment, I was told the waiting list was three months long. Paying no attention to the secretary's comments, I took a plane to Canada. Dina Wolfe fetched me from the airport and drove me straight to the doctor's office where I lay down on the threshold and refused to move unless the doctor agreed to see me. People could not get in or out, and after the other patients complained, the receptionist allowed me in to see the doctor.

The heart specialist examined me thoroughly, said nothing was wrong, and sent me home, but the pain persisted. I was still convinced my heart must be the problem. I returned to Passaic, where Sol Eigen advised me to see Dr. Herman, a top diagnostician. Dr. Herman's office was in a run-down neighborhood of dilapidated houses, boarded-up windows, and broken fences. Before I entered the office, I thought no one in his right mind would come to a doctor in such environs, but I was wrong; the waiting room was full. I waited for two hours before the nurse finally called my name. Dr. Herman put both his hands on my arms and then asked me to lie down on the examining table. After 20 minutes, he spoke frankly. "If you really want to get a heart attack," he said, "you can get one by running around torturing yourself and imagining that you have heart problems. As of now, you do not have a heart problem." This time I left the doctor's office believing the problem was not my heart. So why did the pain persist? Something was wrong.

A few days later, Louis Mayzel and Cecil Rotenberg arrived on their "secret mission" to see the Rebbe. After a good night's sleep, we got into my car and set out for 770 Eastern Parkway in Brooklyn. The traffic was heavy, and when we finally reached our destination, there was not a parking spot within blocks of the building. We went some distance to find a spot, and then we took a cab back to the *shul*.

Outside, policemen and firemen tried to keep the crowd from forcing its way into the already packed *beit ha-midrash* (house of study). Some Hasidim were holding onto columns, some were standing on windowsills, and others hung from railings. It was a sight to see. Never in my life had I witnessed so many human beings crammed into one space. After losing my companions in the crowd and finding myself crushed by strangers, I addressed my Maker, "If what ails me is my heart, then let it cease beating here and now." What a beautiful place to die, amid thousands of pious, praying Jews and in the presence of the Rebbe. I was uplifted, spiritually and literally—literally because I was squeezed so tightly by the surrounding throng that I could actually raise my feet off the floor and not fall. I was among strangers, yet in spirit I felt close to each one of them.

I tried to concentrate on the Rebbe's discourse, which lasted for several hours. He addressed various teachings from the Talmud and Holy Scriptures, interlacing his talk with quotations. From time to time, the lecture was interrupted by joyous melodies bursting from the Rebbe's faithful admirers or calls to drink a *l'hayim*. The *farbrengen* (gathering) lasted late into the night. After midnight, the crowd thinned out. We, too, were ready to return home, yet we kept postponing our departure. We were reluctant to give up on getting a personal audience with the Rebbe while our emotions were still touched by the experience. We decided to explore and found Hasidim of all ages studying heavy texts at long tables in a number of rooms.

At 2 a.m., we came upon a young Hasid who was repeating the Rebbe's four-hour discourse word for word, without notes. When I was listening to the Rebbe, I had been astounded that he was speaking for so long from his own wisdom, from the Talmud, and without a single note card. I thought the Rebbe was a genius, but as I listened to the young Hasid repeating the discourse, I considered him no less of a genius.

I never could pinpoint the cause of my chest pains. It may have been a pulled chest muscle caused by overexerting myself when I blew the shofar; it may have been stress. I'll never know, and I will never know for sure how I got well. What I do know is that, somehow, my chest pains disappeared that night while I was listening to and drinking a *l'hayim* with the Lubavitcher Rebbe.

FRIENDS AND HEROES

Louis Mayzel was a most unusual man. I liked him from the time I first met him in *shul* in September 1958, when he invited us to that unforgettable breakfast. After a while, my whole family was included in the friendship, and we shared many of life's passages. We confided in one another about family and business. Mayzel did not like to watch from the sidelines; he was a man of action and always took a stand.

Mayzel's good works included involvement with the police as a Good Samaritan. Whenever an officer died in the line of duty, Louis took it upon himself to help look after the widow and children. When Louis heard that a poor boy's bike had been stolen, he replaced it without question or fanfare. On *Erev* Sukkoth, Mayzel drove around with a truckload of plywood and a carpenter to put up *sukkahs* for people who could not afford to build their own. Whenever somebody wrote a favorable newspaper article about Israel, Louis sent flowers accompanied by a note of appreciation. Every *Shabes* and holiday, friends and strangers gathered at his table. Whenever somebody needed help, he extended a helping hand, and it was never empty. Louis loved life and people.

Before I went back to the United States, Louis and I got to know each other better after we made a deal on 50 lots for single-family homes in Oakville. We agreed to build more houses on land I would buy from him in stages. I gave him a $25,000 deposit and, without telling me first, Mayzel went to the bank near his office on University Avenue to certify the check. When he returned to his office where I was waiting, Mayzel was all smiles. Louis assured me that neither he nor anyone on his behalf would build houses in that subdivision on their own or with third parties. Doing so would have put them at a decided advantage. I could not compete against a land developer when his land costs were significantly lower than mine.

Louis got heavily into debt on the land and, nearing bankruptcy, made deals with my competitors. I stopped buying lots in the developed area of Oakville to build on Louis's land north of Queen Elisabeth Way and pioneered development there. I built ten model homes, each one unique in style and design, and named them after the provinces of Canada. I advertised them, printed brochures, and made a sizable investment in anticipation of building many more homes in the subdivision.

I was in a difficult situation. When I found out that, contrary to his assurances, Louis had gone into competition with me, I was disillusioned. I could not bear such treatment from a person I loved, admired, and trusted. I doubted my judgment, and the insecurity that doubt created contributed to my decision to return to the United States. Despite my pain, I still liked Louis Mayzel for his heart. He was pushed to the wall and had to do what he did to save his skin, but did he have to hurt me in the process? In the end, Louis took back all the land I had not yet built on, and although those ten model homes were not nearly as profitable as they should have been, they were not a total disaster either.

Years later, when we came back to Canada from the United States, Louis offered me a wonderful opportunity to take over a high-rise site at the corner of University Avenue and Richmond Street in downtown Toronto. It was prime real estate that I could get by paying off the mortgage and clearing the debt to the other Joseph Tannenbaum. I was willing to invest everything I had and borrow whatever I could to be able to build a magnificent high-rise office building. I worked on architectural plans with Eddie Richmond, a well-known architect, and on structural engineering plans with Alex Tobias, an engineer. My motto was, "Sixty-seven stories high for 1967." I had practically three years to realize this once-in-a-lifetime opportunity.

I approached many people to propose a joint venture. I chose individuals I thought had the financial wherewithal and artistic vision for the project. I went to Simon Mintz, a survivor who had started in Canada as a plumbing and heating man and was now a real estate developer. I had known Simon in postwar Germany at the student restaurant on Frauenstrasse in Munich, back when he could barely afford soup for 25 pfennig. The wheel of fortune had turned his way, and Simon was now in a position to undertake very substantial investments.

One Sunday morning when we were discussing the project at Simon's house, his wife suddenly cut the conversation short with one fatal word, "No." I never found the right people to join me in the venture and regretted giving up on the project, but I remain grateful to Mayzel for the wonderful opportunity.

I will never forget the way Mayzel covered his head with a *talis* during *davening*. Addressing the Lord with devotion, Louis cried like a child, reminding me of my own father's prayers on Yom Kippur. Once, on the way home from *shul*, Louis told me how much he enjoyed *Shabes*. He said that *Shabes* observance was so important to him that, if he were forced to choose between his son keeping *Shabes* and forgoing his son saying *kaddish* for him after his death, he would choose *Shabes* observance in an instant.

Another example of Louis's adherence to our sages' dictum, "Speak little and do much," happened when the remains of Ze'ev Jabotinsky were to be transferred from New York for reburial in Israel. The evening before the ceremony, Louis stayed at our house in Passaic, and we spent the night reminiscing, with Louis urging me to return to Toronto. We finally retired at midnight, but about an hour later, I heard Louis fidgeting around and went to check on him. Louis said, "Joey, it bothers me that Jabotinski is in Riverside Memorial Chapel and that I do not know if anybody is there to watch over him." According to Jewish law, a deceased person must not be left alone until interred.

Louis did not hesitate to act in the middle of the night. Unless we went, he said we would regret our inaction. He was absolutely right. We put on our clothes and drove into New York. When we tried to enter the funeral home, we found all doors locked and the windows closed. There seemed to be no way to get inside. We banged on the doors and shouted a little until we woke the chapel attendant who let us in. Louis and I sat with Ze'ev Jabotinsky's body through the night and prayed for the soul of this leader of our generation. We were very proud to be able to render these last respects to our hero.

The next day, tens of thousands of people came to the funeral, and I was one of the marshals who ensured the decorum befitting a visionary who had dedicated his life to the Jewish people. By noon, the funeral home and streets adjacent to it were so packed with people that the police turned people away. When Nathan Silver, national chairman of the Revisionist Party in Canada, arrived with a delegation from Toronto, they were not allowed in. I invented a story on the spot. Thinking that Toronto would not seem important enough to the police officers, I said that Silver and his companions were representatives from South America who had just arrived from Colombia. Nathan Silver and the Toronto contingent were grateful for that little white lie that allowed them into Jabotinsky's funeral service.

Some of the people from Toronto accompanied Jabotinsky's body to Israel, where he was laid to rest on Jerusalem's Mount Herzl next to Zionism's founder, Dr. Theodor Herzl. I have visited their graves on trips to Israel and always feel sorrow and pride as I walk among the heroes' graves. I am filled with sorrow for the too many lives interrupted in their prime, and I am proud that there were Jews who made the supreme sacrifice to uphold the Zionist ideal.

I find solace in knowing that these tombstones will not disappear as did those of my ancestors in Dzialoszyce.

CLOSING A CHAPTER—AGAIN

A joyful event took place in Passaic, New Jersey, on January 10, 1964. Tamara Esther Leah was born. After two boys, the birth of a girl was cause for celebration. From the amount of weight Gena had gained and the size of her pregnancy, we expected twins. (Those were the days before ultrasound confirmed multiple births.) Gena went into labor just as our boys were preparing to go to school. Sidney noticed blood in the toilet and told Gena, who told him that "when a mother's elbow bleeds, it's a sign that the baby is on its way." Sidney, at age nine, immediately ran out to tell the neighbors that the baby was on its way because Gena's elbow was bleeding!

We made sure the boys were taken care of, and I took Gena to the Beth Israel Hospital in Passaic. When Gena was taken to the labor room, I tried to follow, but policy in those days was not to allow fathers to attend the births. As time passed I became increasingly anxious, so I took a chance. The shift was changing, and the new staff at the nursing station did not know me. During my pacing around the halls, I saw a white lab coat hanging in an empty room. I put it on and marched right past the nurse's station without being stopped. Once I was in the delivery room, they let me stay. And instead of twins, I watched with surprise as Gena delivered an eight-and-a-half-pound girl.

We prepared a proper welcome for our princess. My cousin Alex Stanford offered his help, and both of us spent an entire night painting the spare room and crib a pale pink. Alex completely ruined his pants and shirt and had to discard them. Sidney, the proud older brother, bought pink bubble-gum cigars and handed them out to his friends at school, telling them, "It's a girl!"

The whole time we lived in New Jersey, Toronto kept pulling at us like a magnet. If people were not visiting us, we were visiting them.

In Toronto, we stayed with my brother Willie and saw our many friends. During our visit, Gena said she would not mind moving back there. Everyone, including me, was surprised to hear her say that. She had been the primary force behind our return to New York, and when we had lived in Toronto before, Gena missed her parents and Manhattan's cultural life. New York had character and nightlife; Toronto was conservative and had Blue Laws, which meant everything was closed on Sundays.

Passaic was a suburb, and the only thing it had going for it was its proximity to New York City and Gena's parents. We were not happy with the schools in Passaic. The closest day school that taught the modern Hebrew I wanted my children to learn was in Manhattan—too far for the children to commute. To live in a decent Manhattan neighborhood would have stretched us financially. Toronto, though, had an excellent Jewish day school with just the type of curriculum we were looking for, so when Gena said she would not mind moving back, I listened carefully. I asked her how I could know that she would not change her mind again. Gena assured me that she was serious. Finally, we decided to act on it.

We went back to New Jersey and sold everything. To get our boys out from under our feet while we packed, we had them stay with their grandparents in the Bronx. We packed while the boys had fun at the 1964 World's Fair with their grandparents, and when we were finished, we picked them up one evening and literally drove off into the sunset.

ABOVE: Early postwar panorama of the author's hometown, Dzialoszyce.

BELOW: The Tenenbaum home *(third from the left of the corner)* as seen from the market square.

RIGHT: Uncle Shloyme and Aunt Esther, holding their little girl Hanusia, and Esther's sister Yitkele.

BELOW: The *Beit Midrash* in Dzialoszyce.

ABOVE: An early postwar north view of the market, which originally comprised about 100 stalls.

LEFT: The author's sister-in-law Dina's great-grandfather, Avigdor Ezra Silverstein.

BELOW: Estusia Ehrlich, the author's first sweetheart, in 1940.

LEFT: Freed Ebensee inmates, 1945. *Yad Vashem*

RIGHT: The Mauthausen quarry. *USHMM, courtesy of Archiv der KZ-Gede*

ABOVE: The Gusen camp.
USHMM, courtesy of National Archives

RIGHT: Johnnie Stevens *(far right)*, a member of the 761st Tank Battalion, whom the author embraced at liberation and reconnected with in 2002.

LEFT: The author, recovering in the hospital postliberation.

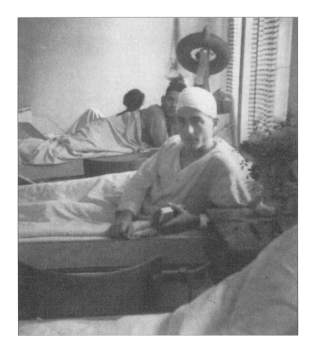

ABOVE: *(front, from the left)* Meyer and Azriel Weinstock; *(back, from the left)* an unidentified survivor, Uncle Shloyme, and the author.

LEFT: The author *(second from the left)* with friends in Italy, where he worked on behalf of *Betar*.

RIGHT: Jabotinsky Memorial Day, 1946.

LEFT: The marble memorial tablet the author had made for each of the Tenenbaum brothers in honor of their parents.

RIGHT: *(from the left)* Art, Chaim-Leizer, Willie, and the author, Toronto, 1960.

ABOVE: Wedding of the author and Gena, with Rabbi Leizerowski and Gena's father.

RIGHT: The author, Tamara, Sidney, and Gary on Tamara's fourth birthday.

RIGHT: The author on his return to Dzialoszyce, at the front door of the Tenenbaum home and store, in 1978.

LEFT: The author indicating the *mezuzah* markings at the back door of the abandoned home.

LEFT: The long-neglected Dzialoszyce *shul*, at the time of the author's return.

RIGHT: The author with Novakova, who helped hide his family's possessions after the German occupation.

ABOVE: Jewish cemetery in Krakow, at the time of the author's return to Poland.

BELOW: The author at the Plaszow monument.

ABOVE: Rav Lau and the author, on behalf of Laniado Hospital, Israel, 2001.

RIGHT: Gena, Yitzchak Shamir, and the author, on Shamir's 2001 visit to Toronto.

LEFT: Menachem Begin (*left*) and the author, 1954.

ABOVE: Nobel Peace Prize laureate Elie Wiesel *(center)* with the author and Gena, at the Elie Wiesel Foundation for Humanity dinner, Lincoln Center, New York, 1989.

PART V

Children begin by loving their parents.
After a time they judge them.
Rarely, if ever, do they forgive them.

Oscar Wilde
A Woman of No Importance

8 STAYNER AVENUE

As soon as we made the decision to move back to Canada, we searched for a place to live. We responded to all kinds of ads and soon found a house for rent on Stayner Avenue, near a park not too far from where we once had lived. The house was just perfect for us. Among the Davis, Pitchosky, Aronoff, and Grammar families, our children had plenty of friends to play with. We lived on a dead-end street that faced Viewmount Park, a safe place for youngsters. Donny Pitchosky had a dog that Gary loved to play with. One summer when Sidney and Gary went to visit their Aunt Anda in Los Angeles, Gary brought back a German shepherd puppy named Sandy, but when our neighbor Sandy took offense, we renamed the dog Omar. Omar came from the breeders of Rin Tin Tin, the famous TV dog, and grew into a huge hound that was very intelligent and loyal. When he was in the park with the children, we did not have to worry about them.

At that time, Viewmount Park was a huge open field with a stream running through it. In the winter, fathers, serving as pull horses, would tow sleds filled with children across the snow-covered expanse. In summer there was baseball and kiting. There was also a tennis court that was the scene of an almost-tragic incident. One evening before dark, I was playing tennis with Sidney while Gary was weaving his bicycle between the poles that supported the nets and did not see the wire tightly strung between two poles. Gary caught the wire across his neck and was thrown off the bike into the air. When I saw what had happened, I nearly died. I ran over and started checking Gary for injuries. When he began to cry, I knew he was fine; I hugged and kissed him, and carried him home.

Except for the few houses occupied by Jewish families, most of the neighborhood was Italian. The young men and teens played soccer in the street, though the park was only a few steps away. I often watched through our living room window or from our front porch, and one time, unable to restrain myself, I asked to participate. At first, they were reluctant to let me join, probably wondering what an older Jewish man knew about soccer.

After a few minutes of play, they realized I must have known something. They screamed, "Go, Giuseppe, go!" After that, they rang my doorbell before every game and asked me to join them. We enjoyed the neighborhood and wanted to continue renting there, but every couple of months, the landlord would ask for a rent increase despite our written agreements. We paid all the utilities and taxes. He held a good job at the post office and, with our payments, had a good income—more than enough to cover the interest he owed on his mortgage—but he was greedy, and no amount of money seemed to satisfy him.

I did some investigating and discovered that the man's ex-wife lived in Bancroft, Ontario. When I first called her, she would not talk to me because she thought her former husband had sent me, and she was afraid of him. I assured her that was not the case.

"Mr. Tenenbaum, my former husband is a very mean man. He is a drunk, and he does not even own the house anymore. He lost it," she told me.

The man appeared to have lied to the poor woman, thereby cheating her out of her share of the house. I offered to buy her half of the house. She repeated that her husband had nothing, and that, consequently, she also had nothing to sell. She advised me not to waste my time and told me that lenders had foreclosed on the house. I asked this woman to come to Toronto and said I would hire a lawyer to act on her behalf—at no cost to her. I offered to pay all expenses. She was so broke she had to call me collect to tell me she would be coming to Toronto on March 20, 1965, if I paid for her bus ticket. I agreed, and then I provided her with an honest lawyer, as promised.

Before she arrived, I had my own lawyer do a title search, and we discovered that the same lawyer who had foreclosed on the house held the mortgage of $3,250. I went to see that lawyer, told him I represented the ex-wife, and demanded an explanation for the foreclosure. He claimed he represented investors, and that no payments had been made on the mortgage, so he foreclosed on the house. When I asked him how much had been invested in the mortgage, he answered, "Many thousands of dollars." I told him that the registry indicated only $3,250 and I doubted whether the sum had been given to my landlord. Then, I handed the lawyer a certified check for $3,250, and told him that if title was not returned to them within 48 hours, I would report the whole transaction to the bar. He would have had to answer for assisting my landlord in defrauding his former wife of her rightful share of the house.

When the papers were ready, she transferred her interest in the house over to me, and I gave her a check for $17,000. I took over the mortgage, paid all her expenses, and made her the happiest person in the world. She called me after she returned to Bancroft to thank me. This time, the call was not collect. For the first time in many years, she could afford to buy food and clothing for her children and have some peace of mind.

A few days later, my landlord arrived at our front door with a check I had mailed to him for $60—half the rent. The former husband threatened to evict us unless I paid $150 per month. When I asked him why he was demanding more money, he said he was increasing our rent by $30. I informed the man that the lease we had both signed had not yet expired, and until then I would only owe half the rent, because I now owned half the house. When it did expire, the rent would be determined by both of us equally or we could go to arbitration. Slowly, the message penetrated, and the man finally understood what had happened. A few years later, we sold our half of the house back to him.

NOT THE MOUSE BUT THE HOLE

As soon as my family was settled again in Toronto, I got back to business. I looked for land on which to build multifamily dwellings. After a few months, two brothers offered to sell me two houses, one on Isabella Street, the other on Sherbourne. They also held an option on two more houses on Sherbourne Street. To prove I was serious about purchasing the entire parcel, I offered to pay them $10,000 more than their best offer. They told me that someone bid $40,000 per house, totaling $160,000 for the four houses. With no discussion, I offered $170,000 and considered the deal done.

After a few weeks, the brothers said they had an offer for $180,000. Again I added $10,000 and gave them a total of $190,000. They repeated this game until the sum reached $224,000. I said I would top the offer only if they signed the agreement on the spot. They agreed, but first demanded a $10,000 deposit. I gave them a certified check, and one of the brothers signed the agreement for $234,000.

A few days later, one of the brothers asked me to come to his house, where he wanted his other brother to sign the agreement. I made a copy of the original and took it with me. When I walked into the house, everyone was waiting, wives included. The first brother told me that he now had an offer for $244,000. If I would be willing to pay $10,000 more, we could close the deal. I reminded them that we had already made a deal when I gave them a certified check for $10,000, which they accepted when we signed the agreement.

"Yes, but you only had one signature; one of us had not yet signed," came the reply. When I saw what they were doing, I moved to leave. The brothers tried to return my check by pushing it into my pocket, but I refused to accept it. They attempted, in vain, to get back the agreement with the one signature, which was in my possession. I left the house and immediately had my lawyer register the agreement in the title records, effectively blocking sale of the land to any other party. In time, the brothers went to their lawyers, who wrote me a letter. I answered, explaining the situation from my point of view. Writing back and forth got us nowhere until they and their attorneys gave the case to another lawyer for litigation. A reputable, well-known litigator, he issued a writ requesting that I appear for discovery.

During discovery, the attorney asked a number of questions. I must have conveyed through my facial expressions some message he did not like because he made several snide remarks, and I did not appreciate it. The discovery process was belligerent on both sides. Obviously, the court recorder could not record facial expressions, but the questions and answers were transcribed. About ten minutes into the discovery, he said, "No more questions."

Shortly, the law firm informed me that it was ready to close the deal on the original terms, but then there was a small complication. I discovered that a knowledgeable builder and his lawyer had an interest in some of the properties. In the end, we settled our differences and closed the deal.

After acquiring title, I hired Grozbord and King, architects who had designed quite a few high-rise buildings in Toronto. Although neither of the men had been licensed to practice architecture by the Ontario Association of Architects, they used Arye Grozbord's license as an engineer, which was based on his degree in refrigeration engineering from Massachusetts Institute of Technology. The firm employed a number of draftsmen to draw plans, and the structural and mechanical aspects of the design were contracted out to firms specializing in those fields. Kazmar Engineering or Alex Tobias & Associates were the structural consultants, and John Garay & Associates the mechanical ones.

While we were working on plans for the Sherbourne building, a real estate broker approached us with a proposition to buy land a block away at the corner of Wellesley Street and Homewood Avenue. The lot had an old three-story apartment building on it and belonged to the broker and his son. It made sense for us to consider building these two sites at the same time. Unfortunately, Joe Wolfe and I did not have enough capital to undertake both projects simultaneously, nor did we want to assume the huge risk involved in constructing so many high-rise apartment units.

Grozbord and King were interested in becoming our partners. We formed a company called Flo Developments, Ltd., with each of the four partners holding an equal share of the company. The signature officers were Arye Grozbord or Abraham King, and I. The relationship started out amicably, with Joe Wolfe and me benefiting from their greater experience with high-rise buildings. Joe and I contributed the land. Together, we applied for and obtained zoning approval. We arranged for two mortgages—one for the 94 suites on Sherbourne Street, from Excelsior Life Insurance at a $6^{1}/_{4}$ percent interest rate; the second, from London Life Insurance, for 114 suites on Wellesley Street, at a 7 percent interest rate. Everything went smoothly in the planning and preparatory stages. Even the demolition of the existing houses on the sites was accomplished without a hitch.

When we started actual construction, Arye Grozbord, who was supposed to be responsible for construction, began traveling for lengthy periods, sometimes for months. We had gone into the partnership primarily because of his reputed expertise, and we expected him to live up to his commitment to oversee the building process. Instead, to satisfy his wanderlust, he traveled to South America, Russia, and Israel (Israel I did not mind; his mother lived there). But his absence created ill-will among the partners.

William Denison, a speech therapist whose home and practice were across the street from our construction site, had many clients who came to his house every day. A friendly and interesting man, he would watch the construction and take pictures of our building's progress. I made a point of being nice to all of our neighbors, especially since we were inconveniencing them with all the noise and dust from the construction site. During one of our conversations, Mr. Denison confided to me that he had decided to run for election as mayor of Toronto. I assured him that he would win, that he deserved the office, and that he had my full support.

Denison kept coming to the site. He invited me for tea at his house, and in turn, I asked him to join me for coffee or lunch at the neighborhood restaurant to talk about the upcoming election. Once, while I stood in front of the unfinished building with Joe Wolfe and Arye, Denison came over, and I introduced him as the next mayor of Toronto. I had hardly finished the introduction when Arye broke into hysterical laughter, his huge frame shaking with mirth. I was shocked by his behavior and embarrassed by his insulting display. Later, I made excuses and explained to Denison that Grozbord was suffering from uncontrollable mood swings so no offense should be taken.

I suggested to Grozbord that we contribute at least $1,000 to Denison's campaign. He offered a big "zero." He was convinced that Denison had no chance of winning, and I could not convince him otherwise. Nevertheless, I made a contribution from the business account I had with Joe Wolfe.

When the elections approached, Denison officially announced his candidacy for mayor. Gena and I were invited to a few fundraisers for him, and we attended to show support. Thus we became social acquaintances. Election Day was dark and rainy. The affluent folks from Rosedale and Forest Hill did not bother voting, but the middle-class constituencies came out in droves. That evening our neighbor William Denison was elected mayor. We were invited to the inauguration, and the following day, Arye Grozbord ate crow.

Some years later I heard a funny story that typified my own frustrations with Grozbord. Aryeh went into partnership with Lou Chesler on 600 apartments built on Gerard Street. For the opening, they flew in Hollywood actor Douglas Fairbanks Jr. as part of a big media campaign. Grozbord went to the airport to pick up Fairbanks and bring him to the buildings where the media were waiting. Instead, Grozbord took him to a tavern near the airport for a few drinks. Fairbanks had left all the details to Arye: if Arye was not rushing, then there probably was no reason to rush; after all, Arye was the host. When they finally arrived at the site several hours late, very few people were left. The opening was a fiasco.

Lou Chesler lived in the Bahamas and was known for his international corporate and business acumen. Somehow, word got to him about a fellow in Toronto named Joe Tenenbaum (me) who had also been Grozbord's partner and managed not to lose money with him. Chesler called me, and we met for lunch in the Captain's Room of the Lord Simcoe Hotel. Lunch proceeded genially, although I was curious about the real reason for our meeting. Finally I said, "Mr. Chesler, it is a pleasure meeting you. I have heard about your business ingenuity. I know I could learn a lot from you, but what is the real purpose of this meeting?"

Chesler looked at me and said, "Believe me, Joe, all I wanted to do was to congratulate you because you are the only one among the many who have done business with Arye Grozbord who didn't end up a loser. I just wanted to know how you did it."

"Just hard work, no more—no less," I said, then added, "Hard work means keeping a constant watch on what's going on, being actively involved in every aspect of planning, contracting, construction, and management. The Talmud says in tractate *Gitten:* 'It's not the mouse that's the thief, rather it's the hole that is the thief.' When you give somebody the opportunity to take advantage of you, chances are he'll get carried away." I went on to tell Chesler that Arye was basically an honest and intelligent person, but that he just had too much on his plate to pay attention to details, and that was what got in his way.

A SQUIRREL AT THE FLOODGATES

After the termination of our partnership with Grozbord and King, I transferred all the papers from the trunk of my car, which had served as a temporary office of sorts, to the basement of my house. That basement was the site of an incident that typifies the thought processes of many Holocaust survivors.

It happened on the first night of Rosh Hashanah in the mid-1960s. The new Shaarei Shomayim Synagogue had recently been built, and we joined because its modern Orthodox point of view was just right for us. I also admired Rabbi Walter Wurtzburger, its spiritual leader. While I was *davening ma'ariv*, Gena ran in and told me that someone had broken into the house and was hiding in the basement. She heard the noise and was frightened to death.

I immediately left the synagogue, ran through the park to our house, took the crowbar I always kept in the entry hall closet, and cautiously walked, step by step, into the basement, yelling, "If you make a move, I'll shoot." I heard a noise, but nobody appeared. I inched toward the source of the sound and discovered that the intruder was a squirrel. Somehow, it had entered the basement through the dryer exhaust, but could not find a way out in the basement clutter. To help it out, I put peanuts—one by one—on a path along the floor, up the steps, and through the door, pleased that I enabled the squirrel to gain its freedom.

The incident opened the floodgates of my memories.

To survive each day, we survivors force ourselves to think and act in ordinary, rational ways. We have to pretend. When we remember the barbarism, the killers, and the silent world, we become capable of destroying our spirit, of becoming insane. Just as a swimmer has to come up for air, we, too, must surface to breathe, above the waves of memory that threaten to engulf us, waves triggered by as simple an act as a squirrel gaining its freedom.

I tried to maintain normalcy for the sake of my children, but I worried about the effect my Holocaust experience would have on them, and while they were very young, we were silent. I wanted them to grow up as normal youngsters, like children whose fathers did not live with toxic memories. I hoped to ensure that the heavy burden I carried would not be transferred to them, and I certainly did not want them to feel sorry for me.

Yet, I must admit that children of survivors, and even their offspring, are different.

Spoken or unspoken, something filters through. For the longest time, I felt that very few people could really speak or write about the Holocaust. Some of the postwar Yiddish and Hebrew poets were eloquent. Later, Elie Wiesel would write moving prose, but although I tried my hand at a few poems, I felt that most discourse or writing on the subject would lead to either banality or pain, and, therefore, what was the point?

My experience has not been recorded in any archives; I am the only one who can open the memories stored in me for more than 50 years. The Talmud says in tractate *Avodah Zarah* (5b): "The proper perspective toward a historical event and the lessons to be derived therefrom may not be obtained until 40 years have elapsed."

Now is the time for me to write. It is painful to do so, but abrogating my responsibility would be even worse. "So that all your future generations will know" (Leviticus 23:43).

FROM WHERE THE LEGS GROW

In my continuing search to do business, I never hesitated to follow up reasonable leads. My friend Mendel Tenenbaum introduced me to his lawyer, Jack Friedman. I told Mr. Friedman, a real estate and corporate lawyer, that I was interested in purchasing a piece of land that would be suitable for building an apartment building and asked if there was anything he could recommend. "As a matter of fact, I can," said Jack, "and I have a survey of the land in my office. I would be glad to show it to you."

I went to Jack's office and learned that the land was in Oshawa, 20 miles east of Toronto. Although I was not overly excited because I wanted land in the city, I thought I might as well check it out in case I could not find what I was looking for in Toronto. Survey in hand, I called Mendel Tenenbaum to tell him what I had gotten from Friedman, because I felt it only fair to share the find with him. At first, Mendel was reluctant to travel all the way to Oshawa, but he decided to consider the deal anyway.

I picked Mendel up and we drove east along Highway 401, took the first Oshawa exit, and followed the map until we reached our destination. I pulled out the survey to double-check that we were in the right place because we were looking at a swampy, low-lying piece of land covered with stagnant water. We looked at each other, bewildered. What had Friedman been thinking? Mendel wanted to go home and not waste any more time. As I scanned the horizon from the valley in which we stood, I noticed apartment buildings in the distance. I told Mendel that since we were already in Oshawa, we might as well see what was going on in the area. I drove in the direction of the apartment houses and stopped the car in front of a simple, one-family house encircled by a cluster of large buildings.

I suggested that we inquire whether the owner wanted to sell. Mendel thought I was crazy. He did not believe we could buy anything in an area that was already built up, much less this house. After some arguing, I asked him to wait in the car while I went to see if the house was for sale. Mendel threatened to call a taxi unless I started back for Toronto immediately, but I pleaded with him to give me just a few minutes.

I walked up to the porch and rang the bell. A middle-aged woman came to the door, stepped out, and looked at me. Without wasting time, I said to her—anticipating all her possible excuses—"Madam, I know you inherited the house and you love it for sentimental reasons, and I am sure you have had many salesmen here asking you to list the house, but you refused. I know that although you have had many offers, you don't want to part with the house, which is why it is standing in the middle of seven high-rise buildings. But Madam, would you consider selling your home if we paid in cash?" The woman told me to wait a minute. She left me on the porch, with the door closed, for more than ten minutes. Mendel was sitting in the car getting impatient and signaling with his hands for me to leave. I thought that perhaps the woman wanted to invite me inside and was tidying up.

In the meantime, a car pulled into the driveway, and a tall, heavyset man stepped out. At first, I was frightened, thinking that maybe the woman had called this person for help in getting rid of me, but as he approached, the man asked me to enter. Standing near the door, I again offered cash for the house and asked how much they wanted. I agreed to pay whatever sum they would name, but I needed seven days to prepare the necessary papers. Until then, we could handwrite a contract with the conditions and schedule a closing in 30 days. I asked for a sheet of paper and wrote down the whole transaction, giving the homeowners a deposit of $200, which was all the cash I had on me. They signed the paper, gave me a receipt for the money, shook my hand, and then I left.

Back in the car, I said to Mendel, who was half asleep, "Mendel, we just bought this house. Do you hear me?"

"Yes, I hear you," he answered. "Not 'we'—perhaps 'you.'"

Noticing that I was not driving toward the main highway, Mendel asked where I was going, adding sarcastically that perhaps I wanted to purchase a second house. I told him we had to close this deal first. I stopped the car in front of the Oshawa City Hall. This time Mendel got out of the car and accompanied me to the planning department, where we inquired about the zoning on the land so that we would know what we would be permitted to build on it. On the way back, we stopped again, this time behind one of the apartment buildings rather than in front of our newly acquired house because we did not want the owners to see us. We checked out vacancies in the surrounding buildings, the rents, the type of tenants living in the area, the builders, the owners, and other pertinent information. This process took a few hours, by which time Mendel was partially cooperating. At last, we headed for Toronto, where I had a formal offer prepared under the name of one of my companies.

The next day we drove back to Oshawa to have the formal offer signed by both the owners, leaving them a copy of the agreement. Driving back with Mendel, we discussed zoning, planning, taxes, and construction. Suddenly Mendel announced that he was not going to travel back and forth to Oshawa every day, even if we got a permit for an 80- or a 100-unit apartment building.

Back in Toronto, Mendel and I kept talking about who was going to supervise the construction. Mendel reiterated that he was not willing to travel 40 miles a day. I politely asked whether he would be willing to travel every other day; we could alternate. Mendel said that there was not enough money in the deal to warrant his going so often. I tried to convince him by calculating that it would be worth at least $500 each time he went to Oshawa. Mendel still did not want to go, so the discussion ended with a difference of opinion. Although I knew we could make a good profit if everything went as planned, I was aware that things do not always go as planned when developing apartment buildings.

The owner of the house called and said he wanted to see me because, he explained, he could not close. I told him that we had already signed a contract, that it was not fair of him that to back out, and that legally I was in the right. My words made no impression on him; he insisted on a meeting. In the meantime, I told Mendel Tenenbaum what had happened, and he said he'd predicted that nothing would come of the deal.

I arranged to meet the owner at my house without Mendel, who refused to waste any more time on something he thought was going nowhere. We started with a few drinks, and I quietly explained the consequences of not closing.

I also reminded him that I had given him the full amount he had requested, without bargaining or without requesting that he take back a mortgage.

The owner told me that he had bought a lot to build a house but later learned that doing so would be more expensive than anticipated. He could not afford the new house. I thought a few thousand dollars might help and asked how much the new house cost. It was more than double what we had paid, so I abandoned the idea. Instead, I asked how much he would pay us for the house, and he could move it to his new location. Without waiting for an answer from him, I told the owner I wanted at least $5,000 because it was large and beautiful, and we could get $10,000 for it from a demolition company. The owner said he could not afford to pay that much, but after bargaining, he agreed to pay $1,000 for the house, moving it to his new lot at his own expense. I accepted the deal on the condition that the owner move the house within seven days, which was before the closing and allowed enough time to get appropriate zoning and building permit applications.

When Mendel saw my progress, he suggested that we transfer the whole transaction to a new company owned by both of us. When I asked why he wanted to incur this additional expense, he said that his lawyer, Jack Friedman, advised him to do so. I said that until we started actual construction, my company, Lebopal Realty, would hold a 50 percent interest in trust for Mendel and his brother Hershel, who was his partner.

After negotiating the number of suites that could be constructed, the city of Oshawa allowed us to build 180 units, but insisted that we transfer land to them to construct a road through the middle of the property. We were forced to split the zoning in two, and instead of a single building, we had one building with 120 units and another with 60 units. Though this condition cut into our bottom line, the project remained profitable. We applied for and received a mortgage from Canada Life Insurance, with a guarantee from the National Housing Authority through the Canadian Housing and Mortgage Corporation. Rolland Spencer, CMHC's general manager for Oshawa, had been the lending officer for Oakville when I had built homes there. With the land transaction closed and the zoning, plans, permits, and mortgage commitment in hand, everything was in place. We could now start construction.

Mendel and I drove to Oshawa, using the time in the car to discuss the project. I asked Mendel if he knew what the mill-rate (property tax) was in Oshawa. "Joe, why do you always want to know *fun vanen di fis vaksn*' [literally, 'from where the legs grow,' idiomatically, 'getting to the root of the matter']?" I explained that I needed to establish the tax rate as part of the total maintenance costs on the project, in relation to income. Before we started digging, I again asked Mendel how much he wanted to make for each trip to Oshawa. He said at least $1,000. I told him that he could have it if we sold the whole package before we finished it. If we constructed the two buildings, he would make far more money in total but much less per trip.

We heard that the three Delzoto brothers, who became famous later as star developers, were looking for ready-to-build properties. We assembled land and received zoning and financing, but building the project with a partner who refused to travel for his fair share was not something I wanted to do. I had already had a partner who did not contribute. I did not need another. With that in mind, we decided to sell to Delzoto. Angelo Delzoto told me that Jews and Italians have something in common, such as names that often end in vowels (Angelo, Yossele). We sold the land at a handsome profit, and Mendel made more than $5,000 for every trip he took to Oshawa.

We had to go to the CMHC to transfer the loan guarantee to the Delzotos, and all three parties had to be present. One of the Delzoto brothers, Elvio, acted as their lawyer, and I cautioned him not to say anything during the meeting with CMHC. I was on good terms with CMHC, especially with Rolland Spencer. As we sat down in Spencer's office to discuss the transfer, Elvio started to talk politics and boost the Liberal Party. Mr. Spencer was a staunch Conservative. When I kicked Elvio under the table to get him to stop, he asked out loud why I had kicked him. I turned red and quickly asked him to take his foot off my shoe. Elvio almost blew the deal by antagonizing Spencer.

Despite Elvio's faux pas, CMHC agreed to the transfer, subject to the approval of Canada Life. Canada Life, however, was not willing to accept the transfer because of a former disagreement with the Delzotos, who had paid off a mortgage sooner than the agreed-upon term, causing Canada Life to lose money. The Delzotos were so eager to begin work that they decided to construct the building while title and advances on the mortgage remained in our company's name. Only after the construction was completed and the contractors had been paid in full were we to transfer title. We cooperated gladly. Though I was not involved in the physical construction of the buildings, it was a good experience for me to deal with civil servants and authorities who had jurisdiction over infrastructure development. The experience gave me the confidence to undertake construction of taller buildings in Toronto and to have the courage to pay higher prices for land.

Around that same time, Consolidated Building Corporation (CBC) started building in Don Mills, north of Sheppard Avenue and Don Mills Road, on land it had previously subdivided. CBC also had a number of building lots in the same neighborhood for sale to other builders. The Tenenbaum brothers (Mendel and Hershel) and I, along with two additional partners, purchased a lot on 35-15 Easterbrook Avenue to build two 180-unit apartment buildings of 16 stories each. My share was supposed to be 25 percent of the total. However, by doing business with friends, I ended up with less than 10 percent. Not long after we started construction—we were not even out of the ground—a buyer materialized who wanted to purchase the whole project. Since I owned only 10 percent of it and did not even have a signed contract to that effect, I was happy to sell. We all made a nice profit.

In the mid-1960s, with land costing in the $2,800 to $3,000 range per apartment suite, I thought we should buy more land. Much later, people from the chicken farms in Vineland arrived in Toronto and purchased land for $4,500 per suite, and they still managed to make a nice profit. Some of them held on to their properties and are now collecting substantial rent. Perhaps the two Tenenbaum brothers and I were worried about holding on to the Don Mills property because so much land was available in the area at the same time that we anticipated a temporary glut in finished apartments.

I concentrated my new efforts on the West Side of Toronto, where I thought demand would be better. I investigated several areas in Etobicoke, Islington, and Weston, and bought a few sites from the Toronto Separate School Board. Murray Hunter, who had built on the northwest corner of Lawrence and Weston Roads, owned a garbage dump site across the street from his project. When I told him I was interested in purchasing it, he first asked for $500,000. When I consented, he raised the price to $525,000. Every time I agreed to the asking price, he increased the sum by another $25,000 until it reached $600,000. By that point, I stopped pursuing the site because I got a better piece of land in Etobicoke at a lower price.

I started to work on the zoning and planning of a project on Capri Road, east of Highway 27. The project was 120 suites in a beautifully designed building 16 stories high. Concurrently, I acquired two houses at 2450 and 2452 Weston Road with the intention of buying more adjacent properties to develop a larger project. I had dropped my pursuit of the Lawrence Avenue/Weston Road site, but figured it would not hurt to go after it anonymously through an intermediary. I found a trustworthy real estate man, told him the story, and armed him with information.

After a few weeks and many sessions between the real estate man and the vendor, I learned that the garbage dump could be bought for $625,000. The Tenenbaum brothers and I immediately formed a company under the name Margoma Holdings and purchased the land. Each of us was supposed to have an equal share—one-third of the project—however, Hershel and Mendel had relatives who wanted in, so I compromised and accepted a cut to 25 percent. I had a choice of having half of 120 apartments on Capri Road with Joe Wolfe, who was still my partner, or keeping 25 percent of 240 suites with the Tenenbaum brothers, who were going to be more active partners.

Because I could not rely on Joe Wolfe's active participation, I decided to sell Capri Road, plans and all, to Yechiel Anisfeld and Nathan Goldlust, and used the proceeds to finance the Lawrence/Weston project. The sale to Anisfeld would not have taken place without the constructive, active involvement of his lawyer, Richard Shiff. (Shiff later became president and chairman of the Bramalea Development Corporation and took it public.) In the end, I owned only 17 percent of the project because each of us had to give up a participating interest to the lender, Canada Packers, in exchange for a mortgage on the buildings.

Despite my hard work on the job, getting the best prices from contractors, and supervising the construction, Mendel objected to my managing the buildings after they were completed. He hired Irving Ross, who did not last long as our property manager. After two years, I sold my interest in the buildings to the two brothers, and they still own and operate it.

All the while, Joe kept promising to give up his fur business and assume an active role in our company. To demonstrate his sincerity, he participated in the purchase of several houses on Lawrence Avenue, a land assembly for an apartment project adjacent to the one I had completed with Mendel and Hershel.

RABBIS

Even before the war, and even as an ultraorthodox boy, I had a healthy skepticism toward authority, which in my world meant rabbis. It was not that I did not admire and respect them, but my experience left me convinced that questioning a rabbi's authority was not necessarily inappropriate.

One *Shabes* in the 1950s, Louis Mayzel took me to *Shabes* lunch at the home of his friends, the Greens. I liked Mrs. Green's apple strudel, and her kindness and hospitality reminded me of the *Shabes* table at our home before the war—when Mother always urged me to eat.

After dinner, Mr. Green said he would like to introduce me to his neighbor, Rabbi Dr. Klein. I felt like I was back in Dzialoszyce, and Father was taking me to Reb Itche Meyer, the *shoykhet,* to be examined on what I had learned during the week. My darling wife was still living in New York with our two young boys, and I was alone in Canada, feeling like a child myself.

I welcomed Mr. Green's invitation and the chance to meet Rabbi Klein. For me, spending an afternoon with three older, experienced men of such stature was a pleasure. We discussed certain tractates of Talmud, and I held my own. We also talked about Hebrew literature until Rabbi Klein hit upon a certain Hebrew poem. We named a flower, *ner halailah (onograceae)* that ended with a vowel and the letter *hey,* which is normally a feminine ending but this word was masculine like the noun *lailah* (night). Rabbi Klein insisted that the word was feminine, and I got a bit upset over his insistence, because I knew that the word was masculine. When I asked him to prove me wrong, he took out a binder with many handwritten pages. "I researched and recorded all of these words," he said. "Are you going to tell me otherwise?"

Standing between the rabbi's two good friends, Mr. Green and Mr. Mayzel, I found myself in a predicament. I wanted to suggest that, although he was a linguistic authority, it might be possible in this case he was wrong. I picked up a *siddur* (prayer book) from the table and opened to the *Shema* (prayer that begins "Hear O Israel," from Deuteronomy 11:13–21). Respectfully, I proceeded to read: "'You shall teach your children.' The Talmud tells us: *'Al tikre* otam *elah* eam' (Do not read *otam*—teach them—but *eam*—with them). One should not only teach them, but you shall study *with* them."

The rabbi got very angry, but I could not accept his interpretation unless he could prove it. I stood by what I knew because to do otherwise would have been an insult to the teachers *with* whom I had studied.

Louis also used to ask me to come with him to Beth Tzedek, at the time, the largest Conservative synagogue in North America. Although it was a far cry from the *shtiblach* of my youth, I went because I liked listening to Rabbi Stuart Rosenberg's sermons. Rabbi Rosenberg led interesting discussions on topics drawn from scripture, and because of his impressive presence, he occasionally intimidated people—a habit that I, as an admirer who later became a friend, did not relish.

On one occasion, Gena and I and a group of friends were invited to the home of Mr. and Mrs. Theodore Richmond for a get-together, and Rabbi Rosenberg was there.

Rabbi Rosenberg did not have the yeshiva type of background that would have put him in the same league as the great rabbinic authorities of our time. When he commented on certain passages from the Torah, and I disagreed with him, he got flustered. Noticing the rabbi's discomfort, the hostess, Florence Richmond, asked him jokingly, "Stuart, do you need a towel? It seems you've found your match." I was simultaneously embarrassed and delighted, I must admit. I did resent pomposity, especially the rabbinic kind, so I took a measure of satisfaction in deflating him to a place where my respect and affection were capable of growing—as they did in the years to come.

In particular, I enjoyed listening to the rabbi when the Beth Tzedek congregation invited Catholic schools to the service. While speaking to such groups, Rabbi Rosenberg did not mince words. He made sure the Christians understood the difference between their faith and ours. When Rosenberg published one of his books, he invited more than a hundred clergymen to the

Park Plaza Hotel, including the Most Rev. Philip F. Pocock, Archbishop of Toronto. The rabbi spoke about his book, *Man Is Free*, a concise explanation of Jewish religion, ethics, and customs.

The volume was ideal for anybody who was ignorant and wanted to learn. Rosenberg was eloquent and straightforward; his harsh words put the blame for our persecution where it belonged. The message Rosenberg conveyed fully echoed my feelings, and I do not think any other rabbi—Orthodox, Conservative, or Reform—would have had the courage to deliver such an impassioned speech to non-Jews, especially clergy. As a result of this gathering, the rabbi's book was introduced into the curriculum of the Catholic parochial schools.

Years later, when Rosenberg became rabbi of Beth Torah Synagogue, the Reverend Roland de Corneille, M.P. (Member of Parliament), told me that he would like to hear Rabbi Rosenberg deliver a sermon. Rev. Corneille was a strong supporter of Jewish institutions such as B'nai B'rith, the Holocaust Memorial, and the Toronto Jewish Board of Education. He was instrumental in obtaining money from the Canadian federal government for the Jewish Board of Education.

Rev. Corneille and I walked into the sanctuary at Beth Torah just as Rabbi Rosenberg was beginning his sermon. When the rabbi saw us, his face lit up. He spoke brilliantly and later acknowledged our presence. Afterward, I invited both the rabbi and the priest to our usual *Shabes* meal, which lasted for hours as we discussed the issues in depth.

Hadassah Rosenberg, the rabbi's wife, was professor of Judaic Studies at the University of Toronto. We often enjoyed the Rosenbergs' company. Gena and Hadassah shared a common language in art. Hadassah admired Gena's sculptures and never missed her exhibitions. Hadassah respected Gena's achievements as national president of the Sculptors Society of Canada, and as Canada's representative in art exhibits at the Ravenna Biennale of Sculpture and in Budapest. Her work was purchased for collections in the University of Rochester and institutions like the Baycrest Centre. When Hadassah asked how I had landed such a talented and beautiful wife, I told her how I had pointed Gena out in the distance from the third-floor window of the Jewish Community Center in Munich, knowing I would marry her, and how I told that to Esther Sniatowski. Gena never fully believed the story until the day we were reunited with Esther, who confirmed the truth, happy that my wish had become reality.

ELIE WIESEL

The mourning process in Judaism is divided into three periods with different restrictions: 7 days, 30 days, and one year. Each period is bound by certain rules. For the first days before the burial, one is not allowed to console the mourner because he is probably beyond consolation. This was true for the first months after the end of the war; we survivors spoke little about our experiences and our losses.

For the seven days of *shivah,* one revisits the past in the company of others. As we survivors renewed our ties with others, we could, slowly, reconstruct events and sit around sharing information about people, places, and things. In 1976, a journalist named Jakki Savan interviewed Elie Wiesel for the *Chronicle Review*. The last question she asked him was, "You survived the Holocaust, but how did you survive the period afterward?"

Ms. Savan wrote: "… the look in his dark brown eyes changed from somber to intense. His voice rose infinitesimally in volume. 'This is a very important question,' stressed Wiesel, who thinks only questions are eternal. The answers, he says, are constantly changing. 'In every single book of mine I try to deal with this question.'" And so it was for us as survivors. Confronted with the realities of having to make a living, resettle ourselves, and build a life, the past, by necessity, receded, waiting in silence to be listened to again. Elie Wiesel—prophet, poet, and mensch—was one of the first to give voice to what was locked in memory. He saved us from relegating the six million to the oblivion of silence and forgetfulness. He saved me from keeping my family's story under lock and key, thereby giving it new life in the next generation.

Were it not for Elie Wiesel and a few others like him, whose untiring work brought the Holocaust to global awareness, this world still would know little about its horrors. "To a very large extent, we were shielded by the Holocaust," Wiesel wrote. "Now, they, the enemies, have realized how strong a shield it was and would like to destroy it. And that we shall not let happen. Ever. Why? Not only do we owe it to those who died. We owe it to ourselves and to the living."

And it is not only our story he has taken upon himself to tell. Wiesel has fought for human rights for all. In 1979 he prodded the world about the Vietnamese "boat people," urging the Geneva Convention not to resemble the Evian Conference. "There exists a link between yesterday and today, and we, the witnesses, are the link. Hence our tendency to weigh and judge all events against the background of what preceded them and perhaps paved the way."

I first met Elie Wiesel in the early 1970s. We were both in a variety store in Miami, Florida, in search of the *New York Times*. Coincidentally, we had stayed in the same hotel and could not get the *Times* in either the hotel or the immediate vicinity. As we walked the few blocks on our way back from the store, we talked. I knew Wiesel was a famous journalist who had written several books and lectured extensively on the Holocaust. Perhaps I had mixed feelings about Wiesel's role. I was happy to meet a man who carried the banner of memory for our departed dear ones, but I questioned whether any person was worthy of writing about the holy victims.

Since the war's end, I had experienced strong, contradictory emotions: on the one hand, I wanted to mourn privately; on the other, I wanted to speak openly and often about the Holocaust. I feared that people might trivialize the tragedy, no matter how eloquent the comments. I felt that speaking about our lost world might well extinguish it. In some situations, silence is truly a virtue. Walking back to our hotel that day, I shared my thoughts and reservations regarding speaking publicly about the Holocaust. Wiesel listened attentively and looked at me with his gentle eyes. "Isn't there *someone* who would be able to talk about it?" he asked. A prolonged silence followed.

I named Uri Zvi Greenberg, the person who wrote:

> *Heym hayu venahagu uvo hachag vaeynam. Ach higiya damam ad el kotel dviram shegam hu rak sarid kepalit beyamam venishar rak hashir vetaamei negunam. Havah nagbir betocheynu rucham ad asher negaeyl ad asher nenucham.*

(They were alive and glowing on the arrival of the holiday—but now they are gone. How can their shed blood reach to the wall of the Temple that is also a remnant and refuge of the nation, and all that is left is the tune and sound of the song. Come let us strengthen their spirit in our midst until we will be comforted and redeemed.)

Even though he had not lived through the Holocaust himself, Uri Zvi Greenberg seemed to have lived it. I felt that he had the power to represent the victims. Writing in Hebrew, the language of the *Shema*, Greenberg spoke in the language of the martyrs. Hebrew, which links us to our forefathers, was one of the treasures the Nazis sought to eradicate from the face of the earth. I felt Greenberg freed the victims from silence and obscurity. Wiesel and I reached the hotel and went our separate ways. Later, we arranged with the maitre d' to make one table large enough to seat both our families. I met Marion Wiesel and the couple's son, Elisha, who was three years old. Friendship blossomed, and we shared food for the soul far more nourishing than the meals from the hotel kitchen.

While at the table, I spoke about Father giving me the watch he received as a bar mitzvah present from his parents, which we buried under the cellar floor. Before I could finish my story, Wiesel excused himself from the table and returned with a book. He opened it to a certain page and showed me a similar story he had written that was based on his personal experience. Wiesel's father, too, had given his son a watch, then buried it to save it from the Nazis. This tale confirmed a link between a child from an Orthodox home in Sighet, and a Gerer Hasid from Dzialoszyce.

One of the great joys was listening to Wiesel chanting *Shabes* and Hasidic songs at our table. I enjoyed Elie's singing so much that the next day I begged him to chant the *haftarah* (Torah supplement from the Books of the Prophets) during services in the hotel synagogue. Although Elie declined the honor, I secretly made arrangements to buy for him *Maftir* (the portion of the Torah that the person who chants the *haftarah* is called up to read). (It is a custom in some synagogues to sell parts of the Torah reading in order not to insult people by favoritism; this way, whoever buys the reading is entitled to it, and the proceeds are used to support various charities.) When Wiesel was called to the Torah by name, he could not refuse. Everyone enjoyed his mellifluous chanting.

Over the years, I have learned so much from Wiesel. Several times I sought his advice and wisdom. He and Marion have always been there for me in word and in deed. Gena and I are proud to be their friends. Marion is a fascinating person in her own right. The three of us often sat together talking at the pool while Elie was writing, studying, or talking on the telephone. Their partnership is inspiring, as is their relationship with Elisha. Although Elisha always had a nanny, his parents spent a lot of time with him—talking, telling stories, and explaining why the little boy could not play with guns and soldiers. Elisha was a bright child, and I sometimes acted as construction manager on his intricate sandcastle projects.

One of the great pleasures of my friendship with Elie is eliciting a smile from this most gentle and serious of people. My escapades in business and my dealings with all sorts of people and situations can occasionally bring a chuckle to his lips. His smile is my greatest reward.

What makes Wiesel so remarkable? I fall back on my study of the Talmud, tractate *Shabes*: "These are the things for which no limit is prescribed," and one of them is kindness. What is kindness? *"Hesed shel emet"* is true kindness, and what is true kindness? True kindness is *"hesed shelo befanav"* (kindness done without the recipient's awareness). Such acts are unconditional, without thanks or reward, like the last honor given during a funeral (burying the casket) when the deceased cannot express gratitude.

Elie Wiesel has had a holy obligation to speak on behalf of the victims, survivors who do not speak, and children affected by their parents' pain. Wiesel has never hesitated to warn the world about the danger of forgetting or to point a finger at Christian complicity in the Holocaust. He did so in a letter that was published in the *New York Times* and addressed to the president of France, Giscard d'Estaing, in which Wiesel protested the release of Abu Daoud, the mastermind in the murder of 11 Israeli athletes participating in the 1972 Munich Olympics.

Wiesel also spoke out at the White House on April 19, 1985, shortly before President Ronald Reagan was to visit the West German cemetery at Bitberg, where Waffen SS were buried. In the packed Roosevelt Room, while millions watched on television, Wiesel spoke truth to power. "May I, Mr. President, if it's possible at all, implore you to do something else, to find a way, to find another way, another site? That place, Mr. President, is not your place. Your place is with the victims of the SS."

Fifty years after the Holocaust, another injustice to the victims of Nazism came to light. During Hitler's reign, in the supposedly neutral country of Switzerland, its banks hoarded vast sums of gold and money looted from victims. For 50 years, these financial institutions kept quiet, hoping to retain money deposited by Jews who did not survive. The sums were not returned to the descendants of the dead or to Jewish institutions. Edgar Bronfman, president of the World Jewish Congress, enlisted the help of political and civic leaders and resolved to reclaim these Jewish assets from the Swiss banks. When the complicity of the Swiss government during the war was also exposed, it disturbed all decent people. To quote Wiesel, "If all the money in all the Swiss banks were turned over, it would not bring back the life of one Jewish child. But the money is a symbol. It is part of the story. If you suppress any part of the story, it comes back later with force and violence."

ROOSTERS, HENS, AND TORN SCROLLS

On April 24, 1979, at Elie Wiesel's invitation, I attended a meeting of the President's Commission on the Holocaust in Washington, D.C. Appointed as chairman by President Jimmy Carter, Elie was spearheading the creation of a Holocaust memorial museum in the nation's capital. It was quite an experience being in the company of Elie and Marion, attending many meetings with various politicians, and meeting personally with Senator Frank Lautenberg (D-NJ), retired U.S. Supreme Court Justice Arthur J. Goldberg, and many other notables.

On my way back to Toronto via New York, I had dinner with the Wiesels at the Russian Tea Room. When I was ready to leave, I called the airline only to find out I had missed the last plane to Toronto. I was forced to remain in New York, where Marion arranged accommodations for me at the Sherry Netherland Hotel, but I was too tired and excited to fall asleep. I was thinking what a waste it was to be here alone. I wished Gena could be with me; she would appreciate all the art in the hotel suite.

I went down to the hotel bar, got a drink, and made a reservation for a morning flight back to Toronto. At about 1:30 a.m., I went back up and tried to fall asleep. After a short sleep that lasted only about three hours, I got up, shaved and showered, had a cup of coffee, and decided to take a bus ride along Fifth Avenue, "down memory lane." I looked right, I looked left, and when the bus reached 23rd Street something compelled me to get off. I walked to Gramercy Park and sat down on a bench. A kaleidoscope of thoughts, faces, and experiences passed through my mind of days long past, when we were living in New York and worked in this very same neighborhood. As I sat on this little bench with my overnight bag, lost in the dreamy world of my past, my eyes began to water.

Suddenly, on the sidewalk just in front of me, there appeared a two-wheeled handcart, loaded with cartons, obscuring the man who was pushing it. He stopped in front of me, and I, thinking he wanted to sit down, picked up my bag to make room for him.

He looked at me and said with a Spanish accent, "Mister, why are you upset, did your wife or girlfriend leave you?" Taken aback by his question, at first I was speechless, but then I said, "Why do you ask?"

"I can see that you are sad, and I would like to help you," was his answer.

I pointed to the fifth-floor window at the corner of 23rd Street and said to him, "Do you see the sign painted in large gold and black letters: ALLIED BRIEFCASES? I used to work there many years ago, doing exactly the same work you are doing now as a shipping clerk. Every day—sometimes twice a day—I used to take the handcart loaded with cartons to the post office." I pulled out of my wallet a picture of the high-rise buildings that I had built and own. I leaned over and showed it to him. "You too can achieve—anything you set your mind to. America and Canada, where I live now, are democracies, and people can better themselves, if only they know how to dream and want to work."

I felt like hugging the guy for caring, so before putting back my wallet, I pulled out a $100 bill and practically had to force him to accept it. When we parted I wished him good luck, and he waited until he saw me enter a cab. I could see tears streaming down his face. He waved, and I looked back, my eyes also not quite dry, until finally, I could no longer see him.

Energized by the trip, I resolved to let my passion guide me in my next project—to help establish a Canadian organization that would involve all the provinces and the federal government in an educational program to raise public awareness of the Holocaust through memorial services, a monument, and a museum.

It took several years to prepare the groundwork that led to a meeting in Washington, D.C., on April 13, 1983. Room 30 of the Convention Center was packed with Canadians who came to Washington to participate in the American Gathering of Jewish Holocaust Survivors. Among those present were Professor Irwin Cotler; Abe Bear, chairman of the Holocaust Committee from Montreal; Nathan Leipziger, president of the Remembrance Committee of Toronto (sponsored by the Toronto Jewish Congress); and many other Canadians connected to the Holocaust or Holocaust issues.

As we waited for the Canadian ambassador to the United States, Alan Gotlieb, who was delayed, people in the audience urged me to address the group. I spoke about the importance of organizing Canadian Jewry in the same manner that the Jews in the United States had organized. Quite a few people offered to help with the project, and I was surprised and gratified by the response.

The next day, I spoke with Elie and Marion Wiesel about my desire for a Canadian memorial to the Holocaust, and they promised their support. They even offered to come to Toronto, if needed. On the same day, I met with J. M. Goldenberg, a prominent Canadian lawyer from Saskatoon, Saskatchewan, who was an active member of the Jewish community and taught at the University of Saskatchewan. Back home in Toronto, I spoke with my wife and children about plans to organize a Holocaust committee. Sidney suggested I meet with his friend Ellen Sokoloff, a capable public relations consultant, who agreed to help. Jack Weinbaum, a survivor I had known in several concentration camps, was now a well-known philanthropist in Toronto who promised to support us and suggested we recruit Yechiel Anisfeld, who was prominent in the Agudath Israel Orthodox community. Also on board were Oscar Hershtahl, a very learned man; his son Zev; and Zev's wife, Sybil. I met with Sidney Midanik, chairman of the Toronto Board of Education and legal counsel to the Canadian Jewish Congress. Albert Kerzner, a lawyer turned real estate developer, got involved and brought along Henry and Gerald Rosenberg, the owners of Dominion Candy, and Sol Rosenberg, who spent the war in the far regions of Russia and later became an electrical contractor.

Sid Midanik invited me to a lunch given by the Canadian Jewish Congress attended by "an unnamed guest" from Israel. It was Dov Shilanski, an old friend with whom I had worked in the underground in Italy, Austria, and Germany. We hugged and spoke about what had happened since we had been separated and discussed mutual friends who worked with us in the *Brihah*.

While I had worked for the *Irgun* in Germany, Shilanski had become head of the *Etzel* in Rome. The freedom fighters destroyed the British Embassy, the center of information on the *Brihah*. The British set up a manhunt for Dov, but he escaped to Germany where we renewed our association and worked intensely for the Altalena Campaign, organizing people and smuggling ammunition. Dov left Europe on the *Altalena;* when he reached Israel, he had to swim to shore. In the Israeli elections of 1981, Shilanski was elected a member of the Knesset and was appointed deputy in the prime minister's office.

Dov's first question to me was, "What are you doing here? Why are you not in Israel?"

"There is a job to do now in Canada," I said. "To work for the victims of the Holocaust." I found my rationale to stay in the Diaspora.

Later that day I spoke to Wiesel, and he proposed a gathering of survivors, partisans, and liberators to commemorate the 40th anniversary of the liberation for May 5 and 6, 1985, in Canada's capital city, Ottawa. Rabbi Gunther Plaut and Irving Cotler were behind the program. I met with Sol Rosenberg and Mel Ostro and obtained a list of Yorkdale B'nai B'rith members, most of them Holocaust survivors. Things appeared to be coming together. The following day, I met with 30 people from the Canadian Jewish Congress.

Suddenly, David Satok, chairman of the Ontario region, walked out. I do not think he was very interested in promoting the cause. I later met with 15 members of the Canadian Jewish Congress Remembrance Committee, including Nathan Leipziger, a professional engineer and partner in the firm of Okins, Leipziger, Cuplinskas, and Kaminker; Gerta Freiberg; Mel Lastman, mayor of North York; Roy McMurtry, former Canadian ambassador to England and now a judge in Ontario; and David Crombie, mayor of Toronto—all gathered to discuss Holocaust remembrance.

Jacob Egit spoke about Israel and the Holocaust. Our discussions also centered on the outrageous news from Alberta about an antisemitic teacher named James Keegstra. I was to take up the matter with Mr. Katz, a member of the Canadian Jewish Congress from Edmonton. I also met Israel's consul to Toronto to discuss the issue. At a meeting of the Canadian Friends of the Hebrew University, I continued my campaign by suggesting they invite Professor Yehuda Bauer to Toronto and help organize a chair for Holocaust studies at either the University of Toronto or York University.

With Sabina Citron, I emphasized the importance of uniting all forces to memorialize victims of the Holocaust. When I saw her again at the Zionist Center on Marlee Avenue, I met Fania Pillersdorf and Helen Smolak. As soon as I walked into the meeting, I noticed that some people became tense. Sabina Citron later told me she thought that I had been sent by the Canadian Jewish

Congress and David Satok, who was in charge of the Congress Holocaust Committee. It was becoming clear to me that this Holocaust memorial was losing its momentum because it was getting bogged down in petty politics. Every individual local organization laid claim to its creation, disregarding the need of the whole for the sake of personal turf.

After endless meetings with community leaders, rabbis, statesmen, educators, Jewish war veterans, editors from the Jewish newspapers, survivors, business people, lawyers, and professionals of all sorts, coordination still remained impossible. A single umbrella organization could not be formed. There was widespread support for a national memorial, but divisiveness appeared insurmountable. Personal ambition, rivalries, and jealousy among individuals and a maze of organizations inhibited progress. Conviction and a good cause are not the only requirements for success. Because of two opposing factions, my work toward establishing a unified Canadian Holocaust memorial organization did not succeed.

I am reminded of a story in the Talmud, tractate *Yevamot* 96B. Rabbi Eliezer said something in a schoolhouse without naming the original author of the statement, Rabbi Johanan, who was annoyed when he heard about the omission. "Rabbi Amni and Rabbi Assi said, 'Did it not happen at the synagogue of Tiberias that Rabbi Eleazar and Rabbi Jose disputed so hotly about an issue that they tore the Scroll of the Law in their excitement?' Rabbi Jose ben Kisma, who was present, exclaimed, I shall be surprised if this synagogue is not turned into a house of idolatry, and so it happened."

In other words, when people fight about frivolous matters, important ones are eclipsed. In our case, personality clashes, distrust, politics, and self-indulgence prevented the formation at that time of a central Holocaust memorial in Canada.

PARTNER

Between September 1958 and September 1970, Joe Wolfe was my only nonactive partner. Our relationship had started long before either of us ever dreamed of being real estate developers. Back in Dzialoszyce, although I was one year older than Joe, I sometimes played with him and his cousin Shyele. They shared a common backyard and alley with Simche, the grandson of Rabbi Staszewski, with whom I had studied Talmud. Simche played the violin, and I loved to listen, hoping he would teach me to play, too.

Another reason for hanging out near Joe's was that he had a beautiful sister my age, and Hershel Lubelski and I enjoyed talking with her. With Hershel next door to the Wolfowich (Joe's family name before the war) family, I always had a pretext to be around.

The Wolfowich family was headed by the patriarch Feivel, whose nickname was Smarklach. He dealt with hats, and that provided another excuse for me to come to their second-floor apartment and catch a glimpse of Joe's beautiful sister, Frieda. The apartment was always full of hats, all over the dining table, on the beds, in the closets. We used to buy three kinds of hats from the Wolfowiches to sell in our store—Polish school hats sewn up on top to form a cross (Father never allowed us to wear these); hats with flat tops for adults, which my two oldest brothers and Father wore; and round hats with a small visor of the type that Willie and I wore. Any other hats Father bought came from Krakow, Lodz, or Warsaw.

Feivel's son, Luser Wolfowich, would come to the store, open the glass doors of the hat display case, and check to see if we had sufficient stock in all sizes and types. Most of his business, however, consisted of selling hats directly to the peasants or farmers on market day in Dzialoszyce and in neighboring towns. I remember Joe's Uncle Leibish and his grandfather, Feivel Smarklach, loading the wagon in front of 14 Market Place, where they lived. Smarklach was a nickname that originated with Feivel, who always had a runny nose but no handkerchief, hence the nickname that describes that phenomenon. "Uncle Leibish," as we all called him, was a powerful man. If the wagon was overloaded, he would walk to the other town and usually get there before the horse and wagon did.

The farmers, or at least the ones who looked for a fight—and there were plenty of them—respected Leibish because he did not hesitate to defend Jews when they were teased or attacked. Once, a few antisemitic hooligans ridiculed and subsequently attacked an ultra-Orthodox Jew as he passed through the marketplace. Leibish, who was close to a parked wagon, immediately untied the ropes, grabbed the wooden bar from the wagon, and started swinging. A couple of Poles ended up flat on their backs and the rest ran off.

Joe's mother, Rivka-Rachel, was a nice lady. She was short, wore glasses, and had a high-pitched voice. His grandmother, Feigele Broiges, and his Aunt Esther were seamstresses who sewed for our store. Like my parents, two brothers (Luser and Leibish) had married two sisters (Rivka-Rachel and Esther). These families were almost totally wiped out by the Nazis and the Poles. Only Leibish, Luser, and the young Joe survived after going through hell in the concentration camps. After liberation, the three survivors went to Italy and from there to Toronto, where Joe married Dina Daniels. Joe and Dina had four children—two boys and two girls. Luser was always at Joe's side, and whenever I met him, he would tell me what a beautiful, smart lady my mother had been. The oldest survivor from our town, Luser Wolfowich, died in 1994 at the age of 94.

Joe is an honorable man. He worked late into the night at his fur factory, and because his business was prosperous, the idea of giving it up proved difficult. After ten years of unfulfilled promises that started in 1958, I got tired of waiting and demanded that Joe contribute equally to the management of our business. I gave him notice and specified a deadline. I also advised him that I would not buy new land or undertake additional projects in partnership with him unless he met that deadline.

Joe agreed, first by managing the Wellesley Street building. He had no real property management experience, so he accompanied me and observed the way I solved problems. One time we received a call from the superintendent about a wild party in progress. Carrying a clipboard and pen, I took Joe and the super with me to see what was happening. When we walked in, we found young men and women sitting around, drinking and smoking marijuana. I shouted, "No one move! Give me your names!"

We stood with our backs to the door, well away from it, and before I had finished writing down the second name, the rest of the gang had slipped out of the apartment. The two people whose names I had managed to record excused themselves, saying that they were only visitors who had been invited over for a drink. I let them go after they promised never to return, and once the apartment was vacant, I changed the lock and rented the apartment to someone else.

Joe also came along when my friend Shlomo Aronowitz from Germany arrived in Toronto, looking to invest in real estate. I wanted him to see a large penthouse in our building, on the 19th floor, with three bedrooms, two bathrooms, a dining room, living room, and two big terraces overlooking the beautiful city vista. I was proud to have built it. We rode the special elevator that opened directly to the penthouse, and as we entered, I saw six men sleeping on the floor. Shocked, I closed the door quietly, went down to my office, and called the police. When the officers arrived, I led them to the penthouse. Apparently, a tenant on a lower floor had smuggled people in from South America. He knew that there was a vacant apartment upstairs and took advantage of the situation. The next night, all his "guests" were sleeping in the custody of the Immigration Department and later deported to their respective countries.

The next day, because the story made the local papers, Joe Tanenbaum, Max's brother, called and asked me to get on the phone with his wife, Faye, and reassure her that he did not own the building on Wellesley—that it was mine! Joe Wolfe and I agreed that we would manage the building two months at a time in rotation. Having learned how to collect rents, handle supers, and respond to emergencies, when Joe's turn came, he did the job pretty well until he discovered students having a noisy party. Joe did exactly what I had shown him a few months earlier, except that instead of standing with his back to the door and away from it, he stood in a position that blocked the occupants' escape. The kids beat him up. After a number of similar confrontations, he refused to be involved on a full-time basis.

When Joe backtracked on his commitment again, I was forced to give up on him. Everything we owned as partners was sold off to third parties or was divided between us. Consequently, the parting was not amicable. Joe and I stopped talking to each other, but that definitely was not my doing.

After about three years, in April 1973, I received a call from Joe. He sounded desperate: "A disaster happened, Joe. I have no one but you. I must talk to you." Within an hour, he showed up at my site office on Weston Road and told me that Dina, his wife, had put all his clothes in boxes on the porch and had changed the locks on their house. He was devastated.

I felt sorry for both Joe and Dina. I could not tell Joe that this fiasco was his own doing, the result of his workaholism. Joe's fur factory had always come first; his business was the god he worshipped. First he lost me, his partner of 12 years, and then he lost his wife. We talked for hours, and I decided to let bygones be bygones, at least as far as friendship was concerned, because deep down, I knew that Joe Wolfe was a good-hearted person.

ON MY OWN

Proceeding on my own with business, I prepared plans for the construction of two apartment buildings in Weston. This was a difficult and complicated project in every respect, especially without the help of a partner, so I followed my old motto: "step by step, one step at a time." To begin with, I needed plans. The architectural part was no problem—I knew to eliminate what was unnecessary. All I had to do was use old plans and fit them to this site. I could not go to Grozbord and King, because we already had severed our business relationship. In addition, Grozbord and King were too expensive, and I did not want anyone to know I was alone on the project. Before long, I was introduced to an English architect licensed to practice in Ontario, and we made a reasonable deal. I took my old plans to him, and we changed everything to a configuration suitable to the buildings if they were ever to be converted to condominiums. We increased the size and number of suites, the ratio of bedrooms, the lobby, and the other amenities accordingly.

I hired an engineer to draw up the structural plans, and after two weeks, when I compared the size and depth of the footings and foundations to those of buildings I had built in the past, I found he had increased the size out of all proportion to the commensurate increase in building size. When I asked him why he had "overdesigned" the project, he said that he did not want to take chances. Instead of fine-tuning his calculations, he had simply enlarged the footings and foundations, giving himself a large margin of safety for design errors. I could not afford his lack of precision because it would have unnecessarily cost me tens of thousands of dollars, so I suggested we part, and I paid him what he asked. I then hired Kazmar Consultants, a group of engineers who had worked for me in the past. Despite their higher fees, they saved me money because thousands of dollars in unnecessary concrete and steel would not be wasted.

I needed money to pay off the mortgages that were due on the land, and asked Willie and his partner (and brother-in-law), Irving Gold, to invest. We agreed on a price per suite, but Irving wanted a guarantee on the number of suites. I offered to guarantee 180, but said there was a good chance of receiving a permit for at least 200 suites. Negotiations dragged on, but nothing was accomplished. Many other builders considered the project, but when money was involved, people changed their minds or broke promises and ignored even written agreements. In several cases, I returned substantial sums I had taken as deposits. Although I was short of cash and legally could have kept the money, I did not want to make enemies in the small development community.

When the preliminary plans were completed, I went to the Borough of York for a building permit. Back then, such permits would normally be issued within two or three weeks. Four weeks passed, then five weeks. I kept checking with the building department, which, for some reason, was stalling. In the meantime I demolished four homes on the site but also wanted to acquire adjacent land on which a fifth house stood. I offered the owner $75,000, but she refused to sell. At that time, the market price for the house was between $40,000 and $50,000. When I offered $100,000, she went to her lawyer, who advised her to ask for $125,000; when I agreed, she demanded $150,000. Before I committed myself to that exorbitant sum, I decided to wait for the two most important items I needed for the project: a building permit and financing.

Blocked on two fronts, I could not move. I turned to Sid Midanik for help. An honest man, Midanik always engaged experts when he doubted his own expertise. In this case, he recommended one of the most knowledgeable lawyers in the field of zoning. I went to the expert's office and told him about my dilemma. After he reviewed all the documents, he prepared papers and had a writ of mandamus served on the proper authority in York. A few days later, the building department invited me to a meeting. The officials wanted to clarify how many suites I wanted because in my original application, I had requested 220, but my lawyer's application specified 600 suites. The mayor of Weston, Mr. Wesley Buddington, decided to act as the arbitrator. Our differences with the building department were soon settled, and I received a permit for two buildings of 212 suites each.

I now had a permit to do a lot of hard work. I needed funds to go forward, but all my cash and borrowed money were tied up in the land, and before building, I had to pay off that mortgage. Mr. Frestacki, chairman of Metropolitan Trust Company and a former banker from Czechoslovakia, lent me some money but not enough. The small sum was like a little bandage on a gaping wound. Initially, I decided to attract a partner by offering a substantial interest in the project and approached Bramalea, a large, reputable real estate company. I also spoke with Alex Rubin, chairman of Revenue Properties (the General Motors of real estate at the time).

I tried many companies—Newstyle, Greenwin Construction, and Cadillac partner Joe Berman, but none was interested. They did not think this project was viable. In fact, Joe Berman advised me to drop it altogether because he considered the building a "losing proposition." To me, every negative statement was like a blow to the head by boxer Muhammad Ali. I could not sleep at night. When I went to lunch at Stubby's, the builders' hangout, I learned that some veteran builders were wagering I would go bankrupt on this project and were betting on how many millions of dollars I would owe. With appetizers like that, I could not eat, so at least I saved money on food.

Though no lives were at stake, the lack of confidence reminded me of when Vladimir Jabotinsky came to his mother with a broken heart and complained that, in spite of all his traveling and speeches, the Diaspora was hopeless. The great Zionist leader urged his people to go to Palestine, yet the Jews of Europe ignored the warning, even as they were sitting on a volcano about to erupt. "The mood is with me but not the vote." Jabotinsky continued, "What should I do, Mother?"

"Son, if you believe your message is just, continue working. If you do not, stop." Unfortunately, time proved Jabotinsky right. Had the Jews listened, they could have avoided a terrible fate at the hands of Nazi murderers. All aspects of my life in Canada and America evoked historical memories of tragic proportions that dwarfed my troubles.

Only one person, Paul Reichman, encouraged me and said my idea had potential. Reichman had just sold all of his residential properties to Jack Weinbaum and Max Wallerstein and was concentrating strictly on commercial buildings. I met Reichman for the first time when Jacob Perlman, founder of Beth Jacob (a girls school), died, and Rabbi Abraham Parshan delivered the eulogy. While the rabbi was speaking, Reichman wiped tears from his eyes.

Later, when I sat in his office, I saw how wise this man was. His charitable statement about the project heartened me. When I left the office, I felt better. Spiritually, I was high; financially, I was low. With no steady or long-term financing, I had to borrow from one place to pay another.

I foresaw the upcoming market for condominiums, which is why I designed these buildings to include many amenities: large suites, swimming pools, and saunas. Financial institutions responded negatively, saying that the public was not yet ready for such product; yet at the same time, there was a shortage of rental apartments. To spur investment in new housing, the Canadian government approved a budget allocating a certain amount for Canada Mortgage and Housing Corporation under the National Housing Act, sections 15 and 16. Five buildings were allotted to metropolitan Toronto, and a call for tenders was made. More than 80 offers were submitted by various companies and institutions, including my proposal for two buildings.

Waiting for the outcome was nerve-wracking. Endless days of hoping evoked old insecurities. I was in danger of losing my hard-earned money, and sums borrowed from others were also at stake. Willie's company, Torpedo Investments, lent me $18,000 in exchange for 20 suites. But if construction did not begin by a certain date, the money had to be returned in full.

Weeks passed as the plans and supporting documents were sent from the Survey Committee to the Appraisal Committee to the Architectural Department. Bureaucratic procedures caused delays. Without adequate financing, delays were my biggest enemy because they resulted in enormous costs. After revising the plans to comply with CMHC's requirements and proving investment in the project, I learned that the total package had been sent to the head office for review.

Finally, the hour I had prayed for arrived. The announcement came that Ateb Developments Ltd., my company, had been chosen to construct two buildings out of the five allotted. That day was one of the better ones in my life, even though the joy did not last. As soon as I was given a commitment to finance the project, I heard from a clerk that Mel Glass was protesting the fact that one company in one borough had received financing for two buildings while other boroughs and builders had received none. The office explained that projects went by tenders, and my buildings were the most suitable for market demands in terms of rents for the suites, which were low.

A day later, I received a telephone call asking me to come to the CMHC office. When I arrived, officials asked if I would mind getting the financing for just one building. I was exploding inside but tried to appear calm. "Yes, I would not mind just one building, but only if the site can be divided into two separate projects." I did not utter another word until I was asked if there was any reason the buildings could not be divided. "Yes, they can be divided, but it would be very complicated with the water service, gas service, easements, curb cuts on a major artery that would have to be approved by Metro Roads, etc. These adjustments will add substantially to the cost of the project because much of the equipment which now serves both buildings would have to be doubled."

The minute CMHC heard that the costs would be higher and they would be on the hook for more money, they stopped me from saying anything else. I left happy but hoping no other surprises were in store. My application to a bank for a bridge loan was rejected because the institution claimed not to know me well enough. Then I went to the bank I had been using on the corner of Spadina Avenue and College Street and spoke with the manager about borrowing $600,000 until I got the first draw from the mortgage. The manager asked me to fill out an application as well as personal and business statements.

Weeks passed, and I heard absolutely nothing. After nearly a month, I went to inquire and was told the bank needed more security. When I asked if the loan could come through in a few days once all demands were met, the manager said yes but announced that the amount would be only $300,000. I explained that this sum was insufficient. After long negotiations, the banker increased the total by three increments of $25,000 each and probably would have added two more, but I did not have time or patience to continue. I requested a piece of paper, drew a river with two banks, and demonstrated that if I chose to jump over the water, falling in the middle, beginning, or even five inches from the other river bank would make little difference—I would still get wet. Landing all the way on dry land was the only acceptable alternative.

"Do you understand now, Mr. Bumstead? That's why I need $600,000 and not even $595,000." Bumstead probably thought I had some nerve talking to him that way.

I picked myself up to leave, but the banker said: "Joe, let me think about it."

"I, too, will think about it," I replied.

Needing to discuss the problem, I turned to Sol Mintz, my accountant, who had an office not far from where I was. After hearing my story over lunch, Sol took me to his bank manager, George Brant, and had me repeat the saga in detail. Mr. Brant told me to contact him in a day or two. I thanked both men and went home. As soon as I sat down at my desk, the telephone rang. Brant wanted me to come to the bank the following morning to sign papers; he was giving me the loan for $600,000.

To facilitate the transaction, I opened my business account at his branch of the Canadian Imperial Bank of Commerce. Now the actual construction could begin. Although I normally chose from among three or four quotes on a particular contract, this time I vowed to shop around for more. This cautious approach would also apply to professionals. I had to prove to my detractors and to myself that the bets on my going bankrupt were wrong. Starting with surveyors, I chose one from Pickering, who offered to work for less than half the price of my old surveyor from Toronto. On my desk I kept a sign that read: "REMEMBER! Mr. Doolittle, Mr. Gagnon, and Mr. Better really is better."

When I had started to build in Passaic, New Jersey, I had engaged a surveyor named Doolittle who quoted the sum of $900 for staking out the footings and foundations for a building. I thought the price was rather steep and approached another surveyor, Mr. Gagnon, who offered to do the same work for $600. Satisfied with having found a reasonable estimate, I had not intended to look further, but one day I was passing the town of Lodi and noticed a surveyor's sign. Just for the fun of it, I paid this man a visit. Mr. Better—the name is real—quoted me the best price at $300. From then on, I applied the same policy to tradesmen, suppliers, and contractors. When contractors saw me standing on the construction site in a heavy blue parka and muddy rubber boots, they asked to talk to the boss. I always answered that a group of lawyers on Bay Street were the owners, but they had no time to bother with building and so had hired me to do the job. I did not want to be vulnerable to the whims of contractors. To this day, one plumbing contractor is embarrassed whenever he sees me because he offered me a bribe of $10,000 to get the job. He was not the only one. Some contractors even threatened me. I gave them a set of plans, specifications, soil tests, and everything else necessary to give me an accurate quote. Following negotiations, after agreement was reached, I would draw up a solid contract detailing obligations of performance along with a payment schedule. Not every contractor adhered to the signed agreement, and some asked to be paid in advance. This time, I could not go along with their demands, especially on a risky project of this magnitude.

I had problems with the excavating contractor. I gave him some money in advance, which was a mistake on my part. I was willing to pay him without delay based on the percentage excavated. He stopped the job, and I was left with a half-excavated garage basement and a big mess. A few days passed, and when he did not show up with his workers, I hired another excavator to finish the job. When the previous contractor noticed new excavating equipment on the site, I soon received a threatening call from someone disguising his voice and telling me to get dressed in my best suit and say good-bye to my wife and children.

I reported the incident to the police. The same day, two detectives told the contractor and his brother that if anything happened to me, they would know who was responsible. The officers added that the contractors were lucky that I had not filed charges against them, or they would have already been taken into custody. The excavators got the message and made sure that no harm came to me—at their hands or those of others.

Like our Patriarch Abraham, who had four doors in his house as a sign of hospitality to welcome guests from all sides, I built an office shack on the job site with four windows to reveal what was going on all around me. It was too much for one person to supervise the work and negotiate prices at the same time. Had I continued in this fashion, the workmanship, the prices, and my health would have all suffered. My friend Abie Blankenstein from Falco Electric was kind enough to lend me his construction superintendent, Joe Skopec, who had been with him for many years. The going rate was $200 a week, but for my peace of mind I decided to hire Skopec at the $350 he had been getting. It was important to have an experienced supervisor oversee the pouring of the footings and foundations on which the stability of the whole building depended. I agreed that, in six or eight months, when Abie was ready to resume his own project, I would release Skopec.

I concentrated on tenders and contracts and wanted Joe to watch the excavation, checking that the plans corresponded to the specifications and the layout. A contractor came to me about bricks and blocks, and as soon as Joe noticed him, he ran to the shack and started talking to the man. I politely hinted that it was premature for Joe to speak to contractors since we did not have a deal yet and said I would let him know when I needed him. As soon as another contractor came to the shack, the same thing happened. I tolerated

Joe observing negotiations but objected to his involvement. Harry Lederman from Lanark Ventilation arrived, and Joe came to the office once more, this time saying he could only work for me if he handled all contracts. I tried to convince him that his job was critical, that supervising footings for two 28-story buildings was more important than speaking with contractors. But Joe was not willing to compromise, so I thanked him for his concern and let him go.

I continued searching for a good construction superintendent; until I found one, I had to do all the work myself. When Sol Mintz came and invited me to lunch, I could not leave the site. "Joe, if you continue the way you're working, this job might be your last. If you learn to take it easy, you could go from project to project without risk to your health," said Sol. Eventually, I hired a capable man.

The time had come to make a deal with the woman who owned the house located next to my land. This acquisition would enable me to add three additional stories to the buildings containing 48 suites. I offered her the $150,000 she had requested earlier, but she asked for $50,000 more. When I finally agreed, she raised the price to $250,000. At this point, I stopped playing the game and went on with construction. Her lawyer soon saw that I had reached the eighth floor and called to say that his client was ready to accept $250,000. I offered $225,000. When I went up two more floors, the lawyer called to accept, but then I suggested $175,000. The higher I built, the lower my offers became. I was no longer interested in buying but wanted to teach a lesson about greed. In the end, the owner sold her house to somebody else for $48,000.

My work was full of surprises. At one point, the union started picketing the project. I had a perfect crew of bricklayers who belonged to the Canadian Union. The group that was picketing insisted I had to hire bricklayers from the American Union. The steel and concrete workers could not continue working because building supplies were not delivered nor would truck drivers and electricians cross the picket line. I had no choice but to go to my lawyer, Midanik. After I explained what was going on, he said, "Joe, I won't act against the union."

I appealed to him, "You are my attorney. To whom should I turn if not you?" Midanik gave me the name of a labor lawyer who specialized in this type of case. The new lawyer had me sign some papers and an affidavit for a court order to stop the picketing. Within three days, the court order was in the hands of the sheriff. When the sheriff arrived at the site and showed the document to the picketers, some hard-liners refused to leave. Only after we obtained a writ for the police to arrest the protesters did they desist, scattering in all directions. Remaining on the premises would have constituted contempt of court and incurred the risk of arrest.

Subsequently, we went to court on this matter because the union falsely claimed that I had signed an agreement. The agreement was in the name of a company in which they claimed I was a shareholder. In court, I proved that this company belonged to a different Tenenbaum. The signature, of course, was someone else's. Consequently, the judge turned down the union application to picket on the site.

In order to make up for lost time, when we started up again, I arranged a competition between the crews working on the two buildings. Whichever foreman finished first would receive a $1,000 bonus. All the men pushed ahead; I did not have to say a single word.

With the forming crews pushing ahead in the race, I was sometimes able to take off half an hour for lunch and went to Stubby's. Mr. Sweet approached me one day and said, "I thought you wanted me for a partner in the project. The people who owed me money paid up the mortgage, and now I have the funds. Let's make a deal." I looked at him and said nothing.

When several other people saw that I was out of the ground and that construction was proceeding floor after floor, they, too, came running, eager to become partners. Being able to refuse their offers gave me great satisfaction. These folks did not realize how ignorant and insensitive they had been in the past. By the time I reached the fourth floor, I received the first draw from CMHC for the cost of the land plus the garage, which amounted to around $400,000. First, I paid the bank the amount I had borrowed. From then on, I was more generous with contractors and suppliers. I paid all invoices and had some money left for contingencies. Now I could breathe.

On the day the first building was topped off, the Canadian flag was raised on the construction crane, and there was a beer and pizza party on the roof. The "losing" foreman received a bonus of $500 because he was only a little more than one floor behind the winner. He finished a week later.

I took my bank manager to lunch and announced that two Canadian flags were proudly flying from the top of the climbing cranes above the roofs. He congratulated me on my achievement but said in surprise, "Joe, I noticed you paid up your loan, and the total amount you borrowed was only $147,000. You insisted that you needed $600,000. I have two questions: why did you pay off the loan so soon, and why did you borrow only $147,000?"

With embarrassment and humility, I told him about the bets made at Stubby's and the rest of what I had endured—how I could not find a partner and how difficult my job was. I needed to be cautious with every penny. The money had been borrowed privately or from banks, and my reputation was at stake. I had to watch every move I made. "You, Mr. Brant, are charging me 8 percent interest on the money, which I appreciate very much, and it was the best rate I could obtain at that time. However, I only pay $7^7/_8$ percent to the government, and that is the reason I paid off your loan. As for the $600,000, it was a safety net in case the bureaucrats and government lawyers took more time than anticipated before giving me the first advance. I could not take any chances." The bank manager complimented me on being a prudent businessman and was happy for me.

Once I had the two skeletons up, I was under pressure to finish the mechanical, electrical, and ventilation systems. The construction superintendent, who in the beginning had been cautious and pushed the job forward, began to fall behind on the inside work. I found whiskey bottles in the ventilation ducts on every third floor, among other places. Whenever I needed the man, I could not find him, so I was forced to let him go. I hired a meticulous finishing expert to supervise completion of the buildings.

During this time, I needed as much help as I could get—including from my family. My oldest son, Sidney, who was then 17, worked during his summer vacation operating the freight elevators. He brought building materials to the designated floors, worked the same hours as the rest of the crew, and ate lunch with the other laborers. When he came to me with a complaint, I explained the hierarchy on a job. "You have a foreman, who has a superintendent above him, and the superintendent comes to me." Sidney no longer brought me complaints.

In January 1972, when the buildings were half-finished inside and looked presentable outside, an article on the building, written by Mac Parliament, appeared on the front page of the *Toronto Star*.

> Everyone appreciates a little luxury in an apartment, and a little is about all those people with an average income get. But the federal

government housing rental scheme, in partnership with private enterprise, produces luxury in unexpected places. Country Club Towers on Weston Road, just south of Highway 401, is one. To achieve this, the buildings and individual apartments were designed to inspire pride of occupancy. Tenenbaum has backed up his respect for the program with long hours on the construction site, working from 6:30 a.m. to 10 p.m. or later for one and a half years to complete the project as superintendent, manager, and troubleshooter.

This concept was the best application of the free-enterprise system to cure some of the city's social and housing problems. It produced two large and gracious apartment buildings overlooking the beautiful Humber River valley and the Weston golf course. It was a significant contribution to the people of Toronto, especially since rents for one-, two-, and three-bedroom apartments were going for $138, $150, and $174, respectively—way below market rates. Although lines of people wanted to reserve apartments for future occupancy, I hired a wonderful couple, Mr. and Mrs. David Weisbrod, to rent out the units. Their job was to make sure prospective tenants complied with the CMHC income requirements, thereby ensuring that those with limited means had a chance at decent, affordable housing.

DEVELOPING LAND

In the 1970s I bought most of my construction hardware from a reliable company, Harvey Building Supplies. Harvey was a professional accountant with whom I liked exchanging business ideas. He was also a part-time builder who invited me, along with about ten partners, to enter into a land deal in Innisfield, Ontario, involving an 800-acre parcel of land on Lake Simcoe. Some of the partners were people I knew, including the Robins brothers from Paramount Construction, experienced developers with a sizable company.

In the beginning, I was reluctant to join a partnership with so many participants. A *minyan* (quorum of ten) may be good for prayer but not for business. Yet, I let myself be influenced to join because of partners like Al G. Brown and Sid Greenstein. Furthermore, the Robins brothers were developers from whom I could learn a great deal. I wanted to observe them throughout all the stages of the development process so that by watching them interact with local municipalities, the Ontario Municipal Board, and other authorities, I could gain greater insight into developing and rezoning farmland.

The reason I wanted to observe their particular method of operation was that my partner Amnon Waksman and I already owned two parcels of land— 10 acres in Kitchener and 100 acres in Ancaster, Ontario, on the outskirts of Hamilton. We purchased the land in Kitchener from Yolles and Rotenberg and the parcel in Ancaster from Jean Letitia Ward in 1974. Constantly hounded by a real estate broker, Jean Ward finally consented to sell the land, which she had inherited from her wealthy parents, to us at a high price.

Mrs. Ward retained a huge house surrounded by ten acres of land, and we had an option to purchase the land whenever she was ready to sell. As soon as we bought the land, we encountered difficulties with local authorities and residents, and it took a long time to begin development. I wanted to see how experts like the Robins brothers operated and to apply what I learned to our situation. In spite of their firm deriving financial benefit from these 800 acres (which, by the way, were never developed by that company), we lost all our equity in the land—quite a substantial sum. Luckily, I was cautious and handled this transaction through a separate, limited corporation, or I would have lost even more. I learned some expensive lessons from this experience, such as the importance of not entering into partnerships where I was not active and had no control. I should never have let others run a project for me unless I had absolute trust in the manager's ability. In the end, the "expert" management company went into receivership.

Gena and I met Amnon and Mary Waksman, an intelligent Israeli couple, at a wedding. We developed a close friendship and vacationed together in Nassau. After we bought land for development in Kitchener and had to travel back and forth, we spent significant amounts of time in the car getting to know each other. Then we purchased the land in Ancaster, which required more commuting and hard work.

It took us years to develop just half of this land. The municipality opposed development, and local officials had been elected to prevent builders from coming into town because the residents wanted to maintain the existing size and ambience. Despite her welcoming smile, Mayor Ann Sloat was adamantly against the construction of new houses in Ancaster. The council passed special bylaws to discourage development. We had to fight an uphill battle step by step, inch by inch.

The council and mayor kept calling public meetings to rally the population against land development. In my heart, I knew this area could support an outstanding community and still keep its picturesque character. The head officer of the loan department of the Toronto Dominion Bank, William Pool, was enthusiastic about this plan when I first took him to inspect it as collateral for a loan of several million dollars for which we had applied. The gentle contours of the land were breathtaking. Surrounding slopes and valleys gave this location a perfect view. Mature trees would provide an oasis of privacy for future residents.

As usual, there was at least one fly in the ointment. Three people who lived on Lovers Lane vehemently objected to the project. At first, they claimed that new houses on the site, right across the road from their homes, would block their view of foliage. These homeowners were up in arms against a couple of "foreigners" from Toronto who bought land they should have purchased. Then the naysayers claimed that traffic would become congested. These grievances were aired during public meetings at City Hall, and the three couples tried to influence all the other citizens of Ancaster to oppose our project.

We countered every claim by bringing in experts with evidence to the contrary. Real estate people and private developers approached us with good offers and a hefty profit for the land, but we turned them down. We believed that, in the end, this project would be a real winner. After a long, hard battle that lasted a few years and entailed numerous meetings with town officials and the Ontario Municipal Board, we finally received approval for the subdivision. The agreement contained 50 articles and more than a hundred pages, in addition to many schedules. The whole process created considerable expense. We also had to donate land for a park, sidewalks, and whatever else the town thought it might need in the future.

The land was marked in blocks labeled from A through I. After we registered the final plan, we called tenders for the infrastructure—storm and domestic sewers, water, electrical and telephone lines, roads, and curbs. As soon as our contractors brought in heavy equipment, a lawsuit was brought against the town of Ancaster and our company to stop development because of potential damage from saltwater running off the roads into a neighbor's well.

At an emergency meeting called by the major to discuss the matter, we agreed to protect the town from any liability concerning the well, guaranteed by a bond. The town already had a performance bond making good on all promises we had made in the subdivision agreement. The bond they now requested was for the cost of the lawsuit brought against the town and our company.

Our chief engineer for this project was Jerry W. Disher of C. C. Parker & Associates in Hamilton. He was one of the kindest people I have ever met. Disher moved slowly but efficiently and working with him was a pleasure. He also piloted his own plane and took us up for a bird's-eye view of the land. We were all in love with this project, but with the looming court case, we feared being forced to stop. At the very least, it would interfere with our progress for a while. Such a delay was unacceptable to us because interest on the borrowed money was mounting every day. We decided to organize a proper defense and countersue for willful damages in obstructing our development.

We hired two university professors. One was a world-renowned expert on water and the damage it can do. The other, from McMaster University, had accumulated thousands of pages of research done by his students. Armed with eight cartons of evidence, we fought in court. We agreed to install a large holding pond with a filtration system that we would maintain. This reservoir would hold any overflow water so that it could be filtered and then diverted in different directions using swales. The water would not harm the neighboring individual's well or land.

Soon we began looking for the best builders in the area to construct houses. The one we chose had shown us exclusive, exquisite homes he had built in Mississauga. We sold him 38 lots on which to build immediately and agreed to sell him all 190 lots once we saw how well he did on the first ones. This builder employed Alec Murray Real Estate Company Ltd., from Hamilton, who, instead of building a few model homes as he had promised, put up a small sales office and started selling from just plans and pictures of houses. He himself went away during the winter on vacation. He did not promote and sell, and he did not even close the deal on the land or pay interest. We eventually replaced him with a couple of local builders who started construction at the other end of the subdivision. These builders sold the houses and bought new lots, and the project started to move slowly. Then interest rates jumped, and houses stopped selling. The project stalled again.

Dr. Mark Nusbaum, his wife Edith, and their four lovely daughters lived near us. Nusbaum had been very helpful when I was gathering signatures for a petition to remove the fertilizer/salt dump on the corner. He was also quite kind in permitting me to use the tennis court adjacent to his house, and we often played together, although I was not at his level; he taught me to play properly. We became good friends, and I cherish that relationship.

HANGOUTS

For the lone entrepreneur, where he has coffee in the morning on the way to work, or where he eats lunch, is significant. Several luncheonettes and coffee shops, none of them fancy, provided me with a forum of peers. The men—and men far outnumbered women—who frequented these places came more for the camaraderie than for the decidedly mundane cuisine. The mix of patrons and proprietors imbued each place with its own particular atmosphere that ensured its status as a hangout.

Stubby's had long ago acquired the status of hangout. People came from all over town and fought over the few seats in this establishment that was half luncheonette and half variety store. The proprietor, "Stubby" to most, Shaye to me, was a Holocaust survivor with an acerbic personality that, instead of alienating customers, drew crowds because people found his insults entertaining. Stubby's was a place where you exchanged information. It was the place my "friends" took bets on how soon my Weston Road project would fail and at what cost. No serious municipal politician would dream of starting a campaign without a visit to Stubby's, even at the risk of a harangue from the boss himself. Stubby's was even the subject of a short Canadian Broadcasting Company documentary produced by Sybil Hershtal, a member of the second generation, the children of survivors.

When Stubby retired, his "main man," Jimmy, tried to keep the institution going in a nearby location, but it did not work. People dispersed to United Dairy, a restaurant that moved from the old Jewish neighborhood on Spadina to Lawrence Plaza, or to Bagel World on Wilson Avenue. Some of us regrouped right across the street from Stubby's in a spot called Hamburger Place—a place where I do not think any of us has ever had a hamburger. The proprietors, Polly and Tony Kuzmas, operate their establishment in a manner completely opposite Stubby's. Polly is a beautiful person of class and character; Tony is smart, understanding, and very quiet, but his silence speaks worlds. Add to this, excellent coffee, superb service, and a feisty, intelligent, talkative clientele, and you have the ingredients for an atmosphere that brings in the regulars.

On any given morning, except for *Shabes* and Sundays, for one or two hours, cultural, literary, and political topics are discussed, debated, and argued on the most profound level. The participants consist mostly of seasoned and experienced entrepreneurs.

The usual bunch included Harry Ungerman, a philanthropist who donated much of his time, effort and money to the Baycrest Center (a top-notch nursing home in Toronto); Milton (Mickey) Snow, a land developer and president of Forest Hill Lions Club for many years, who devoted time and money to many charitable causes; Lawrence Snow, Mickey's younger brother, a real estate broker, very knowledgeable, and always thirsty for more knowledge; and a guy with a golden heart, Stan Goldstein, known as Stash, who is nice, smart, very industrious, and always busy, yet who always finds time to help other people.

There is also Marvin Kalifer, a furrier by trade, who became a property owner and is doing extremely well in managing his apartment holdings. Melvin Richmond, an ex-mortgage broker, financier, and devoted husband, who goes to synagogue every day but "never on Saturday," speaks in a rich baritone voice that is a pleasure to listen to, especially because he does not mince words.

Aaron Barzelai is the only one in the group who understands me when I quote a passage in Hebrew. He is an Israeli, who took part in the 1948 War of Independence, and vividly describes the Arab-Israeli fights in the streets of Jaffa that took place more than 50 years ago while we listen in fascination. Stephen Rukasin is a classy gentleman, honest and sincere, who speaks softly, yet with conviction, when he backs up his statements, a loyal person to just causes. Manly Walters is a well-informed person with much experience, well read, who always listens to others, wanting to learn more. Wayne Tanenbaum is a fabulous host and party animal, well known for distributing *shmurah matzos*, always busily involved in many projects—which is why he shows up when everybody else is about to leave.

Irving Erenberg is the chairman of the board and owner of Irving's Plumbing Supplies Warehouses and Stores. Albert Kerzner, barrister and solicitor, is an experienced developer and entrepreneur, whose first love is really the legal profession. Morton (Morty) Feldbloom is a veteran broker and president of Feldbloom Real Estate Ltd., an honest, trustworthy, capable, and experienced individual. Sol Rosenberg, a real survivor, experienced world traveler, and master electrician, knows and understands, but talks very little; yet, when Sol does say something, it is always meaningful. Harvey Zarnett, the most gentle soul I have ever met, observes, listens, thinks a lot, and comes from a traditional background. We can talk for hours about his parents and grandparents because they come from Chenciny, Poland, the same place as Father and my grandparents of blessed memory. Steven Burnstein, also a licensed real estate broker and developer, loves the outdoors—cottaging, skiing, boating—all pursued with passion, and he is a good debater.

From time to time, other people drop in and add different spice to our discussions. One of them is Murray Goldman, a well-known entrepreneur who develops in Israel as well as in Canada. Another, Sol Mednick, the expert photographer, entrepreneur, developer, and past president of the Lions Club, comes from a traditional Jewish background. The majority of the men in our group belong to the Forest Hill Lions Club, and those who are not official members, like me, nonetheless support that fraternal, humanistic, and charitable organization.

DRINKING WINE BY THE GLASS

In 1975, rent control was instituted in Ontario. I believe that rent control is not good for either landlords or tenants. Nevertheless, it became a reality in Ontario because of three parties: (1) unscrupulous landlords who overcharged tenants and kept raising rents, (2) eloquent politicians such as Stephen Lewis who wanted their oratory to be heard by the New Democratic Party (NDP), and (3) the conservative premier of Ontario, Bill Davis, who sacrificed landlords because tenants represented more votes. I let my views be known to the government and to the public. When Bill Grenier, a former Air Canada pilot turned real estate investor, organized a group to combat rent control, I was among the first to join. I was on the executive committee that formed the Fair Rental Policy Organization of Ontario (FRPO). This organization should have been instituted much earlier to prevent rent control, rather than having been created as an ex post facto reaction to it. Our delegations appeared many times before various government committees.

On August 26, 1986, William Walker wrote in the *Toronto Star*, "Toronto developer Joseph E. Tenenbaum launched a vicious attack on the Ontario government's new rent control proposals yesterday, stunning a legislative committee reviewing the bill." The writer quoted me for more than half a column. "'This is a crisis of monstrous proportions. This legislation has driven all investment out of the province.'" I traveled to various cities throughout Ontario—including Kitchener, Guelph, Barrie, Hamilton, Windsor, and Sarnia—to organize opposition to rent control. I spoke in the Toronto Convention Hall before 1,200 people, detailing the effect rent control can have on property values, new housing, and economic growth. All people in Ontario would be affected. Subsidies for new housing would cost taxpayers enormous sums. Investors would be unwilling to erect new rental housing in the province as a result of the government's action.

Exactly a year after the new legislation was introduced, I decided to stop pursuing construction of any rental housing in Ontario. As a matter of fact, I was spooked by rental housing anywhere because if rent controls could be introduced in Ontario, what was to stop other provinces from introducing similar controls? An opportunity came up in western Canada that Andrew Tylman and I decided to pursue. Our first investment was an existing shopping mall in Saskatoon, Saskatchewan; we purchased the property from Michael O'Byrne, the son of Michael Brian O'Byrne, a Supreme Court justice of the province of Alberta.

While in Saskatoon we found another deal, a joint venture with another builder who had leased land for an office building, but whose project had become too big and complicated for him to handle on his own. Working with the gentleman was not in our best interest in this case, so my partner and I offered him a buyout, which he accepted, and we took over construction of the office building. We incorporated a company called T & T Realty Ltd.—each "T" standing for the first letter of each of our last names.

Our first task at the run-down shopping mall was to improve the tenant mix and customer counts by introducing an anchor store, a main retailer to draw customers. We approached the Saskatchewan Liquor Control Board with a proposition to lease space for a liquor store in our mall. Garry Smulan represented the Liquor Control Board, and he negotiated brilliantly. After quite a long negotiation, we signed a lease, but before the ink was dry on the agreement, I proposed to Smulan that he join our organization. Smulan took our offer as a compliment, and after a few months, he called to ask whether our offer was serious. We were dead serious because I had recognized Smulan's ability. We negotiated again, and Smulan joined our company as manager of the Saskatoon properties.

Despite a few setbacks in the beginning—such as the Canadian Tire Store leaving our mall and McLeod's Department Store going bankrupt, leaving us with 46,000 square feet of empty space—we survived. We eventually renovated and expanded the mall four times, tripling its original size. We completed the downtown office building and purchased the leased land on which the building was erected from Devon Estates Ltd., a subsidiary of Esso Petroleum.

While we were growing as a company in Saskatoon, Patrician Land Corporation Ltd., owned by Peter Pocklington, went into receivership and was put under the management of the appointed receiver, Laventhal and Horwath, according to a March 12, 1984, order of the Alberta Court of the Queen's Bench. Among Patrician's assets was a shopping center known as Sherwood Park Mall, located about nine miles east of Edmonton. Lloyd Levine was managing these assets for Laventhal and Horwath. I had known Lloyd when he was a partner at Pape and Associates.

In order to sell the property, Lloyd procured the best marketing company at that time, Cogan Real Estate, which was owned and operated by Edwin Cogan. Eddie solicited offers from anyone, trying to fetch the highest price. After weeks of negotiations, we flew to Edmonton to inspect the property in order to get a better idea of what we were bidding on when the time came for the tender. As we walked into the management office on the lower level of the shopping mall, I noticed brown stains on the curtains about a foot from the floor. When I asked a secretary what had caused these stains, she replied, "Oh, they're nothing." I explained that we were the prospective owners, and when I confronted her with my guess that the stains had come from a broken pipe, she finally admitted that an adjacent retention pond had overflowed and water had backed up into the mall. Well, I thought to myself, that is one problem to be solved. Despite the water problem, we liked the mall.

Among the many people working for Patrician were the mall manager and his boss, Patrician's general manager, Dennis Bennetu. We arranged to go for dinner at the Westin Hotel, which had the nicest dining room in Edmonton. My partner and I started enumerating the negative aspects of the mall, such as the storm water backing up or the slope of the land that would add costs to future construction. The executives acknowledged these faults yet insisted that the mall would sell for at least $10 million. I replied that whoever offered that price would be overpaying by $2.5 million. When the waiter came to take our orders, Andrew and I each had a glass of wine while the others ordered more potent drinks. During the evening, we kept on expressing regret that the mall was not in the condition we had hoped to find it in.

When we returned to Toronto, the broker for the property already had been informed that we were not big spenders and therefore probably did not have the money to close the deal. Patrician's executives had come to this conclusion because Andrew and I had ordered wine by the glass rather than the bottle. They told the receiver not to count on our offer because it would have little merit. When the time came to submit tenders, ours was the highest. Next was the one submitted by Northern Telecom, which was about half a million less. After the receiver announced that our offer had been accepted, we decided not to risk so much in a single investment, especially since the mall required immediate renovation. We approached Northern Telecom with a proposal to participate in the transaction, which they accepted, thus becoming our partners.

As soon as we closed the deal and title was transferred to us, we undertook two major tasks. The first was to make sure the retention pond was secure. With the help of the county, the sewer system was enlarged, and the berm retaining the water was made higher. We doubled the size of the mall and renovated the existing part to match the modern addition. A new food court and the relocation of Safeway and the Toronto Dominion Bank to a larger area made the complex more interesting. In order to provide for future expansion and additional parking, we purchased two separate parcels of land adjacent to ours, one from Imasco Enterprises and the other from a Croatian organization that had intended to build a church. Not long after the renovation/expansion was completed, the economy in western Canada took a turn for the worse.

Companies went bankrupt, massive unemployment developed, and vacancies opened in the residential, commercial, and industrial sectors. This depression sent a lot of people back east. Large corporations consolidated, others sold assets, banks took over companies, properties changed hands, and authorities closed enterprises for nonpayment of taxes. Andrew and I thought that this was an opportune time to acquire property. Montreal Trust—the trustee for Northern Telecom's pension fund—offered to sell us its share of Sherwood Park Mall, and we accepted.

At about the same time, Bimcor, Bell Canada's pension fund, sold us Royal Square Mall in the Vancouver suburb of New Westminster, British Columbia, and we renovated that mall, too. For a while, we had our hands full with renovating, leasing, and adding to our portfolio. Fortunately, we had the capable and trustworthy Garry Smulan and his staff taking care of our affairs in the west.

Andrew and I traveled often to different locations out west, making sure our investments were safe and properly managed. On one such trip, the director of planning and development for the County of Strathcona approached us to see if we would be interested in purchasing 180 acres of land that were partially serviced with water, sewers, and rough-cut roads. This land, located on Highway 16 north of Sherwood Park, was zoned and subdivided into smaller commercial and industrial lots. This valuable land was owned by the Turbo Corporation, which eventually sold it to us when the economic crunch hit Alberta. After we acquired this parcel, we had to wait for the province to build a ramp off the highway so that we could build and effectively market an industrial park—something the county desperately needed for its economic development and to generate tax revenues. More than 15 years later, we are still waiting for the highway ramp, but have gone ahead and started selling off plots. About half the lots are sold, but at somewhat less profit than if the ramp had been built.

Our mall in British Columbia whet our appetite for acquiring more assets in that province, where the market was cooking. But after we researched a few properties, we decided to wait before acquiring any, because it was hard to compete against buyers from Hong Kong who came to the province in large numbers and paid exorbitant prices to get into the Canadian market. On one of our visits to Saskatoon, Garry Smulan asked if we would consider a proposition from a real estate agent. We arranged a meeting with the broker in Swift Current and, after chartering a plane, flew down to look at the property. After we took a look, however, we decided we were not interested.

The owner of the Swift Current Mall, Thomas Sutherland, learned our names from the agent and set up another appointment to try to convince us to buy. We flew down again to reconsider but came to the same negative conclusion. Sutherland did his best to accommodate Andrew and me. He drove us west in his Jaguar, across the Saskatchewan-Alberta border. When we arrived in Medicine Hat, Alberta, he showed us his farms, several sites for future development, subdivisions with residential lots, and a mall he had built. Everything was interesting, but when Andrew and I saw the shopping mall, we exchanged meaningful glances.

Our rapport with Sutherland improved as we spent time in the car. This relationship was quite different from the cold "trialogue" we had had in Swift Current. Sutherland invited us to join him for lunch in the dining room of a hotel he had built and to stay overnight and enjoy the water slides in the hotel's atrium. We accepted his kind invitation. After a few drinks at dinner, Sutherland bared his soul and told us how Sears, his partner in the Medicine

Hat Mall, was taking advantage of him. He and Sears, which wanted to retain its interest in the mall, had been fighting in court for ten years, practically from the time the mall had opened. We thought this was a good opportunity to take over Sutherland's share of the mall, so we gathered our courage and made a proposal to Sutherland, which was met with prolonged silence. All we could hear was the rattle of cutlery and the munching of food. When Sutherland finally spoke, he said he was not interested in selling the Medicine Hat Mall. We suggested that, in order to avoid his pending court problems, he could sell us his share of Medicine Hat Mall, which would give him the financial wherewithal to be sole owner of the one in Swift Current. Sutherland said he would think about our proposition.

Back in Toronto, we set up an appointment with the people from Sears to see if the company would sell its share in the mall. We also wanted to know if Sears would object if Sutherland decided to sell to us. On the day of our appointment, Rick Atkinson, the manager of the real estate division, led us to the boardroom where Sears's in-house lawyer and his assistant were waiting for us. We introduced ourselves, described the malls we already owned and operated, and offered to purchase Sears's share of Medicine Hat Mall. We received a negative answer because the company remained confident of winning its court battle with Sutherland. Although, according to Sears, Sutherland had not lived up to his agreement with the company, Sears was unwilling to sell as long as it had its department store in the mall. At the same time, Sears had no objection to our purchasing Sutherland's share of the complex.

We did a lot of shuttling between Toronto, Calgary, and Medicine Hat. We had many meetings with Sutherland, conveyed to him our knowledge of the situation, and proposed that he settle out of court with Sears. Sutherland, however, hoped to win, even if the litigation took ten years. We asked simply, "Mr. Sutherland, do you want to sell the Medicine Hat Mall?" He was beginning to waver but requested a steep price. Perhaps he was testing us. Two months passed before we got a signed agreement. He was a mercurial man and negotiations were nerve-racking. Almost every day, he suggested new conditions. We were concerned about a 200-acre parcel of land Sutherland owned nearby. Another mall built there would be catastrophic for us. So we resolved the problem with an agreement that assigned part of the acreage fronting the highway for freestanding commercial blocks and the rest for residential development. We were given the right of first refusal, but had to pay a few hundred thousand dollars for the privilege.

During negotiations, we were unaware of the degree to which Sutherland was indebted to various institutions, mortgage companies, and banks. His financial situation was not as solid as he wanted others to believe, yet he managed to stay afloat for a long time, until the Alberta Treasury Bank took over the mall when the loan it called in was not repaid. At approximately the same time that Alberta Treasury put Sutherland's assets up for sale, Thomas Tucker from Royal Trust foreclosed on Sutherland's mall in Swift Current. The real estate broker called us, asking if we would like to purchase it. We thought that if we took all necessary precautions, introduced innovations, and secured leases with Zellers and Safeway, we might make a go of it. Calculating the cost of marketing through advertising and promotion, we came up with a price: $13 million for the Swift Current Mall. Tom Tucker rejected our offer.

With the passage of time, little improvement took place in the mall. Even the change of management did not help. The mall was offered to us again, but its original value was diminishing. We offered $12 million, although we knew that was more than the facility was worth. Our offer was still not accepted, and the mall's performance kept declining. We came to the conclusion that our first reaction had been sound: the mall was not for us. The Alberta Treasury Bank was patient with Sutherland, giving him every opportunity to redeem his assets, but he could not come up with the necessary funds. As a result, the bank called tenders for the Medicine Hat Mall. On behalf of T & T Properties, I informed the bank that no one had the right to sell the mall as long as our agreement with Sutherland was in force. The bank claimed this agreement was no longer valid or enforceable, likening it to agreements with contractors.

We hired the best law firm in Calgary, registered our agreement on title, and served Alberta Treasury with a notice informing it that we were ready, willing, and able to close the deal according to our agreement. Alberta Treasury claimed that all the commercial properties had to be sold as a package. Though our offer was only for the Medicine Hat Mall, we offered to consider three strip shopping plazas nearby and the adjacent gas station to settle the matter. The bank insisted on including 200 acres adjacent to the mall. Buying that land did not make sense to us from a financial point of view, but the bank held firm. We threatened a lawsuit for damages. After prolonged negotiations, we compromised. Sears retained 40 percent of the Medicine Hat Mall building and Andrew and I acquired a 60 percent interest in it, while we retained a 100 percent interest in the land.

The strip plazas and gas station were purchased by a subsidiary of T & T Properties, our umbrella trade name. Since the emergence of T & T Properties in 1974, the partnership has grown steadily. Administration and leasing offices are located in Toronto and Saskatoon, and we have been successful at redeveloping underperforming or undervalued revenue-producing property. T&T handles only property that it can manage efficiently and in which it holds an equity interest, thus incurring vacancy rates and operating costs far below industry norms. The commercial portfolio consists of shopping centers and office buildings throughout western Canada, and the mall tenants include most of the major retailers in Canada—Sears, Zellers, the Bay, Safeway, Cineplex Odeon, Galaxy Cinemas, Shoppers Drug Mart, the major banks, Burger King, HMV Records, the Sony Store—as well as several hundred other retailers. Revenue Canada, Agriculture Canada, Canada Life Insurance, and the Alberta Treasury Branch are all tenants of T & T, which also owns several parcels at various stages of development.

In addition to being a 50 percent shareholder in T & T, my children and I own 100 percent of Josten Properties. This company has a portfolio of high-rise apartment buildings, commercial and industrial properties, and land in and around Toronto. My companies continually review new investment opportunities and are well positioned to purchase properties that would be enhanced in value by experienced management.

Although involvement with real estate has absorbed much of my time over the years, I did not experience a meteoric rise in what I earned, but the challenge was rewarding. Hillel said in *Ethics of the Fathers,* chapter 2:8, "The more possessions, the more anxiety." The company was growing and with it came stress. What next? became the question. When Andrew and I started working together in 1974, we decided to draft a written agreement defining our relationship as operating partners, joint venturers, risk-takers, borrowers, and lenders.

We went to Sid Midanik and told him we wanted to be partners and needed a contract. Midanik prepared a memo with a list of questions and gave us each a copy to peruse. To date, neither of us has returned the questionnaire, nor do I even remember where it is. We did not even shake hands. We have never had a misunderstanding we could not resolve fairly, nor have we ever taken advantage of each other. When something in our business falls into a gray area, a rare occurrence, we have watched each other's backs. We have been devoted to each other, we trust each other's integrity, and we have confidence in each other. In the almost 30 years we have been in business together, we have encountered plenty of treacherous terrain, yet we have managed to retain composure, dignity, and mutual respect.

Part VI

We have no longer in any country a literature as great as the literature of the old world, and that is because the newspapers, all kinds of second rate books, the preoccupation of men with all kinds of practical changes, have driven the living imagination out of this world.

William Butler Yeats, 1904

MORE RABBIS AND WARRIORS

As a young child, I had no patience to study. Father spent endless hours trying to teach me the value of learning. When they occupied Poland, the Germans robbed me of my youth and the intellectual maturation that would have unfolded as I grew older. I have always carried this void within me. The desire to recapture the study years of my youth propelled me to search for an education.

After the liberation, my emotional survival depended on escape through my preoccupation with business and work for the *Brihah*. I opted to be busy at anything rather than dwell on the past. But, the abrupt halting of my education made me feel like half a person. I understood Father's desire when it was almost too late.

In order to work in the underground, I needed a legitimate cover. I turned to business, and what started out as camouflage provided financial support. One day, a devoted *Betarnik*, Jaacov Slomianski from Vilna, the head of the Jewish students' organization in Munich, said to me, "Erez, listen to me. Enroll in the university. You need a degree. Your education is more important than anything now."

His words shocked me. He, of all people, knew how much work was needed to create a Jewish state. Sacrificing our education, at least temporarily, did not seem too heavy a price to pay. More than 50 years have passed since that conversation, yet I still think about Slomianski's words. He was right, but he was also wrong. If many people like me had agreed with him, what would have happened to Israel, to the Jewish people, to our dream of a homeland?

I did engage a professor from the University of Munich to tutor me privately in exchange for rationed foodstuffs. Slomianski went on to serve as a captain and medical doctor in the U.S. Army. Today, he has a successful practice in New York.

I did not start studying Talmud again on a regular basis until I arrived in New York, when I took those courses with Rabbi Mordechowicz and Rabbi Mordechai Twerski, whose synagogue was on DeKalb Avenue in the Bronx. I also attended annual *halachic* and *aggadic* discourses by Rabbi Dov Soloveitchik at Yeshiva University in Manhattan. These lectures attracted thousands. Once, when it was close to midnight, he said, "Well, you businessmen can go home; it is getting late. But you rabbis, if you want some more material for your sermons in *shul* on *Shabes*, you can stay and listen." Everyone applauded and nobody left.

It was not always easy to satisfy the thirst for spiritual knowledge while meeting the material needs of a family. I was trying to balance a heavy load, despite the constraints of inadequate language skills and my own limitations. The Talmud tells us: If one is a writer, he cannot be a warrior, and if a warrior, he cannot be a writer. I prefer the Talmudic idiom: The sword and the book came down from heaven intertwined. Might and spirit both rule the world.

In the late 1960s, I met Jack Schwartz, a man who worked hard for the community and was especially active in fundraising for the Lubavitcher movement. After we became friends, Jack invited me to attend a Torah study group he had organized that was taught by Rabbi Eliyahu Lipskar. Many professional people attended, among them Richard Shiff; David Goldberg, an accountant; Izzy Eisen, a doctor; Jack Weinbaum, a developer; and Louis Zeifman.

I had met Rabbi Lipskar earlier in a totally different context when he was the next-door neighbor of my friends Jack and Marilyn Kostman. I was always drawn to Jews with long beards and *peyes*, so when I would see Rabbi Lipskar sitting on his porch on my visits to my friends, I would occasionally chat with him. When I came to the rabbi's study group for the first time, he was surprised to see me in the context of religious study, because I was connected to the totally unobservant Kostmans. But Rabbi Lipskar was broad-minded and accepted people without being judgmental. In fact, on college campuses during the 1960s, Rabbi Lipskar was instrumental in keeping Jewish youth off drugs and away from cults, long before the rest of the Orthodox community got involved in such outreach programs. It soon became clear to the rabbi that I was no stranger to Talmud.

Either our group met at the Lubavitch Center on Bathurst Street, north of Wilson Avenue, or we rotated in participants' homes. Ninety percent of our time was devoted to studying *Tanya*, the major opus of Rabbi Schnoer Zalman of Lyady (the old Lubavitcher Rabbi), a great Talmudist and mystic. The *Tanya*, formally titled *Sefer Shel Benonim* (Book of Average [People]), was a guidebook for the "average man" in search of faith and a better understanding of the Torah, a compilation of the Rebbe's discourses published in 1796. I kept challenging Rabbi Lipskar on corresponding passages from scripture or Talmud that seemed to contradict what was in the *Tanya*. The dialogue was not easy for the rabbi or for me.

While I searched for answers that made sense to me, I proceeded with respect as well as affection for the learned man. Once, when I was late for a lesson at the Goodmans' house, the rabbi said with twinkle in his eye, "And I thought for once I would have it easy!" I knew the rabbi enjoyed the challenge just as much as I did. I felt that for both of us, searching through the Torah, Talmud, and *Tanya* for intellectual heights was like mountain climbing. We were tied together with ropes and depended on each other's cooperation to forge ahead. After Rabbi Lipskar died, I got my taste of his teachings when I visited the Lubavitch *shul* in Miami where his son, Sholom Lipskar, is the rabbi. The young Lipskar is every bit as devoted to the Jewish community as his father was and carries on his father's holy work with passion.

Attending Rabbi Lipskar's Sunday morning study group whetted my appetite for learning. When my friend Eugene Feiger, one of my partners in the search for Jewish knowledge, told me about a *shiur* from a scholar, I jumped at the opportunity to join him. The first time I went to the class, the room was packed with people—young and old, professionals and students. The man sitting at the head table, Reb Avraham Schkop, was elderly and clean shaven; he wore glasses and stooped over the book in front of him. He spoke in a quiet, nonchalant voice as if he were speaking to himself, yet every word he uttered was a treasure. After the third or fourth lesson, the number of attendees dwindled, until only a dozen who were seriously involved in study remained. Included in the group were three teachers from Associated Hebrew Schools, two poets, a couple of accountants, a doctor, a lawyer, and a few business people, including Eugene, and me.

Reb Schkop was a genius, yet humble and lovable. He reminded me of Reb Luser Ehrenreich, the fragile old man Father had befriended in Dzialoszyce. I felt the same affection and admiration for both men, but their personalities and teaching skills were worlds apart. Reb Luser Ehrenreich made me think of the Ba'al Shem Tov—a pious, knowledgeable Hasid. Reb Avraham Schkop, by contrast, was a masterful and controversial teacher with a slightly irreverent approach. He was a teacher's teacher.

His older brother, Rabbi Simeon Judah Schkop, had developed a system of Talmudic study that combined the logical analysis of Rav Chaim Soloveitchik and the simplicity of Rabbi Naftali Zwi Berlin. This approach became known as the "Telshe" way of learning. By attending Rabbi Avraham Schkop's classes, I was completing the education from my childhood and adolescence that had been abruptly cut off by the German invasion of Poland and then the Holocaust. The lessons helped me distinguish between truth and falsehood. Studying Talmud as a child had provided me with knowledge and trained me to commit large amounts of information to memory.

While I would have liked to have at my disposal the study aids now widely available, studying in the original Aramaic sharpened my mind. Throughout my life, I applied the wisdom of the Talmud to my experience. For example, when I built an 18-story building on Wellesley Street, the building inspector did not like a particular wall and wanted me to replace it. Reb Mordechai Nussbaum, a Talmudic scholar and owner of the Meteor Block Company, my supplier, happened to be present because he wanted to see how the building was progressing. Reb Nussbaum listened to the way I used translations of paragraphs from *Bave Batra*, one of the Talmud's tractates, to convince the inspector that there was no need to destroy the wall. In the end, he approved my plans.

All my learning as a child—in *heder*, private school, or at home—was much different from my studies with Rabbi Schkop. Father had put little emphasis on Bible study, except once a week on Saturday during the review of the biblical portion of the week. I never understood why questioning the texts in any way other than the traditional rabbinic approach was so strongly discouraged. Rabbi Schkop never said, "Do not ask questions," nor did he ever admonish us for challenging the texts. Instead, he answered our questions in many different ways, always enlightening us in the course of the journey.

HOLOCAUST DENIAL

When our patriarch Jacob had reached a point where he could rest peacefully from the earlier turbulence of his relationships with the likes of Laban and Esau, the woeful news reached him that his beloved son Joseph had disappeared. Once again, he was thrown into turmoil. Likewise, before we had finished mourning our loved ones murdered in the Holocaust, revisionists were hovering over their corpses like vultures, trying to deny their deaths.

In Toronto, Holocaust denial began with John Beatty. He started on a small scale with a few meetings in private homes and then spread out to restaurants and bars where his followers distributed Nazi literature and paraphernalia. Beatty's efforts culminated in a large, widely advertised rally at Allen Gardens in downtown Toronto in the mid-1960s.

Holocaust survivors in Toronto, who had not previously shown any particular interest in baseball, were suddenly interested in the sport, if only to borrow their children's equipment, especially the bats, to take to the park. The bigots were met with full force by the survivors, students, and members of the Jewish community. They vehemently protested the gathering and the granting of a permit for such a rally to a self-professed Nazi group. Fistfights broke out, and there were many injuries. The police, commanded by Officer Adamson, had to get involved.

Adamson, who was later appointed chief of police, called for reinforcements, but he timed his call judiciously, allowing events to transpire in a way that suited the protesters. When the fighting came to a halt, Beatty was removed from the scene "for his own protection." Nazi slander in the public domain subsided, at least on the surface, but the poisonous publications, with their trashy texts denying the Holocaust, persisted. This hatred was disseminated under the protection of "freedom of speech" laws.

While civil rights organizations debated the matter, nothing was done to stop it until Sabina Citron and Helen Smolack, Holocaust survivors and activists, brought the problem of one Ernest Zundel to the attention of Ontario's attorney general in the early 1980s. Eventually, this Holocaust denier ended up in court in Toronto, on trial for "spreading lies and inciting people against a minority"—the Jews. The Honorable Hugh Locke presided. The official charge was "false news." The office of the attorney general appointed Peter Griffith, a deputy crown attorney, as chief prosecutor. Every day during the long trial, the crowded courtroom was packed with people, many of whom had to stand.

The line to enter the court started early each morning, and the authorities, anticipating trouble from Zundel's friends, stationed many guards around them to keep order. Nazi supporters were there every day. A steady attendance by survivors and other Jews faithfully supported the two brave women who had set everything in motion.

I seldom missed a session, and in order to secure a seat, I befriended some of the regular guards. The reason for my involvement, aside from curiosity, was that I wanted to ensure the accuracy of the court interpreter.

As soon as I walked into the courtroom and saw Ernest Zundel sitting on the bench, I could not help thinking of the 21 major German war criminals indicted in the ancient city of Nuremberg, the same city where the Nazi decrees against the Jews had been enacted.

In his opening statement at the Nuremberg Trial, the chief U.S. prosecutor, Justice Robert H. Jackson, declared: "These men know nothing of the evil perpetrated in the German-occupied regions. They [the defendants]—who are responsible not only for the deaths of millions of innocent men, women, and children but also for the loss of countless future generations—they still speak with great admiration for Nazi Germany and Hitlerism. What a pity that besides the testimony already seen and heard here, there could not be present the millions of men, women, and children who perished." The verdicts had been handed down on September 30 and October 1, 1946, as a warning to the civilized world that the day of reckoning had arrived for heinous criminals.

Almost 40 years later, here I was in another packed courtroom, listening to yet another antisemite repeating the plea of "not guilty." I cannot begin to describe Zundel without thinking of him as one of the most despicable of creations. The courtroom was full of interested parties: Holocaust survivors, representatives from the Canadian Jewish Congress and B'nai Brith's Anti-Defamation League, journalists, Nazi sympathizers, and witnesses. The central characters in the drama were Judge Hugh Locke, a tall man in his early 50s; Chief Prosecutor Peter Griffith, a soft-spoken, bespectacled gentleman in his 30s; the lawyer for the accused, Douglas Christie from British Columbia, who also represented another antisemite named Keegstra. The accused, who was about five feet, seven inches tall and weighed 250 pounds, sat in a booth. The prosecutor began his case by reviewing all the reasons it had been brought before the court. Then he called as witnesses regular citizens, expert historians, and others. The defense lawyer tried to obstruct the evidence with constant interruptions.

After 39 tense days of watching Christie perform—and watching him later in Red Deer, Alberta, where he defended Keegstra—I concluded that this lawyer was a Nazi sympathizer. Although I understood Christie had an obligation to represent his client to the best of his ability, there was something about him that made me uncomfortable. He was tall and dark with a stern, mean look, and his abrupt manner reminded me of behavior I had witnessed in concentration camps.

In contrast to Christie's darkness, prosecutor Peter Griffith was a bright ray of light. He presented the case step by step, speaking with respect yet vigor, softly but assertively. Griffith's aim was to convict Zundel of spreading "false news." The destruction of European Jewry, conducted by Zundel's predecessors, had also started with false rumors. All I could offer Peter Griffith was an encouraging word or commentary about an incorrect translation from the German spoken by a witness on the stand. When Griffith needed some documents translated into English over a weekend, I found an expert interpreter and sat with him throughout the night to get the document ready. Sometimes I brought Griffith translated parts from the Talmud that were relevant to the case. Griffith was under constant pressure because of the importance of the case; the eyes of the free world were on him.

The long and difficult trial ended on February 28, 1985, and Zundel was convicted. When I saw the policeman putting handcuffs on this guilty, misbegotten creature and leading him out of the courtroom, I asked excitedly,

"Where is Zundel?" (I knew very well where he was.)

The plainclothes policeman answered, "In custody."

I asked again, "But where is Zundel?"

"Joe, he's in custody," the policeman repeated. When I asked a third time, my other friend in uniform realized I just wanted to hear again and again that the Nazi was going to jail, and hopefully to hell.

Sentencing was supposed to take place on March 25, 1985. On March 2, Douglas Christie filed an appeal with the Supreme Court of Ontario. The grounds for appeal contained 28 items in which Christie claimed the trial judge had erred, incorrectly allowed exhibits, or otherwise acted improperly. In addition, Christie cited "such further grounds as counsel may advise upon reading of the trial's transcript."

Zundel has twice been convicted in Canada, and once in Germany, for denying the Holocaust. Unfortunately, on August 27, 1992, the 1985 Canadian conviction was overturned by a narrow decision, on points of law, but not based on fact. The Supreme Court did not excuse or condone denial of the Holocaust. It stated simply that this type of lie is not a crime under the freedom of speech provision of the Canadian Constitution. By attending Zundel's trial, I learned about court rules and process. In Zundel's own country, Germany, he was convicted, but in liberal Canada—with a tradition of human rights and free speech—the verdict was reversed.

Canada, the nation described so eloquently by Irving Abella in his book *None Is Too Many* was not so liberal when it refused to admit Jewish refugees fleeing Nazi Germany. Zundel's kind of free speech, like yelling "fire" in a crowded theater, is a form of reckless endangerment that can lead to mass murder. We lived through and witnessed the results of hate speech and antisemitism in the past.

One positive feature of the trial was that I met wonderful people. One plainclothes policeman became a good friend. After the trial, he sent me a poem he had written titled "A Friend":

Life's continuing days, that short-change us time;
These days where money and greed, cheating and turmoil brew.
These days where, 'oft times, humane concern is placed aside.
These days where Cruise and Star Wars are man's illustrious toys.
Where serenity and peace seem like misplaced dreams.

Lo!
Into our world, a benign influence slips in as silk and spreads rays of spiritual treasures.
As an Artist's landscape covering threads, he enlightens life.
A true Brother.
Rare,
So very rare.
> R. Williams, March 1985

My small contribution to the Zundel trial was insignificant, but it was appreciated and acknowledged with thanks by the prosecutor. I learned that in the wonderful country of Canada, the phrase "none is too many"—with reference to immigrants—might be recast for hate mongers. Apparently, "one was not enough" when it came to Zundel—we needed to add Keegstra. For 14 years, James Keegstra, a social studies teacher and the mayor of Eckville, Alberta (a village 150 kilometers south of Edmonton), taught junior and senior high school students about the "international Jewish conspiracy." Four hundred students were exposed to a long-discredited theory and antisemitic myths such as *The Protocols of the Elders of Zion*. Instead of following the Alberta social studies curriculum, Keegstra developed his own poisonous teaching plan. Luckily, the whole affair exploded, and Keegstra's lies were exposed to the community, the region, and the nation.

The Lacombe County Board of Education fired Keegstra as a teacher in December 1982. Unfortunately, Keegstra was supported by the Alberta Teachers Association and funded by the Christian Defense League in efforts to be reinstated. Of the school's 116 students, 96 demanded that their teacher be reinstated. When the matter was brought to court, Madam Justice Elisabeth McFayden of the Court of Queen's Bench dismissed Keegstra's appeal, which was based mainly on the support of the large percentage of students he had indoctrinated.

In a 21-page decision, Judge McFayden said: "Mr. Keegstra's students believed his conspiracy theories were fact. While Mr. Keegstra may have prefaced his presentation of the material by a general statement that these were only theories, I am satisfied that the students did not have before them any contrary views or source material which may have led them to conclude that the theories were in error."

McFayden's judgment was a message to teachers that school boards have the authority and responsibility to fire any teacher who betrays the trust of his or her profession. McFayden was not the only judge involved in this case. During the times I visited that trial court, I watched the presiding justice, John McKenzie, listen patiently and display extra courtesy to the antisemitic Keegstra. While on the witness stand, Keegstra rarely moved his tall, well-proportioned figure. He behaved as if he were standing in front of a class. Although Keegstra did not introduce as many pamphlets, photographs, or books as exhibits as had been introduced in the Zundel trial, he presented more than a hundred items.

Keegstra's manner of speaking to the jury and the court resembled that of a preacher, rather than a man accused. I became restless when the defense behaved as though the court case was not about him. The theatrics of the defense lawyer, Douglas Christie, did not surprise me; I was already familiar with them from Zundel's trial in Toronto. Christie used an abrasive technique in examining witnesses and constantly interrupted prosecutor Bruce Fraser.

During recess when we were in the corridor, Christie noticed me. "I see you are here, too," he barked.

"Only because of you, dog," I snapped.

This was Keegstra's third trial, and I did not know how many more would be required to convict him. It was hard for me to travel back and forth to attend all sessions the way I did at Zundel's trial in Toronto. I had to stay at a hotel in Red Deer. But I followed every step of the trial through the media or from people on our side. The anticlimactic end of the case came in the middle of July. After many days of deliberation, the Red Deer jury unanimously found James Keegstra guilty of "unlawfully promoting hatred" against Jews. He was fined a mere $5,000 for this criminal offense.

What was the final outcome of trials like those of Keegstra and Zundel? Did we change the minds of antisemites? There is no evidence to that effect. Just the opposite seems to be true. Not far from where the Keegstra trial took place, a member of the Edmonton legislature, a 38-year-old lawyer named Stephen Stiles, maintained that the slaughter of Jews by the Germans during World War II has never been proven. When Premier Peter Lougheed eventually responded, he said, "History shows that elements of bigotry, such as the antisemitism in this recent [Keegstra] case, can grow like cancer if not challenged and vigorously condemned by those in positions of responsibility."

Lougheed also announced that the government planned to introduce a program to "explain the nature of discrimination and the importance of exposing it." He promised to review school curricula to ensure that it fostered tolerance and respect for minority groups, in order to prevent a repetition of the Keegstra case.

Stiles eventually apologized for his remarks, but how many others who were not public figures made similar statements and did not recant?

"CRUSH THE ARROGANT"

I have encountered many kinds of people in my life—some good, some evil. I have seen denouncers, frauds, and crooks, but traitors to the Jewish people revolt me the most. In the *Shemoneh Esreh,* the prayer *Velamalshinim* reads, "May the slanderers have no hope. May all wickedness perish instantly. May all thy enemies soon be cut down. Do Thou uproot and crush the arrogant; cast them down and humble them speedily in our days."

In 1980, *By Way of Deception*, a book coauthored and published by a Jew, Victor Ostrovsky, created quite a furor. Apparently recruited and trained by the Mossad (the Israeli intelligence service), Ostrovsky later defected and revealed operating secrets. I did not read the book, but when a group of students asked if I would be interested in attending a televised interview and discussion with the author on the *Shirley Show,* I accepted the invitation with an open mind.

When Victor Ostrovsky and coauthor Claire Hoy stepped up to the podium, bodyguards escorted them. Evidently, they anticipated a hostile audience because of the traitorous contents of the book. Widely exposed through the news media, the book incensed the Jewish community. The more Ostrovsky talked, the clearer it became that his only motive was to create a sensation in order to promote his book. Later reports revealed that Ostrovsky had been found incompetent and was discharged by the Mossad; the author's publicity campaign was evidently an attempt at revenge.

I lost patience with Ostrovsky's self-serving deception and asked for an opportunity to speak. On the air, I told the man exactly what I thought of him. I was clearly stating the sentiments of the audience, who applauded enthusiastically. Shirley, the show's host, tried to take the mike away from me, but I would not let her have it. My children, who were in the audience, later told me the show should have been renamed "The Joe Show." I was escorted out of the studio with handshakes and hearty pats on the back. Months later, friends were still congratulating me for my remarks.

ZION, FRIENDS, AND POETS

The death in 1968 of my beloved father-in-law reinvigorated my old ties with Israel, not that they had ever been spiritually severed. I had continued to dream of Zion, as did my father-in-law until he took sick. His passing gave me my first opportunity to make the physical leap to Israel. After a valiant battle with cancer, Joseph Meisels succumbed on *Shushan Purim* in 1968. His last wish was to be buried in Jerusalem.

A memorial service was held in my father-in-law's synagogue on DeKalb Avenue, where Rabbi Twerski delivered a tearful eulogy. The procession set out for the Riverside Funeral Home in Manhattan, where friends and relatives from New York, Toronto, and Los Angeles gathered to pay their last respects. Sons Sidney and Gary flew down with half a planeload of Torontonians (Tammy, Gena, and I were already there), many of them orphaned after the war. My in-laws had "adopted" them, accompanied them to the *hupah,* and stood in for lost parents. Afterward, Gena and I accompanied her father's body to the land of his dreams and buried him in Jerusalem on Har Hamenuhot (Mountain of Rest). His grave faces the Judean hills, overlooking the road approaching Jerusalem, a road saturated in Jewish blood. Whenever any member of our family comes in or out of Jerusalem, we always greet him.

Gena sat *shiva* in Givataim at the home of her father's older brother, Yaakov Leib, who made all the burial arrangements and purchased additional plots next to his brother. Yaakov Leib and his wife Rivkah had lost all their children in the Holocaust and never had children again. A feisty, mischievous type, even during the last weeks of his life in an old age home, Yaakov Leib traded currency and kept a bottle of Scotch hidden from his nurses so that he could entertain his guests in style. This beautiful, bright-eyed man stayed sharp to the end. In 1986, he died, and now the two brothers rest side by side.

After completing the seven days of *shiva* for her father, Gena and I visited my wife's first cousin, Yosef Meisels (Yoshu), and his family in Haifa. I had met Yoshu as a young boy in Munich, where he attended the Hebrew Gymnasium. Yoshu lost his father and an only sister and survived along with his mother. An idealist, Yoshu made *aliyah* from Germany and fought in the Israeli army before continuing his education. He earned a degree in engineering from the Technion and worked all his life for Mekorot, the Israel water utility, eventually becoming chief engineer of the Northern District. He married a wonderful lady, Dina, a talented teacher of geography, history, and Jewish studies at the Reali School in Haifa, and they have two children, Benjamin and Michal.

My good friend Tsemach Tsamriyon lived in Haifa, too. He and his wife, Pnina, were the couple who had walked me down to the *hupah*. Although Tsemach and Pnina were not much older than I, they were both special to me. I respected Tsemach from the moment we met, on the first Passover after liberation, at a seder organized by the Zionist Revisionist movement in Munich.

Tsamriyon joined the Jewish Brigade to support and defend Israel. After the war, he became the publisher of *Unzer Velt* (Our World) in Germany. Upon returning to Israel, he kept away from political activities and focused on community and cultural affairs. From 1950 on, Tsamriyon was chairman of many educational councils, both regional and national. He headed the literary jury for the Arthur Ruppin Prize established by the city council of Haifa and taught at the Central High School of Galilee in Tiberias, later becoming its principal. Tsamriyon was also director of the City High School of Haifa. He became a member of the pedagogic committee of the Israeli Teachers Association and the National Secretariat of Friends of the Hebrew Language in Israel.

He was also editor-in-chief of *Hachinuch*, an education quarterly. This editorship provided him with sufficient income to discontinue teaching as a visiting lecturer at the University of Haifa and senior lecturer in *Tanach* and Jewish history at the Technion, where he was an assistant professor. He contributed articles to a variety of periodicals and wrote a number of books, including *Press of the Jewish Holocaust Survivors in Germany: An Expression of*

Their Problems (1970) and *Three Thinkers—Maimonides, Mendelssohn, and Achad-HaAm* (1979).

Since his return to Israel in the 1950s, Tsemach Tsamriyon had never left the country despite several invitations to lecture abroad. I thought it would be a good opportunity for my friend to travel and visit me, so 12 years after reestablishing contact in 1968, I approached the University of Toronto with a proposal to invite Tsamriyon to deliver a few lectures. The dean, Dr. Arthur Kruger, advised me to contact the new department of Judaic Studies at York University and Arthur Haberman, a professor of history and humanities. The faculty of education at York was also interested in inviting Professor Tsamriyon to lecture in Canada. If arrangements could be made, Tsamriyon would come for a week to ten days in either May or September of 1981. Rabbi Irwin Witty, chairman of the Board of Jewish Education, was enthusiastic and made plans to meet the professor during an upcoming visit to Israel in February.

By October, I had arranged with Professor Haberman to pay all relevant expenses for Professor Tsamriyon's visit, including flights, ground transportation, and hotels. York University would give Dr. Tsamriyon $1,000 for presenting the lectures, since I did not want my friend to know I was funding the trip. After writing many letters to Tsemach informing him of progress made on the lecture series, I received a disappointing note from Haberman and felt terribly hurt. The letter stated, "I regret we are not able to adequately fund a visit by Professor Tsamriyon to York University, as we discussed in our telephone conversation last week. Thank you for your interest in bringing Professor Tsamriyon to York."

More than a year's effort had come to naught. The Jewish students missed the opportunity of meeting a fine educator who was a link to past Jewish culture in Lithuania, Western civilization in Europe, and modern Hebrew culture in Israel.

Another good friend in Israel with whom I renewed contact during our first visit was Levi Shalit. I feel inadequate to describe this great man, yet I can almost hear Levi objecting, "Yosef, God wants your prayers, and not somebody else's. Nobody can pray for you. You have to do it in your own words."

I first met Levi Shalit in the spring of 1946 in The Bristol, a kosher restaurant in Munich. I remember that evening, filled with the fragrance of spring blooms, as Shalit read parts of his newly published book, *This Is the Way We Died*. The restaurant was packed, and while Shalit spoke, people wept openly, thinking of the flower of Jewish youth cut off so cruelly by the Nazis. Shalit kept reading, biting his lips from humbleness while passionately gesticulating with his arms, his black hair falling over his forehead, his Lithuanian Yiddish so perfect that sometimes I had difficulty understanding it. Then came the question-and-answer period followed by a discussion that lasted late into the night. Until I heard Shalit, I thought I knew Yiddish, but that night I discovered quite a few words I did not know. This experience renewed my feelings for a language I had rejected.

Yiddish had been the daily language of my youth, literally my mother tongue—I cried in Yiddish. As the song goes, *"Yidish iz dokh azoy shen; Yidish hot dokh azoy fil kheyn"* (Yiddish is so beautiful; Yiddish has so much charm). As a child, I read the prayers in Yiddish, which were translated from Hebrew. I also read Yiddish books by Shalom Aleichem, Mendele Mocher S'forim, Shalom Asch, and others. Nevertheless, immediately after World War II, I could not bring myself to justify the existence of the Yiddish language. I believed that Jews in Israel and the Diaspora should have one language—Hebrew.

Our people, scattered all over the globe, needed a common tongue to unify us, but the older generation clung to Yiddish. The young were either embarrassed by Yiddish or indifferent. For people who wanted a connection with their heritage, learning both Yiddish and Hebrew might be too much, and Hebrew—the language of our ancestors and our modern country—was certainly the right choice. I felt we must support the study of Hebrew, Torah, language, and literature.

Shalit and I met from time to time over the years, but we were both busy with our occupations. In the early years after the war, Levi was editing newspapers, writing books, and studying law. I was working for the underground and doing business.

We parted in 1951, when I left for what I thought would be a temporary stay in the United States, and Levi went to South Africa. One of Shalit's books, with its hard, gray cover, traveled with me until 1959. When Rabbi David Monson from Beth Shalom Synagogue in Toronto told me he was assembling a Holocaust library and asked if I had any books on the subject to donate, I gave him that book, among others. In 1967, Levi and I met again in Jerusalem, where we spent time reminiscing. We agreed that there is no place on earth like Jerusalem.

In 1974, my dear Levi wrote a book in Yiddish entitled *Time's Tales,* and, in 1980, *Beyond Dachau,* published in Johannesburg. Both were favorably received. *Beyond Dachau* opens with a seven-verse poem that Shalit wrote in 1945, when our wounds were still fresh. The poem describes tanks entering the gates of a concentration camp and thanks the redeemers: "Destiny chose you to be a savior, my liberator."

Levi then admonishes the troops: "You were late in coming. I counted the dead. The numbers climbed into the millions, and still you did not come."

The sixth verse reads: "You lifted me up from my knees but could not comfort me. Like a child fondling a toy, I patted your tank. You took your shirt and gave it to me."

The poet concludes: "You were in a hurry. Your tank hastened. But your warm, embracing shirt remained with me, entrusted to my zealous care."

Shalit's correspondence with me was filled with poetry, history, and wisdom. He wrote to us in several languages; when in English, he penned at the bottom, "Let me add a Jewish word so we will not become totally assimilated."

In another letter from Johannesburg, he wrote, "Now I see you ... Yosef, the youngest of the brethren [referring to Jacob's children] but not a dreamer; always with a sunny smile and an open face, and lips that keep moving with pleasing words."

In 1984, when Gena and I were in Israel, Levi and his wife, Chana, invited us to their home in Ramat Aviv. I told Shalit that I had given some of his books to a library, and he was apologetic about not being able to replace the volumes because they were out of print. He did have a copy of *Messianic Visions of Leivick's Dramatic Poems* (1947) that he gave me.

In 1994, Gena and I learned of Levi Shalit's death. A poet, writer, and revolutionary had passed away. We were shocked to lose a very special friend. We wrote to his wife to offer comfort. In April 1996, I received a book from Chana titled *On the Other Hand: Studies in Jewish History* by Levi Shalit, published posthumously. Levi came back to life in this book.

It was through the Shalits that we met the poet Abraham Sutzkever. When I first met Sutzkever and he showed me books of his Yiddish poetry, I said, "Oy."

"Oy" cannot be translated; it can only be expressed as pain that breaks suddenly from the heart. I thought to myself, "Here we go again, Yiddish!" To add insult to injury, many of the Yiddish poems had been written in the land of Israel—the land of Hebrew! This contradiction upset me. However, once

I read the poems, I forgot what language they were in. Sutzkever converted me and helped me make peace with myself about Yiddish. We developed a friendship and kept in touch by corresponding. I accumulated quite a collection of Sutzkever's books, because he graciously sent them to me as they were published.

Abraham Sutzkever was named an "Honorary Citizen" of Tel Aviv and Yaffa in December 1983 and was presented with an inscribed plaque. He was one of 57 people honored in this way over the years, among them, Albert Einstein, Edmund Rothschild, Lord Balfour, Achad-HaAm, Chaim Nachman Bialik, Ezer Weitzman, Chernichowski, Toscanini, Josef Klausner, Golda Meir, and Uri Zvi Greenberg. A memorial book published to mark the occasion contains a poem by Sutzkever in honor of Uri Zvi Greenberg.

Poets and writers—warriors with words—filled a void in my life left by the dead. These special souls described my background and experience, my people's yearnings, expressing what was in my own heart. I read and reread their works, committing many to memory. Great men like Uri Zvi Greenberg, whom I never met in person, became part of me. I read Greenberg's writings whenever I had an opportunity. I quoted his poems on joyous occasions, at my sons' bar mitzvahs, and at memorials for Holocaust victims.

When I was in Israel, I went to Greenberg's grave on Har Hamenuhot. I hope my feelings of love and admiration reached the poet. The Jewish people and I miss him dearly. Though born into an Orthodox home as the son of a rabbi, Greenberg gravitated toward the political left in his 20s. Like so many young people in those days, he hoped that the Russian Revolution would resolve the Jewish problem. Because of his background, Greenberg decided to make *aliyah* and settle in Palestine, unlike other writers and intellectuals who stayed in the Soviet Union.

Greenberg was warmly received in Palestine by the working classes, whose ideology he shared. Greenberg published his own literary journal, *Sadan— Axle and Anvil,* in which he declared that the time had come for Hebrew poets to reject the confines of pure art and descend from the ivory tower to the level of the masses. Intellectuals, said Greenberg, should share the lives of the common folk. He wrote that composing poetry in the old, classical rhythms did not befit the times in which we lived; the situation of the Jewish people had become too serious.

> I see the eagle of Amalek
> Flying from the Rhine over the heights
> To Westminster ...
> And I see thee
> Going to the ports of Haifa and Jaffa
> On English ships, to escape
> On the backs of your soldiers
> Hot and cold
> As I now feel, writing this song.

Greenberg was distressed by the Arab pogroms in Hebron and Safed, the behavior of the British police forces, and the hypocritical policies of the British Mandate for Palestine. He was also disillusioned by Labor's slow negotiations. Greenberg distanced himself from the workers' movement and joined the Zionist Revisionists. He stopped believing in quiet diplomacy or in accepting negative answers. Greenberg spoke out sharply against the British occupying regime. His protest poems took on a prophetic ring:

> I come from an Exile
> Saved from lakes of blood
> I could have had a harp
> To sing songs of joy
> For my tribe and my people
> But I am nothing but a jackal
> A mean jackal in the vineyards of Judea...

Uri Zvi Greenberg debated with the Almighty, as did Levi Yitzchak of Berdichov. "God the Father, God the Master, who is Lord of Mercies—if you are lonely up there in your world, we, your creatures, are a part of your loneliness." But when the poet fell into despair, overcome by destruction and killing, he poured out his anger: "The sky is not a heaven—it's a covering that conceals poison. There is no God!" This poem is reminiscent of Bialik's outburst in "City of Slaughter" written after the Kishinev pogroms.

When Greenberg was first awarded the Bialik Prize, he donated the money to the children of Jerusalem. In a letter to Ben Zvi, then chairman of the Va'ad Leumi and later president of Israel, Greenberg wrote: "If the Temple were standing today, I would go up to Jerusalem and place a sacrificial gift on the altar. But there is no Temple, so I am consecrating this gift to the children of Jerusalem." Greenberg's love for the holy city, expressed in "Song of Jerusalem," can be compared to Yehuda Ha-Levi (ca. 1080–1141) in his medieval elegy and touched me deeply.

> The one wall of the sanctuary you are unto me
> an outpouring of silence within your cliffs,
> City and Mother, O Jerusalem!
> O that I would raise you up, City and Mother,
> Beheaded one, from the midst of the outpouring of rocky
> Curse, like a dream and a precious gift of the cosmos!
> Then would you be always and forever, O Jerusalem
> As though refreshed after rain, and the moon
> Would be a healing unto you,
> What shall I do for you, O City of my blood?

REVISITING SODOM

In the *Tosefot* commentary to tractate *Niddah* of the Talmud, our sages say, "One does not ask a person who did not see to become a witness, only a person who saw." And so, I decided to take my wife and children to visit the places where my early life unfolded and the atrocities took place.

I wanted them to see my birthplace and that of my parents, grandparents, and great-grandparents. Another catalyst for our trip was that evening in the Florida hotel when Elie Wiesel brought down the book with his story about his return to Sighet, hoping to retrieve the watch his father had given him. I, too, wanted to retrieve the watch my father had given me for my bar mitzvah, but, more than that, I wanted to retrieve a taste of the Poland I knew before the Germans turned it into a land of death.

Of course, recapturing a piece of my childhood would have been difficult in the best of circumstances; in the Poland I returned to, it was more so. There is a legend that the Jews settled in *Polanya* (the Hebrew for Poland) because the name meant *Po* (here) *Lan* (rests) *Ya* (God). I have renamed the country *Pomatnu* (here we died).

We set out on our emotional journey in the spring of 1978. Even before we left, my brothers and survivor friends were telling me I was crazy to take my family to Poland. This was long before the creation of the Holocaust Memorial Museum in Washington and many years before the March of the Living was instituted in Poland. Lech Walesa's *Solidarnosc* movement still had not gained a foothold, and the Communists—the Soviet lackeys—were still in power.

Holocaust awareness was just coming to the fore, because while we were on our trip, the television series *Holocaust* aired. Despite the heavy emotional baggage I carried with me, I resolved to try to maintain some sense of objectivity on our journey. After all, there were many Poles who were not antisemites, and some were even Righteous Gentiles who risked their lives to save Jews during the war.

I thought of what God had said to Abraham: "… if I find in Sodom 50 righteous people, then I will spare the city for their sake" (Genesis 18:26). My resolution was challenged before we had even cleared Polish customs. The official gave us a hard time, and I could not help but feel that it was his awareness of our Jewishness that was behind his attitude. My trip back to Sodom had begun.

We spent our first days in Warsaw. As a child, I had never ventured out of Dzialoszyce farther than Kielce, so Warsaw for me was as new an experience as it was for my family. What was not new about the experience was the feeling of loss when we visited the Jewish institutions. Warsaw, which had had a prewar population of 350,000 Jews, was left with a remnant of only 680, most of them elderly, and several apparatchiks. All that physically remained of a vibrant Jewish presence was a cemetery fallen into disrepair, the dilapidated main synagogue, and a museum of Polish Jewish history housed in the former yeshiva that held a meager collection of desecrated Torah scrolls, damaged Judaica, a few paintings by Jewish artists, and some sketches by concentration camp inmates. A small, brick monument marked the spot where Jews had been loaded onto trains to Treblinka, and an empty square was at the center of what had been the Warsaw ghetto. Poland was waking up to the notion that Jewish tourism would bring hard currency, and not long after our trip, the country began investing in the restoration of its physical Jewish heritage and turning the Holocaust into a local industry.

Though none of my prewar family had a connection to the Warsaw ghetto, my current family did because of the monumental sculpture standing at the center of the square that honored the ghetto fighters. Sidney met the sculptor, Nathan Rappaport, in New York and introduced Gena to him at his studio because they both were sculptors. Gena liked a small sculpture he was working on, *The Burning Bush*, and offered to buy it when it was finished. When Nathan delivered it to Toronto himself, I met a wonderful, unassuming man.

To me, the sculpture signified that just as the bush was consumed in flame and not destroyed, so the Jewish people, even in martyrdom, will never be destroyed. The six-ton bronze Warsaw ghetto monument was set on a stone base that came from the same quarry in Sweden that Hitler wanted to use for his victory monument—a bittersweet irony.

One other institution hinted at the rich Jewish culture that had flourished in Poland before the Nazi destruction. After the war, the Yiddish theater was reestablished, with the help of the government, by Ida Kaminska, daughter of Esther Kaminska, the "mother" of Yiddish theater in Poland. Our time in Warsaw coincided with the 35th anniversary of the Warsaw Ghetto Uprising, and the Yiddish theatre put on a play about the revolt for the benefit of dignitaries from Israel, the United States, and other countries around the world. My family attended the play, which we found contained antireligious overtones from the ruling Communists. The rabbi was portrayed as a coward who tried to discourage people from pursuing armed resistance.

Setting aside the content of the play, the conditions surrounding its production were absurd. The play was performed in Yiddish, but many of the actors were Poles, so they had to learn the language to perform. Though the subject matter was heart wrenching, we could not contain an odd chuckle when the Poles broke their teeth over their newly acquired tongue. To top off the theater of the absurd, half of the audience were Poles who did not understand any Yiddish and consequently wore headsets for the simultaneous translation into Polish of the Polish actors' tortured Yiddish. This is not a Polish joke; it is what actually happened.

At the theater I spotted a man I had not seen in more than 30 years. Gena was, as usual, skeptical and suggested that I was looking for an excuse to meet people. Those who know me know that I do not need a pretext for that! The man was Moshe Beiski, a justice of the Israeli supreme court, a fellow Dzialoszycer, and older brother of my schoolmate Urish Beiski. We also met Gideon Hausner, the Israeli attorney general who led the prosecution at Adolf Eichmann's war crimes trial in Israel.

Gena, the children, and I stayed at the Victoria Hotel, which had been constructed by a Swedish company. Elaborate menus in the restaurant listed many items, but what we were interested in, mainly fruits and vegetables, was unavailable. There were still great shortages in Poland, even for tourists. After three days in Warsaw, we took Lot Airlines to Krakow. Before we boarded the flight, we confirmed that we would be served kosher sandwiches. On board we were told, "No special food! In Poland, everybody same!"

In the late morning, we arrived at the only Holiday Inn in Eastern Europe (in 1978), on the outskirts of Krakow. It was a study in contrasts to look out the windows of this modern high-rise hotel and see a farmer a hundred feet away plowing his field with a donkey. We quickly arranged for a driver and set out to see what we could of Krakow for the remainder of the day. Of course, we were most interested in Jewish sites. We visited Ulitsa Rabina Meiselsa, a street named after the famous Rabbi Meisels, which was Gena's maiden name. We went to the old *shul* of Rabbi Moses Isserles, the Rama, the sixteenth-century codifier of Jewish law, where his remains rest in a mausoleum, a holy shrine visited by observant Jews. People insert written requests into crevices of his tombstone like they do into the Western Wall in Jerusalem. The grave of Rabbi Natan Ben-Solomon Spira, a great seventeenth-century Kabbalist and philosopher, also rested there. Rabbi Spira was known as the *"Megaleh Amukkot"* (Revealer of the Depths) because of the book he wrote. As I tearfully prayed near the graves of these Jewish seers, I wanted them to "reveal in depth" the answer to my question: Why?

The Rama synagogue was completely ruined by the war, but at the initiative of Dr. Boleslaw Drobner, a member of the Soviet-imposed Lubin government, and under the act for protecting historical monuments, it was restored. Another larger synagogue on the same square became the Museum of the History and Culture of Jews, affiliated with the Museum of History of the city of Krakow. The main Jewish cemetery, located some distance away, contained broken monuments and was overgrown with weeds. One North American visitor was so upset at the forsaken state of the cemetery that she arranged to have a memorial wall built of the stone fragments of those monuments that had been completely shattered. We could not get into the main synagogue downtown, but from what we could ascertain, it too was in need of attention.

Krakow was now devoid of Jews. The vibrant Jewish community with its commerce and yeshivas had vanished. That night we retired to our rooms right after dinner. Gena, Tammy, and I were in one room, and the boys were in an adjoining one. We arranged for our driver to meet us at 9 a.m. the next morning to take us to Dzialoszyce. I was so physically exhausted from jet lag and the rainy, oppressive weather that I went to sleep at 8 p.m. I slept fitfully and woke up at about 9:15. When I looked at my watch and saw how late it was, I sprang out of bed, shouting at everyone to wake up and hurry on downstairs or our driver would be gone. But everyone was already up because they had not yet gone to sleep! I was so wound up in anticipation of my return to Dzialoszyce that I had awakened just an hour after having gone to sleep and believed it was morning. The dark skies, which followed us during our entire time in Poland, contributed to my disorientation.

The next morning we set out for my home, whence I had been exiled 36 years earlier. Dzialoszyce, the town I swore never to revisit, the town where I lost my childhood, the town where I used to be happy and carefree, the town of prayers, studies, rivers, and cloudbursts—this town I now wished to share with my dear wife and children. We went to Dzialoszyce because I did not even have a photograph of my parents and relatives to show them, and I wanted them to see something of where I came from.

As we approached Dzialoszyce, I told the driver to stop first in Chmielow, less than a kilometer away. I wanted to show my family how well we were known in the region; the name of our firm, Warshawski, had been emblazoned in large letters on a sign above our store. However, at every house I entered, even one where I vividly remembered hiding merchandise, the residents claimed ignorance. Did they think I was coming back for compensation? It was not possible that these people had not at least heard of the store name, if not the family name.

We went on to Dzialoszyce, passing the swampy soccer field I had played in as a child. I showed my children the sites connected with my memories, street by street and house by house. I found my *heder*, the bookstore owned by Shmuel Levkovitch, the police station on the second floor of Shmuel Piekarz's bakery, the old city hall near the well, and the marketplace. We walked into the church, a building I had never been in during my entire childhood, and looked down over the town from its high vantage point.

I showed my children the spot from which Jew-hating Polish youth would throw stones at us as we passed, and the church retaining wall on which the antisemites had posted their anti-Jewish propaganda. I pointed out the monument of Tadeusz Kosciuszko surrounded by flowerbeds and an iron fence, the place where the town crier made his garbled announcements.

We drove to the home of Wozniakowski, the man who repaired and rented out bicycles before the war. The Jewish cemetery had been across the street. Before the war, there had been hundreds of tombstones and several mausoleums for rabbis, all surrounded by a stone wall. The cemetery no longer existed. Not a single monument or section of wall could be found—no plaque, no cairn, no marker of any kind. Nothing! The cemetery had been planted over with trees, perhaps the better to cover up the physical remains of holy souls who had moved on to a far better place.

I can almost understand why the Poles would obliterate any memory of Dzialoszyce's long Jewish history. To acknowledge it would have been to acknowledge their complicity. If I were generous, I would say that they were embarrassed, but that assumes remorse. Because of the cover-up, I was denied the right to pay my respects to my grandparents at the graves that Mother and I visited on holiday eves.

The synagogue had been a large, imposing structure during my youth. Now it was a coal warehouse. How sad the desecrated house of worship looked! We took pictures to show friends from Dzialoszyce back in Canada. A group of curious onlookers followed us, and two militiamen, seeing the commotion, soon joined the others. The soldiers wore long greatcoats and carried old-fashioned rifles that looked like World War I army surplus. We wanted to photograph the little bridge that had been reconstructed after a cloudburst and flood drowned 36 people when I was a child. The strong current had undermined the bridge and carried it away. Even though the bridge was not much bigger than a footbridge one would find in a Toronto park, it had taken lots of time to rebuild it. As a youngster, I watched its construction every day.

Incredibly, the militiamen decided we were "spies" taking pictures for our Western countries so that they would know over which bridges they could drive their tanks through Poland on their way to invade Russia! The soldiers insisted on seeing our passports, and on scrutinizing them, they could not figure out how I was born in Poland, lived in Canada, and was a citizen of the United States. They demanded explanation. I enjoyed explaining, in a somewhat taunting manner, that in our part of the world, democracy ensured freedom of movement, so those who were citizens of one country could reside in another. Finally, the soldiers let us go but still followed our every move.

We visited the mayor's office, where I hoped to obtain photographs of my parents from old passports, but there was nothing. No title records, tax registrations, or any kind of archival material that could have pointed to their existence as citizens of Dzialoszyce had been preserved. My hope of coming away with any tangible evidence of our prewar existence rapidly disappeared. Perhaps something could yet be retrieved from my old family home.

We approached the house from the direction that I had most used as a child, a courtyard that we had shared with other two- and three-story houses in the neighborhood. Before we were expelled from Dzialoszyce, there had been two communal outhouses for several families to share. On our 1978 trip, four outhouses stood in the yard. I told my kids about the increase in services and then quipped, "Looks like they've made 100 percent progress!" In fact, most of the homes still had not been serviced by a sewage system.

One of the main reasons I returned to Dzialoszyce was to retrieve the watch my father had given me as a bar mitzvah gift. I vividly remembered the pocket watch with its three folding covers and heavy, gold chain. How I wanted to have something of my father's that I could hold in my hand. Alas, this wish would not be granted; we could not even enter the house because it was locked, and nobody was there to grant us permission to enter. All I could show my children was the mark that had been left by our mezuzah on the doorframe of our house.

As we were photographing the front of the house on the main street, a group of people again gathered around us. One blurted out, "The Jews are back! Let's kill them!" Sidney started photographing the crowd, which had the effect of dispersing them. Perhaps, in our long trench coats, they did think we were spies.

Our driver was very agitated and urged us to get into the car and leave immediately. Remembering the pogroms that took place in towns throughout Poland after the war, I took his advice, and we left in a hurry. This time we were not driven out by German murderers but by Polish townspeople, my former neighbors.

Perhaps these were the same Poles who killed my friend Chaim Jurysta or Shmuel Piekarz, the father of another friend, and 16 other Jews who returned to Dzialoszyce in 1945. Maybe these Poles were the ones who threw a grenade into our house in February 1945, because they thought two of my brothers were inside. Luckily, Art and Willie had left Dzialoszyce the day before.

Back in the car, our driver's brow was literally pouring sweat. When I asked him what was bothering him, he first told me that he thought the two policemen were going to stop him because he was carrying one more passenger than Polish regulations allowed. I wanted all my family together and had already told him that I would cover the cost of any fine he received, so I pressed him further. That is when he told us the truth of what was bothering him.

Several months earlier, friends of our driver had been among several drivers who had taken a group of about 20 survivors from Janowicz back to their hometown. The group of survivors was on its way to Israel for a larger gathering of their *landsmen* and had decided to stop off in Poland on the way. While they were in the ruin of a synagogue reciting a memorial *kaddish*, they were surrounded by several armed Polish militiamen. One of the town's children had gone missing, and since the Jews were back conducting some "Jewish ritual," this avenue had to be checked out. It took several hours before the child was found and the Jews were allowed to leave town. Our driver was worried about getting involved in a similar episode. My thoughts immediately went to those poor survivors. I could only imagine what was going through their heads as they were accused of a blood libel.

As we sped out of Dzialoszyce, I was upset that we had not made a single contact who remembered my family, nor had I found any document or object connected to them. Retracing our route through the village of Chmielow, I noticed a bent old woman standing outside a mud house with a thatched roof—a house where there had been no reply to my knock earlier in the day. I asked our driver to stop and hopped out of the car, hoping to give my search one last shot.

The bent old woman was Mrs. Novakova, the wife of Novak, one of the few Polish landed gentry in our area before the war. When I told her that I was Warshawski, she asked me into her humble home, and I summoned Sidney and Gary. Not wanting to overwhelm her with all of us, Gena, Tammy, and the driver stayed in the car. The Novaks had been among the friendlier Poles. I remember giving Mrs. Novakova Mother's Persian lamb coat and personal linens embroidered with our monogram that Mother gave Rose when she married Chaim. When Mrs. Novakova inquired about my parents and other relatives, I told her the sad truth of their murders by the Nazis and their accomplices.

Tears streamed out of her one good eye, and she went on to tell me of her own misfortunes. Her family's land had been seized by the Communists and redistributed, her husband had been killed for being gentry, and the Russians had taken one of her sons away, his whereabouts unknown. Her one remaining son could not make ends meet, and they lived in abject poverty. Looking around at the inside of her cottage, we were witness to that poverty. The thatched roof leaked, the floor was earthen, a tiny 18-inch-high coal stove provided sparse heat, and the available food was a few turnips that looked more like cattle feed than human food.

We reminisced for a while and shed some more tears together. I proudly showed off my family, and then we said our goodbyes. Before we pulled away, I pulled out American dollars and handed them to her, hoping to ease her poverty. When Mrs. Novakova hugged and kissed me, I could sense her feelings were genuine. She was the only person I had met in Poland who had the decency not to pretend to have amnesia. I left knowing that at least one person was left in Poland who knew we existed.

We continued on past Nieszkiev and other villages. Parallel to the road we could see the narrow railroad tracks that had carried the expelled Jews from Dzialoszyce to Miechow. In Miechow, my wife and children saw acres of wide-open, empty fields. I, on the other hand, could picture all my relatives among the many thousands of men, women, and children segregated into two columns by the SS. There was nothing, save my memory, to indicate the catastrophe that had ever taken place there.

The next day we journeyed to Auschwitz. A new Jewish museum had been dedicated the day before, and the opening ceremony had been attended by the same dignitaries who had attended the Yiddish Theatre in Warsaw. When we arrived at Block 27, which held the Jewish museum, the entrance was locked and no sign identified the place. We managed to get in through a side door, but a caretaker told us the brand-new museum was closed for "renovations." It had been open for one day, for a few good "photo ops." Further inquiries were met with evasive answers and lame excuses.

In the other barracks we found lists of inmates, but all the names sounded Polish. There was little sign of the Jewish victims at Auschwitz. The only traces of Jews were mountains of valises taken from the dead; the names written on the suitcases revealed who their Jewish owners had been. (In his book *Holocaust Journey*, Sir Martin Gilbert confirms that, on his 1981 visit to Auschwitz, none of the plaques mentioned the murder of Jews. On his return visit in 1996, he writes that the plaques attesting to the Nazis having murdered mainly Jews were new. I suppose to attract Jewish tourism the authorities had to finally acknowledge the centrality of the Jewish victims.)

The rain outside mixed with the tears flooding our eyes. We drove back to Krakow and to Plaszow, which was the site of the camp at Jerozolimska, one of my first camps. Nothing remained of the abominable concentration camp— no barbed-wire fence, no watch towers manned by guards with machine guns, not one of the hundreds of barracks. All we saw was a monument high on the hill, looking down over empty fields where the soil, nourished by the blood of Jewish victims, allowed the grass to grow lush and green.

Standing there, I remembered *Kommandant* Amon Goeth on his white horse followed by his two vicious Dobermans. I wondered why the camp had not been left intact as a memorial to the Moloch that swallowed so many Jews.

That evening I spotted several newspaper articles about the opening of the Jewish Museum in Auschwitz. An article published in the newspaper *Sztandar Mlodych* described many speakers, including Nahum Goldmann, president of the World Jewish Congress at the time, and Janis Wieczorek, a director of the Council for Preservation of Monuments of the Fighters and Martyrs.

Wieczorek had said, "I am aware of anti-Polish propaganda and accusations against the Polish population in connection with the loss of Jewish lives during the years of occupation, but each one of us knows how he—and the Polish people—acted, and we do not have to justify ourselves before anybody."

I appreciated the Polish underground organization Zegota whose members risked their lives to rescue Jews, but atrocities and pogroms committed by Poles, even after the liberation, are part of the historical record. Even after the end of the war, the Armia Krajowa (army of the country), an underground fighting organization, continued killing Jews.

We all breathed a sigh of relief as our plane left Polish airspace. After the emotionally difficult journey and coming to grips with the fact that absolutely nothing existed for me any longer in Poland, we recuperated in Majorca, where we spent Passover.

This time, we commemorated the departure from Egypt and from Spain and Poland as well. When I was asked to speak after services, I compared the three expulsions: "Elaborating upon the exodus from Egypt is worthy of praise." According to the Haggadah, "In every generation, everyone must view himself as though he himself came forth from Egypt, as it is said, 'And you shall tell your son'" (Exodus 1:14). One must tell and retell our exodus stories to our children and they to theirs for generations to come.

We started the retelling as soon as Sidney's slides were developed back in Toronto. Sidney invited fellow university students, both Jews and non-Jews, to see the slides and to hear about our trip. In those days, not that many people were visiting Poland. Holocaust education was in its infancy, and people were just becoming curious about what had happened during the war.

We also invited the survivors. One Saturday night, my brothers and friends from Dzialoszyce sat from *moytzei Shabes* until 5 a.m. looking at slides and reminiscing, with Sidney recording the conversation. It was amazing to watch one survivor argue with us over whether the church was in fact the Dzialoszyce church. They had seen it last when they were children, and it was the largest structure in their context. Their memory of it was much larger than the reality they saw on screen. For some of the group, it was the first time that they had spoken openly about the Holocaust to any member of the Second Generation, and it was an opening that was to have a positive influence in their own families.

I hope that this book will also serve as a catalyst for those who have not recorded their testimonies.

WOLGELERNTER—AN ALTERNATE RETURN

I was not alone in my urge to go back to the scene of the crime. As gratifying as it was to bring my family to my hometown, I came away with unanswered questions and no concrete remnants of my lost family. This was not always the case. The first time I came across the name Wolgelernter had been when I opened Art's locked dictionary drawer. In it were stored Hebrew letters from his friend Mayer Wolgelernter. Mayer was born in Kazimierz and had three older brothers, Abraham, Chaim, and David. Abraham came to Toronto before the war and settled there. The other brother, David, remained in Kazimierz until Willie rescued him as part of a group of 18 people, which also included my friend Helen Goldstein, whom he brought to Kostrze near Krakow. The rest of the Jews in town were all killed on the spot.

Chaim Yitzhak Wolgelernter studied in yeshiva with the Ostrowcer Rebbe, Yecheskiel Holztock. He was ordained as a rabbi at 18 years of age. Chaim Yitzhak married Chaya Platkiewicz, Yachet's daughter. Chaim and Chaya had a little girl and a boy named Feivel. The daughter, who was about three years old at the time, and Chaya's younger sister Reisel went to the death camps.

While everyone was being murdered, David and Mayer Wolgelernter escaped through the back window and hid in the ritual bath. They then joined Chaim Yitzhak in hiding in Dembowiec, a tiny village of 20 not far from Dzialoszyce, where they found refuge in a barn belonging to a farmer named Biskup.

While in hiding, the surviving Wolgelernters received supplies from the Ehrlich's two daughters, Helen and my dear first love, Estusia (Esther), who were using Aryan papers and passing as Christians. Helen and Esther also provided ammunition to the partisans and the Warsaw ghetto fighters. Esther's cover was that she was selling notions. Normally, these two sisters did not sleep in the barn, but one evening when Esther came to visit, she decided to remain for the night. On June 22, 1944, because of rumors that the hiding place was too dangerous, three people were chosen to leave at two o'clock in the morning. Eight people fatefully stayed behind. The three who left were David Wolgelernter, Feivel Ehrlich, and Avraham Shonfeld (a partisan). They joined another group hiding on Zito's farm in a village one hour away. Once the three were settled, they waited for the others to join them.

Esther was among the eight who remained behind in the first barn. She wanted to ensure that her parents, who were supposed to leave for the second barn the following day, arrived safely. The next day, Zito came into his barn and reported a rumor that eight Jews in a neighboring village had all been killed. He was told that originally there had been more than eight, but some ran away. David and the others pretended to know nothing about the subject and asked who killed the Jews. Zito thought that Biskup had been the murderer.

To date, no one is certain whether Biskup was the killer. Avraham Furman, an underground fighter and liaison between many Jews in hiding, was in the village at the time and had heard that it was the Polish underground army who had slaughtered these Jews. Biskup probably helped. The victims were buried in the fields of Dembowiec.

When David Wolgelernter left the first barn, he took with him some writings by his brother. This testimony, composed while in hiding, documents the suffering of a scholar. David gave the material to his nephew Feivel, Chaim Yitzhak's son, on the young man's wedding day. Years passed, and Feivel's son, Naftali, who grew up in Switzerland, read his grandfather's journal. When Naftali went to study at a yeshiva in Jerusalem, he continued searching for information about his grandfather and great-grandmother. Feivel Ehrlich (one of the three survivors) and Naftali visited Avraham Furman, who told the Ehrlichs about the location of the Polish village where the massacre took place.

Naftali and his brother Chaim made arrangements with Moshe Spiegel, an expert in locating graves and bringing Jewish remains to Israel for reburial. The group boarded a plane for Warsaw and then traveled by car to Dembowiec. Spiegel and his assistant, Boruch Goldberg, secured digging permits, rented a van, and hired strong laborers. They worked extremely hard to locate the remains of the eight Jewish victims. Finally, the grave was found 200 meters from the barn. By examining the skeletons, Naftali, Feivel, and Chaim learned that some of their relatives had been clubbed to death while others were killed with axes or bullets.

The bodies found were those of Yachet Platkiewicz; her daughter Zinale and Zinale's husband, Hershel Ehrlich; Chaim Yitzhak Wolgelernter; Esther and her older brother, Rubin Ehrlich; and one partisan. Miraculously, David Wolgelernter, Feivel Ehrlich, and Avraham Shonfeld lived to tell the tragic story and lay their loved ones to rest.

After liberation, David Wolgelernter went to a French orphanage where he retrieved Jewish children who had been hidden under the care of Christians during the war and raised as Roman Catholics. After completing that rescue mission, David came to Toronto and joined his brother Avraham and his uncle, Rabbi Israel Luser, founder of the Eitz Chaim Orthodox Day School.

In Toronto, David worked as a *shoykhet* and *ba'al koreh*. For my son Sidney's bar mitzvah in 1967, David composed a 100-verse poem of rhyming Yiddish couplets, which he read to everyone's delight. He died in June 1996. Two of David's uncles, Professor Rabbi Maurice Wohlgelernter, a Holocaust scholar, and Rabbi Israel Luser came from New York to deliver eulogies at the funeral. Each of the victims could have made enormous contributions to the world. Every individual was a universe of knowledge.

"TELL THY CHILDREN"

I am blessed that Hashem and Gena have given me three children and seven grandchildren so that I can fulfill the biblical commandment "and you shall tell your children." My children might say that I have told them too much, not about the Holocaust or my life, but about everything else. Having gone through what I have gone through, having lost my parents and other loved ones at a young age, perhaps I have been overprotective. Such overprotection can often boomerang and have catastrophic psychological results.

I will not say that being the children of a complex, protective survivor has had no effect on them, but each of my children seems to have survived my survival and gone on to become a balanced, creative, well-rounded, and successful individual. It must have been Gena's influence on them.

Sidney studied political philosophy at the University of Toronto and earned a degree in architecture from the same institution. After working as an architect in Toronto and New York, he became a developer and recently broadened his entrepreneurial activities to include technology. Sid has always been involved in trying to better the public realm and to that end was vice-chairman of the Planning Advisory Committee of the city of Toronto. Sidney, the sorcerer's apprentice, documented all existing synagogues in Canada, donated the materials to the Canadian Jewish Congress, and produced the book *Treasures of a People—The Synagogues of Canada.*

Sidney is married to Judith Lopes Cardozo, a curator, art critic, and singer, and daughter of Irma and Rabbi Abraham Lopes Cardozo, the Chazan emeritus of the Spanish-Portuguese Congregation in New York City. They have three sons: Ari-Lev, Elie, and Avichai.

Gary studied film at the University of Southern California and completed a degree in film and film finance at York University in Toronto. Gary, a creative entrepreneur from day one, has had a computer and consulting organization that provided business management and automation solutions for such major clients as *The Globe and Mail,* Canadian Broadcasting Corporation, Loblaws, The Barn, Nestle's, and Apple Canada. Gary is currently involved in all aspects of real estate—acquisition, analysis, management, and financing. He has always been Mr. Fix-It for his friends and family—whenever they needed technical or emotional support.

Gary is married to Louise Shimlovsky, a former senior executive at Telefilm Canada, and the daughter of Boris and Kati Shimlovsky of Hamilton. They have one son named Joshua.

Tamara studied at the University of Toronto and the Hebrew University in Jerusalem; she went on to earn her law degree at Osgoode Hall in Toronto. Tammy started out as a criminal lawyer and then moved on to refugee law, where she specialized in helping people who fled brutal persecution in Iran. In one of her cases, she discovered the Iranian equivalent of a Marrano (Jews forced to adopt Christian identities) and helped bring the individual back to his Jewish roots. At a large public event held at the Canadian National Exhibition, the Iranian community of Toronto presented Tammy with an award for her selfless work.

Tammy is married to Uli Friedman, a Judaica silversmith and real estate professional, son of Chaim and Malca Friedman of Jerusalem. They have three children: Odeya Sarah, Daniel, and Eliyah Faye.

As a result of the Holocaust, I no longer had my parents to "tell" me our history. Instead I turned to books and teachers so that I could continue being "told"—so that I would have what to pass on in "telling" to my own children. I am indebted to so many, some of whom I never have had the privilege to know, but whose books have enriched my life: Max Nordau, Theodor Herzl, Vladimir Jabotinsky, Menachem Begin—men who changed the tragic course of Jewish history; Uri Zvi Greenberg, Abraham Sutzkever, Tsemach Tsamriyon, Levi Shalit, Elie Wiesel—men who expressed the tragic course of Jewish history.

In my adulthood, I have continued studying. Learning continues to be my greatest joy. In contrast to many of my childhood teachers in the *heder,* Rabbi J. Immanuel Schochet of Chabad in Toronto, Rabbi Abraham Schkop, Rabbi

Dr. Norman Lamm of Yeshiva University, his son-in-law Rabbi Mark Dratch, and Rabbi Moshe Shulman of Shaarei Shomayim in Toronto—all represent a tolerant and loving approach to Judaism. No question is too controversial; no answer is ever withheld.

The Haggadah (Passover liturgy) says that in B'nai Brak (an ultraorthodox city near Tel Aviv), Rabbi Eliezer, Rabbi Joshua, Rabbi Elazar (son of Azaria), Rabbi Akiva, and Rabbi Tarfon discussed the Exodus from Egypt the entire night, until their students came and said, "Teachers, it is time to say the *Shema*" (Morning Prayer). Ben Zoma explained that the Torah stated, "In order that you remember the day you left Egypt all the days of your life, one has to tell the story" (Deuteronomy 16:3).

Night and day—during the darkness of slavery and the light of redemption—the story must be recounted. According to tradition, silence is not an option. In ancient Israel, five rabbis—plus one who was not a rabbi (Ben Zoma)—were discussing the Exodus.

In my story—my Haggadah (literally, "telling")—I mention rabbis as well as laymen who helped retell the story of the exodus, of surviving the Holocaust. Like Ben Zoma, Elie Wiesel is not a rabbi. Wiesel has spoken about going out of Egypt all his life, day and night. This narration is about who we are. I hope that in my lifetime I have managed to "tell my children" with my entire being.

EPILOGUE

This book began as a letter to my children. In the time it has taken to write, it has become a testament to my children and grandchildren. I also wrote this for myself; I would not be able to rest if I had taken this testimony to the grave. Through writing, I hoped to breathe life into all that had perished; I yearn for loved ones no longer with me.

While struggling to depict awful events, I was plagued by a host of questions. Who am I? Why should I write? Was I composing memoirs out of vanity? I had always kept my personal life private. Yet, a still, small voice, a stronger charge, demanded I expose what was hidden inside. Would the pain disappear with the revealed secret?

In the process of writing this book, I saw the faces of evil spirits at night; by day, I walked with open wounds. Refusing to telescope events for dramatic effect, I related the past as it was. When I was a child, snuggled in the safety of my home, cradled in the embrace of familial love, I could not foresee the end of that life.

I was encouraged by my family and close friends—notably Elie Wiesel—to make my story part of the chorus of testimonies of survivors of the Holocaust. While I have always loved poetry, the struggle of putting thought to paper has been a journey unto itself. I have amassed a large library and I have become computer literate.

I love nothing more than to explore ideas, to remember, and to communicate with people from all walks of life. My hope and my prayer is that I touch a few hearts and minds, and that I do honor to all the silenced voices.

I had to bear witness to the cataclysm of my generation. In that spirit, I offer seven decades of collected memories. The Dzialoszyce of my childhood is no longer. The tears in my heart have never ceased to flow. Each drop, each soul, haunted me and propelled me in the writing of this book—remember, remember, remember …

Tam velo nishlam
(Ended but not finished)

Joseph Tenenbaum, 24 Tishrei 5763